NART SAGAS

ART SAGAS

ANCIENT MYTHS AND LEGENDS OF THE CIRCASSIANS AND ABKHAZIANS

Assembled, Translated, and Annotated by

John Colarusso

With the Assistance of

B. George Hewitt, Zaira Khiba Hewitt,
Majdalin (Habjawqua) Hilmi, Kadir Natkhwa,
and Rashid T'haghapsaw

With a new introduction by Adrienne Mayor

PRINCETON UNIVERSITY PRESS

PRINCETON AND OXFORD

COPYRIGHT © 2002 BY PRINCETON UNIVERSITY PRESS
PUBLISHED BY PRINCETON UNIVERSITY PRESS, 41 WILLIAM STREET,
PRINCETON, NEW JERSEY 08540
IN THE UNITED KINGDOM: PRINCETON UNIVERSITY PRESS,
6 OXFORD STREET, WOODSTOCK, OXFORDSHIRE OX20 1TR

FOURTH PRINTING, FIRST PAPERBACK PRINTING WITH A NEW
INTRODUCTION BY ADRIENNE MAYOR, 2016
PAPERBACK ISBN: 978-0-691-16914-9
THE LIBRARY OF CONGRESS HAS CATALOGED THE CLOTH EDITION
AS FOLLOWS:

NART SAGAS FROM THE CAUCASUS : MYTHS AND LEGENDS FROM THE
CIRCASSIANS, ABAZAS, ABKHAZ, AND UBYKHS / ASSEMBLED,
TRANSLATED, AND ANNOTATED BY JOHN COLARUSSO
WITH THE ASSISTANCE OF B. GEORGE HEWITT . . . [ET.AL.].
P. CM.
INCLUDES BIBLIOGRAPHICAL REFERENCES.
ISBN 0-691-02647-5 (CLOTH : ALK. PAPER)
1. TALES–CAUCASUS. 2. MYTHOLOGY, CAUCASIAN.
3. CIRCASSIANS–FOLKLORE. 4. ABKHAZO-ADYGHIAN LANGUAGES.
I. COLARUSSO, JOHN, 1945–
GR276 M95 2002
398.2'09475–dc21 2001036861

BRITISH LIBRARY CATALOGING-IN-PUBLICATION DATA IS AVAILABLE.

PUBLICATION OF THIS BOOK HAS BEEN SUPPORTED BY A GRANT FROM
THE LOCKERT LIBRARY OF POETRY IN TRANSLATION, MADE POSSIBLE
BY A BEQUEST FROM CHARLES LACY LOCKERT (1888–1974)

THIS BOOK HAS BEEN COMPOSED IN DANTE TYPEFACE,
AND IPA TIMES FROM ECOLOGICAL LINGUISTICS

PRESS.PRINCETON.EDU

4 5 6 7 8 9 10

CONTENTS ❧

Preface ☙

This book began in 1977, shortly after I had earned my degree in linguistics from Harvard University. Characteristic of Harvard's conservatism, and setting it apart from the linguistic efforts centering around Noam Chomsky, who was down the road at MIT, was the requirement that its students have not only theoretical specialties but also a thorough knowledge of at least one language and a commanding knowledge of the family to which it belonged. After looking at Old Georgian, Armenian, and Ossetian, I settled on the Northwest Caucasian languages Ubykh and Circassian and managed to acquire some knowledge of both, the former with the help of the late Hans Vogt of the University of Oslo and the latter through the help of Rashid T'haghapsaw. I also worked on Abaza with the help of material from W. Sidney Allen, passed on to me by Calvert Watkins.

In 1975, finding myself out in the world as a young professor, I was dismayed to feel that this hard-earned knowledge was decaying. Knowing that I lacked the self-discipline to sit on a daily basis and work through material at random, and finding myself in Canada with no handy speakers of Circassian, Abkhaz, or Abaza, I hit on the idea of obtaining a grant to translate folklore. This would force me into a regimen whereby I could maintain my language skills. From 1979 to 1981, the United States National Endowment for the Humanities (administered through the Institute for the Study of Human Issues in Philadelphia) and the Social Sciences and Research Council of Canada (administered through McMaster University in Hamilton, Ontario) generously supported my efforts to translate the Nart sagas. Twenty-two years later I am still not happy with my command of the languages, but I remain amazed at the world opened up to me in the Nart sagas.

The Nart sagas are heroic tales, extremely archaic and varied. They occur across the North Caucasus, among Chechens and Ingush, among Ossetians, among Circassians and their kin, and even among the Kartvelian-speaking Svans and Georgian highlanders of northernmost Georgia. The Circassian corpus was collected largely by a team working under the Circassian scholar A. M. Hadaghatl'a (1968–71), in his *Geroicheskij épos Narty i igo genezis.* Hadaghatl'a's undertaking was enormous, extending to seven volumes, and only a portion, albeit a representative one, appears here. The Northern Abkhaz, or Abaza, sagas were collected by Vladimir Meremkulov and Shota Salakaya, with one story by the late British linguist W. Sidney Allen. The corpus appears in its entirety. The Abkhaz corpus was collected by a team directed by the late Abkhazian scholar Shalva Inal-Ipa and is cited as Inal-Ipa et al. 1962, with one saga from Kh. S. Bgazhba's dialect study of Bzyb. Regrettably, only a small selection of this corpus appears here. The Ubykh corpus—all the available Nart sagas—was collected chiefly by the famous French polyglot and folklorist Georges Dumézil, with one tale collected by the late Norwegian linguist Hans Vogt. The Turkish scholar Sumru Özsoy of Bogaziçi University, Istanbul, has collected seven more sagas from the late Tevfik Esenç. I hope that they will appear shortly.

Quite distinct are the Nart sagas preserved in Ossetic. They are elaborate but a bit less archaic than those of the neighboring Circassians, worked on by Dumézil (1930; 1943; 1960a; 1965; 1968; 1978) and others. They are quite lacking in Mazdaic features (Benveniste 1959, 129) and offer the only glimpse of some of the traditions of the Iranian-speaking steppe nomads of classical antiquity, such as the Scythians, Sarmatians, and Alans, traditions that seem not to have been touched by the great Zoroastrian revolution that characterizes the Iranian civilization of the eastern steppes and of Iran proper. Many of these Iranian features have been brought over into the Northwest Caucasian tradition as well.

Aylin Abayhan of the University of Wisconsin is working on the Karachai-Malkar (Balkar) corpus. The Chechen-Ingush corpus needs a translator, as does the small Svan corpus. Given the differences apparent between the Northwest Caucasian corpora and the Ossetian corpus, these other Nart corpora should make substantial contributions to comparative mythology.

I have labored to produce a readable account that still preserves this ancient material and thereby to render the Nart sagas not only as a body of world mythology but also as a treasure trove for the study of ancient myth in western Eurasia. Where I have invented material to render a smooth narrative, I have included it in square brackets. I have tried to make these bridge passages accord with Caucasian customs (Lotz et al. 1956; Luzbetak 1951; Grigolia 1939; Namitok 1939; Sanazaro 1506; the last one was provided to me by Okan Işcan, my Ubykh milk brother).

What is so exciting about the modern study of myth is the possibility of retrieving lost belief systems that are even more ancient than those represented by the myths that lie before the reader's eyes. Leading this effort has been the late Georges Dumézil (Littleton 1966), whose work is part of a wider effort to retrieve a range of aspects of Indo-European civilization (for example, Polomé 1982; Benveniste 1973; Wikander 1938; Olrick 1922). Puhvel (1987) has taken this effort to new levels of rigor and detail. Although Dumézil of necessity dealt with details, his chief aim was to recover the broad features of social structure that typified the original Indo-Europeans. His result was the well-known and widely accepted tripartite social ideology, reminiscent of the caste system of historical India, with priests, warriors, and agriculturists-artisans.

In my comparative comments and notes, by contrast, I have taken odd details of the myths to be more important than broad outlines or themes and in this regard have come closer to the spirit of Puhvel. Themes may serve some narrative function within a tradition and hence be subject to rationalizations and reinterpretations that reflect the narrator's culture and position within the history of his tradition. The odd details are there, however, only because they have been passed down as relics, often nearly meaningless. Occasionally a wider picture may emerge, but generally such details lend solid support for fairly limited perspectives on original beliefs or iconographies.

This is, in effect, the direct adoption of linguistic techniques in a folkloric setting (Colarusso 1998). For example, when one reconstructs a word for *foot* within Indo-European, what is important are the incidental accidents of sound, so to speak, the fact that the words in Latin and Greek both begin with a *p*, whereas in the Germanic languages they begin with an *f* and in Armenian with an *h*. It is not that Latin, Greek, the Germanic languages, and Armenian all have a word for *foot*. The latter broad structural fact of vocabulary is due to function, that is, to the fact that all these societies had an anatomical recognition of a foot and that their languages reflected this in their lexicons. In fact, nearly all languages have a word for something like a foot. Only a few, however, begin such words with *p* or *f* and show the fortuitous sound pattern that enables one to retrieve a Proto-Indo-European ancestral form. This methodological orientation has made the Northwest Caucasian corpora, with their odd details and garbled plots, extremely valuable for comparative work.

A number of people helped me with this effort. Professor B. George Hewitt and his wife, Zaira Khiba Hewitt, translated all but one of the Abkhaz sagas. Their work was extensive and meticulous. I took the liberty of editing the sagas to render a translation into more colloquial North American tones. I was assisted in my selection and translation of Circassian sagas by Rashid T'haghapsaw (Bzhedukh West Circassian), Kadir Natkhwa (Shapsegh West Circassian), and Majdalin (Habjawqua) Hilmi (Kabardian). Since the cognitive leap from Circassian to English is substantial, any errors are entirely my own. Because I did not have an Abaza speaker to assist me with that corpus, I relied on the Russian renderings provided in the collection by Meremkulov. My Russian was and remains weak, and so to handle the sheer volume of material I hired a recent émigré, Michael Elinson, to translate the Russian. He proved to be a diligent and tireless worker. I then scanned the Abaza originals and compared them with the Russian, often finding discrepancies between the two originals. None of these were due to Elinson's errors; rather they were due, again, either to the cognitive distance between Abaza and Russian or to a tendency to resort to euphemistic renderings when the original waxed a bit lurid. Two of my best students, Rebecca Lee and Bayla Greenberg, also assisted me by transliterating the Abaza original in case I chose later to publish analyses of any of these as specimens. Professor Hans Vogt assisted me by sending me open-reel copies of his Ubykh recordings in 1971 and then assisting me until his death with my questions on this most difficult language. Although Dumézil and Vogt had translated the Ubykh into French, no analysis and gloss had ever been published. I retranslated the corpus, with very few minor corrections, and in the specimen here I provide the first glossed example of this language. In the early stages of translation, Dr. Joel Jutkowitz, director of I.S.H.I., was of great help, and in the later stages of work, Deborah Tegarden of Princeton University Press was a steadfast bulwark of support in times that were often harried and hard. I must also thank the two readers, John Weinstock of the University of Texas, Austin, and Kevin Tuite of the Université de Montréal. The former gave the work a sensitive reading and a strong overall endorsement. The latter did likewise and as a specialist on the Caucasus also offered detailed criticisms and suggestions. Where I have incorporated these, they are credited with a "[KT]" to note their origin or inspiration.

Of course this book would not exist without the efforts of Sara Lerner and the production team at Princeton University Press. I owe them a debt of gratitude. I must also thank Dalia Geffen, my copy editor, who did a thorough and outstanding job. I found it humbling to read all her remarks and to find my writing improved by them almost every time.

For the reader with linguistic interests, and to provide a record of these languages (all of which may become extinct during this century), I have included five specimen texts, with full glosses and analyses, as well as translations. These include the first published analyses of a text in the elaborate Bzhedukh dialect of West Circassian and of a text in the archaic Bzyb dialect of Abkhaz. Also, this is the first time a glossed and analyzed Ubykh text has been published as noted above.

I must add, however, that my comparative claims are solely my own. In particular my Circassian, Abaza, Abkhaz, and Ubykh colleagues do not generally subscribe to such views. Their help in this translation effort should in no way be construed as an endorsement of my own views or proclivities.

A work of this size puts strain not only on the writer but also on those whose lives are linked to his. To my wife and children, the Narts must have seemed a shadowy but never vanishing presence, and this work, an unending quest. I must thank them, Linda and my little Narts, Mark, Tara, and Darren, for their patience, support, and interest. They have quite enjoyed the sagas and made the Narts a part of their lives. I can only trust that the readers will also find the Narts herein a worthy presence and a lasting part of their lives.

Finally, I must conclude by expressing my sadness that the great Indo-Europeanist Edgar Polomé died in March 2000. He recommended this work to Princeton University Press in 1994 but did not live to see it published. The reader, as well as I, owes him a debt of gratitude for what follows.

Introduction to the Paperback Edition ◌

The extraordinarily rich folk literature of the Caucasus is virtually unknown in the West because the region's ancient myths and legends were preserved orally instead of in writing. And the high mountain, thick forests, valleys, craggy cliffs, rocky gorges, isolated valleys, and lonely seas of grass have ensured that the region and its cultures remain little-known today. In antiquity this territory— stretching 1,000 miles from the Black Sea east to the Caspian Sea—was part of Scythia-Sarmatia, home to nomadic and semi-nomadic peoples whose lives centered on fine, fast horses, archery, falconry, herding, hunting, raiding, plundering, and warfare.

A cauldron of myriad ethnicities and languages, the Caucasus has seen geopolitical turmoil for thousands of years. Isolated by topography, restlessly on the move, subject to violent struggles, with entire peoples displaced and some erased altogether, the diverse ethnic groups kept their shared and unique ancient traditions alive in poetry, ballads, proverbs, and oral stories. Outside influences in the mountain fastness arrived quite late: Mongol hordes from the east, Islamic armies from the south, Byzantine-Medieval Christians from the West, and Russians in the modern era. In antiquity, the Caucasus region embraced Pontus, Armenia, Media, Colchis, Abkhazia, Iberia, and Albania. Today the region is divided into southern Russia and a host of republics established (and still disputed) after the Soviet Union's collapse in 1991: modern Abkhazia, Adzharia, Adygea, Karachay-Cherkessia, Karbardino-Balkaria, Chechnya, Ingushetia, Dagestan, North Ossetia-Alania, South Ossetia, Georgia, northeastern Turkey, Armenia, Nagorno-Karabakh, Nakhchevan, and Azerbaijan. And within each of these modern borders, various ethnic groups maintain their own dialects, customs, and histories.

The multiplicity of these names of modern nations harks back to the staggering ethnic diversity and ebb and flow of peoples across the Caucasus in antiquity. Each group, tribe, and clan passed down versions of stories featuring warriors and demigods of the mythic past known as Narts. Narts were imagined as larger-than-life, heroic, and sometimes supernaturally powerful but with mortals' emotions and foibles. As the first saga in this collection relates, given a choice by God, they chose courage, honor, risk, and glory over long lives of comfort, declaring, "If Our Lives Be Short, Let Our Fame Be Great!"

These translations of tales from Circassian, Abkhazian, Abaza, and Ubkh bring to life a nearly forgotten, strange, and wonderful world of primeval giants, evil monsters, magnificent horses, wise elders, impetuous adventurers, sly tricksters, witches and magical spells, earthy humor, and colorful heroes and heroines. The sagas are filled with fantastic exploits as well as realistic details of daily life. Colarusso's commentaries provide historical contexts, explain arcane meanings and local customs, and point out comparative folklore and fascinating mythic parallels.

In contrast with the ancient Mediterranean world, where oral myths were first captured in writing around 700 BC, most Caucasian languages did not possess alphabets until the twentieth century. The myths and chronicles from the heart of Eurasia were preserved in collective memories and perpetuated by the spoken word in countless tongues over generations, preserving themes and motifs related to those in Greek and Asian mythologies layered with Eurasian folk legends of later dates.

The non-Indo-European languages of the Caucasus are extraordinarily complex and subtle. Described by outsiders as mellifluous, percussive, hissing, throaty, and gargling, Caucasian languages are characterized by chains of "harsh" consonants leavened by only one or two vowels. The exotic-sounding, difficult-to-pronounce names in the Nart sagas are typically consonant-heavy.

Many of the numerous languages of the Caucasus appear to have changed little over the last two millennia. Remarkably, some traces of ancient forms of some of these languages were recently discovered, with the expertise of John Colarusso, on a number of ancient Greek vase paintings of the sixth to fourth centuries BC. The vases depicted Scythian and Amazon warriors, dressed and armed like real nomad mounted archers of the same era whose graves have been excavated around the Black Sea and across the steppes. Next to these barbarian figures are strings of "meaningless" Greek letters. Scholars had long assumed that the letters were mere gibberish, signs of illiterate vase painters.

Speculating that the mysterious letters might represent foreign languages spoken by nomads, I enlisted David Saunders, vase specialist at the Getty Museum, and we sought out John Colarusso, the leading expert in Caucasus languages. It was an amazing experience for all of us when John recognized many of the so-called "nonsense" inscriptions as phonetic renditions of phrases and names in ancient forms of Ubykh, Abkhazian, Georgian, and Circassian spelled out in the Greek alphabet. Some of the inscriptions described the actions pictured on the vase, while others were nicknames of Scythian and Amazon warriors, such as "Battle Cry," "Worthy of Armor," "One of the Heroes," "Armed with a Sword," "Noble Princess," "Iron," "Don't Fail," and "Brave Adversary."

This unexpected discovery of ancient Caucasian words on Greek vases, lost in plain sight for more than 2,500 years, surprised historical linguists, vase specialists, historians, and classical scholars. Colarusso's decipherment has significant implications for the history of linguistics and art, with new insights and raising intriguing questions about relations between the Caucasus and the Greek world.[1]

More questions are raised by a recent discovery in the Caucasus of what appears to be ancient writing, a thousand years earlier than the region was thought to have developed alphabets. Archaeologists excavating a seventh century BC temple in ancient Caucasian Iberia (modern Georgia) found an inscription on a stone slab in an unknown tongue. The letters may be the earliest example of alphabetic writing in the Caucasus.[2] Colarusso notes that at least one other undeciphered inscription from the Circassian coast dates to the third millennium BC. The interesting question for historical linguists, notes Colarusso, is why these ancient alphabets did not persist or evolve. He speculates that they may have been lost in the same way that Linear B was lost to the Greeks.

It was not until the late eighteenth and nineteenth century that European and Russian travelers and folklorists began to record traditional customs and stories recited by storytellers in the Caucasus. The eminent French scholar of mythology Nicholas Fréret (1722), Jacob Reineggs (1800) and Count John Potocki some years later, Julius von Klaproth (1807), Edmund Spencer (1838), and James Bryce (1876) are a few examples of Europeans who preserved local traditions in the Caucasus.

Yet, only about 200 of almost 1,000 recorded oral traditions of Caucasia have been translated into English. This collection of Nart sagas is a compelling introduction to the oral literature of a lively cultural crossroads where European and Asian myths, legends, and folklore overlapped and intermingled over millennia. "Historical layering" makes it impossible to pinpoint the original dates of the oral narratives, sagas, songs and ballads, proverbs, and epic poems of Caucasia. But, as Colarusso explains in his commentaries, one can discern threads of Greek, Scandinavian, Central Asian, Indian, and even Bronze Age Hittite myths interwoven in the Nart folklore. The giant Cyclops and the Titan Prometheus of ancient Greek mythology, for example, bear strong resemblances to Caucasian traditions about a one-eyed ogre and a fire-bringing hero in the Caucasus (Sagas 18, 31, 34–37, 52, 55, 91). Circe, the name of the sorceress in Homer's *Odyssey*, means "The Circassian," and the witch Medea, Jason's lover and helper in the *Argonautica*, had a brother whose name is Abkhazian. Both myths bring to mind Nart heroes who are aided or blocked by powerful females. Other Nart sagas have surprising parallels to Norse tales of Odin and the World Tree (Sagas 17 and 28).

According to Caucasian traditions, it was a Nart woman who invented iron-working and the Narts were the first to tame wild horses. At some point, the ancient Greeks must have absorbed these Caucasus traditions because they credited the Amazons with both of these innovations. Two stories in this collection described how Nart women invented iron-working and devised the first iron sickle and other iron tools (Sagas 16 and 49). Another story explains how the Narts were the first to tame wild horses (Saga 81). In the tale, Sasruquo makes a crude bit and reins of braided mulberry bark and jumps on the back of a wild stallion, forcing it into a river with a strong current. The horse thrashes and wears itself out against the raging torrent, then Sasruquo is able to guide the now-docile stallion to the safety of the bank. "From that day onward" people began to tame and ride wild steeds. This Nart technique of breaking horses is still used by horse-people on the steppes and other places around the world; some ride the horses in streams—or deep mud or snow—which has the same effect.

The Caucasus is known for its poisonous snakes, much dreaded in antiquity. According to Saga 3, even the fumes emanating from a dead snake are deadly. Notably, the archers of the Caucasus were feared for their deadly arrows tipped with snake venom. Strabo, the ancient Greek geographer, claimed that one Caucasus tribe concocted an arrow poison so noxious that the mere stench emitted by a whizzing arrow could kill. Several ancient Greek writers preserved Scythian arrow poison recipes calling for viper venom. They also reported that shamans of the Caucasus knew the secrets of how to treat snake bites and how to make medicine from venom. Nart Saga 26 about Lady Amezan claims that she knew how to "counter the poison of the striking serpent." Several sagas recount plots that involve snake venom. In one, enemies plot to place seven venomous vipers in a large drinking horn to kill a powerful hero (Saga 11). In Saga 84, the Nart Narjkhyaw foils a conspiracy to poison his wine cup with a broth of boiled viper venom, blood, and flesh. His steel mustache filters and purifies the venom-infused wine and he quaffs the cup with no ill effects, not even a rumble from his stomach. In fact, venom can be safely digested because it is only harmful in the bloodstream—a nugget of folk knowledge embedded in the saga.

Along with their beloved horses and hounds, Caucasus people hunted with trained raptors, specifically eagles. Many of the Nart sagas describe warriors setting forth with their bows and spears, astride splendid horses, their faithful sight hounds trotting along, and their golden eagles perched on their arms. "Your horse is ready [and] your weapons and armor...your hounds and your eagle too," says the hero's mother as he prepares to ride out. "Whatever your raptor drives out, your dogs will retrieve" (Saga 11). Other ballads (Sagas 12 and 24) describe riders summoning their dogs and eagles and "riding along the empty steppe," confident that whatever game "his dogs flush out his eagle seizes." Traditional falconry with eagles, horses, and sight hounds is still practiced on the steppes.

Geomythology is also featured in the Nart sagas. Some of my favorites tell of the Narts' discoveries of enormous bones and skulls on the steppes. In Sagas 56 and 58, a band of warriors on raid for plunder are traversing a remote, desolate landscape when they come upon an immense boulder with a hole eroding out of the earth. Their leader stays behind to study the rock. When he scrapes away the dirt he discovers that it is a massive bone. His actions summon the ghostly apparition of the giant creature whose skeleton lies embedded in the ground. The giant explains how his bones were scattered, petrified, and inexorably buried by dust, sand, and gravel, only to weather out again. The Caucasus and steppes

contain deposits of fossilized remains of long extinct creatures including dinosaurs, mammoths, mastodons, and other megafauna. These legends arose from
people's observations of massive bones of stone that they identified as belonging
to giant beings of the past.

Audacious, independent heroines abound in the Nart sagas. The harsh lifestyle and unforgiving geography of the Caucasus demands tough, resilient, self-
sufficient men, women, and children. The nomads' mastery of horses combined
with keen archery skills meant that women and youths could be as fast and as
deadly in battle as men. As a result, men and women in the Caucasus enjoyed
egalitarian partnerships that astonished the ancient Greeks and Romans. Reports
of fierce, bold women of the Caucasus and steppes filtered into Hellenic art and
literature after Greeks began to explore and set up colonies around the Black
Sea in the seventh century BC. Indeed, in classical antiquity, Caucasia was recognized as the heartland of the fierce female archers on horseback mythologized by
the ancient Greeks as Amazons. Even the name "Amazon," long assumed to be
Greek, appears to have linguistic roots in Caucasia, perhaps linked to the name of
the warrior woman Lady Amezan in Saga 26, set in the glorious time when the
steppes rang with the "thunderous pounding of horses' hooves." In those days
women buckled on their swords, took up their bows and "rode forth with their
men folk to meet the enemy in battle." Nart women loved and comforted their
male companions but they did not flinch to "cut out an enemy's heart."

Companionable marriages characterized by equality and interdependence
were traditional—and practical—features in many nomadic and semi-nomadic
cultures. Mutual respect was seen as the ideal relationship of husband and wife.
There was tolerance for sexual independence and gender roles were interchangeable in the egalitarian lifestyle of the Caucasus tribes. Early modern European
travelers to the Caucasus remarked on the unusual freedom and respect accorded to women and the affection and friendship of married couples. In the narratives translated here, robust, strong women live the same lusty outdoor life as
the men: they ride, hunt, fight, lead bands, dispense wisdom, choose their own
sexual partners, and star in their own dramatic stories. Shared authority and responsibility, joking camaraderie, and companionship between male and female
"soul-mates" is evident in many of the tales.

One of the most charming examples of egalitarian gender roles is Lady Hero
Gunda, whose name is refreshingly easy to pronounce. Her story evokes the
Greek myth of Atalanta, the athletic heroine who bested male champions in
wrestling contests and would only marry the man who could beat her in a foot-
race. It also resembles similar Central Asian legends about young women who
vow they will only marry the man who can equal their strength in wrestling.
The most famous is Khutulun, a Mongolian warrior princess described by Marco
Polo. In Nart Saga 83, "an army of youths" sought the hand of the beautiful and
valiant Gunda. She wrestled and defeated 99 suitors before finding the lover who

was her match. Gunda is just one of a host of unforgettable characters populating the sagas of the Caucasus.

This marvelous treasury of Nart stories, heretofore unknown in English, is now a vital part of the folklore canon of Eurasia.

Adrienne Mayor

October 7, 2015

Notes to the Introduction

1. Adrienne Mayor, David Saunders, John Colarusso, "Making Sense of Nonsense Inscriptions Associated with Amazons and Scythians on Athenian Vases," *Hesperia* 83, 3 (September 2014): 447–93.

2. Reported in *National Geographic*, September 16, 2015.

PREFACE ◐

This book began in 1977, shortly after I had earned my degree in linguistics from Harvard University. Characteristic of Harvard's conservatism, and setting it apart from the linguistic efforts centering around Noam Chomsky, who was down the road at MIT, was the requirement that its students have not only theoretical specialties but also a thorough knowledge of at least one language and a commanding knowledge of the family to which it belonged. After looking at Old Georgian, Armenian, and Ossetian, I settled on the Northwest Caucasian languages Ubykh and Circassian and managed to acquire some knowledge of both, the former with the help of the late Hans Vogt of the University of Oslo and the latter through the help of Rashid T'haghapsaw. I also worked on Abaza with the help of material from W. Sidney Allen, passed on to me by Calvert Watkins.

In 1975, finding myself out in the world as a young professor, I was dismayed to feel that this hard-earned knowledge was decaying. Knowing that I lacked the self-discipline to sit on a daily basis and work through material at random, and finding myself in Canada with no handy speakers of Circassian, Abkhaz, or Abaza, I hit on the idea of obtaining a grant to translate folklore. This would force me into a regimen whereby I could maintain my language skills. From 1979 to 1981, the United States National Endowment for the Humanities (administered through the Institute for the Study of Human Issues in Philadelphia) and the Social Sciences and Research Council of Canada (administered through McMaster University in Hamilton, Ontario) generously supported my efforts to translate the Nart sagas. Twenty-two years later I am still not happy with my command of the languages, but I remain amazed at the world opened up to me in the Nart sagas.

The Nart sagas are heroic tales, extremely archaic and varied. They occur across the North Caucasus, among Chechens and Ingush, among Ossetians, among Circassians and their kin, and even among the Kartvelian-speaking Svans and Georgian highlanders of northernmost Georgia. The Circassian corpus was collected largely by a team working under the Circassian scholar A. M. Hadaghatl'a (1968–71), in his *Geroicheskij épos Narty i igo genezis.* Hadaghatl'a's undertaking was enormous, extending to seven volumes, and only a portion, albeit a representative one, appears here. The Northern Abkhaz, or Abaza, sagas were collected by Vladimir Merem-kulov and Shota Salakaya, with one story by the late British linguist W. Sidney Allen. The corpus appears in its entirety. The Abkhaz corpus was collected by a team directed by the late Abkhazian scholar Shalva Inal-Ipa and is cited as Inal-Ipa et al. 1962, with one saga from Kh. S. Bgazhba's dialect study of Bzyb. Regrettably, only a small selection of this corpus appears here. The Ubykh corpus—all the available Nart sagas—was collected chiefly by the famous French polyglot and folklorist Georges Dumézil, with one tale collected by the late Norwegian linguist Hans Vogt. The Turkish scholar Sumru Özsoy of Bogaziçi University, Istanbul, has collected seven more sagas from the late Tevfik Esenç. I hope that they will appear shortly.

Quite distinct are the Nart sagas preserved in Ossetic. They are elaborate but a bit less archaic than those of the neighboring Circassians, worked on by Dumézil (1930; 1943; 1960a; 1965; 1968; 1978) and others. They are quite lacking in Mazdaic features (Benveniste 1959, 129) and offer the only glimpse of some of the traditions of the Iranian-speaking steppe nomads of classical antiquity, such as the Scythians, Sarmatians, and Alans, traditions that seem not to have been touched by the great Zoroastrian revolution that characterizes the Iranian civilization of the eastern steppes and of Iran proper. Many of these Iranian features have been brought over into the Northwest Caucasian tradition as well.

Aylin Abayhan of the University of Wisconsin is working on the Karachai-Malkar (Balkar) corpus. The Chechen-Ingush corpus needs a translator, as does the small Svan corpus. Given the differences apparent between the Northwest Caucasian corpora and the Ossetian corpus, these other Nart corpora should make substantial contributions to comparative mythology.

I have labored to produce a readable account that still preserves this ancient material and thereby to render the Nart sagas not only as a body of world mythology but also as a treasure trove for the study of ancient myth in western Eurasia. Where I have invented material to render a smooth narrative, I have included it in square brackets. I have tried to make these bridge passages accord with Caucasian customs (Lotz et al. 1956; Luzbetak 1951; Grigolia 1939; Namitok 1939; Sanazaro 1506; the last one was provided to me by Okan Işcan, my Ubykh milk brother).

What is so exciting about the modern study of myth is the possibility of retrieving lost belief systems that are even more ancient than those represented by the myths that lie before the reader's eyes. Leading this effort has been the late Georges Dumézil (Littleton 1966), whose work is part of a wider effort to retrieve a range of aspects of Indo-European civilization (for example, Polomé 1982; Benveniste 1973; Wikander 1938; Olrick 1922). Puhvel (1987) has taken this effort to new levels of rigor and detail. Although Dumézil of necessity dealt with details, his chief aim was to recover the broad features of social structure that typified the original Indo-Europeans. His result was the well-known and widely accepted tripartite social ideology, reminiscent of the caste system of historical India, with priests, warriors, and agriculturists-artisans.

In my comparative comments and notes, by contrast, I have taken odd details of the myths to be more important than broad outlines or themes and in this regard have come closer to the spirit of Puhvel. Themes may serve some narrative function within a tradition and hence be subject to rationalizations and reinterpretations that reflect the narrator's culture and position within the history of his tradition. The odd details are there, however, only because they have been passed down as relics, often nearly meaningless. Occasionally a wider picture may emerge, but generally such details lend solid support for fairly limited perspectives on original beliefs or iconographies.

This is, in effect, the direct adoption of linguistic techniques in a folkloric setting (Colarusso 1998). For example, when one reconstructs a word for *foot* within Indo-European, what is important are the incidental accidents of sound, so to speak, the fact that the words in Latin and Greek both begin with a *p*, whereas in the Germanic languages they begin with an *f* and in Armenian with an *h*. It is not that Latin, Greek, the Germanic languages, and Armenian all have a word for *foot*. The latter broad structural fact of vocabulary is due to function, that is, to the fact that all these societies had an anatomical recognition of a foot and that their languages reflected this in their lexicons. In fact, nearly all languages have a word for something like a foot. Only a few, however, begin such words with *p* or *f* and show the fortuitous sound pattern that enables one to retrieve a Proto-Indo-European ancestral form. This methodological orientation has made the Northwest Caucasian corpora, with their odd details and garbled plots, extremely valuable for comparative work.

A number of people helped me with this effort. Professor B. George Hewitt and his wife, Zaira Khiba Hewitt, translated all but one of the Abkhaz sagas. Their work was extensive and meticulous. I took the liberty of editing the sagas to render a translation into more colloquial North American tones. I was assisted in my selection and translation of Circassian sagas by Rashid T'haghapsaw (Bzhedukh West Circassian), Kadir Natkhwa (Shapsegh West Circassian), and Majdalin (Habjawqua) Hilmi (Kabardian). Since the cognitive leap from Circassian to English is substantial, any errors are entirely my own. Because I did not have an Abaza speaker to assist me with that corpus, I relied on the Russian renderings provided in the collection by Meremkulov. My Russian was and remains weak, and so to handle the sheer volume of material I hired a recent émigré, Michael Elinson, to translate the Russian. He proved to be a diligent and tireless worker. I then scanned the Abaza originals and compared them with the Russian, often finding discrepancies between the two originals. None of these were due to Elinson's errors; rather they were due, again, either to the cognitive distance between Abaza and Russian or to a tendency to resort to euphemistic renderings when the original waxed a bit lurid. Two of my best students, Rebecca Lee and Bayla Greenberg, also assisted me by transliterating the Abaza original in case I chose later to publish analyses of any of these as specimens. Professor Hans Vogt assisted me by sending me open-reel copies of his Ubykh recordings in 1971 and then assisting me until his death with my questions on this most difficult language. Although Dumézil and Vogt had translated the Ubykh into French, no analysis and gloss had ever been published. I retranslated the corpus, with very few minor corrections, and in the specimen here I provide the first glossed example of this language. In the early stages of translation, Dr. Joel Jutkowitz, director of I.S.H.I., was of great help, and in the later stages of work, Deborah Tegarden of Princeton University Press was a steadfast bulwark of support in times that were often harried and hard. I must also thank the two readers, John Weinstock of the University of Texas, Austin, and Kevin Tuite of the Université de Montréal. The former gave the work a sensitive reading and a strong overall endorsement. The latter did likewise and as a specialist on the Caucasus also offered detailed criticisms and suggestions. Where I have incorporated these, they are credited with a "[KT]" to note their origin or inspiration.

Of course this book would not exist without the efforts of Sara Lerner and the production team at Princeton University Press. I owe them a debt of gratitude. I must also thank Dalia Geffen, my copy editor, who did a thorough and outstanding job. I found it humbling to read all her remarks and to find my writing improved by them almost every time.

For the reader with linguistic interests, and to provide a record of these languages (all of which may become extinct during this century), I have included five specimen texts, with full glosses and analyses, as well as translations. These include the first published analyses of a text in the elaborate Bzhedukh dialect of West Circassian and of a text in the archaic Bzyb dialect of Abkhaz. Also, this is the first time a glossed and analyzed Ubykh text has been published as noted above.

I must add, however, that my comparative claims are solely my own. In particular my Circassian, Abaza, Abkhaz, and Ubykh colleagues do not generally subscribe to such views. Their help in this translation effort should in no way be construed as an endorsement of my own views or proclivities.

A work of this size puts strain not only on the writer but also on those whose lives are linked to his. To my wife and children, the Narts must have seemed a shadowy but never vanishing presence, and this work, an unending quest. I must thank them, Linda and my little Narts, Mark, Tara, and Darren, for their patience, support, and interest. They have quite enjoyed the sagas and made the Narts a part of their lives. I can only trust that the readers will also find the Narts herein a worthy presence and a lasting part of their lives.

Finally, I must conclude by expressing my sadness that the great Indo-Europeanist Edgar Polomé died in March 2000. He recommended this work to Princeton University Press in 1994 but did not live to see it published. The reader, as well as I, owes him a debt of gratitude for what follows.

SYMBOLS AND ABBREVIATIONS ✑

v́	= vowel with primary stress
v̀	= vowel with secondary stress
V	= abstract vowel slot in the vocalic tier, used to explain word shape
3	= "he," "she," "it," "him," "her"
*	= a reconstructed form
—	= morpheme boundary for inflectional or productive morphology
+	= morpheme boundary for unproductive derivational morphology
abs	= absolutive case (subject of intransitives, direct object of transitives)
act	= active
adj	= adjective
adv	= adverb
aff	= affirmative mood
asp	= aspect of present continuous verb
ATR	= advanced tongue root, an articulatory gesture that bunches up the tongue body and produces a palatal y-like quality
cause	= causative ("caused," "made," "allowed," "enabled")
ch.of.st	= change of state preverb
conn	= connective, used in compounds and sometimes with the causative
dat	= dative ("to," "at")
detri	= detrimentive ("against," "despite")
dir	= direction
dist	= distributed through space or time
dur	= durative
dyn	= dynamic
emph	= emphatic ("indeed")
ep.v	= epenthetic vowel (a vowel inserted for phonetic reasons)
fem	= feminine

fut	=	future
gen	=	genitive ("belonging to")
genr	=	general (unspecified)
ger	=	gerund (a participlelike form that can take case endings)
hor	=	horizon of interest (object of action is of interest to the speaker, or action is toward the speaker)
hum	=	human
immed	=	immediate, soon to happen
imp	=	imperative
inal	=	inalienable possession (inseparable from the possessor)
indef	=	indefinite
inf	=	infinitive
inst	=	instrumental
int	=	intimate possession (used for a spouse or parents)
intr	=	intransitive
invis	=	invisible
irreal	=	irrealis ("contrary to fact," "unreal")
iter	=	iterative ("again and again")
loc	=	locative
masc	=	masculine
neg	=	negative
neg.tns	=	negative tense suffix
non.pr	=	nonpresent tense vowel /ə/ of Bzhedukh verbs
obl	=	oblique case (subject of transitives, indirect objects, objects of postpositions)
obl.conn	=	an affix found in Circassian compound nouns of the form /-n-/ or /-m-/ and reminiscent of the oblique case
opt	=	optative (used for wishes or contrary-to-fact statements)
part	=	participle
PIE	=	Proto-Indo-European
pl	=	plural
pl.conn	=	plural or numerical connective found in Circassian between a noun and its numerical, specifically a cardinal adjective
poss	=	possessive
pred	=	predicative case, being a certain way or in a certain state
pres	=	present tense
preV	=	preverb without a separate sense from the verb root
pro	=	pronominal suffix

prog	=	progressive aspect
prol	=	prolongation suffix
pro.tns	=	"pro-tense," which stands for a supressed or missing tense
prox.fut	=	proximate or near future
Q	=	question suffix, question complementizer
recip	=	reciprocal ("each other")
refl	=	reflexive ("to one's self")
sg	=	singular
stat	=	stative affirmative
subj	=	subjunctive ("maybe")
th.v.	=	thematic vowel (used to form stems for inflection)
val	=	valence (adds an argument to a verb or increases its activity)
voc	=	vocative, form used in address
WCirc	=	West Circassian

NART SAGAS from the CAUCASUS

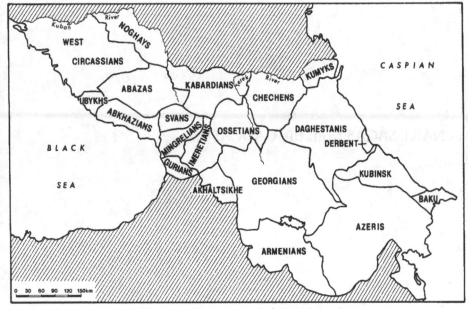

Caucasian Peoples and Districts, End of the Eighteenth-Century

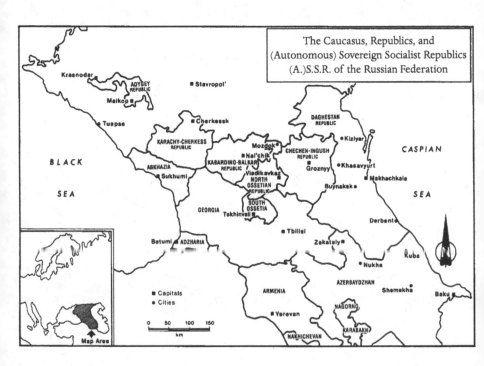

A ship sailing across the Black Sea in the year 1780 eventually would have come upon a lush shore at the eastern end of the dark gray waters (compare Odell 1977; Lotz et al. 1956; and the earliest account, Sanazaro 1506). If the course setting had been east-northeast, then this would have been the Circassian coast, a rolling land with distant mountains rising behind it. If due east, then the ship would have come upon the Abkhazian coast, with the hills and mountains descending to the beach and at a few points dipping into the sea. This stretch of shoreline might well be the same on which Jason and his argonauts are said to have landed three millennia earlier. In that year these were the watery boundaries of two large nations, Circassia and Abkhazia, with the land of the Ubykh falling between them and sharing allegiances with both. In Abkhazia the traveler would have encountered a state with a ruler, albeit under the thumb of the Ottoman Empire, whose inner boundary petered out in the high reaches of the mountains (see Lak'oba 1998). The nobles of Abkhazia shared pedigrees with the nobles of the small Ubykh tribe farther up the coast, on the far side of the river Psow. In Circassia the traveler would have encountered a series of tribes structured by clan lineages and allegiances, all of whom called themselves Adyghey, including the small Ubykh tribe. This realm would extend eastward through tribes, each having its own dialect, across the Caucasus Mountains, which run for one thousand kilometers from the northwest to the southeast, and along the south bank of the Kuban River, to the very center of the North Caucasus. Here, in the shadow of Mount Elbruz, the highest mountain in Europe, the Kabardian tribe dominated with an almost statelike cohesion over the Turkic-speaking Noghay nomads of the plains and the Iranian-speaking Ossetian mountaineers. Here too the Terek River began its eastward flow to form the northern boundary of the Northeast Caucasus. In the mountain pastures of the Circassian realm lived Turkic-speaking pastoralists, the Karachais and Malkars (or Balkars). Some northern Abkhaz, the Abazas, also lived among them. Across the Kuban and Terek Rivers were settlements of Russian- and Ukrainian-speaking people who had fled the system of serfdom farther north and who had intermarried with many of the Caucasian and Turkic women.

These were the Cossacks. In many ways they resembled their Caucasian neighbors but traditionally maintained a hostile relationship with them. They were the vanguard of the invasion that was to come in the next century.

In this lush realm at this time may have lived as many as 2 million people, all sharing a set of striking features of language, dress, and custom (Hewitt and Watson 1994; Colarusso 1994a; Volkova 1994; Shamanov 1994; Khodorkovsky and Stewart 1994; Fritz 1994). In peace, the peoples were organized into a number of tribes, each with its own language or dialect. In war, they united and behaved like a conventional state. The Circassian tribes of the coast, the Shapsegh and Natukhay, practiced trade and exhibited a loose social structure, but farther along the coast, among the Ubykh and Abkhaz, and inland among the other Circassians, an elaborate social structure existed. These people were warlike, and their society was highly structured to enforce a discipline and order that served them on the battlefield. They were ranked into princes, nobles, freemen, and serfs, the last serving the nobility and chiefly descended from prisoners of war. Clans and lineages interpenetrated with this hierarchy and shaped almost all social interactions. Despite this social order, feuding was rampant, and no man was without his weapons. Since social rank was inherited and prestige was measured by valor, material goods were not socially important outside of the trading tribes. In fact, a sort of sporting theft was common, so that goods tended to circulate in the community. Although the princes and nobles entrusted their children to retainers, family values as a whole were strong, and this fosterage actually served to tie the serfs to their overlords not as slave to master but as family member to clan leader. In fact, the visitor, if all went well in following social decorum and restraint, might eventually receive the great and lifelong honor of being adopted by a clan. Despite the strict codes of conduct, the concern with honor and social face, and the elaborate hierarchy, the overall social values reflected ideals of individual freedom and democratic participation in comunity life. The power of the princes and nobles was moderated by the views of the elders of the community, and these in turn were sensitive to the needs of all the community's members.

The economy of the region was varied. Aside from traders with fortified outposts, people lived in villages strung along rivers deep in the forest. In the higher hills, stone houses with single towers predominated. Each of these was like a self-contained fortress. The mountain pastures, however, were by and large the domain of the Karachays and Malkars, Turkic pastoralists, who like the Cossacks and the other Caucasians had simpler social systems. The Circassians, Abkhaz, and Ubykhs bred horses, cows, oxen, sheep, pigs, and chickens, and grew abundant fruits and vegetables. Apiculture and the gathering of walnuts were also vital parts of their agricultural economy, as was hunting. Felt rugs were a prime manufactured good. Splendid horses were also traded, with the Kabardian breed being one of the most prestigious. The skill of the men on horseback was most impressive.

The peoples were highly variable in appearance, some being dark and others light, with light eyes and blond or red hair. Some looked like northern Europeans, and others had a distinctly Mongol cast to their features. Their varied appearances testified to their long and complex history. Many of the princes and nobles were tall. Many individuals were strikingly handsome, with both genders frequently showing expressive faces, lithe physiques, and graceful movements. The men of this region accorded their women great freedom and respect, even if their economic roles were traditionally set. Elders were revered, and many lived to be well over a hundred. Even in advanced age—and many claimed to be more than a century old—they remained an integral part of society, and perhaps most strikingly, they were accorded passions and hopes just like the younger members of their clans.

Dance was a crucial aspect of social life, the men spinning and leaping with astonishing speed and power and the women gliding about with fluid grace, the motion of their legs hidden by their long, gownlike dresses. Women's clothing consisted of a gown with false sleeves. On their heads they wore a hat shaped like an acorn, usually with a scarf trailing from the crown. They walked on platform shoes. The men's clothing was also striking, consisting of loose trousers tucked into soft leather, soleless knee boots, resembling leather knee socks. Their high-collared shirts were covered by a *cherkesska*, a robelike coat with a fitted torso and a flaring lower portion that draped over their horse's haunches while riding. Across their chest, they had a series of sewn cylindrical pouches into which silver tubes were placed. Each of these contained a measured charge of powder for the muskets, which they always bore, along with swords and daggers.

The religions were many, with some Christians among the Abadzakh of the hills and some Jews living intermixed with other Circassians. Islam dominated the region, but no mosques were to be seen. In fact, religious tolerance was a feature of the Caucasus as a whole, and strong pagan traditions still shaped many beliefs among the peoples and lay behind most of their rituals. Great feasts were often held, especially at times of seasonal rituals, and these were headed by a toastmaster, *t'hamada*, a term destined to spread north into Russia and south into Persia. At such feasts bards, both male and female, would recount old legends in their various languages. These languages were most remarkable and complex, ranging from the mellifluous Kabardian to the percussive and subtle Bzhedukh and Shapsegh to the hissing and throaty Ubykh and Abkhaz to the startling Abaza with its almost gargled quality. They clearly bore no links with any of the more familiar languages around them. Great buildings and monuments were absent, but the chief monument of their civilization resided in the languages and the folklore these enshrined. Most varied and revered among the various tales was a body of lore in which a band of heroes was depicted, all of whose members were said to have a single mother, an ageless beauty. These were the Nart sagas, legends found across the North Caucasus.

In the coming decades Russia was to expand into this area, and war would rage across the North Caucasus. The resistance the Circassians, Ubykhs, Abkhaz, and Abaza offered is only scantily known (Berzeg 1998; Tsutsiev and Dzugaev 1997, maps 2–6; Henze 1992), in contrast to that of the Chechens and Daghestanis (Gammer 1994; Blanch 1960; Baddeley 1969), which has become the stuff of legends. It must have been ferocious, however, because the Caucasian campaign dragged on a full five years longer in the west (which ended in 1864) than in the east (which ended in 1859) and resulted in the wholesale deportation of the population into the Balkan region of the Ottoman Empire (Brooks 1996, 1995). Today the majority of the Circassians, Abkhaz, and Abazas and all the Ubykhs live in Turkey, with enclaves in Jordan, Iraq, Syria, and Israel. Recently small immigrant communities have been established in the United States (Colarusso 1997). Those remaining behind in their homeland are a distinct minority but nevertheless enjoy more cultural continuity than their cousins abroad. Russian authorities have devised literary languages in Adyghey (based on the Chemgwi dialect of West Circassian), Kabardian, Abkhaz (Abzhwi dialect), and Abaza (Tapanta dialect) and have established cultural institutions, such as museums, dance companies, and folklore institutes. Scholars have gathered the surviving portions of the old traditions. The Nart sagas have been recorded intensively, and large portions of the corpora have been published (see also Khamytsaeva and Bjazyrov 1989 [Ossetian]; Dalgat 1972 [Chechen and Ingush]; Aliev 1994 [Karachai and Balkar]; Dzidziguri 1971 [highland Georgian dialects and Svan]).

In a sharp irony of history, contemporary Russians, descendants of those who, caught in the juggernaut of nineteenth-century imperial expansion, sought to destroy this civilization, have provided the essentials for preserving and disseminating some of its most valuable aspects. For the Nart sagas the crucial step was the creation of literary languages in which this oral, bardic tradition, told by both men and women, could be collected and to some extent codified. In addition, museums, dance companies, and grade schools were founded. In fact, near the close of the Soviet period Moscow initiated a repatriation program (Colarusso 1991) and has since permitted the various Circassian republics to fly their traditional flag and has even promoted the singing of a national anthem. The Abkhaz, after their secession from Georgia in 1993 (Hewitt 1998; Colarusso 1995), have also flown their flag and taken on the trappings of nationhood. Following Moscow's earlier example, the Abkhaz have also invited the exiled Ubykh who also have a flag, to return to a part of their traditional territory in northern Abkhazia. Thus, after many tragedies and a hiatus of nearly two centuries, this realm may yet enter the world stage as two pluralistic states with large supporting diasporas.

The Nart sagas, which are not sagas in the usual sense of semihistorical accounts of a prominent person's life, closely resemble the myths of the pagan Norse (Davidson 1964) and Ancient Greece (Burkert 1985, especially pp. 119–225). Bards, male and female, render them through song, verse, and simple prose. Although the exploits of the characters have the magic and bravura of gods, only a few figures retain genuine deity status. In this sense they are once removed from the status of myth (note this designation by Özbay 1990), but starting with the first account of Circassian lore by the Kabardian Shora Begmurzin Nogma (Bergé 1866), the term *saga* has been used. Despite occasional references to tales (Dirr 1920; Nat'ho 1969) or legends (Dumézil 1930), I shall abide with this usage, since it has come to dominate later scholarship (Lang 1954; Özbek 1982). These sagas are of interest not only in their own right as a testament to the civilization of this lost world, but also because they show striking parallels with the traditions of the ancient peoples who at one time were in contact with the North Caucasus. They have been largely viewed as a relic of the old Iranian-speaking culture of the Scythians, Sarmatians, and Alans, with only passing reference made to Circassian lore (chiefly Dumézil 1978; see pp. 34–49, 146–68). That there is an ancient Iranian core in the various corpora is not to be denied (Dumézil 1934, 1956; Bjazyrty 1992). The name Nart is of

Indo-Iranian origin (PIE *əₙn−(ə) r-, Greek āné-r, Lincoln 1981, 97 and n. 4); Sabine Nerō- 'strong' (personal name), Umbrian nerus, Old Irish nert, Vedic Sanskrit ńrtama 'most manly' (an epithet of Indra), Sanskrit nā́, náram (accusative) 'man, hero', Avestan nar-, nərə-(gara-) (Pisani 1947, 147, §302), Ossetic nart (Benveniste 1959, 37 and n. 1). Such a view distorts the sagas' value, however, especially the value of this tradition as preserved among the Circassians and their kin. The Ossetian material (May, Salbiev, and Colarusso 2002) has been reworked to form a smooth narrative. The Chechen-Ingush lore has a great deal of material peculiar to the Northeast Caucasus in it. The Northwest lore, however, has been published in virtually a raw form, with all the odd details constituting the detritus of earlier traditions and beliefs.

Details survive millennia (epithets, names, specific features, such as size and color, social patterns, for example, as with the hero or god who has one hundred or ninety-nine followers or brothers). Thus the nonsensical and functionless features of a tradition are the oldest. One must be wary of folk reinterpretations along the lines of later cultural patterns and developments.

The relevant features may also be scattered among an array of figures, but details still survive due to the rote nature of the bard's task of learning a saga. Other details may be ascribed to different figures as the fortunes of a cult shift down through the tradition of a people. In the Nart sagas heroes are almost interchangeable in their roles, and Satanaya and her last son, Sosruquo, have expanded to assume the roles of a wide range of earlier figures, especially in the Abaza and Abkhaz corpora.

By judiciously sifting the folklore at hand for, in effect, nonsense and odd details, including names (see also Knobloch 1991), and by carefully using external controlling factors, for example, archaeological, historical, and linguistic information, one may reconstruct ancient myths and cultic beliefs from very remote periods with as much certainty as the data permit and as much certainty as any historical reconstruction may have, as the present cases show. This can be done at least for the basic lineaments of the myths, enriched by the occasional peculiar detail that may safely be posited on the basis of its survival in the attested traditions. Much more of the unwritten past may now be recoverable by such techniques than many ever dreamed possible.

The reader will gain an idea of the significance of this lore for comparative mythology by reading some of the parallels I have proposed. For Ancient Greece there are Nart figures with clear links to Aphrodite and her shepherd lover, Anchises, with the Gorgons, with Prometheus, with the Cyclopes, and with the Amazons (Colarusso 1989a, 1988). For Ancient India as depicted in the *Rig-Veda*, the Nart hero offers close ties to and insight into the great hero Indra, who slays the monster Vrtra atop a mountain and thereby releases the waters of life (Colarusso 1984b). More surprising are the striking parallels between the grim Norse war god Odin and a Nart named Wa(r)dana, as well as between the Norse world tree Yggdrasil and Lady Tree of the Narts (Colarusso 1989b, 1989c, 1984b). There may even be parallels between this Nart tradition and a myth of the ancient Hittites (see my comments at the end of sagas 23 and 60). Parallels with the Arthurian cycle are also undeniable (Littleton and Malcor 1994; Colarusso 1994b, 1994c) but are more evident in the Ossetian Nart tradition (May, Salbiev, and Colarusso 2002). I have made notes at the end of each saga regarding some of these parallels. For a few of the more important parallels, I have offered discussions in the end comments.

Good tales, like useful words, can jump language barriers. So even though the languages of the present corpora are non-Indo-European, many of the details preserved in them seem to have Indo-European parallels. Some of these, however, such as the giant atop the mountain, may ultimately be of Caucasian origin, as is most of the material in the sagas. I have suggested the dates and paths of such borrowings in a few places, but most cases present difficult questions of historical layering that can be answered only with further study. The Ossetian Nart tradition has already offered some insights into Indo-European myth (Dumézil 1978; Puhvel 1987, 217–18). Surely experts whose knowledge lies beyond my own will draw further links from the present corpora, links not only with the traditions that I have already examined but further afield, both within Indo-European and in the Turkic and Mongol traditions. It is safe to say that an incisive analysis of ancient Eurasian myth will not be possible in the future without an examination of the Nart sagas. It is also safe to say that the lover of myth will not be truly satisfied without the pleasure of having read them.

A SELECTION OF THE CIRCASSIAN NART CORPUS

Translated and Edited by
John Colarusso

with the Assistance of
Rashid T'haghapsaw
Majdalin (Habjawqua) Hilmi
Kadir Natkhwa
and others

SAGA 1 ✑ If Our Lives Be Short,

Let Our Fame Be Great

The Narts were courageous, energetic, bold, and good-hearted. Thus they lived until God sent down a small swallow.

"Do you want to be few and live a short life but have great fame and have your courage be an example for others forevermore?" asked the swallow. "Or perhaps you would prefer that there will be many of you, that your numbers will be great, that you will have whatever you wish to eat and drink, and that you will all live long lives but without ever knowing battle or glory?"

Then without calling a council, but with a reply as quick as thought itself, the Narts said, "We do not want to be like cattle. We do not want to reproduce in great numbers. We want to live with human dignity.

> If our lives are to be short,
> Then let our fame be great!
> Let us not depart from truth!
> Let fairness be our path!
> Let us not know grief!
> Let us live in freedom!"

In this way they chose to be small in numbers but to perform deeds of courage and boldness. This was the answer they gave to that small swallow to take back to God. And so their fame has remained undying among people. The Natuquaja[1] are their descendants.

From GENEG, 362, recorded in Syria in Abadzakh West Circassian.

✑ The heroic spirit articulated here is reminiscent of the Ancient Greek concept of *kleos aphthiton* 'imperishable glory' [KT]. This is the first of numerous parallels between the Nart tradition and the lore and civilization of Ancient Greece. Many of these parallels may have arisen during the long period of Greek colonization of the Black Sea coast (see Ascherson 1995, 49–88).

[1] I do not recognize the Natuquaja, the tribe referred to, as one of the historical Circassian tribes. The name seems to be a Shapsegh-derived form [nɑ(r)tʼəqʷáɡʲe] ← / nahrtʼ-

ə-q°a-a-gʸa /, with the sense of 'Nart-inal-son-conn.vowel-instr' (as a derivational suffix), literally, "the sons of the Narts." In a note Hadaghatl'a claims that this was one of the ancient Circassian tribes that lived along the Black Sea coast and that one village in this region is descended from them.

I have adopted a deep phonological representation of Circassian vowels (Kuipers 1960), whereby the neutral vowel is / ə / ([ə]), the mid, central, or front vowel is / a / ([ɛ], [æ], [a]), and the open back vowel, which also fills syllable codas, ([ɑ·]), is either / aa / if it reduces when unstressed—because it arises from two / a / s—or / ah / if it persists regardless of stress—because it seems to be patterned after the plural allomorph / -ah- / in prefixes (/ -ha- / in suffixes). Once the equivalence of persistent [ɑ] with / ah / has been made, I have assumed that the speaker extends this equivalence to those persistent [ɑ]s found also in loanwords. A more conventional analysis of / ɪ, e, a / would be closer to the Cyrillic orthography but would ignore a host of phonological patterns that link [e] as well as /ʔ/ with reducible [a]. For more on Circassian phonology and vowels, see the introductory remarks in Appendix A.

SAGA 2 ☙ *The Tale of How Warzameg and Yimis Came to Be*

It is told that the Narts had a golden tree. This was no ordinary tree, not least because it was golden. If an apple were to sprout from it in the morning, then by the evening of the same day it would have fully ripened. This same apple held within it an amazing magical power. One side of the fruit was red, and the other was white. It was said of it:

> If a barren woman tastes of the white side,
> Then to her will be born a daughter
> With hair silken white.
> If a barren woman tastes of the red side,
> Then to her will be born a Nart son,
> A great son, a white son,
> With hair silken white.

But it came to pass that the Narts could no longer enjoy the wonders of this marvelous apple. Each time an apple would sprout forth, it would be secretly stolen in the dark of night. For a long time no one could discover this thief.

"Now, alas! What are we to do?" said the Narts as they sat together at their council. Some of the wisest among them said, "A guard must be set!" And so a guard was posted by the tree. But, alas, this effort was to no avail, for during the night the apple once again disappeared.

"We must enclose the tree within a high fence made of thorns!" others then said, and a fence of sharp thorns was built around the tree. But, alas, this too was to no avail. Once more the apple disappeared during the following night.

"Now, surely we must surround the tree with a whole band of mounted warriors!" some said, and so a mighty band of armed horsemen was set around the tree. But, alas, this too was in vain. No one was able to catch a single glimpse of the thief, not even of his feet or his footprints. And in this way the theft of the apples continued for a long time.

There was one Nart, Tatemquo,[1] who had two sons. The elder was called Pija,[2] the younger Pizighash.[3] These two brothers were famous throughout the land of the Narts and beyond for their skills in battle. Their arrows never went astray; their swords never failed to slash. They came to sit guard through the night beneath the golden tree of the Narts. While they were thus sitting, the elder brother, perhaps being more tired than the younger, fell asleep. Pizighash, the younger brother, remained sitting, however, with his bow and arrows at the ready. Suddenly three doves flew up to the golden tree of the Narts and alighted on it.

"Ah, now! What should I do?" he asked himself, but he did not waste much time in thought. Quickly he took aim and shot at one of the doves and wounded it. Despite this, the three doves rose up and flew back from whence they had come, taking with them the golden apple.

Pizighash took out his white handkerchief and blotted some of the blood that the wounded dove had spilled, then he called to his brother and woke him up. He told him all that had happened, and together they set off. They followed the trail of blood left by the wounded bird until they came to the shore of the Sea of Azov.[4] There the trail disappeared.

"Now," said Pizighash, "you and I sprang from the same mother and father. So if we turn back without discovering who these thieves are, then not only will we surely be disgraced, but so will our mother and father. These three doves who returned to this sea, I shall go after them. Stay here on the shore. Wait one year for me, and if I have not returned by that time, you must assume that I am dead."

"So be it," said his elder brother. "Seek them upon the waves! Seek them in the depths! May your quest be blessed!"

Nart Pizighash struck the sea with his sword. The waters parted and he descended straightaway to the seafloor.[5] Once in the dark depths, he set off and traveled far until he came upon a mist-filled ravine. There, nestled deep within it, was a beautiful white house. He entered, and as he did so there appeared seven brothers, all of the exact same size and appearance, who followed behind him.

"Welcome!" they said. They bowed before him and showed him great respect. They stood ready to serve his every need. Two young women then entered, one carrying an ewer, the other a snow-white towel. They let him wash himself and then they retired. In a few moments they returned, bearing a small three-legged serving table laden with food. First Pizighash saw only the sumptuous array of food on the table, but then he discovered the apple that sprouts from the golden tree of the Narts lying among the delicacies.

"Aha! What is unfolding is a marvel," said the Nart youth as he sat there. "As things have happened, I have chanced upon the exact spot where my quest lies!"

They fed him and gave him drink. These men sat together as one and they stood together as one. All that they did they did as one. Finally they said to him, "We are the children of the goddess of water. In all we are seven brothers and three sisters. If you will speak honestly, then why should we keep secrets? Those you see before you are our two sisters. The third is unable to wait upon you."

"What is amiss with her? Is there any way at all that I can be of help?" asked Pizighash.

"We shall speak to you of what has befallen her," said the sons of the Lady of Flowing Waters,[6] "if it does not seem importunate."

"Speak," replied their guest.

"The three sisters used to put on the skins of doves and in this guise would fly to Nartia, land of the Narts, in search of husbands. They would bring back the apple, which sprouts in one day on the golden tree of the Narts. Until now no one has ever followed them back here, but after this flight the youngest of the three sisters, the damsel Meghazash, returned wounded. Now she lies in bed, bleeding and in need of help."

"Well then, what is needed?" asked the young Nart.

"You would not be able to find it. Her cure is some of that same blood that she shed in Nartia," they replied.

"If that is so," said the young Nart, "then I happen to have some of that very same spilled blood."

He then reached into his pocket and brought forth the white handkerchief with some of the dove's blood on it. The brothers took it from him and moistened the cloth. When they applied it to her wound, the lovely damsel Meghazash was suddenly restored to health.

The sons of the water goddess were overjoyed and sang Pizighash's praises:

"The sea's floor and the land's plane for you are both alike
But nowhere have we seen a man who is your like.
Here from our three lovely sisters, dear guest, choose you one.
We shall give you her who is dearest to your heart."

"Then if that is so," said the young Nart, "give me the one whom I have restored to health."

"The one you healed is the damsel Meghazash,[7] and so the damsel Meghazash is your good fortune," said they. So saying, the brothers gave the youngest of their three sisters to Nart Pizighash as his boon and his bride, as his reward and good fortune.

Thus the Nart who came from the dry land and the damsel who lived on the seafloor were joined together, and their families became linked one to another.

The brothers then showed great respect to Nart Pizighash and held him in the highest esteem. A great banquet was held in his honor, and he departed with the damsel Meghazash as his companion.

When Nart Pizighash returned from the sea and approached the place he had left, his brother was waiting for him. Pija was overjoyed when he saw him. "As long as you have returned alive, nothing else matters." With the maiden as companion, the three set off for their people. Once back among the Narts, a great feast was given to honor them. For seven days and nights the Narts were overjoyed. They were as happy as dogs or pigs:[8] they ate, they drank, and they danced. The feast lacked nothing.

They remained together, and as life passed Meghazash gave birth to two boys. The youngest they named Warzameg,[9] and the elder they called Yimis.[10] These sons of Meghazash rose to become the leading men in Nartia, the Circassians say, but this is another tale.

From Hadaghatl'a 1968, vol. 1, no. 3.1, pp. 86–90, in Shapsegh West Circassian.

෨ This is one of the few tales centering on an earlier generation of Narts. Spearer and Slasher, the sons of a hero whose name can be read as "Grandfather," embark on an adventure in which one of them wins a maiden, whose name means "many offspring" or "the one who is not abandoned." In doing so, they unite the realms of the earth and of the water. From this union will come one of the great heroes, Warzameg, who will in turn be leader of a yet younger generation of heroes. Parallels with the Indo-European Divine Twins, in Greek the "Dioskouroi," and their rescue of the maiden Dawn are evident, these associations themselves leading into the watery origins of the prime Greek fertility figure, Aphrodite. The golden apples have correlates also in the life-giving golden apples of the Hesperides, mentioned in the Labors of Herakles of Ancient Greece, or the magic life-giving apples of the goddess Idun, of the pagan Norse pantheon. In both traditions these apples are stolen and must be recovered so that life can continue.

[1] The name [tɑtémq°e] ← / t-ah-tá-m-q°a / 'father-intimate.possession-father-obl-son / naming.suffix' would appear to mean "grandfather." He represents the oldest of four generations of Narts, of which only oblique references such as the present one survive.

[2] Pija [pə́gʲe] ← / pʼə́-gʲ-a / 'sever-spear-in,' "he who spears."

[3] Pizigash [pʼəzəɣéś] ← / pʼə-zə-ɣá-ś / 'sever-who-causes-fall.off', "he who severs" or "he who causes parts to fall off, to be lopped off."

[4] In Circassian / mə-wə́+tʼa / 'not-val+dig', that is, "that which cannot be dammed up," the source of the Greek name for this sea, Maeotis. Note also Circassian [tʼáne] ← / tʼáana / 'the Don River', Greek *Tanais*, the name for the Don and its vicinity, and Iranian *don* 'river', perhaps a borrowing from a northern Circassian-like language.

[5] Note the obvious biblical parallel. God tells Moses: "But lift thou up thy rod, and stretch out thine hand over the sea, and divide it: and the children of Israel shall go on dry ground through the midst of the sea" (Exod. 14:16).

[6] The name of this water goddess is [pséthe g°áśʲe] ← / psə́-tha g°áaśʲa / 'water-god lady', at one point, and /psə́-x̌°a g°áaśʲa / 'water-flow (river) lady' at another.

[7] This may be an Iranian name, *maga-zač*, Sanskrit *maha*, Greek *mega-*, English *much*, and for the second stem Ossetic *zæic* 'offspring', that is, "(she with) many offspring," similar in sense to *Setenaya*, Iranian *sata*, Latin *centum*, Lithuanian *šimtas*, English *hund(red)*, Circassian / na-ya / 'mother-the.one.of', "mother of one hundred," the fertility figure of the next generation. In purely Circassian terms, it would be /mə-ɣa-za-čʲʸ/ 'not-let-(be)one-inst', "the one who is not abandoned," which in fact accords well with the tale and therefore probably reflects a folk etymology.

[8] Literally, [ħekʲʸefqʼ°əkʲʸef] ← / ħa-kʲʸaf-qʼ°ə-kʲʸaf / 'dog-happy-pig-happy'. The Circassians consider dogs and pigs the happiest of animals.

[9] The name has no clear etymology within Circassian. It appears in various Circassian dialects as 'Warzamayg', 'Warzamaj', or 'Warzamas.' It reflects the form *warza-māka*, borrowed from an Iranian language other than Ossetian, which has *Uryzmæg*. The name would be an adjective (-*māka*) based on the Indo-European stem *Hwerg-* 'to strangle', as in several Germanic legal terms that have an association with strangling or being hanged, such as Old Norse *vargr* 'wolf, outlaw', Old English *wearg* 'monster, outlaw', Modern English

worry, and even Hittite *hurkel* 'outlaw, sex criminal' (see Gerstein 1974, 172), though for the last one Held, Schmalstieg, and Gertz (1987, 151) have only the gloss 'outrage, offense'.

So, originally he was the great wolf or outlaw, which is in keeping with his scruffy appearance in some accounts. This etymology receives support for the tale of the rape of Setenaya, something now expressed through the separate figure of the Gorgon swineherd (saga 4) but perhaps originally a deed performed by proto-Warzameg.

Abaev (1996, 4:127; 1990, pp. 246–47) does not know what to make of this root, noting only that it has an Iranian pedigree and belongs to that group of names ending with -*maka*. Knobloch (1991, 64, §218) takes the form back to Iranian *warāza-* 'wild boar' solely on the basis of the Armenian form (borrowed from Iranian) *Varazman*, which may or may not be relevant. Benveniste (1959, 129) takes it back to a hypothetical *(a)varazmaka-*, but notes that it is devoid of sense even if of obvious Iranian form.

[10] This name would appear to be linked with an Indo-Iranian source; cf. Sanskrit *Yama* and Avestan *Yima*, both gods of death. Circassian folk etymology takes the name to be / yə-mə́-s / 'inside-not-sit', "the one who is never home, the wanderer." In fact, the Circassian form may have been reshaped from an earlier Iranian one to fit this folk etymology. The link to an Indo-Iranian death figure, specifically to the Iranian form *yima-*, is strengthened by the fact that in the saga "How Warzameg, Son of Meghazash, Won the Damsel Psatina" (saga 3) a third brother is added after Yimis, Pshimaruquo, whose name means "Prince of Death" (see the end comments in saga 39). He would seem merely to be an epithet of Yimis elevated to the status of a character.

SAGA 3 ◑ *How Warzameg, Son of Meghazash, Won the Damsel Psatina*

The Nart Lady Meghazash had three sons[1], Warzameg, Yimis, and Pshimaruquo[2], and three daughters also. The latter had no equals in beauty.

When the time drew near for Meghazash to die, she gathered her sons about her and conveyed to them her last wishes. "Sons," she said, "you will give each of my three daughters to a good man thus. When seven months have passed after my death, you will be visited in the middle of the night by a horseman who will ride into the center of our courtyard and cry out to you, 'Are you ready?' Give to him your eldest sister. Then, when a further three months have passed, another horseman will come in the night just like the first. You will give to him your middle sister. Finally, one night a third horseman will come as the others will have, and to him you will give the youngest. There is one further demand I must make of you: do not ask these horsemen to which clans they belong.[3]

"Aside from this, you will find three horses ready and standing in the stable. May they bring you happiness. May you test yourselves on them and award the best horse to the best man.[4] Divide the remaining livestock among yourselves. After this, when the time has come for you to marry and live apart, let the Nart council divide the property among you. Then live apart. I shall not divide this property among you myself, because you would then say, 'You gave this one more and the other one less,' and saying this you would curse me in your hearts."

Seven months after Meghazash died, a horseman came in the middle of the night, just as she had foreseen. He cried out, "Are you ready?" The youngest son, Warzameg, came out of the house and bade him welcome; he then went back in to tell his eldest brother what was happening and to ask him what he should do. This brother told Warzameg, "I shall not give my sister to a man whose clan I do not know. Go back to bed!" But Warzameg obeyed his mother's last wishes, and instead of returning to bed, he went to his eldest sister and helped her prepare for the journey. Then he led her outside into the courtyard and gave her away to the horseman.[5]

Three months later a second rider came in the night, rode into the courtyard, and cried out, "Are you ready?" Again Warzameg came out of the house and bade him welcome. Then he went to his middle brother, told him what was happening, and asked him what they should do. This brother told Warzameg, "I cannot give my sister to a man whose clan I do not know. Go back to bed!" But once more Warzameg obeyed his mother's last wishes and helped prepare the middle girl for the journey. Then he led her outside into the courtyard, as he had the first, and gave her to the horseman.

Finally the last horseman came in the night, as had the others, and cried out, "Are you ready?" Warzameg came out and bade him welcome. Then he, as youngest brother, went back in to his youngest sister's room. He told her what was happening and asked her, "Will you go with him?"

"I shall. All this was preordained for me long ago," she said.

"Then so be it! Dress yourself!" He then helped her to prepare for the journey. He led her outside into the courtyard and gave her to the horseman.

Some time later the three brothers were speaking among themselves. The two elder brothers suddenly asked Warzameg, "Where are our sisters?"

"They have left us for husbands. Each has married by her own wishes," he replied.

"No! You have sullied our honor. You have given them away to those horsemen in the night," they said and grew furious at him. "If a guest should come, then the obligations of the host will rest entirely on you. You yourself must do anything and everything that our sisters would have done." So they sought to punish him for what they saw as his treachery.

For a long time Warzameg did all the chores of the household. Soon he grew tired and could no longer carry on with his tasks. He sought the help of his friends, and they advised him to seek wives for his elder brothers so that the women could then aid him in his work about the house. He followed their advice. All went well, and soon the elder brothers had brides.

Then one day Warzameg's brothers were talking between themselves and decided that it was their younger brother's turn to find himself a wife. When they broached this subject to him, he said, "I shall not marry as you did. The one whom I shall marry is the damsel Psatina,[6] sister of the Nart Lady Setenaya. Among all the Narts there is no other whom I would marry."

His brothers laughed at him and mocked him cruelly, saying, "How can you marry her? We have had word that she lives in a land far away that you could never even reach."

"I shall go!" said Warzameg.

Warzameg had received a bay horse when he and his brothers had divided their mother's estate. Now Warzameg readied himself and his horse for the long journey. As he was about to leave, he said to his brothers' wives, "If I live, I shall return. If I die, then my mortal remains will be brought back to you. Until you see my corpse, do not mourn me or raise a grave mound for me." Upon saying this, he turned and rode out of the courtyard and off into the empty plain.

No one knows whether he traveled long or a little, but finally he came to a village. Warzameg rode up to a little old shepherd who was tending his flock on the outskirts.

"May your herd be bountiful!" Warzameg said in a customary greeting.

"Thank you! Please come to my house and be my guest," the little old man replied.

"Thank you, but no. This I cannot do, nor can I tell you the reason for my journey. Where, though, might I find good lodging?" Warzameg asked, quite oblivious of the insult he was giving to the old man by declining his offer of hospitality.[7]

"Well then, enter yonder," the little old man said, ignoring the young man's blunder, and he pointed a house out to Warzameg. "But if you ever need the wisdom of an old man," he added, "do not hesitate to seek me out."

Warzameg entered the courtyard of the house he was shown. There the people greeted him, helped him dismount, and led him to the guest quarters. They then went to the mistress of the house and said, "We have a weary guest and he must be served promptly."

As the mistress of the house stepped out into her courtyard to draw water from the well, she at once recognized the bay horse as belonging to her youngest brother. She was Warzameg's eldest sister. She ran to the guest quarters to see if her brother had really come.

"Ah, Warzameg! I knew I was fated to aid you in your quest, for you cannot fulfill it alone. But you are no mere guest. Come with me!" she said and led him to the main house. There he washed up. Then they sat down and began to eat together.

Warzameg asked his sister, "Is your husband one of the men I met in the guest quarters?"

"No. He is at the wedding celebration of the damsel Psatina, but he should return soon," she replied.

Even as she was saying this her husband rode into the courtyard. He dismounted and led his horse into the stable. There he saw a bay horse standing in the place normally reserved for his own. "We must have a guest," he thought and entered the guest quarters to greet him. Those therein said, "There is no guest here. The lady of the house came in and said, 'You are no mere guest!' and led him out."

"This must be a special guest, indeed," he thought as he went to the main house. He entered and saw Warzameg seated on the decorated cot, reserved for the most honored guests. The man bade Warzameg welcome and then sat down.

The sister noticed that her husband sat troubled and silent, and she asked him, "Do you not know who it is that sits here with us?"

"Of course I know! He is your brother."

"Well, yes," she said, "but he is my youngest brother, the one who led me out to you in the courtyard that night."

Still her husband sat glumly, and so she asked him, "Why are you so sad? Do you think that he has come to ask for me back or to demand a bride-price from you?"

"No, that isn't it at all. How could it ever be that he and I could not resolve any problem that arose between us? If he says, 'I want her back,' then I shall give you back. If he says, 'I want wealth for her,' then I shall gladly give him cattle or whatever he wants. What troubles me is something else altogether," he replied, and then he began to relate the tale of his journey.

"I was thinking instead of the wedding celebration that my brother and I went to. The family had chosen my younger brother and me to be responsible for the festivities for the three days required, and so as lords of the dance and feast we took our rightful place in the center of the festivities. The celebration was over the day before yesterday, but we had to stay and tally up all the expenses for them and so could not return right away. Earlier today we finished everything and set off for home, but as we came to the forest road we heard someone screaming. We scattered and took cover. Someone was abducting the damsel Psatina! We cried out to the kidnapper and offered to hold a parlay, but he ignored our pleas. We fought with him, but in the end he escaped with her. He was riding a horse called Zhaqa. No other horse alive today can catch up to it.[8] We were not able to help her, and I do not know what we should have done. It is this which bothers me," said the master of the house.

Warzameg saw his chance and said, "If someone has taken the damsel Psatina and carried her off, I shall bring her back, dead or alive."

No one could hold back Warzameg, son of Meghazash. In the middle of the night he went to his horse and rode off into the darkness. He did not know which way to go, but soon he came upon a road and set off on that. He came to a little old shepherd tending his flock on the outskirts of a village.

"Welcome, young man! Please be my guest at my home!" said the little old man.

"No, thank you. I am not a rider who can stay and chat. I have urgent business. Tell me where I may spend the night."

The little old man pointed out a nearby house to him and sent him on his way. "But if you ever need the wisdom of an old man, do not hesitate to come to me," said the little old shepherd.

When Warzameg the Nart entered the courtyard that the little old man had shown to him, some people came out to greet him and help him dismount. Then they led him into the guest quarters.

Soon thereafter the mistress of the house came out into the courtyard and recognized the visitor's bay horse. She was Warzameg's middle sister. Like her sister before her, she went into the guest quarters and led Warzameg out, saying to him as she did so, "You are no mere guest."

They sat down together to talk, and while thus seated the woman's husband returned and entered the courtyard. He went to the guest quarters, but finding no one there he went to the main house. There he welcomed Warzameg and sat down, but soon he was lost in thought. When his wife saw that her husband was brooding, she asked him, "What troubles you?"

"When we were crossing through the forest, we saw the great scaly giant Arkhon Arkhozh[9] abducting the damsel Psatina, who was crying out for help. But alas, we could do nothing. We tried to stop him, but he killed some of us and wounded others. He escaped with her, without suffering a scratch."

"I shall find the damsel Psatina. I shall bring her back, either alive or dead," Warzameg said. He mounted his horse again and once more rode off.

He rode on for a long time until finally he came upon a little old shepherd tending his flock on the outskirts of a village. The little old man approached and bade him welcome in good Circassian manner. Warzameg, however, would not accept his hospitality because he feared that he would be a burden to one so old and that his quest would be delayed by the little old man's slowness. Rather, he insisted that the little old man point out a place where he could stay. Warzameg then went into the courtyard that had been pointed out to him and hitched his horse to a post. He was greeted by men who led him to the guest quarters. Soon the mistress of the house came out into the courtyard and saw the bay horse. She recognized it at once, for she was Warzameg's youngest sister. She went to the guest quarters and led Warzameg back to the main house.[10]

Warzameg asked his sister, "Where is the master of the house?"

"He has a great many cattle and has gone to count them," she replied. "He should return shortly."

Just then the master of the house rode back into the courtyard. As with the others, he eventually came to the main house, where he sat down and began to brood.

"This is my youngest brother who sits here, the one who brought me out to you in the courtyard that night," she said to her husband, "and yet you show him no courtesy."

"Forgive me," said her husband to Warzameg, "but as I was returning here I met some people who were coming back from the wedding feast of the damsel Psatina. They brought me terrible tidings and I worry now about these."

"I know whereof you speak. The damsel Psatina has been carried off," replied Warzameg. "It is she whom I seek. I must go now."

"No. You mustn't. You would never be able to overcome him by your-self," the husband warned him. "He is carrying her off not to be his bride but rather to prove his might. This is his way of seeking a worthy oppo-nent from among the Narts, a hero capable of defeating him."

Despite these words, he was not able to dissuade Warzameg. The hus-band said, "Your horse will not be able to carry you there," and he offered him another horse. "You will come to a river too wide for you to cross. Do not enter it! Go up along the bank and you will find a boatman. Persuade him to convey you to the other side."[11]

Thus Warzameg set off and eventually came to an enormous river. As told to do, he went along the bank until he came upon a little old man sit-ting there.

"Where are you going, young man?" asked the little old man. "An evil scaly giant lives on the other side of this river. He kills everybody. He will not allow even a bird to fly about in his domain. You will surely perish at his hands."

"No," insisted Warzameg, "I will not die at his hands. Help me cross this river!" The little old man gave in to Warzameg's plea and ferried him across the river.

When they had reached the other side, the little old man advised him, "Now perhaps you need the wisdom of an old man. During the day do not leave the protection of the forest. Travel only at night! At dawn you will draw near his garden, and you might see him there. Beware if you fail to catch a glimpse of him, for you yourself might be seen and killed."

So Warzameg set off, traveling only at night. As the sun was beginning to rise, he came to a garden. He heard weeping and looked about. There in the garden sat the damsel Psatina.

"Come over here, my lady," he whispered to her. "Come up to the fence. Is it possible to get in?" he asked her. The damsel Psatina went to a spot in the fence, opened a hidden gate, and let him in.

"Psatin,[12] I have come for you. I shall take you back."

"No! You would be in terrible trouble and so would I. Even if the scaly giant does not awaken, his horse Zhaqa is certain to hear us and crush us with his hooves. The giant sleeps until noon."

"Trust me! Let us go!" urged Warzameg. "We can go far by the noon hour." He helped Psatina onto his horse and rode off with her seated behind him. They rode until they reached the river and came up to the little old man.

"The evil scaly giant will kill you," said the little old man. "The ride that you made in the span of a morning he can make in a moment. He will catch up with you and kill you. Do not ride out into the open steppe! Travel along the edge of the forest!"

Again they set off. They had been riding a while when Warzameg looked back and saw a horseman coming after them.

"That must be him. What should we do?" he asked Psatina. "If we turn off into this field, his shepherds and those who tend his horses will see us and our lives will not be safe with them. They will betray us, for if they didn't, he would kill them all. He is crazed. We can't leave the forest's edge. We must stay where we are."

Psatina said, "Let me stay here. You go into the forest and hide. If I perish at his hands, then at least you will survive. If I cannot handle him, then you must not try either."

Warzameg agreed. He took cover in the forest so that he could still watch over the damsel Psatina. The scaly giant rode up alongside Psatina. "You and I agreed that I would keep you for a span of seven years. If during this time no Nart came to challenge me for you, then I was to take you back to your home. Was this not what we agreed to do? Who was the man you were riding with? Where is he?"

"I did not mean to break our agreement, but the horseman was waiting, and I was sure that I could not awaken you. So I went off with him," she replied.

"Where is this horseman?" demanded the giant.

"Here!" cried Warzameg and he strode forth.

"Who are you? What do you want?" bellowed the scaly giant.

"I have come for the damsel Psatina. If you give her to me, then I shall take her back. If you refuse, then I shall attack and slay you."

The scaly giant reached over, grabbed the youth, and with contempt hurled him back into the forest. "Now come here!" he ordered Psatina. He grabbed the maiden and carried her off again, warning her, "Never do that again! When the seven years have passed, I myself shall take you back to your home."

When Warzameg's sister and her husband saw his horse return without its rider, they thought, "Surely, he has been killed." They set off to look for his body. Soon they came upon the cloak that Warzameg had sat on while hiding in the forest. Suspecting that Warzameg himself might be near, they looked all about and finally found him still clinging to life. Carefully they bore him back with them.

They tended to him carefully, and when he had been nursed back to health, he said to them, "Now I must go." They tried to dissuade him, but he refused to heed their words. Once more he mounted the horse that they had given him and rode off. He came once more to the little old man sitting in his boat.

"Grandfather, I have come again. The scaly giant caught up with me and took the damsel Psatina away from me. If you know how I can save her, then tell me! Surely you must know a way."

"I shall tell you how you may save her if you can. I know that the horse that gave birth to Zhaqa is still alive. Ask Psatina to find out from the giant its whereabouts. He will certainly tell her where to find that horse. There is no one else who can persuade him. Also, pay heed to those in need! Never pass by someone in distress without offering your help to him!"

The old man ferried the youth across the river once more, and Warzameg set off. Again he came to the giant's garden and entered by the hidden gate. When Psatina saw him she said, "Why won't you stop risking your life? Our lives were spared the first time we tried to escape. But if I go off with you again, he'll only catch us as he did before and we both may perish."

"No, I have not come to make things worse for you. I have come this time not to take you back but rather seek your help. I must know the whereabouts of the horse that gave birth to Zhaqa. You must trick the scaly giant into telling you where this horse is kept. Only when I have found this horse can I return for you. Then I shall be able to carry you back, and no one will be able to stop us."

"Go back into the forest and hide," she said to him. "Don't let him see even your shadow. If I can, I shall make him tell me about this horse," she said.

Arkhon Arkhozh awoke and went out into his courtyard. He began to exercise with some steel bars and to bend them and toss them about. After a short time he went over to the maiden.

"What do you think of that?" he bragged.

"That is all very amazing, but I suspect that Zhaqa taught you how to do to that," she replied. "Tell me, what sort of mare gave birth to Zhaqa?"

The scaly giant was surprised at her question and grew suspicious. Sensing this, Psatina took great care to remain calm, and eventually she succeeded in making him divulge all to her. Psatina discovered that the mare that had given birth to Zhaqa still lived and was kept near a cove among a herd of horses. These belonged to a sorceress called the Bitch of the Flying Wagon.[13] She now had all the information that Warzameg needed. The next time they met, she passed all this along to him.

Warzameg said, "Do not worry. If I survive, I will make my way back to you. If the horses are there, I will find the mare." With these words he was off.

In the course of his long quest, Warzameg came out into an open plain. There along the trail he stopped under a nearby tree. While he was resting there, a hawk, in headlong flight, swooped down and alighted on him.

"Ah, Lord!" he said. "I must help this poor creature." He then took the hawk in his hands.

"Save me!" cried the hawk. "But you can't save me this way." So Warzameg stuffed the hawk under the folds at the chest of his coat. An enormous hawk suddenly flew up and asked Warzameg if he had seen a fleeing hawk. Warzameg did not reply, and the giant hawk flew away. Warzameg reached into his coat and set the smaller hawk free. Before it flew away it said, "I cannot help you now, but if later you find yourself in trouble, call my name." Then it flew off.

Warzameg had set off again when after a short time he came upon a wolf who had fallen into a hidden ravine that opened up in the steppe. Warzameg thought, "I shall lower a rope down to this wolf and help it back up." "Help me!" cried the wolf. "But you cannot help me that way; you will fall in yourself. Instead, search the surrounding countryside and find a shepherd. Buy a sheep from him, slaughter it, and give it to me bit by bit. Then with your help I shall be strong enough to climb out." Warzameg set off and soon came upon a shepherd. He told him that he needed a sheep.

"Welcome!" said the shepherd. "I shall kill a sheep for you." He picked one out, killed it, and gave it to Warzameg.

Warzameg brought the carcass back to the ravine and skinned it. He gave some to the wolf, and when it had finished that mouthful, he gave it some more. Bit by bit, the wolf ate the whole sheep and in this way regained its strength.

"Now," said the wolf, "lower the rope. Tie the rope to a tree. Don't try to hold it yourself! Do as I say and I shall be able to crawl out."

Warzameg did as the wolf said, and the wolf crawled out of the ravine.

"Was that enough to satisfy you, wolf? No? Then if you are still hungry, have what is left," and he gave it the lungs, which were all that was left.

The wolf said, "The dogs of the shepherd chased me away from the sheep, and I fell into the ravine. If ever you find yourself in trouble, call my name and I shall come to your aid." Then the wolf loped off.

Warzameg traveled a great distance until he reached a great lake. The tide had receded and stranded a catfish on the shore. "I shall help this poor creature," said Warzameg. He picked up the catfish, gave it food, washed the dirt off it, and set it free in the lake.

"If ever trouble befalls you, call my name and I shall come to your aid," said the catfish before it swam out of sight.

Warzameg went yet farther and eventually passed beyond the shore of the great lake and into an immense forest. Deep in the forest he heard a voice crying from an eagle's nest in the top of a tree. Remembering what the little old boatman had told him, he stopped to offer help. He tied his horse up and began to climb toward the nest. As he climbed higher, he saw that two baby birds had fled their nest in an effort to escape a snake that had wound its way up the tree after them. Warzameg struck and killed the snake. The little birds were grateful to him, but before they could say anything, Warzameg had passed out from the poisonous fumes given off by the dead snake and fell to the ground. The mother eagle returned. She did not see him lying unconscious at the foot of the tree.

"Pfew! There are humans about. I smell them!" she said.

"He saved us and killed the snake," said her little ones. They showed her Warzameg, lying below.

The mother eagle then went to fetch water to revive the man who had saved her chicks. She returned with a beakful and forced some into Warzameg's mouth.

"What are you seeking?" she asked.

"I passed by your tree on my way to the horses of the sorceress," he said. "I seek to become her herdsman."

"No," said the eagle. "You must not go to her. You will surely perish if you do."

"I must go, even if I am to die," he swore.

"Then so be it," said the eagle. "I shall take you, both you and your horse, but the sorceress must not see me. Now let me set off to hunt so that tonight I can leave enough food for my little ones until I come back."

She then flew off and after a while came back with food for her brood. Then she bore Warzameg and his horse over the sea. There, on the far shore, she showed him a house with a fence around it.

"Don't go in there now!" she said. "Wait until night and then make an opening in the fence. In the morning you will be able to sneak in. At that time the sorceress will come outside and look all around her land. She will sit down over there." The eagle pointed to a spot. "Creep up on her and put your mouth to her breast."[14] Then the eagle flew back across the sea.

That night the youth dug a tunnel under the fence. The next morning when the sorceress came out into her yard to survey her land, the youth crept up to her, and before she could stop him he put his mouth to one of her breasts. Then in dismay she began to beat on her own eyes and ears.

"Why, Mother, do you beat yourself so?" asked her new foster son.

"I beat them because my eyes did not see and my ears did not hear. What is it that you want?"

"I want to be the herdsman of your horses," he replied.

"No! You wouldn't be able to do it," she said. "But if you stay around the house instead and watch what goes on in the courtyard for a year, then you will come of age."

The youth refused to listen to her advice.

"So be it!" she said. "However, if you lose any of those which I place under your protection, I shall eat you!"

They sat down together in her coach[15] and set off. When they reached the forest, the sorceress's coachman found the youth's horse and took it along with them until they came to her herd. The sorceress showed the boy her horses and made her way back home. The youth spent the day riding to and fro and watching over the herd. When night fell, the sorceress's horses lay down to sleep. He himself lay down intending only to rest but fell asleep. Upon awakening, the horses were gone, and although he searched hither and yon, he could find them nowhere. Finally, while riding along the edge of a stream, he came upon a catfish lying on the bank. It spoke to him and asked, "Why, boy, are you crying?"

"I have lost the horses," he replied.

"If that is so," said the catfish, "then stay here and I shall find them," and off it went.

Not much time had gone by when the catfish drove the horses back to him.

"Now, do not think of me again," it said. "My debt to you has been paid." Then it slid back into the water.

At dawn the old witch set off, convinced that Warzameg would have lost the horses. So when she arrived in the forest where her herd was kept, she said to him, "Surely, you have lost all the horses!"

"No," he replied. "I have not lost them."

"Then you have earned my first praises. Hobble your horse, set it out to graze, and then come and sit in the cart with me," she said. When he had done this, she let the youth sit down in the cart, and they rode back together.

Back at her house she made him hot cornmeal with milk. When he had finished eating, she told him, "Rest, sleep well, and don't worry about anything. You must ready yourself for two more nights of testing to prove yourself worthy of being my herdsman."

Again in the morning she made him hot cornmeal with milk for breakfast. Then she made him sit in the cart, brought him back to watch over the horses, and returned to the house.

When the youth found his own horse among the others, he mounted it and drove the other horses to the edge of the forest. There, while watching them, he grew drowsy. "I'll just take a little nap," he said, and so he dismounted, sat down, and fell asleep.

He awoke and again found that his horses had disappeared. He followed their trail but could not find them. While riding in the thick forest high up on a mountainside, he chanced upon a wolf.

"What has caused you such sorrow, boy?" the wolf asked him.

"To my sorrow," said Warzameg, "I have lost the horses once again."

"Say no more," it said. "Stay here and I shall drive them back to you," and the wolf loped off into the forest.

A long time passed, but at dawn the wolf drove the horses back to him.

"Boy," it said, "more remains of your ordeal, so don't let them wander off again. I have paid my debt to you; think of me no more." And with that the wolf went back into the forest.

The old witch returned. "Since you have once more kept the horses from disappearing," she said, "you have earned my second praises." She made the youth turn his horse free among the herd and let him climb into the cart to carry him back. Once there, she let him eat and lie down to rest.

The following morning when the youth went back to the herd for the third time, he drove the horses into an open field. This time he became drowsy and fell asleep in the saddle. When he opened his eyes the horses were no longer there. He went in search of them but could not find a single one. When he stopped to catch his breath, a hawk alighted next to him.

Warzameg said to it, "I was watching over a herd of horses and I let them go astray."

"Sit here for a while," said the hawk, "and I shall find them for you," and so it flew off.

A long time passed before the hawk returned driving the horses before it. "Now only a little time remains in your ordeal, so do not fall asleep again. My debt to you has been paid; think of me no more," it said and flew away for the last time.

The old witch arrived. "Now you have earned my third praises, my boy! Now there is no one who can surpass you. The horse that I will give you is about to be born." As before, she made the youth sit in the cart and carried him back to the house. She let the youth rest long and well that night, and in the morning the two of them went to the horses. Two new colts had been born in the night, one with a bad foot. When it came time to choose, Warzameg chose the lame one.

"That one is bad," she said. But he insisted on having it.[16]

Thus Warzameg set off and began his journey homeward. Eventually he, his horse, and the lame colt came to a riverbank. They sat for a while and pondered how they might ford the river. Then the little colt spoke and said, "I do not have the strength that you hope for, but if you set me free, I will suckle from my mother for a while, and then there will be no one who can conquer me." So he set the colt free.

The colt suckled with its mother for one whole day and returned in the evening.

"Now I have the strength to carry you across the river," it said, "but don't let anything come in front of me to impede me."

The youth mounted the colt and held the other horse beside him as they crossed the river. On the other shore he stopped by the little old man and told him how he had found the horse. Warzameg then set off for his home but stopped on the way back where Princess Psatina was being held captive.[17] When he reached the stronghold of Arkhon Arkhozh, he called to her.

"Why did you come again?" Psatina wept.

Warzameg said, "Don't be afraid. Mount my horse. I shall ride the colt." They set off for home, but while riding back they saw a horseman riding after them. The colt spoke and said, "Neither of you say a word. I'll talk with this rider's horse."

They were standing in a little group when Zhaqa approached with the scaly giant on his back. As it turned out, Zhaqa was the elder brother of the lame colt, and so the younger brother said to his elder brother, "What sort of giant is sitting on your back? Where are you taking him?"

"You know full well that I bear the evil scaly giant," replied Zhaqa. "What can I do?"

"I have a plan," said the colt. "Go slowly and he will whip you. Then bolt and throw him, and trample him against the stones. Then we can kill him."

As the colt had said, Zhaqa did do, and then Warzameg killed the evil scaly giant. Warzameg and Psatina sat on his horse, Zhaqa, and started off to the first of Warzameg's brothers-in-law, carrying with them the giant's head.

They stuck the head of Arkhon Arkhozh on a stake of a wattle fence and then went into the house. They were greeted joyfully. The people of the village assembled and passed judgment on the dead giant, "Every year this giant extorted much wealth from us. Let us go together and bring back from his stronghold all our belongings." And off they went. They brought back people whom the scaly giant had enslaved, livestock, and everything else that was there. They set the slaves free. They distributed the livestock among themselves. Of the former slaves, those who wanted to go back to their homes did so; those who wanted to remain stayed. They said to Warzameg, "Now that you have endured so much hardship for Psatina, we think that it is fitting that you take her as your wife."[18]

"Indeed, I want her," he said, "but what matters is what she herself says."

When they asked her, she assented and said that she would stay by him.

The youngest sister made the first three-day wedding feast for them. They then went to his middle sister, already having been given every gift they could possibly need. The middle sister did as the youngest had done. They then left her and passed on to the eldest. She did likewise. Then with his brothers' wives and his sisters, he returned to his brothers' house. There his three sisters and sisters-in-law made a seven-day feast for him.

Nart Warzameg lived in abundance and good health for a long time. Not long after he had begun living with the damsel Psatina she bore him a son. That was Shebatinuquo,[19] of whom it is told that he accomplished many brave deeds. For this reason they say that Shebatinuquo and Sawseruquo are cousins.[20] They say too that the damsel Psatina was also the mother of the Nart Yasharuquo.[21]

From Hadaghatl'a 1968, vol. 1, no. 12, pp. 113–24, in Bzhedukh West Circassian.

☙ Here the female fertility figure has the transparent name of Life-Giving Mother, *Psa-ti-na*. She is said to be the sister of Setenaya, the female fertility figure who is later associated with Warzameg as his consort (West Circassian 'Setenaya' /sat'anáaya/, Kabardian East Circassian 'Seteney' /satanáy/, Abaza and Ubykh 'Satanaya' /satanáya/, and Abkhaz 'Satanay' /satanáy/). She is probably an old epithet of Setenaya elevated to the status of a person. Psatina is rescued by the young Warzamas, elsewhere depicted as old. In the course of this rescue, he visits a land where nothing stirs, not even a bird in the sky. Her abductor, whose name has reptilian connotations, rides the fastest horse, called Grave Mound. This steed is reminiscent of the horse in saga 28, ridden by Wardana, and which has a parallel in the horse Sleipnir of the Norse myths, the horse of the god of war and of the dead, Odin. Unlike the Greek goddess Persephone, who was destined to spend half the year with her husband, Hades, after he had abducted her, Psatina is fully returned to the world of the living. One may note the further Greek parallel between Charon, the boatman who ferries the dead across the river Styx into Hades, and the little old man whom the hero encounters repeatedly, the last time as a ferryman. This little old man appears in another saga (31), along with a little old woman. Together they are the guardians of the souls of the Narts.

[1] The verb "won" in the title is "lead back." The sense is one of abducting the woman, the customary form of marriage in the Caucasus. Usually these abductions were prearranged with the cooperation of the family of the bride-to-be.

[2] The figure of Pshimaruquo has been added to the Warzameg-Yimis duo (see saga 2, "The Tale of How Warzameg and Yimis Came to Be") merely to make it a trio. The name means "Prince of Death," / pš'ə-mahrə́-q°a / 'prince-death.spirit gd-son', probably merely an epithet of Yimis if the latter is related to the Indo-Iranian god of death, Sanskrit *Yama*, Avestan *Yima*. The / -mahrə- / in his name is an Indo-European loan and appears in such words as Latin *mortis* 'death (gen)', *mori* 'to die', Greek *brotós* from **mrotós* 'mortal', German *Mord*, English *murder*, and *(night-)mare*. (See the end comments in saga 39.)

[3] This is a gross breach of etiquette. "Abductions" are proper only if both families are familiar with each other's pedigrees and if their intentions are known to each other beforehand. Otherwise the abduction is a criminal offense.

[4] This odd custom involves assigning the horses in an estate to the best riders among the heirs. The heirs hold a contest, riding on various mounts. The goal is, I believe, to match the best horse with the best rider. I am indebted to B. George Hewitt and Zaira Khiba Hewitt for this explanation.

[5] The original text is quite garbled here and in the next few lines. Warzameg goes to his eldest sister, skips over her to go to his middle sister while failing to give the elder away, and so forth. It is clear, however, from later developments in the story that he is the only one of his brothers to follow his mother's dying wishes and to give each of his sisters away.

[6] The name is /psa-t'ə́-na/ 'life-give-mother', "Life-Giving Mother." In this text the dialect (Bzhedukh) has Warzamas. Here Psatina's true identity is hidden in a kinship bond. Setenaya and Psatina are indistinguishable. In all other sagas Warzameg is married to Setenaya.

[7] The rules of guest and host are among the strongest in Caucasian culture insofar as they take on the form of a transient symbolic kinship. Warzameg is depicted as a callow

youth who is unaware of even the rudiments of social conduct. The little old man, who appears in several guises throughout this saga, remains unoffended, however, and offers his aid to the youth at a future time.

[8] The whole significance of this saga is revealed by the etymology of this name. The name means "grave mound," / ža- / as in Bzhedukh / žáɣ°ə / 'foot hill', Ubykh / ʒarɣa / 'mountain slope', or for the sense of 'mound' in Bzhedukh / ža / 'lower jaw', / ža-pq / 'jawbone', "chin," / ƛa-g°á-a-n-ʒa / 'leg-zone-conn-obl.conn-mound', "knee." The / -qʿa / is simply Bzhedukh 'grave'. Thus this is the horse of the grave mound, which carries souls to the land of death. This finds an exact parallel in the Scythian burial custom of interring a horse in the grave mound of a chieftain, recorded by Herodotus. Psatina's name as "Life-Giving Mother" now takes on added significance. Her abduction represents the loss of the life force to the world of death. Warzameg's quest to free her recalls the Vedic Indra's effort to free the life-giving waters from the clutches of a strangling serpent. A striking corroboration of this interpretation is the fact that the giant who has abducted Psatina appears in other variants with the same name but with the form of a giant serpent or dragon. (See the next note.)

[9] This name, / arx̌°án arx̌°an-ə́ź /, with the suffix / -əź / 'old, venerable; ugly, evil', refers to a giant, the ruler of the realm of the dead. In some variants of this saga, this name was applied to a giant serpent or dragon that lived underground. By some accounts he is a "lizard man," a quasi-human reptilian demon. If a serpent is intended, then one might see in the name */a-r-x̌°a-n/ 'the-gliding.motion-turn-inf', "the one who glides in coils," a good epithet for a serpent, for / x̌°a- / '(to) coil, turn'; cf. Bzhedukh / x̌°aráy / 'winding, turning', Ubykh / x̌°ə́x̌°dá / '(to) slide, slither, coil' (Vogt 1963, 210, entry 2170).

One should note that in the Kabardian saga "Wazermas Takes Dadukha for a Wife" in Hadaghatl'a (1968, vol. 1, no. 6, pp. 101–4), this villain's role is taken by a wild man of the forest, a sort of yeti or a bigfootlike creature (see Ubykh sagas 90 and 91).

[10] The Circassians and their kin once lived in enclosed properties with several buildings. In addition to stables and storage facilities, there was a guest house and a main house. Large families would even have several houses for married sons within the complex.

[11] This little old man appears in several sagas, occasionally with a little old woman as his wife. He is generally associated with danger and the land of the dead, often with safe conduct to and from this realm. He recalls the Greek Charon, the boatman of the ferry over the river Styx, who carries the dead to Hades.

[12] In vocative forms (as well as copular or predicative ones) the last vowel is dropped.

[13] The witch has the elaborate name / k°ə-x̌aráyna ḥà-a-bzə-wə́də / 'wagon-flying / swinging dog-conn-female-witch / demon / sorcerer', so this literally means "the Bitch Witch of the Flying Wagon." Despite her important role in this story and her fascinating name, she remains an enigmatic figure.

[14] This gesture symbolizes an adoption. Often a man in desperate straits and fleeing from his enemies would accost a woman in this way and thus gain the protection of her family as an adopted son. Even someone who was subject to blood vengeance because he had killed a member of a clan could find sanctuary within that clan by forcing himself on one

of its women in this way, thus becoming a member of the clan that had originally sworn vengeance on him.

[15] The coach is the "flying wagon" of note 14. It does not appear to do any flying in this saga. The term could also mean a swinging or swaying wagon and might refer to a wagon with a body suspended from a chassis by leather straps.

[16] This is an extension of the theme of befriending animals in trouble, also prevalent in Russian lore, which dominates this section of the quest for the magic horse (Propp 1968).

[17] Warzameg's original quest appears to be taken up again almost as an afterthought. This tone is a strong indication that another quest saga has been intercalated into the main one, namely the saga of befriending animals and being helped by them in turn in difficult circumstances. This popular theme is found throughout the Caucasus and up into Russia. The animal saga ends here, and the matrix saga in which it was embedded resumes in a somewhat awkward fashion.

[18] This comment is quite oblivious of the fact that Psatina was already married, to one whose name we never learn, and that she was abducted from her own wedding feast. It is characteristic of both Psatina and Setenaya that their nuptial abduction or celebration is interrupted by an abduction at the hands of a powerful, undesirable figure, often one who takes the virginity of his victim, as is the case with Setenaya (saga 4).

[19] This son is one of the mightiest of the Narts, / šʸa bahtənə́qᵒa / the 'Hunter Batinuquo', the god of the hunt, regarding whom there are many sagas (10, 11, 12, 67, 68, 88).

[20] This son is the smallest of the Narts, / sahwsərə́qᵒa /, a trickster figure, the bastard son of Setenaya and her abductor (note 18). He is powerful but small, often relying on his wits or magic to defeat his enemies. He is one of the most popular figures in all the sagas and is the enemy of Shebatinuquo (saga 88).

[21] The name Yasharuquo has several variants: / yašʸarqáw/, /yašʸarə́qᵒa/, /yarəšʸáqᵒa /, Ubykh / yarə̌čʸx̌áaw/, /yarašx̌aw /, Abkhaz / yarčʸx̌ʸaw /, /narǯʸx̌ʸaw /, of which the Abkhaz appears to be the original and the others efforts to render the alien Abkhaz cluster / -rčʸx̌- / (see my comments at the end of saga 89). This figure is the last of the Narts. Much like Warzameg, he tries to rescue a beautiful maiden from the clutches of a giant, this time from an underground cavern, but turns to stone, along with his maiden and his enemy, and remains forever underground (see the Ubykh saga "Les Nartes" [Vogt 1963, 58–63], translated here as saga 90).

Saga 4 ⌖ Setenaya and Argwana

In the time of the Narts there stood a city called Ghund-Ghund.[1] Its streets were narrow and twisted. A man could easily become lost and never find his way out! Therein lived a woman named Lady Setenaya whose beauty was unsurpassed. In that city there was also a great treasure, a magical three-legged table of the type that one sat at for meals.[2] All one had to do was tap on it and command it to bring food, and it would bring whatever was desired. Unlike most tables, the top of this one was made of leather. The following song tells how the Narts set out to capture both Setenaya and this magical table.

> A woreda-woreda, a woreda-rau!
> Warzameg was a Nart.
> He was their prince and *t'hamata*,[3]
> The leader of the feast.
> For a long time he had been a widower.
> Now the Nart page[4] went forth
> And came to Warzameg.
> "Let us find you a bride," said he.
> "To whom shall we go?" replied his lord.
> "Setenaya sits alone like a fair maid."
> "She won't go with me. No, she won't, my page."
> "May you have many descendants, my lord!
> A man does not let the drinking horn pass him by.
> She will go with you. She will go with you, Warzameg."
> The suitors set off on their way.
> They came to Setenaya's abode in the city.
> She went out to meet them
> And invited them in.
> She led them through the door
> And readied a place for them to sit.
> She bade them to sit down,
> Then she stood back and awaited their wishes.
> "We come for a purpose."
> "Please speak," said she.
> "Sit down, dear girl," urged the page.
> "We will cause you no harm
> If you sit here with us.
> We are not guests who shall stay long.
> We are guests who shall leave soon.
> We shall tell you our intentions.
> Warzameg is a widower.
> He remains without a wife.

So, we have come to court you."
Then said Warzameg to the young beauty,
"Come away with me, Setenay!"
"I will not marry you, Warzameg."
"What is wrong with me, Setenay?"
"When I gaze upon you, you are black;
When I look at myself, I am white.
How could I ever marry you?"
"Do not let that stop you!
Many white sheep stand among our herds.
Black give birth to white.
White give birth to black."
"By my mother's soul, I will not go off with you!
When the wool sheared from our sheep
Is not enough to make
Even the sleeves of your cherkesska,[5]
How could I ever marry you?
The whole hide of a three-year-old calf
Is the leather of your shoes,
Your old hat is in tatters,
Your old cloak has been dragged through the underbrush,
How could I ever marry you?
God strike me down!
God snatch me away, O Page of the Narts!
How could I ever marry the likes of him?
You bring before me a white-bearded old man."
Then Warzameg said to the young beauty,
"What I wear I'll find myself.
You would never have to make a coat for me.
Among our sheep are ones with white hair too.[6]
If I am still a man,
I will not let you stay here.
I will still take you, despite your words,
... If you will go with me."
Again Setenaya replied,
"By my mother's soul, I'll not go with you!"
Now a frown came over Warzameg and he said,
"The two braids of your hair are a tangle, my Lady,

Your two breasts are like old, bouncing pumpkins.[7]
I'll make you a swineherd's wife,
Or you can shave off my mustache
And flaunt your laziness in my face,
You witch!"[8]

A woreda-woreda, a woreda-rau!
Then Warzameg left and rode home.
He sent a messenger on horseback
Among his people
And called together a great meeting.
They brought together all the herdsmen.
They brought the one who husks the barley
And the one who grinds the millet.
They brought too the one who runs the mill.
When the Narts had assembled,
Warzameg asked, "Who is absent?"
"Argwana,[9] whose beard could be fodder
For two yearlings to graze upon
Has not heeded your call."
Wusara the Venerable[10] knew all,
What chance and fate had ordained.
"Without Argwana the mighty,
Ghund-Ghund City will not be yours."
"Let us bring him!" cried Warzameg.
So a young rider was sent for him.
"Argwana, you must come," commanded he.
"The Narts have been insulted."
Great Argwana replied,
"If so, then I will come,
But first you must tell me
The number of my pigs."[11]
Alas, the youth could not count so high,
And so he returned to the Narts.
The Nart clan stood ready to ride forth
When the youth gave them the bad news.
They knew not what to do.
There was among them one Yermyl,

An Armenian trader,[12] who said:
"Let me go for him.
He will heed my words."
So they set him on a horse
And sent him to Argwana.
"Greetings, Argwana!
May your hogs be fruitful!
I bid you join the Narts!"
"Listen well, trader!
You must tell me their number
If you are to be a swineherd."
"Mother pigs—nine,
Tuskers—ten,
Buff—eleven,
Shaggy ones—twelve,
Half-grays—eighteen,
Their mothers—thirty,
And their fathers—thirty.
Another thirty behind each of these.
Trailing each sow is a piglet.
Thousands upon thousands,
They stand in the mountain valleys."
"Yes, that is the size of my brood.
If I leave, you must care for them.
You must not lose one!"
The Armenian could count!
Now, as for Argwana the Ugly,
One hundred pork sausages
And eight hundred spoonfuls of mush,
This was his food,
And all this he did eat.
Then he went to his stable
And led out rat-tailed Shwayekhwacha,
And he took his boar's saddle[13]
And placed it on his mount.
Then Argwana mounted
And set off and came to the place[14]
Where the Nart tribe stood assembled.

The other Narts grew frightened at his approach
And feared that he would seize
The young beauty for himself.
Wily Sawseruquo was among the Narts.
He said, "Argwana cannot be restrained
By force alone, but he is a fool.
Tonight let us make him stand watch.
When he sleeps, we shall set off on our quest
And be gone at his waking."
So they gave him the night watch,
And he fell asleep despite all,
Just as Sawseruquo had said.
Then the horsemen set off,
Unheard by Argwana,
And rode a great distance.
When Argwana awoke at dawn,
He set off after them,
Astride rat-tailed Shwayekhwacha,
And easily overtook them
And fell in with them.
That night they drew near the walls of Ghund-Ghund
And prepared to storm the city by dark.
"The snorting of our horses
Will reveal us," said Warzameg.
"Each man tie the snout of his horse!"
The Narts used reeds to muzzle their horses,
But Argwana took out his wineskin of pig's hide,
Tied its thong around his horse's nose,
And jerked the wineskin upward
So that it covered the poor horse's entire head.
Soon his horse, Shwayekhwacha,
Began to stagger and sway.
"My horse is dying, Narts!" cried Argwana.
"No, Argwana," they replied.
"He's not dying.
He's dancing for joy!"
Poor Shwayekhwacha finally fell down and died.
Argwana picked the whole horse up,

Threw the carcass over his shoulders
So that the four legs came together
In front of his chin, and carried it off,
Running after the rest, who had already set off.
Despite his burden, Old Argwana overtook the others.

A woreda-woreda, a woreda-rau!
Argwana went to battle in the forefront of the Narts.
He was the first to smash through the gates.
He was the first to run through the twisted dark streets,
He was the first to find the magic table.
He was the first to reach the elevated platform
Upon which Lady Setenaya was seated.[15]
He seized her and carried her back,
Pushing his way through their ranks,
Both of Nart warrior and of foe,
Thwarting all efforts to stop him.
He went to his dead horse
And strapped the girl and table to its back,
Then hefted his burden and started home.
From the back of the dead horse
Setenaya saw Warzameg and pleaded,
"One side of your mustache is white gold,
The other side is white silk!
Save me from this ugly swineherd
And forever will I be your wife."
"You haughty sorceress,
I have kept my promise to you!"
The Narts pursued him,
But they could not stop Argwana.
Quickly they held a council.
"This disgusting man will carry off this lovely lady
If we do not do something," they said.
"Let us make him our warlord," said wily Sawseruquo.
"Then he must award her as booty
To our prince, Warzameg.
Otherwise, he will never relinquish her."[16]
Then the fastest among them flew like an arrow

And drew near the mighty swineherd.
"Now you are our leader of good fortune!"
Argwana stopped and untied Setenaya.
"May God make her a curse to you,"
He said as he gave her to them.

A woreda-woreda, a woreda-rau!
Then they took her to the House of Adleg[17]
And kept her there
Until the wedding feast.
The magical leather table
Was taken to the House of the Guides[18]
And left there for safekeeping.
The Narts feared that Argwana
Might try to steal her back,
And so they set a guard over her.
Then they diverted a stream
So that it flowed around the House of Adleg
In a circle and formed a great mire.
Finally they made eight oxen drag an enormous log
To the front of the courtyard
And roll it up against the front gate.
But while the wedding feast was being readied,
Setenaya went outside to bathe
In the clear upper reaches
Of that glittering nearby stream.
There Argwana spotted her.
He still lusted after her.
When no one was looking,
He seized her,
Dragged her crying into a thicket,
And there forced himself into her
And spurted into her his seed.
From this rape would come a child,
The mighty hunter, Wild She-Batinuquo.
When Argwana had withdrawn
And once more returned to his swine,
Setenaya bathed again

To wash away the dirt and disgrace.
Then she returned to partake
Of her own wedding feast.

A woreda-woreda, a woreda-rau!
That night Warzameg sat her
Upon his bed, [and with tender hands
Undid the many knots of her nuptial corset.]¹⁹
Then he saw her bruises and cuts.
"My lady, what has befallen you?"
"By the stream as I bathed
Mighty Argwana did seize me,
And in a thicket he took
[What you denied him before."]
Warzameg now felt sorrow
For the suffering she bore,
And he said, "My dearest lady,
You shall stay by my side!"
Day dawned and Warzameg called the Narts.
"Brave Narts, we spoke of abducting a maiden
When in truth we took someone's wife!
By right of battle she is now mine.
[She will stay by my side.
My honor is henceforth her honor."]
Yet Warzameg was full of anguish,
As wily Sawseruquo could see.
One day when Warzameg was alone,
Sawseruquo came up to him,
And without greeting whispered,
"Two brothers live nearby,
The sons of Anaya.²⁰
If you can find them,
They will stand up against Argwana.
They can kill him."
"So be it! I shall do as you say."
Warzameg sent a messenger
To the grim sons of Anaya.
"Warzameg bids you prosper!
He invites you to dine with him."
"We shall accept his hospitality."

They came to Warzameg,
When he was alone,
When Lady Setenaya was away,
Visiting with the Nart women.
Warzameg greeted them and
They were served marvelous food
By the magical table. Then he said,
"That night at Ghund-Ghund City
Argwana fought in the forefront of battle,
Where he took Setenaya and this,
The magical leather table.
Yet still may he want them,
And no Nart can withstand him."
"We will bring peace to your heart,"
Said they to him and quietly they withdrew.
Then soon one evening
The grim pair set upon Argwana
As he was rounding up his pigs.
For seven nights and seven days
They fought with the mighty swineherd,
And on the eighth evening they slew him.
The two brothers then brought his ugly head
To their leader and prince,
And with many horses for reward
Returned to their home.
Thenceforth Lady Setenaya remained Warzameg's wife
Forevermore.

This tale is an amalgamation of four sagas (Hadaghatl'a 1968, vol. 1, no. 8, pp. 104–6, no. 13, pp. 124–26, no. 17, pp. 137–40; GENEG, pp. 269–73), together with some cultural material I have used for the wedding night of Warzameg and Setenaya, which I have drawn from the wedding rites of the Caucasus (Luzbetak 1951).

➋ This saga is a story of rape and redemption, with Setenaya again in a central role, this time as a young woman. The tale exhibits a number of parallels with other traditions. The city of Setenaya's origin, bearing the odd name of Ghund-Ghund, is a labyrinth, recalling the Greek hero Theseus's exploits against the Minotaur. Setenaya herself is wooed by a much older Warzameg in an exchange that is almost comical in its bluntness. Here one is reminded of the widespread folk motif of the young wife and the old husband, perhaps the most famous ex-

ample of which is Mary and Joseph in the New Testament. Most notable, however, is the figure of Argwana (see n. 9), whose name seems to be a variant of an
old word for "rapist." He is a strange mixture of the absurd and the fearsome. In
one variant, 17 (on which saga 11 is in part based), he is simply called Old Cow
Herder (/čʸama-x̌°á-ź/ 'cow-herder-old; ugly; evil'), and the child he sires later
rescues him from a banquet where he is to be poisoned. This is more properly a
tale of She-Batinuquo, the Hunter, who has an anomalous origin and emerges
from a grave mound to rescue Warzameg, who then adopts him (saga 11). I have
omitted this portion here, focusing instead on the abduction and rape of Setenaya
by this monstrous swineherd.

Warzameg uses Argwana to humble Setenaya, and in this aspect of the tale one
is reminded of King David, himself originally a shepherd, lusting after Bathsheba
at her rooftop bath. (I am indebted to Alvin Lee of McMaster University for help
with this parallel.) In fact, the Old Testament account and this saga are in many
ways inverses of one another. In the Nart version, the ruler is not smitten with
lust at the sight of the bathing maiden, nor was he ever a shepherd, but much of
the plot's machinery and the three main characters—king, shepherd, and maiden
at her bath—are recognizable even if used for different ends. Argwana triumphs
in the forefront of battle. Uriah the Hittite is sent to the forefront of battle so that
he might be killed and David might marry the widowed Bathsheba. Argwana
threatens the ruler's house to regain his "war bride," whereas Uriah sleeps before
the king's door to protect the king. Argwana rapes Setenaya, whereas King David
has illicit sex with Bathsheba.

In this way this Nart saga serves as a bridge between the Old Testament traditions and those of Ancient Greece, in which Anchises, the shepherd king, and
lovely Aphrodite have assumed roles similar to those in the previous saga, and the
three Gorgons have been marginalized with only one of their number, Medusa,
serving as a dramatic foil for the hero Perseus. The saga further sets the ground-
work both for Setenaya's odd marginality in Nart society and for Warzameg's later
concern that she is stealing his glory (saga 13).

---

[1] Ghund-Ghund /ɣ°ənd-ɣ°ə́nd/. The meaning of this name is unclear. Ghund, the root
/ɣ°ənd/ alone, means "gadfly." Most interestingly, however, the city is depicted as a labyrinth
on small wooden palettes or tables (see Hadaghatl'a 1, no. 17·139, with a photo of a tablet
in the Circassian regional museum of Maikop). The Circassian word for "labyrinth" is /da-
ḥa-dá-čʸ/ 'open.space-enter-open.space-exit', that is, "to go in and out of many rooms /
areas," possibly implying that a labyrinth was originally any structure with several internal
walls dividing it into more than just a few rooms. Such an older sense would be historically
plausible, since older structures (for example, the nearby Bronze Age and early Iron Age remains in the Mediterranean and Near Eastern areas) are generally quite simple.

² These individual eating tables are round and supported by three legs. The modern supported circular trays that serve as eating tables throughout the Middle East and in the Georgian highlands are similar. Graves (1955), perhaps fancifully, has interpreted some of the swastika patterns found in Mycenaean and early Classical Greek art as depictions of tables of this sort, which in turn were depictions of the disc of the sun or moon. Such tables may be ancient simply because they function well on uneven floors, where a four-legged table would wobble [KT].

³ The Bzhedukh form of this Circassian term, / ṭha-a-m-áh-ta / 'god-pl.(archaic)-obl-int-father,' "father of the gods," (suggested to me by Stephen Anderson in a personal communication), now refers to the one who conducts the activities at a feast. This is a position of great prestige and is accorded the greatest respect. The term (in the Kabardian form / ṭhamáada /) is one of the few that have spread outside the family to such neighboring languages as Russian, Georgian, and Persian, where it has taken on the sense of "toastmaster." Attempts to find an Iranian origin for this word (Abaev 1996, 3:227) ignore its transparent semantics when set in the Circassian Nart tradition with its Olympian feastlike motif.

⁴ Shawa / śáawa / in normal speech is 'boy, lad, page boy to a warrior', but in the sagas it is still the title of a person who does the bidding of a lord or leader, and in some of the older sung forms it even seems to mean "warrior" (saga 71). The present sense reflects the feature of youth from the original. Therefore, I have rendered the word here as "page," since the present sense seems very close to that of the medieval term for a youth apprenticed to a knight. Although this word does not look Circassian, efforts to compare it with the Ossetian / sau / run up against the semantic problem that this Iranian word means "black" (Bielmeier 1977, 209). Setenaya's odd allusion to Warzameg as black, however, may hark back to some old color symbology in which warriors were black or dark, and so the word may be of Iranian origin after all. The few black people of African origin living in the Caucasus today seem to have settled in Abkhazia in early modern times, and it is therefore doubtful that this is what is intended by this old epithet.

⁵ The cherkesska, a caftanlike coat, tight fitting in the torso and flaring below the waist, is the national male costume in the Caucasus. It usually has full sleeves and is made of a fine, waterproof wool called / c'ə-ya / 'wool-one.of'.

⁶ There are a number of ways of interpreting the significance of this line and the squabble between a white maiden and a black warrior. This may reflect an old ethnic antagonism between light and dark peoples, between light- and dark-haired peoples, an old regional one—with white for west and black for north (a long-standing Central Asian color symbolism that has spilled over into parts of the Caucasus)—or, last but also most likely, a Zoroastrian one characteristic of Iranian culture in Central Asia, which opposes white (good) to black (evil). See also note 4.

⁷ Warzameg lists some revealing cultural values here. In earlier times Circassian men found large breasts ugly. The term is "jumping," so that the image is one of full, bouncing breasts, perhaps an enhancement of Setenaya's fertility image. Warzameg intends this as a great insult to her. Muslim or even early Christian influence may have stigmatized this aspect of the old fertility goddess that Setenaya must once have been, thus converting the assets of a rival religious figure into objects of opprobrium.

[8] To have his mustache shaved off would be a great humiliation to Warzameg, a sort of emasculation. Warzameg is thus staking his manhood to back his oath.

By Circassian standards, laziness is a terrible fault in a woman, particularly a hostess, as Setenaya is here. An energetic hostess is considered a beautiful woman, regardless of her appearance. The neighboring Abkhazians have similar attitudes (see Iskander 1983, 70).

[9] Argwana / arg°áana / has as variants / yarg°án / and in Abaza / g°arg°ána / (Allen 1965, saga 55). This is an extraordinary name, clearly linked with the Greek *Gorgon*. It gives clear evidence of an ancient theme that has been preserved as the stories of three monstrous sisters in Greek and a giant savage herder in Circassian. The name has no obvious etymology in Greek but shows a confused history: *gorgós* 'fierce', nominative *Gorgṓ* ← **gorgón*, older genitive *Gorgoús* ← **gorgón-s*, with this underlying *n*-stem dominating in later forms: younger genitive *Gorgónos*. Certainly *Gorgṓ* is a difficult word and is one of a set of feminines in omega, *Lētṓ* (Dorian *Lātṓ*), *Saphṓ*, all of which present problems [KT]. The root is clearly *gorg-* (which simply means "fierce, grim, terrible") and may be of Indo-European origin, **gor-g^y-*, compare Russian *groz(nyj)*. For *Gorgṓ* and *Lētṓ* the stem clearly ended in ** / -y- /* (Buck 1933, 202–3, §271); note *Lētói* (vocative) or *Lētóos* (gen, sg) ← ** Lātóyos* ← ** Lātósyos* which suggests that *Gorgoús* (gen, sg) was originally **Gorgósyos* and therefore also an **-oy-* stem. Somewhat like *egṓ*, *egǫ́n* 'I', both names show variants with / -n /, though one must go to the Latin form of *Leto* to see this: compare Greek *Gorgṓ*, *Gorgónos* (gen, sg), Latin *La-to-na*. This / -n- / might be viewed simply as a case of a name forming suffix seen in such theonyms as the Germanic *Wodan* and Gaulish *Mappona*. Curiously, even the Latin shows the two variants: *Latonius* (fem.), an appellation for Diana, Latona's daughter, but *Latous* (masc.) for Apollo, Latona's son. This suggests that the -y / -n variation is extremely old and that both names have been subject to reworking.

The variants in the Circassian form reinforce the impression that this obscure Greek name is of Northwest Caucasian origin. In these one might see an old root for 'vagina'; compare Ubykh / g°á /, Circassian / g°ədə / with a derivational suffix. Thus the Abaza and Circassian forms may be read as / g°a-r-g°á-na / 'vagina-loc-stuff, cram-inf', "to stuff the vagina," / y-a-r-g°áa-na / '3-in-loc-stuff, cram-inf', (the lengthened vowel -aa- is automatic in Circassian when an / -a- / is stressed and followed in the next syllable by an / -a- /) "to stuff her," / a-r-g°áa-na / 'the-loc-stuff, cram-inf', "the stuffer," all appropriate, if crude, terms alluding in order of descending explicitness to this character's role as a rapist and despoiler of Setenaya.

In Greek there were three Gorgon sisters, Euryalé ("broad"), Sthéno ("mighty"), and Medusa ("guardian") (Médoisa), who were endowed with boar's tusks, among other bizarre attributes. The Greeks seem to have inverted the original gender of the Gorgons to produce a monstrous female triad, each with one of his attributes. Such attributes are typically abstract nouns of feminine gender in Greek (and in the ancestral Indo-European), thus giving rise to the gender change. Only Sthéno might have a masculine referent. By contrast, the Circassians have conflated an earlier group of Gorgons (see note 13) into the figure of Argwana, who has assumed the herdsman role of Aphrodite's lover Anchises, the warrior role of her other lover, Ares, god of war, and the crudeness of her husband, Hephaistos, god of the forge. Only Hephaistos is retained within Circassian to the extent that Setenaya relies on Tlepsh, god of the forge. Taken with saga 8, the Circassian tales suggest an original tradition in which the goddess of fertility had at least three liaisons: with a crude shepherd, with a fierce god of war, and with a god of the forge. Such a threefold sexual linkage would make her a transfunctional goddess (see Puhvel's [p. 62] extension of Dumézil's theory [1968]), uniting her with the agricultural, the warrior, and the priestly Indo-European functions if the smith group is taken as divine [KT]. The last assumption is plausible since the figure of Tlepsh, the smith, is the only one to have retained his divine status. Saga 11 also suggests a marriage to a kind but crude older man who was a leader or a king. This figure seems also to have been cuckolded (saga 9), as was the case with King Arthur and Guinevere (Littleton and Malcor 1994).

[10] This figure conflates the functions of poet and seer, as in Celtic lore: / wəsa-rá-ź / 'compose-part-old, venerable', literally, the venerable one who composes, the name for a seer or poet, probably from / wə+s+a / 'val+sit+in', that is, "to put things together," hence "to compose."

[11] The swineherd's tale is always associated with this odd enumeration of his swine. The formulas involved are no longer of any significance, if they ever had any. The sum itself works out to 900 piglets for each mated pair, for a total of 27,000 piglets, truly an enormous number, but everything associated with Argwana is enormous and superabundant.

[12] Note in the text: Circassian / yarmáλ / 'Armenian'. The Armenians among the Circassians performed the role of small traders. Here the term might only mean "one who can count," thus an accountant. Contemporary Circassian Armenians, centered around the city of Armavir in the North Caucasus, have fully assimilated in language and culture to the Circassians. Even today Circassians say, "Learn to be eloquent from the Armenian." General Aleksei Petrovich Yermolov, who set about to conquer the Caucasus for Tsar Alexander I (Gammer 1994, 29–38) at the beginning of the nineteenth century, has a surname that is derived from this Circassian word.

[13] In the variant from GENEG, this is a saddle made of boar's hide. This phrase may imply that in older versions he rode a boar, as he still does in variant 13. This would explain why his horse is called One with the Tail of a Male Rat in variant 8, / š°aya-x̌°á-č'ʸa/ 'rat-male-tail', literally "(one with the) tail of a male rat." A rat's tail is naked and tends to twist, much like a pig's tail, so that this horse, Shwayekhwacha, might originally have been a boar.

[14] This is a confusion here in the variant from GENEG. The Armenian was supposed to remain behind with the herd, but the bard has conjoined him with Argwana to account for the plurality of "Argwana" in the following sentence, which has "at their approach." This is the only version where such a plurality is found for the name Argwana. The plurality is evidently old and is the reason the bard has forced the Armenian into companionship with Argwana in an attempt to make sense of this otherwise meaningless historical plural. This suggests that originally the Gorgons were a group, and this has been lost in Circassian but preserved in Greek.

[15] Shandaka, / š'ʸandáaqa / 'elevated platform, tower'. This was an elevated platform on which noblewomen would sit. It was high enough to offer them a good view of whatever

competition or activity was conducted in their honor while removing them from direct contact with the participants. This platform has a precise analogue in the medieval platforms from which the European nobility watched tournaments. With this platform, the Circassian saga has faithfully preserved a medieval European tradition, whether it originated independently or was borrowed. Setenaya is often depicted as so seated.

[16] This odd strategy seems to have the following rationale behind it. The Narts intend to make Argwana the leader of the raid, and as such he would have to distribute wealth, property, and booty among his followers. Thus, once Argwana is made leader of the raid, someone eminent among them can demand Setenaya, and he must give her to him, or at least consider doing so. The position also seems to have entailed some religious status. Thus, he is called "luck-bringing" leader, the one who provides good fortune. Argwana's parting curse to the Narts upon giving Setenaya over to them therefore not only reflects his understanding that he has been duped by them but also carries with it a degree of prophetic, religious significance and represents a serious curse, foreshadowing trouble to come.

[17] This name, $/a\lambda \acute{s}g^y/$, appears to come from the Ossetic alæg, itself from the Iranian *arya-ka- 'Aryan one' (for the ultimate origin of this name, see Colarusso 1997b, 141, item 67). This figure is the one who summons the Narts to conferences and feasts at which important legal and social matters are discussed. His house is thus a central point in the Nart world, one where Setenaya's fate is properly decided.

[18] Literally, "the orienters," $/\gamma \acute{a}-a-z-a/$ 'purpose-conn-turn-in', that is, the guides. These appear to have formed a distinct profession or league among the Narts, one that enjoyed some prestige.

[19] In the Caucasus the bride, on her wedding night, usually wore a leather corset tied with numerous knots. It had to be presented the next morning with all its thongs intact as a sign of the groom's consideration and self-restraint (Luzbetak 1951).

[20] Anaya /ha-ná-ya/ 'int-mother-character/bad', "the motherly one" or "the bad mother." The latter might seem odd, but a treacherous mother plays a crucial role in some of the myths. Her sons remain enigmatic despite their crucial role in this tale.

SAGA 5 ❧ The Blossom of Lady Setenaya

Once, long ago, the Lady, Setenaya[1], was walking along the banks of the Kuban River and gazing at the dense foliage that grew near the water's edge. She came upon a sheltered clearing that opened onto the bank. In this clearing grew some flowering plants with the most beautiful blossoms she had ever seen. "I shall plant one of these flowers before the front door of our house. It will grow so that whoever passes by shall see it and be awed by its loveliness." So saying, she dug one up, took it back, and planted it.

The following day when she looked at it, its leaves were curled and brown. It had dried out. She was greatly saddened.

Sometime later she returned to the glade on the riverbank and brought back another one, as lovely as the first. "Although the first one did not thrive," she said, "perhaps this one will grow." Thus, she planted a second flower. The next day it too was dry and wilted.

Seeing how sad she was at the loss of these flowers, a Nart took pity on her and, going himself to the clearing, brought back a third plant as a gift for her.

"This one will not be like the first ones. This one will not wilt," she said as she planted it before her door as she had the others. But, as with the others, its leaves soon drooped.

Then with sorrow and remorse she thought to herself, "Why did I not leave them alone in the glade where I found them? There they were full of life and loveliness." Then, without warning, the clouds began to gather. The sky grew dark and soon a great rain fell. The following day when she looked at her flower, she was amazed. Once again it stood tall, fresh, and lovely.

Setenaya rejoiced. The rainwater had restored the last flower to life and made it bloom once again.

In this way the first people came to know that there was power and goodness in water. The Narts used to say, "Water is like the soul."

From Hadaghat'la 1968, vol. 1, no. 1, p. 81, in Hatiquoya West Circassian.

◌ Here Setenaya shows her skill at general knowledge. What is striking about her is that she acquires this knowledge in an empirical fashion and not by magic.

¹ The Circassian word for the rose is *Setenaya-blossom*, /sətənay-qayáaya/, so the plant in this tale is a rose. In some myths Setenaya's association with the rose degenerates into a mere association with thorns.

SAGA 6 ◌ *Why the Sun Pauses on the Horizon at Sunset*

Have you seen how as evening approaches the sun pauses in its course for just a moment at the horizon, on the sky's lower flank, just before it sets? I shall tell you why this is so.

One day, long ago, Setenaya and a lad of the Narts, who made harnesses, decided to compete against one another in traditional skills.

She said, "Today I shall sew a *saya*, a woman's gown." Setenaya was unique. There was no one else like her, they say.

"Then it will take me only one day to make a saddle," replied the youth.

As the day passed, they sat, each laboring at their separate tasks. The Nart youth was an experienced craftsman. He finished his saddle and rested. As the sun approached the horizon, there remained for Setenaya just a little more work than she could finish.

"O, Sun!" she pleaded. "If only you would halt awhile!"

In the time of the Narts wishes would come true. So the sun halted its descent for a little while and sat waiting at the edge of the earth until she had finished sewing. Having sat all day, Setenaya grew tired. She stood up, stretched, and then donned the gown. Then she invited the youth to look at her.

"You are just as they say you are, Setenaya! You have made it well!" the Nart youth replied as he gazed on her.

From that day forward, as evening approaches, the sun pauses in its course for a little while on the sky's lower flank. To do so has become part of its nature.

From GENEG, p. 266, in Abadzakh West Circassian.

☙ Here Lady Setenaya makes her appearance, characteristically exhibiting not only her beauty but also her consummate skill at crafts.

SAGA 7 ☙ *Lady Setenaya and the Magic Apple*

The golden tree of the Narts had many powers. Once each year, at the very top of the tree, an apple would sprout. For six months it would grow and slowly ripen, and during the next six months it would gradually shrink. In appearance and size it was not like the other apples that ripened in one day. This apple always grew bigger, rounder, and firmer than the others.

Over a long time the Lady Setenaya had been able to discover what powers lay within this special apple. When the first frost came and the leaves fell from the trees, she would pick the apple and set it in a wooden chest. So Setenaya kept this apple for the Narts and used it in her ministrations to their sick, for many things can befall a person in this life, and sometimes he fares well and other times poorly.

The person who tasted of this magical apple would grow gentle in heart and compassionate and would not grow older, but as the years passed would grow younger instead. That apple would add to the span of a man's life as many years as he had already lived.

No one ever said that Lady Setenaya grew old or became unsteady in her step or that her face ever bore a wrinkle. And in truth how could they? For Setenaya never grew old!

She would smear on her face the pulp from the core of the apple, which was like fresh butter. Thus her face would become white, clean, and so shiny that like a mirror you could see your reflection in it. She would also boil the apple's skin and make a broth, which when drunk would make your heart grow happy and your spirit turn tender and compassionate.

Yaminizh,[1] Old Cholera, heard of this magical apple. He feigned blindness and lameness, and so he went to Lady Setenaya. He went disguised as an aged and ailing Nart so that his youth might be restored and he could go on tormenting humankind.

"Setenay!" he called.[2]

"What?" she asked.

"My legs no longer carry me. My eyes no longer see. My head has grown stupid. My heart throbs like an inflamed nerve in my chest. The life left to me is short. Help me!" begged Yaminizh. "Will you dare pretend that I don't know of the magic stored within your apple?"

"I will let you partake of neither the broth nor the paste of the apple," she said, seeing him for the wicked disease he was. "You have brought too much evil into the world," and so saying she withheld the remedies from him.

"If that is how things are to be and the apple's goodness is denied to me, I will make certain that it will be of no good to anyone!" he replied. Sometime later, in the dark of the night, Yaminizh crept up to the golden apple tree of the Narts and cut it down.

The tree is now gone. If the Narts had not lost their tree, then even today they would enjoy good health, live in abundance, and be forever young.

From Hadaghatl'a 1968, vol. 1, no. 3, variant 2, pp. 86–90, in Shapsegh West Circassian.

◈ Here, with this unique apple, Setenaya is said to come by her knowledge after a long period of study. The portrayal of a disease, cholera, as a person is common in South Caucasian folklore [KT].

[1] Yaminizh is a personification of cholera, so that the literal form of his name, / y-a-mə-nə́-ź / 'it-in-not-remain (in)-old, evil', that is, "(that which) won't stay inside" plus the suffix "evil," is a fair rendering of this dreaded disease's chief symptom, catastrophic and frequently fatal diarrhea. This is probably a folk etymology, however, since this name may be a borrowing of the name of the Iranian god of death, Yima (saga 2 n. 9) (see Puhvel 1987, 284–90), with an / -n- / suffix appended (saga 4 n. 8).

[2] In vocative forms (as well as copular or predicative ones), the last vowel is dropped. Since this effect is absent in Ubykh, Abkhaz, and Abaza, this may be an example of Greek influence on Circassian [KT], since in Greek final consonants are dropped or final syllables are shortened in vocatives.

SAGA 8 ◈ Lady Setenaya and the Shepherd:
The Birth of Sawseruquo

There were two brothers, the sons of Sajem. The elder was named Zartyzh, the younger Shawey.[1]

One day Setenaya was bathing by the river. On the water's other side stood one of these brothers, the Nart herdsman Sajemuquo Zartyzh, also called Tezhidada, the "Eldest Ram." From where he stood he was able to see Lady Setenaya. When that brother saw the beautiful temptress[2] going back and forth, not standing still, strewing her clothes about, he could no longer control his passion.[3] He was enchanted by her beauty and so let loose an arrow of manly fluid.

"Setenaya! It is coming to you."

"So, let it come, but why did you do that?" said Setenaya.[4]

"Hey, Setenaya! By day I tend the sheep. By night, when I come to you, the lance is always stuck in the ground in front of your house.[5] So how would you have me do it?" said the shepherd.

Heavy steam arose as the bolt skimmed over the water, tracing a path until it reached Setenaya, but the bolt of lust just missed her and instead fell on a stone that was lying beside her on the riverbank. Setenaya picked up the stone, wrapped it in a warm cloth, brought it home, and placed it in the stove. Day by day the stone grew. It lay for nine months and nine days. During this time it grew in size and became very big. Lady Setenaya had her people bring the stone to Tlepsh's smithy. There she bade Tlepsh, the god of the forge, to break open the stone.

Tlepsh did as she had bidden him. From inside the stone emerged a baby boy, glowing as bright as fire. The baby fell on the front part of Setenaya's dress and burned through it until he fell to the ground. Tlepsh seized him with his blacksmith's tongs, and holding him by the thighs plunged him into the water for the grindstone[6] seven times, thus cooling the baby. Then once again Tlepsh picked up the little child with his metal tongs by his thighs and hardened him seven times, so that the child's skin became a little bit more flexible.[7] The child became like a human being, but his skin remained tough, like tempered steel. Tlepsh named the baby Sawseruquo and gave him back to Setenaya.

On his thighs, where Tlepsh had held him with the tongs, Sawseruquo's skin remained soft like human skin, and because his thighs had been squeezed, he was bowlegged.

I compiled this account by using variants from GENEG, p. 284, from a saga recorded in 1954 in Gustanfeld, Germany, and from Hadaghatl'a 1969, vol. 2, no. 83, pp. 31–32.

 Variants have Setenaya washing clothes, dishes, or her own body by the bank of a river. In all cases her conduct is unwittingly revealing. Here Setenaya is reminiscent of Indo-European Dawn washing clothes by the shore as well as of Greek Aphrodite, inextricably tied to water, as her name implies ("Foam-Born"), who made love with the shepherd prince Anchises and conceived the god Adonis. In some accounts Setenaya accepts the shepherd's sperm gladly, in others she is angered either by being hit herself or by being subject to an indignity even though the stone is hit (for infants born from stones see Ardzinba 1985), and in still others she is raped outright when he swims over to her. In the variant in which she herself is pregnant, she runs a high fever before bearing a flaming infant. The fiery hero, thus conceived, is quenched and tempered like steel but has a vulnerable point. He recalls the Greek hero Achilles (Akhilleus in Greek) (see Tuite 1998), with his vulnerable heel, or the Germanic Siegfried, with the soft spot on his back.

The herdsman is stated to be the brother of one Shawafizh, the "White Boy," who later, as Toterash, is a dreadful enemy to his own nephew Sawseruquo.[8] This tale thus provides a genealogical framework for strife that in later tales is related without much motivation. The motif of the hot rock as womb has a parallel in the goddess Thetis "cooking" the fetal Achilles in an oven to drive the mortal portion out of him (again, see Tuite 1998). The attributes of being sired by a shepherd, made of steel with metallic eyes, bowlegged, vulnerable in the thighs, and the "unborn" or adopted son characterize Sawseruquo in all his sagas. He is also said to be dark, with dark eyes of steel, wearing unusual boots or shoes, endowed with magical powers, treacherous, and merciless toward his enemies. He remains marginal to the Nart community because of a birth that is considered abnormal or because of a sire who is considered lowly.

[1] These names have an Iranian look to them, "Son of Saje(m)," "Old Zart" (but with an ejective-t / zahrt' /), and "Shawa" or "Shaway," with the / -y / perhaps a Circassian suffix meaning "bad" or "the one of." His alternative name is, in Bzhedukh West Circassian, / t'a-ź ə-dəda / 'ram-old-superlative', "the eldest ram," perhaps an old term for *shepherd*, since the eldest ram leads the flock and the shepherd does the same for the villagers.

[2] Circassian / ḥa-a-bz(a) wəd(a) / 'dog-conn-female witch.sorceress' translates literally as "bitch witch." It is not clear what the older significance of this epithet might have been, but currently this seems to have a pejorative tone. After the early conversion of the Circassians to Christianity and later to Islam, Setenaya seems to have persisted in folklore by undergoing a moral bifurcation into a temptress sorceress, on one hand, and a fertile wise mother, on the other.

[3] Version three has her being courted by the shepherd.

[4] In the courting version (GENEG) the bard says the following: "This same Sajemuquo the herdsman did not want to be a bad man. At that time Setenaya's husband was very old. It was nothing special for a woman to enter and sit with our guests, or so the old men tell." This suggests older sexual customs in which women enjoyed substantial latitude.

[5] The goddess of fertility, or her human descendants, such as Queen Guinevere of the Arthurian romance, is frequently marked by promiscuity. Here her sexual visitors mark their presence by thrusting their lances in the ground before her home. The marginal role of the shepherd in village life places him at a disadvantage in gaining her favors. In this way he tries to excuse his actions.

[6] One variant has / məź°a š'araX̌-ə-psə / 'stone wheel-ep.v-water'. It is not clear what this may be, but one could read it simply as "water wheel stone," some sort of stone basin, round like a wheel.

[7] This double dunking suggests an older metallurgical technique by which steel was quenched once to harden it, then annealed (softened by slow heating) and quenched a second time to impart flexibility to it. Sawseruquo has the aspect of a living weapon.

[8] The hero puts in an anachronistic appearance in saga 4. This is the West Circassian form of the name, / sahwsərśq°a /, whereas the East Circassian one is / sawsrśq'°a /. I have used the western form throughout the Circassian corpus, using the eastern one only for the Abaza corpus.

When the time came for Warzameg to set off on a quest, he turned to his wife, Setenaya, and said, "If I am absent for too long, then take an awl and puncture the palm of your hand. If blood comes out, then I am dead and will not return. If milk spurts out, then I am still alive and will come back to you."

After her husband had left, the Nart Tughuzhipsh[1] came to visit her. She served him food and treated him as a guest should be treated, but when Tughuzhipsh revealed to her what lay in his heart, she drove him out of the house.

Word of Tughuzhipsh's misadventure came to Nagurashkho, the son of Tlepsh.[2] As he was a master blacksmith, he set about fashioning two small daggers. He finished them in fine chasing and filigree and then imbued them with magic. When his work was done he brought them to Setenaya.

To serve her new guest, she asked him to help her slaughter a sheep.[3] He then took from his pocket the two daggers. No sooner had he drawn them out than one of them turned into a handsome youth and the other into a comely maiden. The youth killed the sheep and the girl dressed its meat. When they had finished their tasks, they returned to Tlepsh's son and turned back into daggers. He picked them up and put them away.

A great desire arose in Setenaya to have these magic daggers. She begged him to give them to her, but he refused.[4]

"If tonight you let me sleep on your bosom," he said to her, "then I shall give them to you."

She coveted those daggers so badly that she let Tlepsh's son sleep that night on her bosom.

At daybreak Warzameg returned driving before him a multitude of cattle. He called to his wife from the courtyard. Setenaya did not know what to do or say and so kept silent. When she did not open the door to greet him, he became suspicious and went out again.

Then Lady Setenaya was stricken with remorse for what she had done. She resolved to run away and so dressed herself in men's clothing and ran off.

In her flight she came upon a shepherd's hut and decided to spend the night there, but when she went inside she found herself face to face again with Warzameg! Trying her best to prevent him from recognizing her, she drew forth the two magic daggers and showed them to him. Just as she had coveted them, so too did he. "Please give them to me!" he begged, but she refused, saying, "Only if you give me a woman will I part with them. Nothing else will do."

"If I had been born a woman, even I myself would sleep with you!" swore Warzameg. Then she revealed herself and told Warzameg what had happened to her. Then they forgave one another and their hearts grew close once more. As inseparable companions, they returned to their home.

From Hadaghatl'a 1968, vol. 1, no. 23, p. 155, in Hatiquoya West Circassian.

◯ This tale exemplifies the ideal of sexual tolerance found among the Circassians and their kin. It also rises above the traditional formality between husband and wife to depict an intimate and enduring marital bond. In this dialect, Warzameg's name is Warzamaj.

[1] Tughuzhipsh /təɣ°ə-ẑə́-psʸ/ 'thief-old-prince', that is, "Prince (Old) Wolf" ("old thief" means "wolf," the original word for 'wolf', / ḥa /, now meaning "dog").

[2] Nagurashkho /na-g°ə-rá-ŝx̌°a/ 'eye-zone-locus-big', "Wide about the Eyes, Big Area around the Eyes"; perhaps a Mongoloid physiognomy is intended. Tlepsh is the blacksmith of the Narts and is intimately associated with Setenaya in tales in which she gives birth to Sawseruquo. Tlepsh's son, by contrast, is a shadowy figure, rarely encountered.

[3] A woman was not to touch a weapon, and this may account for imposing on her guest the slaughter of a sheep. Kevin Tuite notes that in premodern times only men slaughtered meat, either in their capacity as hunters or when presiding over the domestic circle. Here one may glimpse an old complex of taboos involving women, weapons, hunting, and the slaughtering and butchering of animals.

[4] This is a gross breach of etiquette on Nagurashkho's part. In Caucasian culture, if someone admires something, one must give it to him as a gift, particularly if one is staying as a guest.

Saga 10   ◯   *The Childhood of Shebatinuquo*

Some say that the Nart Warzameg was of the Nart lineage, but others say that he came originally from Chinta.[1] He was the ruler and lawgiver in the land of the Narts. One of his rivals was the Nart Adleg,[2] who lived on a mountain called the Querghwa Ridge, near the banks of the Pshish'ha River.[3] It was Warzameg's custom to go there, promulgate laws, and make rulings before the Narts who had gathered for the Nart council. Warzameg was a big man, handsome, with eyebrows that met above the bridge of his nose. He was a generous, noble, and good-hearted man. Despite his strength and manly bearing, he was unable to beget a child.

The Lady Setenaya, wife of Warzameg, had become pregnant when she was raped by the mighty swineherd Argwana. While Warzameg was away, this child was born. Setenaya knew all and could see all—what was, is, and will be. She entrusted the babe to a valiant woman, the wife of mighty Shebatin the Hunter, to raise in fosterage as her own until he should reach his fifteenth year. She said to Shebatin's wife, "Raise him as your own. Let no one know that he is mine. Keep him safe until I send for him." Setenaya then spent her time keeping vigil in the courtyard, waiting for her husband to return. When she saw him coming back, she began to dig at the foundation of a small storage shed, and she had already begun to stamp down the loosened earth when he entered.

"Setenaya! What are you doing around there? Tell me!" he called.

"Alas! The child whom I had been bearing has died, and I am burying him under this shed," she said in reply.

"Alas! What has happened cannot be undone," and saying this Warzameg entered the house. Hearing nothing more about the matter, he eventually forgot about it.

Then a time came when the army of Chinta entered the land of the Narts to wage war. The Chintas devastated the land of the Narts. They put the houses to the torch and killed old men, women, and small children. And so they came, committing many atrocities.

When this happened, all men who were able to sit on horseback throughout the Nart land arose as one. They rode into battle against the Chintas. The Narts fought bravely, but their number was small. The Chintas were far more numerous than the Narts. Every Nart horseman faced a hundred Chinta enemies on horseback, and even though the Narts killed many Chintas, they were so numerous that you would not have noticed a drop in their multitude. But when even one Nart was killed, you at once noticed his loss, since they were so few. To the Narts it seemed that if the war were to last for any length of time, the Chintas would defeat them and the Nart race would vanish from the earth.

Things proceeded in this way until, without anyone's noticing, what appeared to be a horseman showed up in their midst. To either side of this rider ran two hounds, staying ever near, and above him soared a great eagle circling in the air. This is how they tell of his manner and appearance. The horse on which he rode had a neck like a snake's. His lance, which he wielded against the Chintas, rumbled like thunder. On his head was a gleaming helmet that shone like the sun. He struck fear into the hearts of the Chintas when they saw him, and in their panic they could not escape from before him. That horseman came among them and hewed them down, destroying the army that had invaded the land of the Narts.

Then each Nart turned to the one next to him, and all began to wonder and ask aloud, "Who is this horseman? Where has he been until now? Where has he fought before?" Hope was restored to the hearts of the Narts, and they began to drive what remained of their enemy up into the mountain valleys.

The Chintas were unable to withstand the Nart horsemen, who now rode down on them. They were mown down like blades of grass in great swaths. The strange horseman fought with great inner strength. He hewed down the Chinta army until only one man was left alive from among the enemy.

The horse rider bore down on this lone survivor like a whirlwind and riding over him threw a burning brand on him so as to mark him with a great weal. Then he said to him to return home and bear the tidings of the destruction of the Chintas. "If you come back again, I will kill you," he said to him. Then he let the Chinta go free and set him on the road back to his homeland.

Now the Narts marveled at the deeds of this horseman and asked themselves, "To which clan does this horseman belong? How did he happen upon our battle without our noticing? Where does he live? Who are his friends and kinfolk?"

The Narts asked one another such questions, but no one knew who this rider was who had destroyed the Chinta army.

Long-bearded Nasren did not know to what clan the mysterious rider belonged. Ashamez said, "I have heard no word about him." Even wily Sosruquo knew nothing at all about the horseman. None of the Narts knew where he had come from. No one would approach him to ask him of his origins. Then the mysterious rider came up to the main body of the Narts.

The Narts in their joy praised him and said to him, "May God grant you life! You saved us from today's evil." Among the Narts was one Tlabetsa[4] the Short, a liar and blasphemer. He ran up to the rider and asked him where he was from.

"I am just like you. I am of Nart lineage. Why did you let these Chintas enter the land of the Narts without sending one voice to bring me word? It is our duty to stand as one, to defend the land of the Narts together," said the rider. "Now I am returning home. Once again misfortune befell you. This seems to be the way of people. We come to know one another chiefly when misfortune befalls us," and so saying the rider set off for home.

The Narts had failed to ask him his name or where he was from. The Narts regretted this and were sad.

Then Tlabetsa the Short decided to find out whence this horseman had come. Tlabetsa deemed that it would be to his advantage to win this rider over as his friend. Tlabetsa dreamed in his heart of setting himself above all other Narts, of becoming their leader. He thought that with this warrior's help his dreams might come true.

Tlabetsa the Short mounted his horse and set off on the trail that the rider had taken to return home.

One rider followed behind the other until they both came in turn to the mountain valley where Nart Shebatin's house stood.

Tlabetsa saw the mysterious rider enter the courtyard of the house, dismount, and take his horse to the paddock. Then he went into the house. As Tlabetsa followed, the thought flashed into his mind that perhaps here he could find a wife as well as a friend.

When he entered the yard, a woman came out to meet him, holding a drinking horn full of wine in her hands.

"You are our guest, decent and brave Tlabetsa! Do not feel slighted and say, 'A mere woman comes to greet me!' Do not think that no man lives in our house. All our men remain away on their quests. Do not say, 'The one who offers a horn to me is a mere woman!' Drink the wine!"

"May it be so!" said Tlabetsa the Short, and he drained the horn of wine.

The woman issued an order to slaughter seven oxen for the newly arrived guest. In her husband's absence the woman made a banquet in honor of Tlabetsa. Tlabetsa entertained himself with eating and drinking, but his mind soon turned back to the secret matter for which he had come, and he thought to himself, "Where did the man go whom I saw enter this yard? Now in this house there is not a single man. I saw the rider enter this yard, enter this house. Where is he?"

Then Tlabetsa the Short decided to walk about the grounds. When he stepped out from the house, he saw some women in the courtyard cleaning the horse of the mysterious warrior. Tlabetsa recognized the horse from its neck. This horse's neck resembled that of a snake, like the neck of the horse that the brave rider had mounted.

Tlabetsa decided not to ask whose horse it was. Instead, without saying anything to anyone, he returned to the house, went back in, and began to eat and drink once more.

In the evening, when they had finished with the drinking, Tlabetsa went from the house to the stables. He entered the stable where he had seen the horse with the snake's neck. He had decided to steal it. But the stall of the snake-necked horse was underground, with a huge stone lying over the door. Tlabetsa' strength was no match for the task of moving the massive stone, no matter how hard he tried.

Then Tlabetsa thought, "Perhaps the rider's strength lies in his battle garments, in his chain mail and helmet. I shall go and steal these, and then I will be able to move this boulder." But of the rider's battle garb he could find no trace. Tlabetsa despaired because he was unable either to find the battle garments or to move the boulder. And so he returned to the kitchen, where he lay down and tried to fall asleep, but sleep would not come to him, and he lay on the floor, turning first to one side and then the other.

When dawn broke the Nart Shebatin the Hunter returned from his quest.

His people came out to meet him and said, "You have an important guest!"

Shebatin said to them, "If he is so important, then why have you led him into the kitchen and not to the rightful guest house?"

For the sake of honor and propriety, Shebatin sent them to take Tlabetsa from the kitchen to the guest house. He then commanded that seven fatted sheep be slaughtered in honor of the guest. Once again Tlabetsa set to feasting, but his appetite failed him, for he realized from Shebatin's noble manner that he would never join Tlabetsa as an ally.

Shebatin's wife brought the wine horn to Tlabetsa and gave it to him to drink. As she bent forward to hand it to him, Tlabetsa thought he heard an infant cry out. Tlabetsa accepted the wine horn and acted as though he had heard nothing. He had seen no infant in the house, no sign of one. Perhaps it had cried out from her belly, though she seemed slender, with a flat stomach.

For seven days and seven nights they feasted. On the eighth day Tlabetsa returned home.

Tlabetsa had hoped to be lord over the Narts. He had hoped that no man among them would be higher than he, that all the Nart land would be in his hands. This was the reason he had hoped to make the unknown rider his friend and ally. But now he understood that Shebatin would never be his ally. He had thought to steal the rider's horse and battle garb so as to steal his strength. Then he would not have needed him as an ally, but here too his plans had failed because he had been unable to steal the horse or to find the battle garb.

Now Tlabetsa the Short was the sort of man who would lie and deceive the Narts at every turn. No matter what truth they were told, about what was or was to be, they would always believe Tlabetsa's lies instead. Tlabetsa feared that the child he had heard at the home of Shebatin might one day grow to manhood, if he was a boy, and challenge Tlabetsa's rule of the Narts. Therefore Tlabetsa decided to destroy the infant.

As soon as he returned from the home of Nart Shebatin, he convened a meeting of the Narts. When the Narts met, Warzameg was usually their t'hamata, master of the feast, and if Warzameg was away, then Shebatin took his place. Tlabetsa knew that Warzameg was away, and he took care that Shebatin should not hear of the gathering. He was free to give tongue to the myriad lies teeming in his heart. When the meeting opened, Tlabetsa said to those gathered before him, "Narts, not long ago I went before God and asked Him the following: 'Will the Narts endure longer on this earth?' In reply God said to me, 'The Narts will not long endure on this earth.' And then I said to God, 'When will the Narts perish?' and he replied, 'There is a Nart woman who has conceived. If a girl will be born to her, then when that girl grows up and marries, no other Nart woman will conceive thenceforth. If a boy will be born to her, the boy, when he grows to manhood, will walk to a wall and take down a great sword. On the day when he takes that sword, all men who dwell in the land of the Narts will die.' That is what he said to me.

"Then I asked God once more, 'There are many Nart women who have given birth to girls and will still give birth to them. There are many Nart women who have given birth to boys and will still give birth to them. How can I tell which child will be the doom of the Narts?' To this God replied: 'Among the Nart women there will be a woman who will have conceived even though she seems empty of child. Within the first three months, the child will cry out from her belly. If that infant who cries out is a girl, then the day will come when the Nart women will not longer lie in childbirth. If that infant who cries out is a boy, then the Nart men will disappear, the Nart men will all die.' This is what God did tell me," said Tlabetsa in this meeting, speaking loudly for all to hear.

Tlabetsa was able to convince all the Narts gathered there of what he had said.

"So, Narts, heed my words. I was recently at Shebatin's house. Shebatin's wife extended to me the wine horn to drink, and as she bent over to hand it to me, I heard an infant crying out from her belly. From the cry I could tell that the infant would be a boy," said Tlabetsa. "When that boy reaches manhood, he will destroy us all. We must destroy him even though he is an infant, lest he destroy us."

The Narts pondered his words and became exceedingly frightened. The Narts were sore at heart to think that they might have to kill an infant, but the liar Tlabetsa had convinced them that when this child grew up he would take sword in hand and hew them all down. What they should do they did not know.

Now the Narts conferred among themselves and decided that when the wife of Nart Shebatin bore her child, the Narts would kidnap him, but they did not know how to do this.

"How will this child come into our hands?" they asked Tlabetsa.

"We have Byaramupkhw[5] as a midwife and nurse for the Narts. The women in childbirth and the new mothers are always sending for her. There is no older woman in the land of the Narts. When the wife of Shebatin bears her child, we shall send old Byaramupkhw to her," said Tlabetsa.

So the Narts decided to send her.

Byaramupkhw went to the house of Shebatin and found there a young infant boy. One day, while pretending to help by taking care of the infant, she stole the child and brought him to the Narts.

When the Narts looked on the child, he smiled, and it seemed to the Narts that his smile was like sunshine.

The Nart Shaway said that because the child had smiled, there must be some hidden meaning in the events at hand, and so they decided not to kill him but to let him live. The Narts cut down a large oak tree and hewed from its trunk a canoe. They set the infant down in it. Then they carried the canoe to the mountains with the child lying in it. They placed it and the infant down in one of the deepest ravines. After leaving the canoe in the ravine, they returned home and told Tlabetsa that they had carried out his wishes, that they had killed the child.

When he heard these words, Tlabetsa was glad because he feared that when the child grew up he would be a threat to him and would challenge him to the leadership of the Narts.

That night a great wind arose in the ravine where the child was lying. A great cloud swept in, and it began to pour rain. Lightning flashed and thunder roared. The heavy rain began to fill the ravine. As the water rose, it lifted the canoe bearing the child and began to carry it down the mountainside. The torrent bore the child with it until it flowed out into a wide plain, and there the canoe came to rest with the infant in it.

In that plain, tending the geese of the Narts, was a lone old Nart woman. Suddenly there reached her ears the voice of a crying child. The old woman looked behind her and saw a canoe. She walked up to it, and when she looked in she saw a child lying in it. The child smiled and laughed at her. When he laughed, it seemed to her like sunshine.

The old woman picked up the child and set off for home. "I shall bring him as a present to my old man," she said to herself. The old woman carried the infant home with her, and she and her husband, the little old Nart man, began to care for him as their own in their underground house.

At about the same time, many of the Narts gathered for a meeting. To this meeting came the old woman Byaramupkhw, and she said to those gathered, "Do you recall the one who came to our rescue when the army of the Chintas had invaded our land, the one who saved us, the brave horseman? That horseman was not a man. Rather, it was the wife of Nart Shebatin. There is no man in all of Nart land who could overpower that woman. Now let me tell you that a misfortune has befallen that brave woman. The child whom she has borne has disappeared. She is searching for him now. It is you who have stolen this child. If she learns of this, then she will make you plow the fields with your bare hands. Take heed for yourselves!"

The Narts grew frightened and they scattered. The very first to flee in dread was Tlabetsa the Short. He was never seen again.

The wife of Nart Shebatin searched for the child. Eventually she came to the lowlands, and there she came upon the old woman who tended the geese. Shebatin's wife asked the old woman, "Against my wishes my child has disappeared. Do you know anything of him? His name was Shebatinuquo."

The instant she uttered his name all the geese took wing and soared into the sky with a great honking. When she beheld this, Shebatin's wife grew joyous, threw herself on the old woman, and embraced her.

The old woman took her by the hand and led her to her underground house. There she showed her a crib, and in it was lying the infant.

When Shebatinuquo saw his mother, he smiled and his smile was like sunshine. His mother wept for joy, gathered him up, and took him to Setenaya to tell her all that had happened.

Setenaya was a wise woman and had foreseen all. She sent some of her people to bring the little old woman and the little old man to her. When they came, she told them how someone among the Narts was seeking the child in order to destroy him. The old woman then told Setenaya and the wife of Shebatin how she had found the child lying in a canoe. Setenaya and Shebatin's wife feared that the child was still in danger. Wise Setenaya commanded that an underground house be built and that the child be raised therein by the little old woman and the little old man.

To the little goose herder she said, "I am Shebatinuquo's true mother. You rescued him. So despite the fact that you did not give birth to him, he is no stranger to you. Someone among the Narts wishes to kill Shebatinuquo. So I set Shebatinuquo with you to be your foster son, to raise in this underground house. Let no one among the Narts know one word of the child's existence, not even his own father. Raise him and train him as your own until he is able to sit on horseback."

When they heard her words, the little old woman and the little old man were glad in their hearts, for Setenaya had conferred on them a great honor, and they loved little Shebatinuquo as though he were their own child.

"May the sky be our witness! We swear that we will let no man see the child. We will raise him so that no other woman will bear his equal among the Narts! Also we will breed for him a winged horse, an 'alp,'" they said. "Furthermore, we will give you our word that he will train the sharp-taloned eagles and the dogs of the 'samer' breed."

"May it be so!" Setenaya and Shebatin's wife both replied. "But when he cries, let no man hear his voice."

"I know from having cared for the child that when he cries he wants to eat," the little old woman replied.

Lady Setenaya then told the little old woman to feed Shebatinuquo the marrow of bucks and does. Then he was placed in the underground house, and a mighty horse, a sharp eagle, and a swift hound were all brought and placed there together with him so that they might be raised together. All this was part of her plan to prevent the child's father, Warzameg, from dying at the hands of his enemies.

The old woman and the old man guarded Shebatinuquo in the underground house, caring for him and nurturing him. What another child would grow in one year, Shabatinuquo would grow in one day.

Soon Shebatinuquo would no longer fit in his crib. So in the dark of night the old woman and the old man yoked eight oxen into a team and dragged a huge oak into the underground house. From this they fashioned a huge crib. They made a cradle strap from the hide of a deer.

Shebatin's wife had let him suckle from her breast seven times a day. Now the old woman fed him with the choicest foods: the marrow from deer, walnuts, and the honey of the bee. The old woman would rock the huge cradle and sing, "Today is a special day, a sacred day! May what I sing quickly come to be! When you go into battle, your coming will be like the dawning of the day. You will be glorious like the day. A shining Nart horseman will you be. The alp on which you will sit will be like the whirlwind. On your right the swift hounds will lope. On your left the swift hounds will lope. Above your head will soar the sharp-taloned eagles. On your helmet the sunlight will glint. From your lance's head will peal thunder. You will pass from one end of the foe to the other. You will vanquish all armies."

When the old woman had ceased her song, Shebatinuquo seized his crib band and tore it asunder. He arose from his crib and stood on the floor. He strode to the wall from which hung a great sword. He took it down and began to swing it before him to get its feel. Then he went to the eagle, stroked its head, and accustomed it to his touch. Likewise he went to the samer hound, stroked its head, and accustomed it to his touch.

This was the manner of Shebatinuquo's birth and childhood.

This saga and the following one draw on Hadaghat'la 1970, vol. 3, no. 243, pp. 103–7, in Bzhedukh West Circassian; 1968, vol. 1, no. 27, pp. 158–64, in Bzhedukh, and no. 32, pp. 172–78, in Shapsegh West Circassian.

☙ These sagas deal with the rescue of Warzameg from a banquet where he is to be assassinated. His wife, who is clairvoyant and has foreseen this crisis, saves him. To avert it, she has conceived a child who, in effect, dies and is raised in a grave mound by the guardians of the souls of the Narts, the little old Nart woman and man. The child comes back from the dead and saves Warzameg. Warzameg then takes him as his son. In variant 32 this child is Sawseruquo, but this seems to be an expropriation of an earlier myth by this highly popular trickster figure. In variant 27 the child is Pataraz, who, as a gigantic Nart, seems to have displaced the earlier gigantic Nart, Shebatinuquo. In other accounts, the child is Shebatinuquo, or more precisely Warzamegyuquo Shebatinuquo. His name is a double patronymic, which is found only with one of Warzameg's other sons, the minor figure Warzamegyuquo Yareshuquo in saga 29 (see, in addition, *Hadaghat'la*, vol. 1, nos. 79–82, pp. 269–81). Shebatinuquo has two fathers and two mothers. He seems to be an ancient figure, the son of Shebatin (the Ubykh name points to an original Shebartin), which is literally (the) Hunter (she-) Bartin. His wife is an Amazon but otherwise nameless. The tale of his childhood is one of treachery and abduction at the instigation of evil Tlabetsa. He is raised underground and is resurrected, but otherwise the rescue theme is absent. Much like the Greek hero Achilles, who was fed animal entrails by Charon, the boatman to Hades, he is linked to death and an unusual diet [KT]. He is later subsumed into the Warzameg-Setenaya cycle, where again he is resurrected but this time goes on to fulfill his destiny.

The Shebatinuquo saga provides rare but strong evidence of an earlier, purely Caucasian tradition on which the later Iranian Nart apparatus has been erected. I have exploited the Circassian practice of fosterage, practiced until recently, and subsumed the earlier myth under the later saga, thus explaining Shebatinuquo's dual parentage. In all other regards, however, I have remained faithful to the originals.

[1] Chinta / č̣ʷʼə́tʼa /, / ṣ̌ʷʼə́ntʼa /, the name of a region often referred to in the Nart sagas. Its location has been forgotten, but this story points to its having been north of the land of the Narts. It is odd, to say the least, that the Nart Warzameg, ostensibly the ruler of the Narts, seems to live in a place other than Nart land. This suggests that originally Warzameg was not a Nart but rather some important personage who visited Nart land and was the intended victim of treachery. This is only one of several themes suggesting that the Nart sagas reflect an old animosity between the Narts and another ethnic group.

[2] In Bzhedukh / ʔahλáǯʸ /, in Shapsegh / ʔahλáǵʸ /, from the Iranian Ossetic name for this Nart, / alæg /, itself from Alanic */ālag-/, in turn from a Proto-Iranian */ārya-ka-/, an old adjectival form of the ethnic name, 'Aryan'; compare also Iron Ossetic / ir / 'noble' from simple */ārya-/. This Nart's name is, therefore, simply Aryan One, a fitting epithet for a ruler of a group, the Narts, which itself bears an Iranian name. At the end of the story he is called a prince, further evidence that he is the local ruler of the Narts.

[3] Pshish'ha / pṣ̌ʸə́sʼa /, see Paris (1974, 14, map) for the river Pchich.

[4] Tlabetsa / λabə́-cʼa / 'heel-hair', "Hairy Heels", (see saga 72). He appears as Tleguts, "Hairy Legs," in saga 39. He is a trickster figure, much like the Ossetian Nart Syrdon [KT].

[5] This name is literally / byara-m-ə-px̌° / 'Byara-obl-inal-daughter'. Byara is not a Circassian name but rather has an Iranian or Slavic look. Elsewhere her name is Baramupkh or Barambukh (see sagas 50 and 64).

[Now, although Tlabetsa the Short had fled at the words of Byaramupkhw and had never been seen again, other Narts still resented Warzameg and planned his destruction. Warzameg knew that he had many enemies, but he paid little heed to them.] Being wise and intelligent, Setenaya knew what plans the Nart Aleg, Lord of the Council House, had in his heart. So she had made fully ready Shebatinuquo's horse, hounds, eagle, and armor so that he might one day vanquish these enemies.

At the Nart councils it was the custom for the other Narts to give the drinking horn first to the Nart Warzameg. Holding the horn he would say, "Whoever has a heavy heart, let him speak of it now. Once I have raised this cup high, I shall not accept complaints from anyone, no matter what he says," and so saying he would drink from the cup and then pass it to the others. Now in that drinking horn Aleg had planned to put seven poisonous snakes. The Narts would let Warzameg drink from it as usual, and as he drained it these snakes would bite him and kill him. All this Setenaya the Beautiful had understood. She knew too that Nart Aleg had laid plans so that the position of lawgiver—of supreme ruler of the Narts—would devolve upon himself. Knowing all this, she had made everything ready for that terrible day so that Shebatinuquo might save Warzameg. Setenaya the Wise, with her keen mind, had seen far and knew all that was to be.

As this evil was afoot, Shebatinuquo was growing to manhood without knowing what the world was like. From infancy he had lived in the underground house, never seeing anything but a pine torch for a lamp and knowing no one save the old man and the old woman of the Narts. Meanwhile, the enemies of Warzameg had decided that the time had come to carry out their plan, and so they invited Warzameg to the Nart meeting.

The Narts made a strict pact among themselves: "Let six days pass. On the seventh come to the Great House." And you see, after they had dispersed, having spelled out their plan, one of them, without the others knowing, went in secret to Warzameg and told him all. That is what happened. He told Warzameg what was afoot because he did not want to bring slander and disgrace on his head. The one who told him, who brought these bad tidings back to Warzameg, was the son of his sister, his nephew.[1]

"Do not go. That of which they have accused you is not good. It is dangerous. You might be killed. They have decided that when six days have passed, they will gather for a feast on the seventh and summon you there," said his nephew. "Pretend to be sick, whatever, but do not go. If it were up to me, I would not let you go among them."

Thus, this having been done, six days passed. The appointed day came, and as they had agreed, the tribe of Narts gathered in the old house, bringing food and provisions.

"Who will bring Warzameg for us?" they asked and began to discuss this among themselves.

They asked one man, but he said, "He must already have heard of our plan by now. I would not let him kill me, furious as he is, by going near him," and he would not give one word of acquiescence to their request that he summon Warzameg.

Then they asked among themselves: "Who, indeed, will go for us?"

"I shall go," answered the Nart Zhemadu,[2] giving them his word.

"Do not say too much to him. Do not add anything to what we shall tell you to say," they warned him.

"What should I tell him?" he asked them.

Then they entreated the messenger to say only the following: "'The Narts are holding a feast. They need you. They must see you. They have prepared the horn for you and have it waiting. They wish for you to enter among them.' If you should say more than that to him, he shall harm you and we shall know nothing from him but misfortune."

"I shall tell him what you have said, but I shall not be able to refrain from saying more if my wits tell me to," said Zhemadu and he set off.

Warzameg, pretending to be sick, lay in bed.

"What kind of illness does he have? Nothing seems to ail him, and yet why did he lie down?" Warzameg's wife wondered, but she was afraid to ask him.

Zhemadu arrived. He tied his horse to the hitching post and went inside. Setenaya, intending to eavesdrop on them, crept close to the door.

As Zhemadu entered, he realized that Warzameg was lying down.

"We did not realize that you were sick. If you are ill, may God speed your recovery," said Zhemadu.

"Sit," Warzameg told him.

"If I were to sit whenever someone said 'sit!' then I would not be the kind of man of whom legends are told. I shall not sit, but by your leave I shall tell you my concern," said the messenger.

"Speak," replied Warzameg.

"I shall. The Narts have gathered. They hope to have you as a guest and so have prepared a drinking horn for you. It is waiting. They wish you to come among them," said Zhemadu.

"I have come down with diarrhea. My stomach has liquefied. My horse, Pefizh Usha,[3] is a very rough horse. If I ride him now, he will kill me," said Warzameg.

"You are the one to say, 'I shall go there' or, 'I shall not go there.' It is your choice," said Zhemadu. "I have told you what I came to say. There is little courage in you, Warzameg. My heart is a fiery, parched gully. My eyes burn with fire. The courage in my two wrists is more than you have altogether," said Zhemadu and he left the house.

Although Zhemadu had said to the Narts that he would not say anything excessive to Warzameg, he used his keen tongue and said that much to him. Setenaya, who was standing near the door, heard what the two men had said to each other without missing a word. Not letting the Nart, who was mounting his horse, see her, she sneaked out from behind the corner of the door and went back into her house unobserved. After Zhemadu had mounted and ridden off, she went into her husband's room.

"Until now I have lived with you thinking that there was worthy courage in your heart, but today I see that this is not so. For three days, with nothing at all ailing you, you have been lying around. The lies that you told that man you should not have concocted. Why don't you get up when they've gone to such trouble to send for you? Why shouldn't you go?" she reproached him.

"The Narts have evil planned in their hearts against me. You would have me go among them and have me be killed by them? Then perhaps you intend to marry one of them. You rebuked me in an effort to trick me," Warzameg said to her, and he picked up his riding whip, intending to strike her. His wife then pleaded with him.

"Warzameg, put away the whip! Don't hit me! Let me have my say! I did not say those things to you with such cruelty in my mind. Do not sit here in idleness and despair. Get ready and go! I shall send after you a man who is no less a hero than you are. The one I shall send, if he finds you alive, will lead you safely back from them."

So Warzameg led out Pefizh Usha. He put a saddle of finest pigskin on it and in all his splendor set off. Warzameg left Chinta, crossed the Pshiza,[4] and set off on the way to the council, which was held in what was called the old domain of the Nart Aleg, the so-called Hill of Querghwa,[5] near the banks of the Pshish'ha.

When Zhemadu rejoined the Narts back at their territory, they asked him: "Did you tell him more than we said or did you say correctly just what we told you to say?"

"Just what you told me to tell him I told him, but my sharp tongue added a bit more," he said to them.

When he spoke thus he made the others tremble. So that they could see when Warzameg approached, they set lookouts in the tops of the trees. They began to quarrel with Zhemadu. "You said too much to him and have brought down his wrath upon us." The lookouts kept a keen vigil and soon saw a horseman coming. From his manner and appearance they recognized Warzameg.

The lookouts brought back the news of his coming, saying, "The breath from his horse's nose sets the road and embankments afire. The clods from beneath the hooves of his horse fly up into the air like black-and-white birds. These are the tokens of his horse."

Then they said, "If he is coming relentlessly like that, then we must set down our fur cloaks as a welcoming mat, otherwise we shall not be able to calm him." So they set their cloaks down end to end to form a welcoming mat that reached out to the road, and they stood there holding food for him.

Warzameg kept coming and finally arrived among them.

They said to him, "Warzameg, calm yourself and your horse too! You are not too late for the feast."

They helped him dismount and made him stand on the fur cloaks. They let him taste the food, and with a man in waiting standing on each side of him, they led him down the line of cloaks. In this manner they brought him to the house and led him inside. Among those gathered were men both younger and older than he was, but they did not set him among these; rather they led him to the place of honor, placing him above all others.[6] When Warzameg was seated, they gave a sign, a wink, to Khimish's son, Pataraz, and said, "The horn!" They intended to give him the drinking horn first and to withhold the food, so as to make him drunk. Pataraz picked up the drinking horn, which could hold six pails of wine, with his right hand alone, not even balancing it against his left hand, and extended it to Warzameg.

Pataraz was young at this time and did not know of their treacherous plans. His was the privilege to wait on the most honored guest.[7] He then said, "This horn is for you. It is meant for no other man. It is yours. Drink this home brew down to the bottom!"

"May you, the draft pourer, live long.[8]
May you, the cupbearer, live long.
I know not what is afoot,
But lest I lie on this horn,
I shall not drink from it," said Warzameg.

He took the horn and without drinking from it stood there at the seat
of honor. Pataraz, the son of Khimish, stood there waiting for the horn.
Pataraz, son of Khimish, said, "Do not delay the horn, Blessed Lord of the
Feast![9] Do not keep those sitting at your side hungry."

"The Narts have more than one draft and one horn.
The Narts do not have merely a single horn,
But let them find another horn.
Let not our comrades hunger, but give them a horn,"
    said Warzameg.

Meanwhile, Lady Setenaya, knowing what business awaited Warzameg
at this meeting, led Shebatinuquo from the underground house in which
he had been reared and led him into the world of daylight for the first time.
Shebatinuquo looked around him for a long time. He had never before
seen the sun or the moon or stars. Everything amazed him greatly and he
gazed in wonderment all about him. He asked his mother, Setenaya, "Our
mother,[10] what is this into which you have brought me?"

His mother replied, "This is what is called the world." Then she showed
him the sun, the moon, and the stars.

"Do you know who your father is, my child?" she asked him.

"How would I know him? I have never seen him," replied Shebatinuquo.

"Your father is Warzameg," Setenaya the Beautiful told him.

"Where is he? Why have I never seen my father?" Shebatinuquo asked.

"I shall tell you all, my child," she replied.

"Today is your father's day. Your father is the lawgiver. At this moment
he is at the old home of Aleg. When the Narts have finished with their
council, when they have sat down together to eat and drink, then they will
let your father drink from a horn containing seven poisonous snakes.
These snakes will strike and kill your father."

"But, our mother, if they are going to have these snakes kill my father
this way, why didn't you tell me before now?" he asked his mother, Setenaya the Beautiful.

"My child," said Setenaya, "for all these years I have allowed them to rear you, nourishing you with the marrow of bucks and does that your father brought back from the hunt, because, my child, I knew that this day would come to confront your father with its awful treachery." So saying, the Lady Setenaya answered Shebatinuquo. "With my acquiescence and knowledge, I have sent my own husband among the Narts. He is there now. You will go there and send him back to me alive. Then you must go to visit your cousin Sawseruquo. But if you find that he is dead, that they have killed him, then bring his body back to me," said Setenaya.

"As I have never seen him, how shall I recognize him from among the men with whom he is standing?"

Setenaya said, "They have given him the drinking horn and made him take the place of honor. He is standing there waiting for you. Thus, as soon as you enter, he will extend the horn. Do not err and strike him! He is the one whom you must bring back, lead back."

"Well then, our mother, what must I do to ready myself?" he asked her.

"Your horse is ready, my child, along with all the belongings you must carry with it. Your weapons and all your armor and clothes are ready.[11] Your hounds are ready and your eagle too. What your eagle drives out, your hounds will retrieve. Your lance is also ready. All you need do is saddle your horse, gather your arms, and set off. There is nothing else," said Lady Setenaya.

He led out his horse and put the saddle on it. He took up his arms and clothing. Then his mother attached the *hajitsas*[12] to his elbows, knees, and heels.

Shebatinuquo asked Setenaya, "Our mother, what are these things that are attached to my arms and legs?"

"My child," she replied, "bring your forearm back toward you," and she made him flex one of his arms so that his hand went toward his chest. When he did this, the blade of the hajitsa shot out to the side. "Now, raise your knee upward," she said and made him flex his leg. When he did this, the blade of this hajitsa shot out toward the front. "Their function is this: the hajitsas at your elbows will strike down whoever comes at you from the side. The hajitsas on your knees will stab whoever rushes you from the front. The blade on your heel will strike off the horse's leg of your enemy when he draws alongside you. Now you know what they are for," she said.

"Good, our mother!" he replied. "Now, point me to the road that I must take."

"My child, head south! At night the North Star, the star of Taymir the

Kazak, should be above your right shoulder. Orient yourself by the moon! Should there be no moon, then the Big Dipper should be above your left shoulder," said Setenaya.[13]

"I am off!" he said and rode on his mission.

Shebatinuquo traveled far and finally came to the Narts' country. When he entered their territory, he encountered the herdsman of the Narts.

"May your herds be fruitful!" Shebatinuquo said to him in greeting.

"May God give you life!" responded the herdsman.

Shebatinuquo then asked him, "Will you tell me where the house of Aleg is, wherein the Narts hold their council?"

The Nart herdsman then replied, "Aye! The house of Aleg the Nart is a house that bends this way and that.[14] Many pillars support it. The floor of the front porch reaches up to the breast of a horse. Eight ox-drawn carts are needed to haul its main support pillar. A girl lives therein of whom it is said, 'She goes in with the squirrel but comes out with the fox.'[15] The courtyard has many hitching posts. The front of the house is a whole week's journey in breadth and has before it a slippery quagmire. When you see the girl, you will fall down in it and be disgraced."

Then Shebatinuquo replied to the herdsman of the Narts in this way: "Old stupid herdsman of the Narts, would I ever have left Chinta and come to the Narts' land if I were the sort to fall down in the mud and make a fool of myself every time I saw an ugly old bitch? Old stupid herdsman of the Narts, if I did not respect God and honor forgiveness, I would make you crawl through the hoop of my fingers!"[16]

The girl of whom the herdsman had spoken was Akwanda the Beautiful,[17] the daughter of the master of the house, Aleg. She was looking out from her tower[18] when she saw a horseman enter the courtyard. He was Shebatinuquo. Akwanda the Beautiful went running to her mother (her mother was also a Setenaya beauty)[19] and said to her, "Our mother, we have a guest coming. Until now we have never had a guest. I see dust rising, too little for a group but too much for one man, you might say. His mustache glitters like gold.[20] If food has been cooked, please set it out! If it is not ready, please go and prepare it as fast as possible! Up to now no man has ever come to Nart land like the one who is coming. Whatever his eagle flushes, his hounds bring back. For all I know, he might even be from Chinta."

Her mother was very wise and said, "If it is as you say, my daughter, then he will be Shebatinuquo, the son of Warzameg."

In less time than it took her to say these words, Shebatinuquo rode up and entered the courtyard. He did not go to the hitching posts intended for suitors but tied his horse's reins to a post intended for guests of the council. As a gesture of peace he thrust his lance into the ground.

Akwanda the Beautiful ran out to meet him and stepped lightly out of her slippers,[21] saying as she did so, "Welcome, our guest, to the great house!"[22]

"I shall accept your hospitality but not your invitation," replied Shebatinuquo to the girl. "I am not bound for the great house but have come to be a guest at the council gathering." So he walked off toward the meetinghouse to take a place at the council gathering.

She turned about and went back into the great house. Therein were many Nart youths sitting about, hoping to gain her favor. These suitors laughed when she entered and said to her, "Who was that ugly, stupid fool who did not accept your invitation?"

Even though she had not known such humiliation before, the girl could not forget him.

"I shall agree with you and call him an ugly, stupid fool if any one of you can pull his lance out of the ground," she replied. "Furthermore, I shall give my hand in betrothal to the one who can do it."

At this they all began to shout, "I can do it! It will be easy!" They ran out of the house and one by one tried to pull the lance out of the ground, but without success.

"Who is this person who has stuck this lance in the ground?" they wondered. "What is his lineage? We cannot pull it out!"

"He is the kind of hero that I thought he was!" the beautiful Akwanda said, taunting them. "I do not go out into the courtyard to greet just anyone who enters!"[23]

When the guards at the council's door saw Shebatinuquo coming, they hooked the door with the head of a lance to keep him from entering.

"Is this your mighty dagger, Narts?" he called to them.

"For you a dagger will suffice. As for us, our dagger, our stronghold, we shall not show it to you," they replied.

"It may be enough to slow me down, but I shall show you right now that it will not stop me," he said. Then he drew his sword, broke the lance head out of its hook, and used it to smash to pieces the lances of the guards, sending sharp shards flying in all directions. Then he strode toward the council room.

Shebatinuquo entered the Nart council and stood in a corner until they had finished the meeting. Then they brought in serving tables and set one before each guest. They brought in drink. Then too they brought in the poisoned drinking horn and placed it before Warzameg. Each man had his own eating table before him, and all was ready. It was time for Warzameg to take up the horn and signal the beginning of the feast. Warzameg stood up and raised the horn. He stood there for a moment and shook the horn, saying, "Hearken to me! Whoever has a heavy heart, let him speak! Let him say now before I have drunk from this cup, for once I have raised high this cup and drunk therefrom, nothing can be done for anyone who has a grievance."

His mother, Setenaya the Beautiful, had told Shebatinuquo what was about to happen.

"I am one with a heavy heart!" he called out, and with the sound that came from the youth's mouth all the Narts sitting there were struck with great fear and turned to look at him.

Warzameg, his father, then said to Shebatinuquo, "If you stand over there, I will have trouble understanding you. Come closer and tell me your troubles." As Shebatinuquo approached, Warzameg said to himself, "Could a Nart ever be this big?" Shebatinuquo was not like the others. He was much larger. He came before Warzameg's table and struck the horn that Warzameg was holding from his hand, smashing it and spilling the drink. Seven venomous snakes slithered out of the horn and reared up to strike Shebatinuquo. With one swipe of his sword he cut them all in two. He then turned to where Aleg, the one who had planned this perfidy, was sitting by Warzameg's side, and with one sweep of his blade he struck off his head. He cut the ear from the side of one. Another Nart he slit down the ribs. A third he hit a mighty, crushing blow with the flat of his sword. Another he pushed down until he broke his back. When the Narts realized what was happening, they were stricken with panic. They rushed to the door, pushing against each other until they finally smashed through the door frame and scattered, forgetting their horses and running off into the forest. The other, the old man Warzameg, thought that he would be the last to be struck down. He stood there trembling, then sat back down in the center, alone, and awaited his fate. The old man remained like that, and Shebatinuquo said nothing to him but simply strode to the door. He stopped at the threshold. Then he turned about and approached Warzameg, intending to take the old man with him. He realized then that Warzameg was not preparing to leave but rather was afraid of him because he had fought so fiercely and bravely. When the old man just sat there and showed no sign at all of starting back, Shebatinuquo thought a bit and said,

"Unlucky old man with the big mustache, who may never enter this house again, don't you know how to leave?" Then he broke a window with the hilt of his sword, picked Warzameg up with one hand, and threw him onto the veranda, hurting three of his ribs in the process.

The old man, full of fright, sprang up, ran back to his horse, the clever Pefizh Usha, sprang into the pigskin saddle, and headed off toward his home.

As his mother, the Lady Setenaya, had said he must do, Shebatinuquo set off on a visit to his cousin Sawseruquo.

Warzameg set off for Chinta. He drew near home and finally entered his own courtyard, where he dismounted. The Lady Setenaya came out to greet him and led him back into the house.

"What news?" she asked him. "What did you see? What judgments did you pass? You were at the Nart council, were you not?"

"Alas! What I saw was a bitter sight. What we said was worthless. But there was a youth present there of such manly bearing and stature that he was unlike any that I have ever seen before."

"Yes, but what kind of young man?" said the Lady Setenaya to Warzameg with feigned astonishment.

"Alas! If you have not heard him or seen him for yourself, you would find him hard to imagine. I have never seen his like among the race of Narts. His like is simply not to be found in Nart land. He is larger than the Narts. When he walks, you think that many people are walking. We had finished the meeting and the tables had been brought out. We sat down at a table, and they set down my drinking horn. I took the horn and stood up, saying, 'Today, whoever has a heavy heart, let him say so now before I raise the cup. After I have raised high this horn, I shall not be able to offer succor to anyone with a grievance.' I spoke thus, took the horn, and stood up, whereupon someone rose from the corner and called out. The Narts were frightened. I have never seen a Nart like him. I bade him draw near me so that I could ask him what was wrong. I wanted to look him over closely to see what manner of youth he was. When he was close to me, he struck the cup from my hand with his sword and broke it. Then one of the poisonous snakes that they had put inside came out, and he cut it in two. Then he cut off Aleg's head. The Narts fled in panic. He cleaned his sword, resheathed it, and left without saying a word to me. I went after him and looked everywhere for him, but he had mounted his horse and ridden off. That is what happened to me," said Warzameg.

Setenaya then asked the old man, Warzameg, "My dear old husband, what kind of bond between you and him would be acceptable to you?"

"Ah, if I could have him for a son," replied Warzameg, "then even if all the treasure of the Narts were lying here at my feet, I would not touch it!"

"He is your son," said the Lady Setenaya.

"The only child you ever bore, the only son I ever had," protested Warzameg, "died. Where then would I get a son?"

"In fact, he is that very child I was carrying. He is your son," insisted Setenaya. "I gave him to the old Nart man and the old Nart woman to rear him in an underground house. I have known all along that this day's treachery would be lying in wait for you. I did all so that he could save you."

(Later Shebatinuquo, the son of Warzameg, met his end at the hands of blind Aleg, the younger brother of Prince Aleg. I have forgotten his real name![24] Shebatinuquo met his end at Razyanska grounds. Blind Aleg killed him in Danji Valley with an arrow that he had Tlepsh, the god of the forge, make for him. This, though, is another story.)

From Hadaghat'la 1968, vol. 1, no. 27, pp. 158–64, in Bzhedukh West Circassian and no. 32, pp. 172–78 in Shapsegh West Circassian.

[1] The term / px°ə-rá-ƛfə / 'daughter-by-be.born' may denote either one's sister's children or the children of one's daughter, that is, the children of an immediate female blood relative of one's own or of a descending generation. Such children share the same status as one's own children. As Warzameg is taken to be sterile, I have chosen the word *nephew*. This is the only known reference to Warzameg's having a sister.

[2] Zhemadu / ž̍ʸa-m-ah-dɔ́-w / 'jaw, mouth-obl-int-sharp-pred', "the one with the sharp mouth," that is, the one who says what he thinks. For / də / as "sharp" see reduplicated intensive root, / dɔ́də / 'awl' ('sharp-sharp'). I am indebted to my informant Kadir I. Natkhwa, for this etymology.

[3] Pefizh Usha / p'a-fɔ́-ž̍ʸ ʔɔ́-ˢʸ-a / 'nose-white-color mouth-bent-in', that is, "the horse with the white and crooked muzzle."

[4] Bzhedukh / pš̍ɔ́za /, the Kuban River. Warzameg seems to be heading from the present-day Ukraine down into the Caucasus. The Kuban was the northern border of the Circassians prior to the czarist conquest.

[5] In some variants this is / q°ərɣ°ə-táama / 'Querghwa-wing', meaning "a ridge." Here it is / q°ərɣ°ə-ž̍á-pq / 'Querghwa-mound-frame', meaning a "hill" or "tumulus."

[6] The terms for this position of honor, the point within a house farthest from the door, and hence from the drafts, are / ƚɔ́-ɣ°a t'ɔ-ʁ-ɔ́-p'ʔ / 'old-character down sit dyn place", "place where elders sit down," and / ž̍a-n-t'á-a-śḥa / 'old-obl.conn-stand upright-conn-head', "the head (of the house) where the elders stand," near the hearth.

In a personal communication Kevin Tuite has stated, "In a number of highland Caucasian cultures, the space around the hearth was divided into halves or quadrants, with one half for women, the other for men. One portion of the men's half was reserved for the chief of the household or for a guest. In Svaneti, the guest and elder men still sit facing the hearth, with the young menfolk on the other side of them. The latter are usually on the same side as the door, presumably as a first line of defense against intruders."

⁷ Traditionally, young men could participate at feasts and have the honor of serving their elders. These young men were termed / p̄ʿš̱ʸa-rá-hə / 'cooked.things-inst-bear', "(he who) carries the cooked items."

⁸ This remark is directed to the one who has filled the cup, and not to Pataraz, who is always depicted as blameless. The second remark is the one directed to him.

⁹ The feast cannot start until the tʼhamata decrees it. Circassian / tha-a-m-áh-ta / 'god-pl.(archaic)-obl-int-father', "the father of the god(s)," preserves the old role of the leader and father of the gods at a divine feast. The term, in its Kabardian form / thamáhda /, has spread into both Russian and Persian as *tamada*.

¹⁰ This acknowledges that she is the mother of all the Narts.

¹¹ The arming of a warrior son by his mother seems to have been an ancient and widespread tradition common not only in Spartan Greece but in Celtic and Germanic traditions as well (see Graves 1955, 1:327, 2:100).

¹² Bzhedukh / ḥaaǯʸə́-ca / 'Haji's tooth', probably a weapon brought back from the Middle East by Muslim pilgrims. It seems to have been a set of long spurs attached to various joints of the arms and legs.

¹³ These directions orient him from south to west to north, depending on the time of year. A southward course across the Kuban (/ pš̌ə́za /), with the North Star on his right and the Big Dipper (/ ž́ʸaɣ°a-bə́nə / 'star-family') on his left, would place the journey in late July or early August.

¹⁴ Bzhedukh / q-y-a-ba-ná-a-ba / 'hither-dir-to-bend-thither-dir-to-bend', literally "to bend this way and that," perhaps an image of treacherousness and complexity. Labyrinths also appear in some Circassian sagas (see saga 4), and this may be one name for such a structure.

¹⁵ In other words, she is tricky and deceitful.

¹⁶ This refers to the tunnel formed by holding the hand, palm down on a surface, but with the four fingers arched so that their tips are touching the surface.

¹⁷ Bzhedukh / ʔahkʿ°áanda / or / akʿ°áanda /, but elsewhere in West Circassian simply / k°áanda / and in Kabardian / g°áanda /. This name appears in Ubykh as / g°ə́ndʿ°a / or / g°ə́nda /; the latter form is also found in Abkhaz and Abaza, and in the Iranian Ossetic as / agunda /. Her name is always accompanied by the epithet "beautiful," Circassian / dáaʀa /, Ubykh / nə́ʀ°a /, Abaza / pš̌ə́ʒa /, Abkhaz / pš̌ʒa /, and Ossetic / ræsuxd /. See saga 12 n. 3 for an etymology of this name.

¹⁸ Bzhedukh / š̱ʸandáaqa /, a sort of elevated viewing platform from which noblewomen observed the activity of their surroundings. The following account, wherein the young maiden reports to her mother about the approach of a marvelous warrior, has strong Celtic parallels in Findabair's account to her mother Medb (Meave) of the approach of the warriors Leary, Conall, and Cúchulainn (Delaney 1994, 30–32), (see also saga 53).

¹⁹ Here "Setenaya" is clearly a title, rather than a name.

²⁰ In the Ancient Indian tradition, the hero Indra is wounded in the mouth during his

fight with the demon Vrtra and loses his jaws. These are replaced with golden jaws, (Rig-Veda 1.32.2, 4.18.9). In a Kabardian tale told in Ubykh (Dumézil 1960b, 432–50, saga 86), Tutaresh (Circassian Totaresh) is seen from afar by the glitter of his golden mustache, one of his characteristic features. Similarly, Shebatinuquo has a golden mustache (Hadaghat'la 3:103–11). Although a golden mustache is not a golden jaw, in both the Vedic and Circassian-Ubykh traditions the lower part of the hero's face is characteristically golden and glittering.

[21] This seems to be a gesture of respect and perhaps a mild act of flirtation. The shoes, Bzhedukh /pahpə́šˈʸ/, are strikingly modern; they are backless, with a closed toe, a high heel, and a wooden sole (see Hat'ana and K'erashya 1960, 440).

[22] Bzhedukh /wəná-šk°a/ 'house-big', the main living quarters, as opposed to the smaller guest house (/ḥaač̌ˈʸá-šʸ/ guest-shelter). Suitors are normally accommodated in a special room in the main living quarters.

[23] The hero has proven his true worth by inserting his weapon into the ground in such a way that no one but he can extract it. This theme is familiar to Western readers from the sword-in-the-stone motif of the Arthurian romance (Littleton and Malcor 1994; Littleton 1982). This may have been a more widespread motif at one time (Graves 1955, 1:327 n. 5). In an Abaza Nart saga (Allen 1965, 165), the young Sosruquo proves his heroic nature by "pulling an anvil out of the earth's seven layers and thrusting it back into its nine layers." The theme of the earth or cosmos containing nine layers recurs in Dante's "Inferno" and "Paradiso." This test of the weapon or anvil (source of the weapon) seems to derive its sanctity and force from the hero's unique ability to touch all the layers of creation.

[24] Here one of the Aleg brothers is referred to explicitly as "prince," in keeping with the Iranian etymology of his name *ārya-ka- 'Aryan-one,' the ancient rulers of much of the Caucasus and the Eurasian steppes.

Saga 12 ⁊ *The Ballad of Warzamegyuquo Shebatinuquo*

Eh, ah—Nart Shebatinuquo,[1]
Ay, ay—From the Narts,
Ah, ah—Always full of envy,
Ah, ah—Boiling with malice,
Ah, ah—Never without his horse.
Ah, ah—Pshiza River, which is without a ford,
Ah, ah—Reaches only his horse's belly.
Ah, ah—The horse Bzezhi on whom he sits—oh-oh,
Ah, ah—He tightens its saddle girth,

Ah, ah—And rides along the empty steppe—ey-ey,
Ah, ah—As he is riding across it—oh-ey.
Er, ar—He meets one sent for water,
That Radem, Wheel[2] of the Narts.
"I am a wayward guest—ghey-ghey,
Please show me
Eh, ah—The way to the Narts.
Ah, ah—I would be very grateful," he said.
Eh, eh—"How should I know,
The direction of the Nart road?—yo-yo,
Eh, eh—I am but the Narts' milkmaid.
Eh, ah—I go out at night.
Eh, ah—I come back at night."
Oh, ah—She says to him there.
Eh, ah—"How should I know the Nart way?"
"That devil bitch!
Yer—You great bitch!
Yeh, yeh—If I did not respect God,
Eh, ah—If I did not respect breast milk,
Eh, ah—Through the hoop of my great finger and thumb
Ari-yey—I would force you to crawl!"
"Ah, don't be so harsh with me!
Ah, ah—Whose pain would I bear
Eh, eh—When you climb that hill?
Eh, eh—It is one whole day's travel.
Eh, eh—In the middle of a field stands
Eh, eh—A white-shouldered house.
Ah, ah—That house is long and wide,
Oh, eh—Running this way and that,
Oh, eh—With many columns.
Ra, ah—The porch floor alone
Oh, eh—Under these columns
Ra, eh—Reaches to your horse's breast.
Ay, ay—Therein sits a beautiful maiden.
Eh, ah—Wicked suitors
Ay, ay—Have made a mess near the gate
Ay, ay—So that if your horse makes a misstep,
Eh, eh—You may fall down.
Eh, eh—You might be killed there.

Eh, eh—It is an evil place," she said.
"Oh, you bitch of a sorceress,
Oh, you dishonorable witch!
Eh, eh—When I entered the mire,
Eh, ey—Even if my horse fell,
Eh, ay—Would I lose face
Eh, ay—When I saw just a bitch?
Eh, ay, ay—Have I not come from Chita?
Eh, ay, ay—Have I not come to Nartiya?
Eh, eh—I have come
Eh, eh—To exact of the Narts
Eh, eh—My father's blood price," oh, gha!
Eh, eh—Bzezhi, whom he was riding,
Eh, ah—Stretched out the reins
Eh, ah—And across the barren steppe
Eh, ah—They went riding.
Eh, ah—From beneath his hooves
Eh, ah—Flew black clods and white.
Eh, ah—They fly into the air.
Eh, ah—His two hunting dogs
Eh, ah—Run about him—a, gha!
Eh, ah—Flame issues from his horse's nostrils,
Eh, ah—Setting fire to the side of the road.
Eh, ah—Foam comes from its mouth
Eh, ah—And falls upon the ground.
Eh, ah—Whatever his two dogs flush out
Eh, ah—His eagle seizes, ay, ay!
Eh, ah—From beneath her brows
Eh, ah—The beautiful maid gazed out.
Eh, ah—She saw him from afar.
"Our mother, Setenaya!
Oh, ah—Setenaya, Lady!
Eh, ay, ay—There comes a horseman,
Eh, ar—He must be from Chita!
Eh, ah—His like is not in Nartiya, ah!"
"A salt bread and mush meal
Er—Prepare for him!
Er—If we can be ready for him,
Er—We will invite him in," replied

Eh, ah—Mother Setenaya.
Eh, ah—She rolled up
Eh, ah—Both pants' legs.
Eh, ah—She rolled up
Eh, ah—Both sleeves.
Eh, ay, ay—She prepared a meal
Eh, ah—Neither too hot nor too cold.
Eh, ah—She readied it for him.
Ye, ah—Then making a bow,
"Welcome!" she said to him.
"I am not a party boy.
Eh, ah—I am not a lad bent on lust.
Eh, ah—I must find
Ra, ah—Aleg's old house.
Ra, ah—I have come from Chita.
Ay, ay—I have come to Nartiya.
Eh, ah—I am not a lad bent on lust.
Eh, ah—I am not a party boy," he said to her.
"Welcome, Shebatinuquo!
Eh, ah—From our fat sheep
Eh, ah—We have readied our gravy.
Eh, ah—From our fat old oxen
Eh, ah—We have made our broth.
Ay, ay—We have readied our Akwanda[3] beauties—ra
To caress your head," said Aleg.
"May your fat sheep
Ra, eh—Meet their ends!
May God strike down
Re, ah—The Akwanda beauties!"
"Welcome, Shebatinuquo!
Ah, ay, ay—Do not pass by!"
Eh, eh—They brought him into the house.
Eh, eh—He took off his weapons
Eh, eh—And gave them to a youth.
Ay, eh—The youth's eyelashes began to flutter.
Vay, ay—His two legs
Ah, eh—Began to shake.
Ay, ay—When he hung his weapons from a post
Ray, ay, ay—That post sank down.

Ra, eh—When he laid across the bed board
Ra, eh—That board upon which he laid it
Ra, eh—Broke asunder.
"O God, let him devour you all!
Ra, eh—Their place of rest
Eh, ah—Must be the very smallest place!"
Eh, ah—He took back his weapons.
Ay, ay—They brought a serving table for him.
Eh, ah—He placed his hat upon his head.
Eh, ah—He began to dance thereon.
Eh, ah—The beams began to give way,
Eh, ah—And those standing at the back
Eh, ah—Were hurt on the head.
"Shebatinuquo!" said Aleg.
Ay, ay—"Don't bring the Narts' Old House
Ay, ay—Down upon our heads!"
"If you Narts don't pay
Eh, ah—My father's blood price,
Eh, ah—Then I will return," he said.
"Bring me water in a sieve.
Eh, eh—Grill butter for me on a spit!
Eh, eh—That's what I'll take for my father's blood."
Eh, ah—The most foolish of the Narts
Eh, ah—Scattered in all directions.
Ey, ay—They had gone to fetch water in a sieve.
Ey, ay—They had gone to fry butter on a spit.
Ey, ay—But it was impossible to do as he said.
"Nart Shebatinuquo!
Prince Shebatinuquo!
Yer—You ask of us the impossible," they said.
"Find a bulrush as an axle,
For Wheel, for me!
Wheel, if you can find her,
Wheel, I will take," he said.
Spinning about—yi, ay
A bulrush axle
For Wheel they could not find.
"All the swarthy people among the Narts
You must bring together,

And there on Haram Hill you must slash them.
If it flows up to Bzezhi's side,
If you can satisfy Wheel,
Then as my father's blood price
I will take Radem," he said.
Yeh, eh—"Take all the silk in Nart land,
Yeh, eh—Gather it up,
Yer—Burn it atop Haram Hill.
Yer—Fill my game bag
Ye, eh—With the ashes—
Ye, eh—As our[4] father's blood price
I will take the Radem, the Wheel," he said.

From GENEG, 323–27.

⚬ This ballad has close parallels to saga 31, wherein Pataraz takes the place of Shebatinuquo. The fate of Shebatinuquo's father, known in the Abaza corpus simply as Badan, remains unclear in the Circassian corpus. In the Circassian material, Shebatinuquo saves at least his stepfather, Warzameg. Shebatinuquo appears to be the older, pagan hunting god superseded by Pataraz, who shows Christian influences.

[1] I have recorded the filler words in this song because of their odd dramatic use; they are omitted when a sharp reply is made. This song is in an extremely obscure dialect that is transitional between Shapsegh and Bzhedukh West Circassian. I suspect the language is poetic and archaic. Even the Russian translation (GENEG, 327–32) often seems to be something of a guess.

[2] The name of this maiden is Radem, which seems to come from an Indo-European language, most likely Iranian, and to mean originally "(spoke of a) wheel" and here perhaps even "cart" (Proto-Indo-European *rot-ə₃- [more concretely probably two-suffixed variants */rat'-h°-/ and, perhaps, older, unassimilated */rat'-ʕ°-/]; compare Sanskrit *ráthah*, Latin *rota*, Old Irish *roth*, all from the first form, Old High German *rad*, and perhaps English *(hot)rod* from the second form. Thus in these closing lines a pun is being made on her name. Shebatinuquo seems to be willing to forgo vengeance and to take the humble maid who offered to share his pain. This sets him at odds with a similar account given of the utterly implacable Pataraz, with whom he shares other characteristics: large size, great ferocity, a blood grievance. Thus, although this song is very similar to that of Khimishuquo Pataraz, its import is different: it offers the taming of implacable vengeance through kinship ties, namely by marriage to a woman of the enemy, the triumph of individual love over group hate.

[3] This name, /ak°áanda/, usually belongs to the spurned beauty who first greets the hero. Here it seems to belong to a type of serving girl who offers intimate comfort. The

root may be related to that for Gunda, / g°ónda /, another famous beauty. In the history of Circassian, the final / a / has triggered / aa / in the preceding syllable, so that the original would have been * / ak°ónda /. Curiously, in accord with the Iranian name Radem, / rah-dam / 'cart,' this name may be based on the proto-Circassian root / k°ə / '(two-wheeled) cart' (Kuipers 1975, p. 58, §83), so that originally the milkmaid and the spurned beauty were probably the same woman.

⁴ The form here, / t-y-áh-ta /, is ambiguous and can mean either "our father" (our-poss-int-father) or "grandfather" (father-poss-int-father). I have used the first reading because plural possession seems to emerge occasionally in some of the sagas with regard to Sete-naya, where it implies a group kinship. I think this saga may offer evidence that Shebatin-uquo's father was ruler, perhaps even the "all father," of the Narts and the people of Chita.

Saga 13 ❧ *Setenaya and the Great Nart Warzameg*

The Great Nart[1] Warzameg would set out on a quest and return driving a multitude of cattle before him. These he would distribute among the people of his village. As they were leaving, the people would say, "The Great Nart is no better a man than we. The one who brings him his good fortune is his wife, Setenaya." Despite the fact that the people attributed his great feats to Setenaya, he never complained to her and for a year or two more lived with her as his wife.

Then one day he again drove a herd of cattle back to the village and distributed it among the villagers.

"Surely, the Great Nart is a very good man!" said some, but others said, "He is no better a man than we are. It is Setenaya who brings him his good fortune!" This time the great Nart returned home bitter in his heart. He went back in his house and sat down. In a little while Setenaya brought the serving table and set if before him.[2] Her husband was not much interested in eating. He sat a bit and then said, "Setenaya, I must give you your freedom. We can no longer live together."

Setenaya asked her husband, "What has happened now? How have I fallen from your good graces? How have I angered you?"

"The people say that every brave deed I do you make me do, that if it were not for you, I would never be able to carry out such feats, that you are the one behind my manly deeds," he replied. "I wish to make the people understand that I would still be able to carry out these deeds even if you were no longer my companion."

"If that is how it is, then what can I do? Divorce me!" said Setenaya.

The Great Nart then said, "Even though I speak thus, I shall let you take from the house whatever you say is dear to your heart."

Then Setenaya spoke, "Nart, I ask of you only one thing. Grant me this last favor. I would like to hold a three-day feast for the people in the village whom I liked and who spoke well of me in turn, among whom I have lived for two or three years, those older and honorable people."

"If you have lived here for two or three years," said the Great Nart, "then you can certainly live here for one more week. Say to them what you wish to say and do for them what you wish to do."

Setenaya set to work, making food and ordering drink. Her guests partied for two days, eating and drinking the whole time. More than a hundred became tipsy and had to be helped about. The Great Nart, however, did not become drunk. Setenaya went among the people and asked, "Why isn't the Great Nart drunk?"

The guests replied, "The Great Nart is huge, mighty. The liquor did not affect him, even though he drank as much as we did and drank from the same brew as we did."

But Setenaya entreated some of them, "Make him drunk for me. When you exchange toasts with him say, 'Drink yet one more hornful with me for my sake!'" This ruse of enticing the Great Nart to drink twice his usual amount worked, and he finally became drunk.

Thereupon Setenaya said to those present, "Now my party is over. May God give good life to all those here! You may leave now whenever you wish." The guests dispersed and returned home.

Setenaya asked one of the remaining youths to hitch the horses to the wagon. She herself laid a mattress and pillow in the wagon, then had the Great Nart laid down on them. She climbed into the wagon and drove off. They traveled to the border of his region and crossed into her territory, which she had left long before as a bride. The Great Nart awoke.

"What happened to me?" the Great Nart asked his wife. "How did I get here?"

"Nothing at all has happened to you," she replied softly. "You said to me, 'I will let you take from this house, as your very own, whatever you want most.' But what would I do with wealth and possessions? What I wanted most that was in the house was you, so I took you."

"If you were to leave," he replied, "I would lose everything I have. You are even smarter than they say. Turn the wagon about!" Sitting side by side, they turned around and headed back to their home.

From Hadaghatl'a 1968, vol. 1, no. 20, pp. 145–46, in Bzhedukh West Circassian.

ᴓ This charming saga gives some insight into traditional matters regarding social standing, envy, pride, love, and divorce. This tale is found in the Jewish folklore of eastern Europe (Janarno Lawson, personal communication).

[1] Great Nart / nahrt´-ɔ́-šk°a / or / nahrt´-ɔ́-šx̌°a / 'Nart-ep.v-big', "Big Nart," most likely originally an epithet of Warzameg, and so I have named him here. Huge size is indicative of a true hero. This feature is common to heroes in many Indo-European traditions, perhaps most notably of Indra in the Rig-Veda.

[2] A small, round, three-legged serving table, the Circassian / ʔáana / .

SAGA 14 ᴓ *Nart Wazarmeg and His Friends Decide What to Do about a Black Fox*

Nart Wazarmeg went to hunt with Nart Sawsaruquo and Nart Khimisha,[1] they say, at Sh'hagwa Ford.[2] They reached the hunting grounds and began to hunt. They hunted for a while, then they found a black fox running from the forest before them. All three men simultaneously shot and killed the fox. Since Nart Sawsaruquo was the most talkative, he said, "My arrow hit." Nart Khimisha said, "My arrow hit," and Nart Wazarmeg said, "My arrow hit." When all three men reached the dead fox and looked at it, they all were right. Three arrows were placed in it.

Only one of the three hunters would get the skin of the black fox, but they did not know what to do because all three were eager to have the skin. None of the hunters had any desire to give up the skin to one of his friends. Then Nart Sawsaruquo suggested that the one who had experienced the most interesting episode in his life could have the skin. The others agreed to that and said, "Good idea! Then you are the first to tell your story."

Nart Sawsaruquo said, "Once upon a time, I had been hunting with one man in the forest. Since I did not find any deer to kill, I got a fish from the sea, gave it to my cook, and told him to bake it. So I lay down and slept for a while. When I was awakened, I saw that the boy was still sitting by the fire, but he had not baked the fish. I asked him then, 'Where is the fish?' The cook said, 'I cut the fish, cleaned it, put it on the skewer, and was baking it on the fire, when I thought that it should be salted. So I tried to salt it in saltwater, when it became alive again. It came off the skewer and jumped back into the sea.' 'How can you fool someone with that nonsense?' I said and killed the boy. When I had thought it over a bit, I changed my mind. I was ashamed for killing the boy, just for a lie. How could I commit this kind of atrocity? Then I thought that I should find out if it was really true what the boy had said about the fish. So I took the boy's corpse to the sea, and when I put it in the water he became alive again. That really happened to me."

So, when Sawsaruquo had finished his most interesting tale, Khimisha began his tale.

"Once upon a time I went with my friends to hunt," said Nart Khimisha. "We found some deer and killed them. We had to spend the night in the forest. We were far from home. So we found a site where we could spend the night at the edge of the Kwirghwa Forest.[3] We skinned the deer that we had killed. I cut the deer in two, put it on the big skewer, and gave it to my cook to roast. I thought I should rest while the boy roasted the meat, and I fell asleep. I did not know how long I slept, but when I awoke it appeared that the boy sitting beside the fire was looking very sad. 'Did you roast it already?' The boy said, 'No.' 'Why not?' The boy said, 'While I was roasting the meat my wrists became so tired that the meat fell from my hands. When it fell into the fire it became alive again. It placed its skin onto itself anew and ran back to the mountain forest.' I was very angry and said, 'Who could ever believe a thing like that?' So when I hit him, he died. But when I had thought a bit, I changed my mind and felt very sorry. Even if he had told an unbelievable story, why should I have killed him? However, this boy had said that when the deer fell into the fire it became alive again. Well, then I would see if the fire would make the dead boy alive again. So I took his body and put it in the fire. The boy became alive once more. I personally experienced that," said Nart Khimisha.

The two listeners did not say anything. They were preparing to hear the story of Wazarmeg.

Wazarmeg began. "I went to hunt alone by the mountain Fishti.[4] I did not find anything to hunt or to kill. So I was just walking in the forest, when suddenly I came upon a house. I was very, very hungry. When I came to the courtyard and entered the house, I found two tables covered with food.

On the first table there was lamb meat. On the second was human meat. I did not want to eat from the table of human meat, so I started to eat at the table with lamb meat. Somebody yelled at me and said, 'Do not eat from that table! Eat from the other table!' I did not see the one who had roared at me and did not obey the voice. I kept eating. The second time, he or she was very angry with me and roared with the same voice. I heard the voice but could not tell where he or she was. Suddenly something jumped down from the attic, holding a short whip. 'Let him become a skinny greyhound!' I became a dog and remained in the courtyard over there. I was praised all over the region, and no one could overcome me. Nart Pshekyach's[5] sheep had been stolen by a wolf, but he could not catch the beast. So when he heard about me, he came to the courtyard where I lived and begged my master, 'A wolf is eating my sheep. He is destroying me. Lend me your dog!' 'I will lend you my dog, but if you do not take good care of it, it will not help you with anything.' 'Certainly I shall take care of it. I shall take very good care of it.' And with that my master lent me to Nart Pshekyach.

"So he led me to his sheep pasture and camp. He told the cooks in the camp to take good care of this dog and then returned home. The shepherds did not care for me at all. They did not feed me well, nor did they make a decent place for me to sleep. Yet these shepherds thought that this skinny greyhound would guard the sheep all night long, and they went to bed and slept. Since they were not good to me and did not care much about me, no matter what happened all night, I didn't move. That night the wolf came and killed and wounded a good many sheep. When Nart Pshekyach arrived the next morning and learned the news, he said, 'I wish you will become a useless animal for your master, who lent you to me,' and beat me very hard with his whip and drove me from his property. What could I do now? So I came back to my master's courtyard and lived there, but my condition was very bad, as if God had condemned me.

"At a neighboring village an old bear came and disturbed the inhabitants. When the village people heard that I was a very good dog, they sent a man to my master. He begged, 'Would you lend us your dog?' 'I will lend you my dog, but if you do not take good care of it, it will not help you.' 'Whatever you say, we shall do it for the dog.' 'You must keep it clean and feed it well.' 'We shall take as good care of it as we can,' they promised.

"So he lent me to them and I was led to their village. They fed me well and kept me clean. And while I was living there a bear came to the village.

"'Please, skinny greyhound. The bear has come to the village. Help!'

"I started running and jumping fast at the bear, and when it saw me, it turned back to the forest. I had to catch up to it, but I couldn't because it was running very fast. I was chasing the bear and it was running to the mountain, which was not far from the area, and I lost it there. Yet I did not give up. I went after the bear up into the mountain.

"The old bear said to me, 'Nart, don't attack me! Stop there!' When it spoke to me, I had to stop immediately. 'The village where I used to go, I went there not to harm anyone but to go there because of you. I knew that they would bring you there. I wanted to free you from this curse that has befallen you. This curse was cast by a woman. Now, return to your master, and when you enter the courtyard, pretend to be very sick. Try to walk unsteadily, try to crawl. When you get up on your feet, pretend to fall on the ground again. Crawl right to the house door and lie down there. Don't accept any food, no matter what she gives you. When you stay there for three days or so in this condition, she will say that you are not useful anymore and will drag you off and leave you somewhere, but she won't bury you because you will still be alive. The short whip that she used to strike you is still under her pillowcase. She will have to leave the house and it will be unlocked. Thus, when she leaves the house, you have to get up, run into the room, take the short whip from under her pillowcase, and say, "Make me a human being again as I was before!" and strike yourself. When you return to your human form, you can do what you want.'

"After those things happened to me, I returned to my master and did precisely as the bear had told me to do. I made myself very sick, crawled to the door, and was in critical condition there. I did everything the bear had advised me to do, and when I got hold of the short whip, I struck myself with it and returned to my human form once more.

"I just sat down and was sitting there when my master returned home and entered the room. 'We have a guest,' she said, and she drew near the pillowcase. When she approached the pillowcase, she found that the short whip was no longer there. I saw what she wanted and said, 'Let her become a male donkey!' and struck her with the short whip. Thus, she became a male donkey, and I sat on its back and returned to my home again. All that happened to me," said Nart Wazarmeg. "Now to whom shall we give the black fox fur?"

They consulted together, but when no one openly confessed his desire to have it, they decided that the problem be presented to the Nart council to determine who should be the owner of the fur. So they skinned the black fox, and all three Narts returned home with the skin.

The men went before the Nart council and told their stories. The council gave the fur to one of them, but to whom was the fox fur given?

From Hadaghatl'a 1968, vol. 1, no. 34, pp. 183–87, in Shapsegh West Circassian.

◑ Here a dispute among friends over a prized pelt serves as the basis for three wild yarns. Similar tales occur in highland Georgian lore [KT].

[1] The dialect in which this tale was related, a form of West Circassian Shapsegh, has an odd variant of "Sawseruquo" / sawsarə́q°a /, with an open second vowel, a form of "Khimish" with a final vowel, / xəmə́š'ʸa /, and a scrambled form of "Warzameg," / wazarmagʸ /. The word / sawsaruquo / is from */ šwas-alān(ām)(-ə-q°a) / 'breath-Alan(gen.pl)(his-son)," "Breath of the Alans" (earlier "Aryans"), and so is an old form preserving the original second vowel.

[2] Sh'hagwa Ford is one of several place-names in this tale whose modern equivalents are unknown: / šḥa-g°ə-š'ʸ-a-rə́-k'ʸə / 'head (hill)-zone-there-at-by.means.of-exit', with / -rə-k'ʸə / used especially in the sense of "to cross a river," whence "ford near a hill or mountain."

[3] Perhaps this is / k°ə́-r-ɣ°a / 'twig-by-red', "with reddish twigs"; compare Shapsegh / k°a / twig.

[4] Fishti / fə́-š'tə q°ə́šḥa / 'white-freeze mountain', "frozen white mountain," one of the higher members of the range, with a snow-capped peak.

[5] Pshekyach / pš'a-k'ʸáč'ʸə / 'Psha-short', a typical public name, since family names are used only in a restricted sphere.

Saga 15 ◑ *The Old Age of the Great Nart*

The Great Nart grew old with his wife, Setenaya.[1] Now that he had grown old, the people no longer came to him for advice as they once had done.

The Great Nart went among the lawgivers, who were gathered in the Great House, and said, "I am worth nothing anymore. The people no longer respect me. I have grown old. I am no longer of any use to you." He begged them, "Let them make a big chest and place me inside it. Then throw me into the sea."[2]

But the lawgivers said to him, "You are our honored elder and are still our adviser. We shall not cast you into the sea. Now return to your home and stay there." The Great Nart was thus sent home.

Yet a second time he went and beseeched them to cast him into the sea.

This time they released him from his responsibilities as adviser, but they steadfastly refused to cast him into the sea. As he was returning home, however, he came upon a gang of youths.[3]

"This ugly old man is always going before the lawgivers," they said. "Let's throw him into the sea and see what he'll do!" They made a huge chest for him. They set the Great Nart down inside it and gave him enough dried meat to last one month. They smeared the chest with pitch so that the seawater would not leak in, carried it to the sea, and threw it on the waves. The sea carried the chest for one month before it was stranded on the beach of an island. Not far away, there were cowherds, who saw the chest.

"What can this be?" they said in amazement, drawing closer to examine it. They opened the chest and found a little old man sitting inside.[4]

"Who are you?" the cowherds demanded of the Great Nart. "Why are you sitting in there?"

He answered them, "It so happens, I am the Great Nart."

"Ah! We have caught the man who never let the emperor rule in peace over his own kingdom!" they said, brought the Great Nart to the court, and gave him over to the emperor. The emperor recognized him at once and had him carried away to prison.

After fifteen days had passed, the Great Nart called to the man who brought food to him, "This can't be! This emperor is so stupid, such an animal!"

The man said to him, "Don't say that! The emperor will have you killed."

"He is free to have me killed if he wishes, but he's an idiot and a savage," the Great Nart said again. The man went to the emperor and told him all that had been said against him.

"Bring that son of a dog here!" bellowed the emperor, and so the Great Nart was brought before him.

The emperor said to the Great Nart, "Why are you jabbering? I know you say that I am an idiot and an animal."

The Nart calmly replied, "You, O King, are still an idiot and an animal."

The evil emperor grew furious and demanded of the Great Nart, "Why am I an idiot? How am I an animal?"

"Certainly I shall tell you, Emperor, just why you are an idiot and how you are an animal," replied the Great Nart calmly. "If you kill me, would you be killing a man? If you imprison me, would you be imprisoning a man? The Narts will offer a ransom for me and buy me back. This would be more to your advantage. You are stupid because you do not have any understanding of things like this."

The emperor then asked, "What ransom will they offer for you?"

"They will give three hundred oxen for me: one hundred oxen with one horn, one hundred oxen with two horns, and one hundred oxen with three horns. That will be the size of my ransom," said the Great Nart casually.

The evil emperor did not comprehend his words and asked, "Whom should I send there?"

"Send one dark-haired man and one light-haired man.[5] Where the lawgivers sit together is like so.[6] When the dark-haired man and light-haired man reach there, they should say to them, 'We have been sent to the Narts so that you may tell us about the three hundred oxen that are to be sent back with us,'" said the old man.

So the emperor ordered brought before him one dark-haired and one light-haired man. He gave them their instructions and sent them forth after the ransom. The two men traveled as the Great Nart had directed and eventually came to the house of the lawgivers. When they entered, the lawgivers interrogated them, but none understood the meaning of what the two men said.

"Clearly we have to ask the Great Nart's wife, Setenaya, what the meaning of this message is. If she knows, then we will no longer be in this muddle," said the Narts. They went to Setenaya and asked her what meaning these strange words of the Great Nart could hold.

She pondered for a while, but finally she said, "I shall tell you the meaning of these words. 'One hundred oxen with one horn' means one hundred men armed with rifles.[7] 'One hundred oxen with two horns' means one hundred men armed with rifles and sabers. 'One hundred oxen with three horns' means one hundred men armed with rifles, sabers, and daggers. These three hundred men must be sent armed with weapons. That is the meaning of his ransom."

Immediately three hundred armed men were chosen. They set off with the dark-haired man and light-haired man at their front. As they were traveling, one of the men realized the Narts' intention to kill the emperor and attempted to lead the troops along the wrong road. But the Narts realized his plan and struck him down, killing him. When the other man saw how they had killed his companion, he feared for his own life and so did his best to lead them along the correct path. They journeyed until they entered the emperor's domains.

As fate would have it, the emperor was saying to the Great Nart at that moment, "Little old man, let us climb the tower[8] and look out. Perhaps we can see my men driving your ransom before them." And together they climbed the tower. When they looked out, they saw the Narts approaching in the distance like a great black herd.

"Now, King, send forth all your men, but without weapons. If they go armed," said the Great Nart, "the oxen will take fright, scatter, and be lost." And so the emperor sent out all his men unarmed. The emperor and the Great Nart remained watching together from the tower.

The emperor asked the Great Nart, "Why is there a heavy haze suddenly rising from the midst of your ransom?"

"Some of the men you have sent out must have taken weapons along," replied the Great Nart. "The oxen have been frightened and are stampeding. What you see is the dust that they are raising."

The three hundred men who had been sent by Setenaya killed the unarmed men who had gone out to meet them. When the Narts drew near the castle, the Great Nart seized the emperor and threw him from the tower to his death. When all was concluded, the Great Nart rejoined his people and returned home with them.

From Hadaghatl'a 1968, vol. 1, no. 20, pp. 146–49, in Bzhedukh West Circassian.

⌁ Here Warzameg appears in his extreme old age as a little old man, who nonetheless is wily enough to defeat his lifelong enemy.

[1] This tale was taken from the second half of a narrative in the source. The tale is interesting in that it presents Setenaya and a Warzameg-like figure, the Great Nart (probably originally merely an epithet of Warzameg), as aging, something the other sagas do not do, at least with regard to Setenaya (see note 4).

[2] This is the fate of unwanted infants who are destined to prove their worth as heroes. Here, instead of an infant undergoing this test, a worn-out hero is the subject. He shall later prove to have diminished in size (note 4), a sign that his heroic stature has been temporarily lost.

[3] Gang of youths / č"aλa-γ°áλa / 'child, youth gang', a gang of young ruffians or undisciplined youths. A gang of toughs would hardly provision their victim the way these youths do. This appears as a lapse in tone in the saga (nowhere else does such a gang appear) and may be an addition on the part of the bard, replacing a possible older sequence in which the lawgivers oblige the Great Nart and seal him in a chest. This dissonance is repeated in the previous sentence, where the lawgivers relieve the Great Nart of his responsibilities, which is clearly at odds with what they would do if they wanted to reassure him of his worth.

On the basis of these oddities, I would reconstruct an earlier myth, in which the Great Nart goes to the lawgivers three times to beg them to cast him into the sea. The first time they refuse, the second time they relieve him of his position, and the third time they oblige him and cast him into the sea.

[4] Although a Warzameg-like figure is referred to, with an epithet serving as his name, this seems to be one of very few stories about a little old man, the Charon-like figure of the Narts seen in saga 3. This saga may indicate that earlier this little old man was merely an avatar, a geriatric form, of one of the heroes. His peripheral appearance in a number of sagas, often in conjunction with a little old lady (see Paris 1974, 30–39, story 1), may reflect a late severance of this earlier link with a hero.

If the little old man of the Narts is an avatar of Warzameg, then the little old woman of the Narts, who protects the souls of the dead (saga 31), might also have been merely an avatar of Setenaya. This would explain Setenaya's anomalous aging in this saga. This aged avatar, coupled with Setenaya's otherwise perennial youth, would give her a role much like that of the Greek Persephone, who was, when above the earth, a lovely maiden, but when ruling with her husband over Hades and the souls of the dead, she was an old woman.

[5] This recalls the symbolism of white and black in Warzameg's wooing of Setenaya (saga 4).

[6] Northwest Caucasian narratives can be maddeningly terse. Where the scholar would hope for detailed instructions that might reveal interesting geographic or political traditions, only a lone adverb can be found, as in this tale. Only some Abaza sagas form exceptions to this rule.

[7] Rifles / šk°a-n-č̓ʸ/ 'big(?)-conn-arrow, bullet', originally "big arrow" (= javelin [?], as 'spear' is / pč̓ʸə / and so cannot be intended here); now it refers to rifles or shotguns. Whatever the antiquity of the Nart sagas, the armaments found in them are often modern, or relatively so.

[8] Tower /š̓ʸandáaqa /, here a watchtower and not an elevated platform from which noblewomen would view surrounding activities. The South Caucasian Svans still have stone houses with watch towers, once widespread in the Caucasus (see Lyons 1977, 149; Rice 1965, 247, for photographs of these structures).

SAGA 16 ❧ *How They Made Tlepsh*

Fashion the First Sickle

This happened in very olden times. Then in our land dwelled the Narts. Their graves stand in great numbers near the Ubin Ford.[1] The Narts near the seashore used to fish with nets. They were exceptionally good at making white wine. They used to work in the fields. The Narts raised mainly millet as a crop. They used to plant millet, and when it ripened, they pulled the kernels of grain from it. But would you go on forever like that?

"Tlepsh!"[2] called the Narts.

"What?" responded Tlepsh.

"Make something for us to bear in our hands that we can thus use for reaping millet. We are tired of keeping at the reaping. We spend too long a time at it," they said.

"How should I fashion something that will do?" Tlepsh asked them.

"We do not know," they said. "But you must be able to make something for us that we can hold comfortably in one hand so that we can do our reaping."

"In that case," said Tlepsh, "you consult T'haghalig's old wife."[3]

"All right, then," they said, and they went to T'haghalig's old wife and asked her.

When they asked the old Nart woman, she replied, "By this firmament,[4] Lady Isp[5] shall well tell us," she said, and she sent them after Lady Isp.

Lady Isp, Pataraz's mother, was sensitive and vulnerable.

They sat making conversation with one another waiting for Lady Isp to arrive.

When she arrived and attempted to cross the threshold, which was unusually high, she tripped.[6]

T'haghalig's old wife often joked with a sharp tongue:

"Ah, welcome, welcome,
Lady Isp, our beloved,
Before arriving you are rolling."

She let this quip spring from her mouth and ridiculed Lady Isp a little, so they say.

In her heart, Lady Isp did not like this and grew displeased. She was ashamed before those who were standing about, but because she was an old woman also she refrained from speaking back.

"This is the reason I called you," said T'haghalig's old wife, and she told Lady Isp what she wanted.

Lady Isp, without telling her anything, turned back and, being very careful of herself, recrossed the threshold and left.

"Aha! Now if you have done any good, it will be taken back from you!" thought Lady Isp.

T'haghalig's old wife was clever and knew well Lady Isp's nature:

> "Let someone here follow her,
> Let him listen.
> It is possible that she might say something."

She told this to the Narts. Therefore, they set the youngest one after her to listen.

Lady Isp was walking along, and this Nart lad was following her. He listened to her as she spoke and repeated things to herself in her anger:

> "To you I will not tell it,
> You, you will not know it.
> Like a rooster's tail you should bend it,
> Like a baby snake's tooth you should sharpen it.
> To you I will not tell it,
> You, you will not know it!"

The Nart lad overheard again what Lady Isp was saying.

> "Like a rooster's tail you should bend it,
> Like a baby snake's tooth you should sharpen it.
> To you I will not tell it,
> You, you will not know it!"

All the time she was making a sound like *gherts-gherts* and wagging her head as she headed home.

Now they had discovered what form the tool should have. They were happy and laughing.

The Narts went to Tlepsh and said: "Like a rooster's tail you should bend it, / Like a baby snake's tooth you should sharpen it," they told him.

Tlepsh was their leader and a blacksmith, the likes of whom has never been born. Whatever you told him you wanted he would make instantly for you. Then he would give it to you.

Therefore, he made a tool bent like a rooster's tail and sharp like the tooth of a baby snake. It bit and cut off whatever it touched. A remarkable sickle he made for them.

"Here, Narts, this can reap enough. May God not let you lack for anything!" he said to them. "If you work, then you eat."

According to Tlepsh's words, while the Narts lived, their sickle cut down enough so that they never lacked for anything. Regardless of how much they used it, the sickle that Tlepsh had made for them never grew dull.

That was the nature of the sickle that Tlepsh made.

From Hadaghatl'a 1968, vol. 1, no. 55, pp. 218–20, in Shapsegh West Circassian.

ᴥ This is a comical tale of one of the little people, in this case the water sprite Lady Isp, humorously mother of the largest Nart, Pataraz.

[1] Ubin Ford / wəbən-rək˺ʸə/, /wəbən/, the name of a river; /rək˺ʸə/ derives from the verb /yə-k˺ʸə-n/ 'dir-exit-inf', "to leave, to cross, especially to cross a river." The Ubykh take their Circassian name from this river: / wəbə-ʁ/ 'river.name-region', uby-kh, yielding Ubykh.

[2] Tlepsh /λəpś/ the god of the forge and of blacksmiths.

[3] She is the wife (literally "woman" with an intimate possession prefix, /y-ah-/) of the god of the harvest, /tḥa-ya-λəgʸa/ 'god-caus-be.surplus', an archaic adjective, now with a sense of 'leftover, excessive, harmful' (Kuipers 1975, 46–47), but see the comment in saga 41 for the likely original sense of this god.

[4] Originally, this was the supreme god, addressed as / yə-wa-n/ 'O-god-obl', and it is still such among the Ubykh.

[5] This figure is a female water sprite, wife of Khimish and so mother of Pataraz. She can sometimes have a batrachian aspect, as with the strange noises she makes in this account. She is noted for her extreme sensitivity, especially regarding her diminutive size.

[6] In a few tales small people trip over a threshold when visiting Narts who wish to discover a secret from them. They are humiliated, become angry, and leave without speaking. A Nart must follow them to learn what is desired, because these small people mumble to themselves when angered. See the Abaza saga 54 about the dwarf Shardan.

Tlepsh could not make those things for the Narts that they needed in life. He could not find the necessary knowledge. He remained in this quandary until he grew desperate. When he could no longer bear this situation, he went to Lady Setenaya and beseeched her: "Lady Setenaya, I am desperate. I cannot uncover what I need to know. I cannot discover it by my own powers. I have pounded out flat all the iron that I have. They say that there is no one who has even a part of your wisdom. Recall that knowledge which I must have."

"What is there to recall?" said Lady Setenaya, being selfish. "If the Narts need weapons, you make them for them; when the Narts needed a sickle, you made it for them. You have made what people need to live. Now get ready to leave and travel the world. See how other peoples live and bring this knowledge back for the Narts. If God does not find you utterly odious, you shall find something."

"What will I need to travel the world?"

"Do not stop because you have some pressing need. Just take some clothes for yourself and set off. He who grows millet will love you, and he who breeds cattle is your friend. Because of this, they will not let you die."

Tlepsh tarried no longer. He took a pair of shoes that he had made from the hardest steel, and with these in his hand he set off. Thus Tlepsh traveled swiftly for a long time. For one day he traveled along a forest road. For one year he traveled through a forest. When he came to cliffs, he strode over them. When he came to rivers, he leaped across them. Bounding along, he crossed seven rivers and came to the shore of the Taingyiz Sea.[1] He walked among a hundred trees. He cut them into logs and bound them together to make a raft. He launched it into the water and stayed on the Taingyiz Sea until he had crossed it. He came ashore and saw, playing and sitting on the beach, a group of girls with the loveliest eyes he had ever seen. Tlepsh was instantly enthralled by the girls, but although he tried hard to grasp one, he was unable to catch a single one. As he pursued them, they slipped past him and darted away. He did not tackle any of them and eventually turned pale. Then he asked them: "I enjoin you to swear by God. Tell me what manner of women you are. I have never seen your like among my folk. I have not made such a fool of myself in all my experience," he said.

"We are the devotees of Lady Tree," the group of girls replied.[2] "Our lady will invite you to her house and honor you."

"Set forth! Lead me there!" replied Tlepsh, and he went along, following the path of the devotees. When he reached the place, there stood a tree that you would not have recognized. It was a tree and yet not a tree, a person and yet not a person. You would not be able to comprehend its true nature. Its roots ran deep into the earth. Its hair, like a cloud, rose high into the sky. Its two arms were like a person's, and the cheeks of its face were the loveliest of the lovelies. Gold and silver were everywhere. Lady Tree fell in love with Tlepsh and invited him in. She let him eat and drink and made him lie down to rest. In the middle of the night, Tlepsh awoke and said to her, "I must seek something," and he resolved to leave.

"This will not do!" Lady Tree protested. "I am a princess. Until now no mere mortal has reached me."

"I am one of the gods," replied Tlepsh. He stood up and made love to her.

The lady loved Tlepsh and beseeched him, "Don't go! Stay!"

"No, I cannot stay," protested Tlepsh. "I must find the edge of the earth and from there bring back knowledge for the Narts."

"Do not set off, Tlepsh. I shall give you the knowledge that you need. My roots run deep into the ground. I know the life that lies under the earth. My hair rises into the sky, and I know the life that is in the heavens. The earth has no edge."[3] But Tlepsh would not be her beloved.

"Would you set off into the world, which doesn't have a boundary? It doesn't exist. Don't go! I shall acquaint you with the stars of heaven. I shall place in your palm that life which lies beneath the earth, and I shall give you all that is on the surface of the earth."

After all that Lady Tree had said, he still would not become her beloved. He put the shoes that he had made on his feet, hefted in his palm the walking stick that he had made, took his hat down from the wall, and put his torques about his neck. He set off and traveled all over, but he did not find the edge of the earth. He turned back and returned to Lady Tree.

"Did you find the earth's edge?" asked Lady Tree.

"No."

"So what did you find?"

"Nothing."

"So what did you learn?"

"I learned how the earth has no boundary."

"Then what?"

"I learned how a person's body is harder than iron."

"Then what?"

"I learned how there is no road more difficult than that which is traveled alone."

"And that life is beautiful," replied Lady Tree. "But what did you learn for the welfare of the Narts? What did you find for them?"

"Not a thing."

"So there is nothing from your traveling about apart from that. If you had stayed and listened to what I said, I would have given you the knowledge so that the life in your limbs might not end. You Narts are a stubborn people. You are proud. You shall perish from this. But I give you this in which sit life and survival," she said, and she placed in Tlepsh's arms a baby sun.[4] "I carried this within me as your son. The knowledge that I hold I have placed in it. Will you not look after its growth until it matures?"

Tlepsh returned carrying the infant. He let loose the words of his tongue and said to the Narts, "Do you see the Milky Way in the sky above?"

"We see it."

"Then, when you go forth at night on a raid and when you return, if you do not lose him, you will not be lost," he said.

"Lord! If that were to happen, it would be considered a calamity. He needs someone to rear him and take care of him," said seven women.[5] They stayed by his side and reared him, looking after him.

After this, one day the infant went out and disappeared. He became lost while playing and vanished. The women no longer sensed the infant's presence and scattered to look for him. They could not find him.

When the Narts learned that this had happened, they went on horseback to search for him. They turned this way and that and looked about, but they were unable to find him. He was not to be found.

"He must have gone back to his mother," they said, and so they sent Tlepsh after him. But the infant had not gone back to her.

"What should we do? What is our remedy?" Tlepsh asked her.

"There is no remedy. A time may come when he returns on his own.[6] But God knows if he will return. If you all return alive from your raids, then you will be happy. If you do not return, then it will be your calamity and you will have perished because of this," she replied to him.

Tlepsh returned home, his head hanging in dejection.

From Hadaghat'la 1968, vol. 1, no. 76, pp. 263–65, in Kabardian East Circassian.

◌ At one time the worship or veneration of trees was widespread across Eurasia. The Norse had the world tree, Yggdrasil. The Celts had their druids (based on the word for 'tree' and sacred oaks and groves. The Romans had a special link between their supreme god, Jupiter, and the oak. The Greeks had sacred groves; one of their gods, Dionysus (Roman Bacchus), had a tree incarnation; and there is evidence for local tree goddess cults. The nomadic Iranians of Classical Antiquity, who roamed the steppes of Central Asia and the Ukraine, left a burial at Pazyryk in Siberia, which shows a goddess on a throne holding a tree while a horseman pays homage to her. In India a pole festooned with flowers and ornaments, called Indra's Tree, is the center of a round dance. This Indic tree has a clear parallel in the European practice of dancing around the Maypole, which must have been a tree originally. Tree images abound in early Mesopotamian art, and the Bible makes good use of trees. In the Caucasus the Abkhazians also have sacred trees and groves.

Interestingly, the Circassian saga provides us with an excellent insight into why trees were venerated. In an age prior to technology, humans were utterly earthbound. They could attain heights only by climbing a mountain or a tree. In fact, in all the world only trees had, as part of their essential nature, the ability to span all three realms that humans seem to have deemed part of the world: by their roots they reached deeply into the earth from which all vegetative life, and hence all life, seemed to have sprung; by their branches they reached high into the realm of air and hence had a natural communion with the heavens and the celestial objects in them; and by their trunks they occupied the realm that belonged to humans, offering them shade, wood, bark, and fruit. This unique ontological status is obvious in this myth.

Surprisingly, however, there are a host of other features. The closest parallels to these are found in the Norse world tree. Both the Circassian and the Norse trees are cosmic in their grasp: their branches lead up to heaven, encompassing the stars; their trunks occupy the world of humans; and their roots extend downward into the subterranean realms. Yggdrasil, the Norse tree, means *ygg-* 'terrible' and *drasil* 'steed' and was taken to be an incarnation of the horse of the Norse supreme god, Odin, which he rode on his exploits. The link between Tlepsh, knowledge, and the world tree is also similar to Odin's link between the quest for runes and his hanging on Yggdrasil [KT]. Also, the trees of both traditions are intimately associated with raids. In this saga these raids are nocturnal and are illumined by the child of the tree, the Milky Way. Perhaps related to this theme is the fact that in the Norse myths women are said to have cooked and eaten the fruit of Yggdrasil to ensure a safe childbirth, so there is a procreative dimension here as well. The Circassian tree possesses the life that lies beneath the earth, and Yggdrasil's three roots reach down one by one into a well of memory and understanding, a well of fate and destiny, and into the mouth of a dragon of destruction, so that the Norse netherworld is more elaborate than the Circassian. Nevertheless, Yggdrasil's root to the well of fate and destiny is guarded by three women, the Norns, so that the Norse tree may, at an earlier date, have had a more pronounced feminine aspect, much more like the Circassian. Tlepsh himself resembles Odin, who is closely associated with Yggdrasil in a number of ways. Both gods have large hats, both make use of walking sticks, and both travel vast distances in a short time.

This Circassian myth has a remarkable celestial significance, absent from any Norse Yggdrasil myth. Lady Tree gives birth to the Milky Way, which in Circassian is "Milky Foot-Path." That the Milky Way is considered a baby sun is most striking. Perhaps the Milky Way is thought of as inchoate celestial light, which in its mature form is manifested preeminently as the sun. The seven women who tend to this celestial infant seem to parallel the Seven Sisters, the Greek Pleiades, a tight grouping of stars in the winter sky, near the Milky Way. Equally striking is the theme that the world has no edge (see also Myzhaev 1994). This is not a modern interpolation, for this theme alone is the subject of other myths about Tlepsh and his wanderings. I leave it to the reader to puzzle over the planetary and astronomical wisdom that is hinted at by these aspects.

[1] The Taingyiz Sea is the Sea of Azov, just northwest of the traditional home of the Circassians. The name is Turkic for "heaven."

[2] Lady Tree appears to be a female personification of a world tree, similar to the Norse world tree, Yggdrasil. A felt carpet preserved in the permafrost at the Siberian grave site of Pazyryk shows a male rider with a prominent mustache before a large figure seated on a throne, holding a curling, decorated tree. Having no mustache and dressed in an ankle-length caftan, the figure is assumed to be female. I would venture to suggest that this carpet depicts an eastern, Iranian variant of the same saga (Rice 1965).

[3] This appears to be a remarkable bit of folk knowledge regarding the spherical geometry of the earth.

[4] The baby sun proves to be the Milky Way, /šə-ƛá-a-ɣ°a/ 'milk-foot, leg-conn-path'.

[5] These seven women may be the seven sisters of the star cluster, the Pleiades.

[6] The Milky Way may have been a useful guide on the moonless nights favored during cattle raids. The Milky Way is high in the night sky, however, only during the winter and summer months. This saga explains its seasonal character.

SAGA 18 ✑ The One Who Committed
One Hundred Sins

The Narts used to have great compassion. The mighty would not attack the weak, nor were the poor compelled into service, but one who committed one hundred sins was, by their law, not to be forgiven.

Thus things were with them. Old Khimish had been killed by Shewafizh,[1] the Wide Wristed. Pataraz too was no longer living, he who was left alone, sitting in a mud house by his mother, Lady Isp. Lady Isp was the mother of Khimish's son, Pataraz, but once some discord came between her and Khimish. She became offended and returned to her people, they say.

Well, this woman grew to be very old and lonely. The Narts called a council and resolved that while she lived, they would provide for her and that no one would be allowed to be cruel to her. He who treated her wrongly would be considered as having committed one hundred sins and would be put in fetters and nailed to a mountaintop. When Tlepsh had made the first sickle, it was she who had hinted to him how a sickle should look.

In those times the giants were the enemies of the humans. So the giant Sh'habgho[2] came forth, with malice, to attack her, to take the little booty that her husband had left her and anything else she might have. All this he gathered up and took back with him.

The law of the Narts was strong, and no living Nart would betray his word. They said that one who had attacked another was not allowed to go free. Therefore, they sent Tlepsh's son, Nagurashkho, after Sh'habgho to bring back his head. Nagurashkho was a robust man, enormously strong. If he stood on his feet, you could not knock him down.

He accepted their mission without objection, for she, the old woman Lady Isp, had done much for him, caring for him like one of her dear sons. As soon as Nagurashkho got to the giant's abode, Sh'habgho reached out from behind an old tree, grabbed him with a bear hug, and tried to lift him so that he could dash him against the ground, but Nagurashkho stood immovable with his feet planted firmly on the ground. No one could knock down Nagurashkho when he was standing on the ground. The giant grew furious and exerted all his might. He managed to pin the Nart to the ground for a moment and then to lift him in the air so as to throw him into a nearby ravine, but Tlepsh's son, Nagurashkho, simply squeezed the giant's head and flattened it so that the giant collapsed. Then he wasted no time; he tied the giant up, tossed him across his back, and set off for home. He brought him to the Nart council and set him before them.

The Narts were angered and said, "We should not show mercy to him who showed no mercy to Lady Isp, who behaved disgracefully, who committed one hundred sins. So they resolved to fashion a chain, *zhghau-sau*,[3] to fetter him in it, and to beset him with one hundred torments to endure. During the day they set the sun upon his face so that it would bake his visage and dry out his mouth. At night he would have moisture so as not to die, but again during the day he would suffer thirst and have only dried kasha and barley to eat, which they would put before him. They lifted him up on the mountain brow and nailed him there so that other evildoers would see him as a warning. They said, "Let no one forget that a Nart never breaks his word. Let all know the punishment."

In such a fashion, they say, the chained giant is nailed to the mountain, neither alive nor dead, and he suffers one hundred torments in return for his evildoing. The kasha that he eats during the day is replenished at night. By day the sun dries up his mouth, but during the cool night the dew descends and moistens his mouth once again.

In this way the giant is atoning for the one hundred sins he committed.

From Hadaghatl'a 1968, vol. 1, no. 69, pp. 249–50, in Shapsegh West Circassian.

◌ This saga seems to be a primitive version of the Prometheus myth (Charachidzé 1986). There is no mention here of any challenge being made to a high god, which in the Greek results in Prometheus's punishment. See sagas 31, 34, 35, 36, 37, 52, 53, 55, and 91 for more complete accounts.

---

[1] Shewafizh / śaawa-fə-ž' / 'warrior-white-color.suffix', "the White Warrior," another name for Tutarish; see sagas 22, 23, 24, and 60. The color white is reminiscent of the Indic god Shiva and of the pagan Germanic Wodan (Colarusso 1984b).

[2] Sh'habgho / šḥá-a-bɣ°a / 'head-conn-broad', "the One with the Wide Head," a reference to his defeat at the hands of Nagurashkho.

[3] / ž̂ỳàaw(a)-sáaw(a) / of unclear etymology, perhaps 'black chains'. See Iranian *saw* 'black'.

SAGA 19 ∾ *The Lament for Nagura Tlepshuquo*

He led the way across the burning hot path,[1]
He took honey from Sham.[2]
Striking down all before him
Was the sword of Nagura.
Smashing down doors
Was short Nagura.
Not thinking of booty,
Not troubling about life,
He dismounted at last,
Did Nart Nagura.
"Cruel Chadlakhstan of the sharp beard
Murdered Nagura,
Leaving me bereft!"
So goes the song
Of Tlepsh's daughter-in-law.

From GENEG, 336, in Bzhedukh West Circassian.

∾ This tale is unique within the corpora in that it alludes to a raid into Syria from the Northwest Caucasus, though one must note that Georgian folklore [KT] cites Sham as a fabulous and remote destination where heroes prove themselves. Therefore, this tale may show Georgian influence. The murderer is the cowardly Chadlakhstan, an otherwise minor figure. In the next tale, the murderer is Bearded Yamina, or Cholera. This song seems to imply that Nagura was treacherously murdered when he returned, carefree, from a valorous raid.

[1] This phrase refers to a route through a desert, part of a raid from the Caucasus into Mesopotamia.

[2] *Sham* is Circassian (and Georgian) for Damascus or the region of Syria, hence the desert route

SAGA 20 ❧ How Nart Tlepsh Killed Bearded Yamina
with the Avenging Sword

Bearded Yamina had murdered Tlepsh's son, so Tlepsh vowed to avenge his son's death. Tlepsh had grown old, and such an act was beyond his hands, so he fashioned a sword that could move under its own power. It could cut through anything. He laid this razor-sharp sword inside a chest. Then he had one of the most trustworthy men brought before him. He ordered this man to go to Bearded Yamina and to take this chest with him.

"But," Tlepsh said to him, "he must view this gift, which I am sending to him with you, only in some private and dark room of his house."

When the chest reached Bearded Yamina, the man did not tell him what handiwork Tlepsh had fashioned therein, nor did he tell him for whom it was intended. When evening fell, Yamina went into a room alone to examine the sword thoroughly. When he opened the chest, the sword, which had lain at the bottom, rose of its own, sliced through Bearded Yamina, and so killed him.

This is how I heard it told.

From GENEG, 358–59, in Hatiquoya West Circassian.

SAGA 21 ❧ Tlepsh's Gold Cellar

Khotkhoshdemyr,[1] grandson of Tlepsh by his daughter, was brought to his grandfather's to stay and learn to be a blacksmith.

Tlepsh used to train young men, to build for them smithies, and to settle them down in families.

One day they had worked for a long time, and Tlepsh had grown greatly tired, so he lay down in the smithy and dozed off. Khotkhoshdemyr stood above Tlepsh gazing on him and did not know what to do. Then a fly came out of Tlepsh's nose, crawled across his face, walked on his chest, and descended by his foot. It crossed the floor and went into the iron that lay on top of the barrel that held the water supply, and then it went into the coal that was piled in the corner and disappeared. When the fly had gone into the corner, Tlepsh began to sleep more calmly.

After quite a while had passed, Khotkhoshdemyr saw the fly returning, going back exactly the way it had left before. When the fly reached the iron on top of the barrel, he reached out and picked up the piece it was on. As soon as he did this, Tlepsh became greatly troubled in his sleep. For a while Khotkhoshdemyr watched the uneasiness of Tlepsh and the fly, finding it astonishing, and then he replaced the iron where it had lain.

When the fly found that the iron was back in its place, it went onto Tlepsh, climbed on the tip of his foot, went up his leg, across his chest, and returned into his nose.

At that instant Tlepsh awoke with perspiration running off him and said, "Oh, my God! While I slept I saw an interesting dream."

Khotkhoshdemyr said, "May God make it propitious! Relate it to me!"

"I was going somewhere and crossed a certain iron bridge. I went for a while, then the earth opened up and I entered a cavern. Beneath the cavern was buried a hoard of gold. I looked at the gold and said, 'I shall return and tell the people, and I shall let them take home all this gold.' While returning, I reached a chasm filled with water where the bridge had been, but the iron bridge was no longer lying over the chasm, and I grew greatly worried, but carpenters and blacksmiths came and suddenly rebuilt the bridge. Having crossed back over it, I woke up," said Tlepsh.

Khotkhoshdemyr told his mother about the fly and about Tlepsh's dream.

"When my father finishes training you, he will build for you a smithy and arrange for you to start your own family. Do not agree to this. You must tell him, 'Upon my word, I have grown completely used to this smithy. I will not be able to work in this new smithy at all.' Then he will leave his smithy to you. Then we shall go where the fly went and where the gold is buried, and we shall dig it out," said his mother, and in such wise she enlightened Khotkhoshdemyr.

Khotkhoshdemyr did as his mother had said.

They relate that when Tlepsh died, Khotkhoshdemyr obtained much gold from beneath the smithy and grew very rich.

From Hadaghatl'a 1968, vol. 1, no. 72, pp. 253–54, in Shapsegh West Circassian.

෴ This saga portrays the belief that a sleeping person's consciousness or soul wanders about as a fly, seeing the world from an insect's point of view. Tlepsh's grandson, Khotkhoshdemyr, does not share his grandfather's lofty generosity.

¹ This colorful name appears to be a compound. The second half is Turkic / demir / "iron," which resembles the forms / tamər /, /taymər /, found elsewhere across the North Caucasus. The first part is pure Circassian and may be / x̌°a-tx̌°a-ṣ̌ʸ / 'praise-flatter-name.suffix', which matches the behavior of this figure toward his grandfather.

SAGA 22 ෴ *The Story of Nart Totaresh*
and the Chinta Leader

Yerey, Albech's son Totaresh,
Mighty Totaresh, as a lone horseman
You entered the Nart council.
The leader, Nart Aleg,
And the elders sat in the council.
Nart Chadlakhstan also sat among them.
Aleg lifted the hero's horn.
"Chadlakhstan is the leader of the Chintas.¹
Does anyone challenge him?"
So saying, he proffered the horn to Chadlakhstan.
Chadlakhstan then said, "Pshimaruquo, do you challenge me?"
Pshimaruquo then said, "Khimish, do you challenge him?"
Khimish then said, "Yimis, do you challenge him?"
Yimis then said, "Totaresh, do you challenge him?"
Then Totaresh seized the horn from Aleg and drank it dry.
"Narts, may a horn of misfortune be your lot!"
And so saying, he strode from among them and returned home.
"Our mother, the Nart council was gathered.
Nart Chadlakhstan also sat among them.
I challenged the leader of the Chintas,
And I drained the hero's horn.

The leader of the Chintas, what is his speech,
What is his look, what manner of man is he?"
"The leader of the Chintas
After whom you inquire, my poor luckless one,
Is clad in tempered mail.
He is a horseman clad in chain mail
Who has carried away the heads
Of many a luckless horseman.
My poor luckless one,
Do not let him carry off yours!
If you go to challenge him,
Then feed and water your wild slender steed.
Your arc-headed lance rests against the column,
And with your tempered wide sword
And with your shoulder like a bison's,
Strike him on his helm and drive him down!
Pin him to the ground with your arc-headed lance!
And take his soul with your *hajitsas*!"
Yerey, mighty Totaresh, a lone horseman,
Gazed forth from Old Dog's Tail Ridge.
He rode forth into Tyuman Field.
The hooves of his wild horse danced.
The copper of his chain mail glittered
And flashed into the eyes of the Chinta leader,
So that he stumbled and lost face.
The leader of the Chinta did not retreat
But bore his blunder bravely.
Totaresh whipped his wild slender steed
And rode forth into Tamber Field,
Where the Chinta leader turned to meet him.
Yerey, Albech's son Totaresh,
With the shoulder of a bison,
With his tempered wide sword,
He struck him on his helm
And drove him down.
With his arc-headed lance
He pinned him to the ground,
And he took his soul with his hajitsa.
"He-hay!" he cried.

When the Chinta army came
And he let them pursue him,
Between two seas he led them,
And there he struck and annihilated them.
He turned about, and one by one
He struck them down.
As before, the Nart council sat in session,
But Chadlakhstan himself was not among them.
Totaresh entered among them and said,
"The steed of the Chinta leader carries an empty saddle.
The army of Chinta is now food for vultures and eagles.
That I am saying the truth
I swear by this blue sky,
Which is our God unbetrayable.
If what I am saying is a lie,
Let God dry up the wine that stands in this barrel.
If what I am saying is true,
Let God increase the wine that stands therein."
All this he said to the assembled Narts.
The cover of the barrel blew off
And the wine flowed out.
Having humbled the Narts,
Totaresh left and returned home.

Kube Shaban, Adegha Folklore *(Paris, 1959), in Bzhedukh West Circassian.*

✍ This account presents the archvillain Totaresh (also Tutarish) as a young hero, with many of the exploits normally ascribed in other sagas to Sawseruquo.

[1] The Chintas are rivals of the Narts (see saga 10).

SAGA 23 *⌒ Two Fragments of the Ballad of Sawseruquo*

I

Armi, dark Sawseruquo,
Armi a black man with iron eyes,
This horseman apart, who would not stay!
From the mounted Nart horsemen,
Sawseruquo fell behind;
Seven nights and seven days the sky stormed,
The wicked Narts really began to freeze;
These asked one another:
"You, Yimis, do you have fire?"
"You, Sosem, do you have fire?"
"Bearded Zhyandew, do you have fire?"
"Araqshaw, do you have fire?"
"Wazermas,¹ do you have fire?"
"Bearded Nasran, do you have fire?"
"Asha's son Ashamaz, do you have fire?"
"Khimish's son Bataraz, do you have fire?"
"Sebelshey, do you have fire?"
"Albek's son Totaresh, do you have fire?"
Of the Nart troop that was traveling
None came forth from among them with fire.
Mother's² two sons prayed to God,
"If evil is not to befall us,
And if Sawseruquo is not to ride among us,
Then we ought not to go farther."
Just as they spoke and argued,
Sawseruquo arrived among them.
"For this our golden lineage,
Armi, our goodly lineage,
For fire shall we die out!"
"Ay hay! I have some," he said.
Then he kindled a great fire for them,
But when the whole troop went to him
Sawseruquo grew angry.

He threw away the fire,
Threw it into the water;
Now the old Narts remained without fire.
"Armi, our Sawseruquo,
For this other our golden lineage,
Armi, our goodly lineage,
You have fire. Make it for us!" they said.
Thus then did they beseech him.
"May the great sky stay in its place! I have none,
But even if I have none, I shall make some for you," he replied.
Upon Little Gray he leaped,
He ascended Harama Mountain and peered about:
Some ruined towers,
From which a little smoke issued forth,
This Sawseruquo saw;
He crept up on foot and stole within.
This was the house of a giant.
His head leaned upon his legs,
And a fire burned nigh his middle;
This giant was sleeping.
Sawseruquo quietly went back.
About this giant he asked:
"Truly, my Little Gray Ram,[3]
Whose legs cannot be beaten,
Over there is a giant's house,
His head leans on his legs,
And a fire burns nigh his middle.
That giant is sleeping.
How will we take his fire?" said he.
Armi, dark Sawseruquo,
Armi, a black man with iron eyes,
This horseman apart, who would not stay, [said,]
"Sit on my back.
The sound of my horse's hooves
I shall make like the sound of a dog's paws,
The sound of my dog's legs
I shall make like the sound of a cat's paws.
In such fashion I shall start to run
And we shall steal one firebrand."

Sawseruquo mounted
And approached those towers.
They stole one firebrand.
For seven days and seven nights they galloped,
But one ember had fallen from the fire,
Had alighted upon the skin of the giant's thigh,
And the giant awoke with a start.
As he had before, he counted his firebrands.
One was missing!
"Would they bring disgrace to my father!
What wicked wretch of theirs has stolen it from me?" he said.
Not moving, sitting where he was,
He stretched himself out to the ends of seven roads to try
    to catch them
Where they had run to after seven days and seven nights.
"O warrior of the Narts!
I shall eat you raw surely
If you do not tell me what manner of man is Sawseruquo."
"I have not seen him,
But I have heard about him.
I do not know what manner of man he is."
"But even if you do not know him,
Teach me his amusements!"
"Ay, hay! I shall tell you of his games!"
He proceeded as this giant had commanded.
"Sawseruquo, they say,
Stops at the weathered foothills
And makes them throw down to him a stone of heaven.
This he butts with his forehead
So that it flies up more swiftly than it fell down."
"Do likewise with me!" said the giant.
Sawseruquo climbed a nearby hill
And threw down an iron meteorite that he found there.
The giant butted this with his forehead,
And it flew back up more swiftly than it had fallen down.
Then the giant squatted down on his haunches.
He started again,
"That is a wonderful game!
And if you know it, teach me a more wondrous one.

This one will drive away any ache from your forehead."
The giant's death would be God's vengeance,
Because Sawseruquo did not know how to kill the gaint.
"Tell me a more wonderful game!"
Commanded this giant.
"Sawseruquo, they say,
Kneels on his knees
While white-hot arrowheads
Are shot into his wide-open mouth.
He chews the heads up
And then spits out the shafts."
"Do likewise to me!" said he,
And the giant kneeled down
And opened his mouth wide.
Sawseruquo took short white-hot arrows
And shot them into his mouth,
But the giant chewed them up
And then spat out the shafts.
"O warrior of the Narts,
That is a wonderful game!
It has driven away my sore throat.
If you know one, teach me yet a more wondrous game."
The giant's death would be God's vengeance,
Because Sawseruquo did not know how to kill the gaint.
"Teach me a yet more wonderful game!" said he.
"Sawseruquo, they say, opens his mouth,
And they throw in plowshares that are red hot.
His stomach cools them off,
And he vomits them back up."
"Do likewise to me!" said he.
Sawseruquo gathered up plowshares and heated them
    to a red heat.
He threw them into the giant's mouth.
But the giant's stomach cooled them,
And he vomited them out again.
"O warrior of the Narts,
That was a wonderful game!
Show me something still more wonderful!"
The giant's death would be God's vengeance

Because Sawseruquo did not know how to kill the gaint.
"Wait! Wait, giant!
One game yet remains.
Sawseruquo, they say,
Is led to seven turbulent seas
And stops at the deepest spot,
Where his legs cannot touch bottom
But where the water does not touch his mouth.
For seven days and seven nights he lets the water freeze,
And then with a heave he comes back out again."
And when the giant said, "Do likewise with me!"
Sawseruquo let him freeze in the sea.
"Now give a heave," he said,
And the giant heaved
And broke the ice to pieces.
"Wait! Wait, giant!
To grow strong from head to toe,
It will be useful to have the ice freeze harder."
The giant rushed to stand on the sea bottom
And let the ice freeze more solidly.
And when Sawseruquo said, "Give a heave now!" that wicked giant
Replied, "I have, but cannot free myself!"
To seize that giant's sword
Sawseruquo then dashed off on his horse.
"Uff!" grunted the giant as he continued to heave.
It was nearly noon
When his winged mount returned,
And Sawseruquo drew forth the sword.
As he stepped forward to strike off the giant's head,
The giant said, "I am no giant! I am a fool!
You yourself are Sawseruquo.
I should have recognized you by your knees!"
He cut off that giant's head
And returned, bringing fire.
He brought fire back to the Nart troop and offered help to all.
Some there had died of cold.
Some there had died of heat.
A few had survived in the middle.
For these he made a great fire.

Then Sawseruquo sent them out on raids,
And he led them back again.

II

Sawseruquo, our *qan!*[4]
Sawseruquo, our light!
Whose great sword, Irresistible, gleams of gold,
Whose chain-mail shirt reaches down to his thighs
Whose hat shines in the sun,
Who, having clapped his hands, mounted his horse
And set off for the Nart council.
When he reached there,
Two honor guards of the gate stood facing one another.
The two dared not
Go to announce him.
Sawseruquo drew up to them
And falsely presented himself as a messenger,
And the two honor guards led him in.
He dashed to pieces his own drinking horn
And took from them the sana[5] warrior horn.
With his dog as his only companion,
With not one Nart horsemen, he set off again.
He circled around Lake Areqe
And came out of Quablana.
He encountered a darkness.
He shouted to it, but it did not heed him.
He set out for it but could not overtake it.
Of its own accord the darkness turned about.
He heard it shout.
This darkness began to move and to bear down on him.
With the two-headed lance of the Narts,
It reached out to his saddle,
Then tore the reins from his hands.
With his shoulder the darkness made him plow
Ten furrows in the sky.
The snot of eight plow oxen dripped
From his nostrils.
His golden mustache
Was rubbed in the foul dirt.

All the mother's milk he had drunk
Was forced up from this stomach.
[A huge man formed from the darkness and] drew forth
    a great sword.
This [dark giant] drew near to take his head.
"Wait! Wait, warrior of the Narts!
You, you are a dog and a coward."
"I am not a dog! I am not a coward!"
"Today the Narts drink their sana.
We must not muddy the vat.
On a day like today we of our lineage must not kill.
He who kills today is doomed.
Give me a place and a day!"
"Harama Hill is our place,
Tomorrow our time. If you betray this,
Then you will wear a woman's hat."
Totaresh, of the raging darkness, stepped back.
Sawseruquo went back to his home.
"My mother, Lady Setenay!
Let your scissors cut for me!
Let your needle stitch for me!
Let them fetch my sword Jumping Flesh!
"My unborn son,[6]
My dear son,
When you went to the Nart council,
Tell me what you heard."
"My mother, Lady Setenaya,
Your woman's head is unfit for it."
"You ask a woman's counsel!
You drew nigh to ask a woman something!
By the enduring blue sky above I shall kill myself!" she said.
"Wait! Wait, our mother!
Of those cowards who let themselves be killed
And those in the world who kill themselves
Leave nothing behind
For those little people who are to come after us."[7]
I shall tell you what I have heard
When I went to the Nart council.
I encountered a great battle there.

When two honor guards at the gate,
Who stood facing one another,
Dared not go among them to announce me,
I went up to them and falsely presented myself as a messenger
And tricked them into fighting one another.
My own drinking horn I dashed to bits,
And I took from them the warrior's horn.
With my dog as my companion,
With no Nart horseman by my side,
I departed from their midst.
I circled around Areqe.
I came out from Quablana Ravine.
I drew near a darkness.
I set off for it but could not catch up to it.
I called to it, but it did not heed me.
This darkness turned about of its own accord
And set off after me, catching up to me.
The two-headed spear of the Narts came out to my saddle
And then tore the reins from my hands.
This darkness forced the snot of eight plow oxen out of my nostrils
And rubbed my golden mustache in the foul dirt.
All the mother's milk that I have drunk
It made me vomit up.
It drew forth a great sword
And stepped forward [as a man] to take my head.
By crooked cunning I escaped
And came back to your house."
"Your mother is a solace for your troubled head.
And much trouble have you brought back.
Confide to me
What he and his horse were like."
"The [tawny] steed on which he rode had the head of a deer,
And its head reached into the heavens,
And from its fetlocks sprouted long tusks.
When it dashes out, it gallops.
When it gallops, you cannot see it.
The warrior who rides him
Is a white youth with mighty arms and thick wrists.
He goes about with his chest bare

And shows no care in his wanderings."
"Oh, your mother is a solace to your troubled head!
My sister, Bahrambupkh,
Bore nine brothers.
I have had you bring me the heads of eight.
The ninth is unique.
May such evil never again befall you
As has befallen you now!
I shall enable you to bring his head.
The horse on which he sits was born in a witch's hut,
Raised in a savage house.
I shall bring for you
The tolling bells from a boat and
I shall plait them into your horse's tail.
I shall plait them into your horse's mane.
When you make your horse's head shake and
When you make your horse's tail jingle,
The tawny horse will be frightened and bolt.
His horse will turn its back to you.
Then what you must do you will do."
"My mother, Lady Setenaya,
Do thus for me," he said.
Sawseruquo went back
To his horse, Little Gray.
"There you are, my Little Gray Ram!
Fleet-footed one!
The offense of yesterday, which the tawny horse gave us,
     is a disgrace.
Is it my disgrace alone
Or is it our disgrace?"
"Eh, puny Sawseruquo!
Eh, you bow-legged one,
Sired by this other cowherd
And born by this sorceress!
Do I not fill my throat
When a cold stream is flowing by?
Do I not graze my fill
When the wild garlic is round about?"
"More than anything this is my disgrace.

My father is covered in shame.
My mother nags at me.
And now my horse reproaches me!"
Sawseruquo grew angry.
He mounted Little Gray,
Galloped out the gate, and rode in a circle.
Setenaya saw him and said,
"My unborn son,
My beloved son,
By all the oaths made before God
Do not go to the Nart council,
But come back here instead.
We have plaited your horse's tail
With the tolling bells of ships!"
With his horse's tail plaited,
With the tolling bells of ships,
He set off to Harama Mountain
To meet Albek's son Totaresh.
The appointed time had come
And Sawseruquo conjured forth
A small mist, a black mist.
"My father has been covered in disgrace!
Where did this evil black mist come from?"
Totaresh asked himself as he drew nigh,
And his head nodded as sleepiness suddenly came upon him.
Sawseruquo was there
And reined in his horse's head
And made the horse's tail ring.
The tawny horse grew frightened and whirled about.
"May the dogs eat you!
You are taking me back toward the women!" said Totaresh,
And he struck his horse in the mouth
So that the two jaws were broken
And dangled from its mouth.
Sawseruquo set on him there
And leaped on his head.
He drew forth his curved sword.
When he went to cut off his head, Totaresh said,
"Wait! Wait, warrior of the Narts!

Yesterday I granted you a reprieve.
Today you in turn must grant me one."
"Foolish warrior, you die!
Once you gave me a reprieve,
But if I give one to you,
The Narts will not stand around and wait for us," said Sawseruquo,
And with that he cut off his head and returned to his mother.

From Hadaghatl'a 1969, vol. 2, no. 136, pp. 106–17, in Old Kabardian, first published in 1864 in an archaic dialect of Kabardian East Circassian.

◌ This saga is the oldest piece of literature recorded in any Circassian language. I have preserved the older forms of the names. For example, in contemporary Kabardian the hero is called Sosruquo, but in this old text his name retains the older West Circassian form Sawseruquo. (See saga 8 n. 8 and saga 24 n. 1.) Other names, such as Ashyamaz for the usual Ashamaz, may reflect a mid-nineteenth century effort to transcribe the language more than any actual difference between Old Kabardian and New. Hadaghat'la has supplied glosses for some of the more obscure words of the texts, based on dialect forms or modern equivalents of the Russian translation that accompanied the original.

Kevin Tuite (personal communication) remarks that the first part of this saga contains material that is closely parallel with the theft of fire by Amiran (or Prometheus) (Charachidzé 1986) in Georgian folklore. The otherwise senseless word "Armi" in the refrain may be an older name for the hero and represent an original South Caucasian "Amiran," with the / -n / taken as a name suffix. "Amiran" itself seems to be derived ultimately from the Zoroastrian (Iranian) god of darkness and evil, Angra Mainyu.

This text deserves an extensive commentary on parallels that it seems to show with an ancient Hittite myth. The majority of Hittite myths have clear Middle Eastern origins, mainly Hurrian, but an account of a battle between a storm god and a dragon (Güterbock 1961, 150–54) has close parallels with the rest of Indo-European, even though the storm god bears the Hattic name Zaskhapuna (with the 'z' apparently a 'ts' and the 'kh' the velar fricative, as with the German 'ch').

Zaskhapuna, a storm god of Nerik (a city), fights a dragon, Illuyanka (a Hurrian name). The dragon first defeats Zaskhapuna, robbing him of his heart and eyes. Blinded, Zaskhapuna marries a mortal woman, the daughter of a poor man, with whom he has a son. Upon reaching maturity, their son marries the daughter of the dragon. As a bride-price, he asks for his father's heart and eyes back. Regaining these, Zaskhapuna is restored. In a second encounter by the sea, Zaskhapuna kills Illuyanka but must also kill his own son, who has sworn allegiance to his father-in-law. Despite her humble mortal origins, Zaskhapuna's wife, Zaliyanu, is a mountain.

Critical features of the two myths, Hittite and Circassian, persist despite a general confusion between them of who is what and who bears which features, but this is not unusual after four thousand years. In some ways, however, the Circassian variant retains enough clarity to offer some insights into the much older Hittite form. In the Circassian variant the storm god, Sosruquo's older identity, is defeated in his first encounter with the monster (monstrous Toterash), probably a rival storm figure and possibly his kinsman who already has his glowing eyes. It is an insult to make a warrior do an agriculturist's work, as Toterash forces Sosruquo to plow the sky, but this is only proper as a storm god whose domain is celestial. His plowing with his shoulder may be linked to an old Hurrian myth that shows other parallels with the tale of Sosruquo. Kumarbi (Hurrian) mates with a rock (as Sosran sires Sosruquo), and stony Ullikumi is eventually born therefrom to fight one Teshub (Hurrian). The rock itself is the shoulder of Ubelluri, an amorphous figure on whom heaven and earth are built and from whom heaven and earth were later sundered by a "cutter." Ubelluri says to Ea, king of the gods (?), "my right shoulder hurts." This proves to be Ullikumi, who is then sundered from Ubelluri by the "cutter," Ea playing the role of the god of the smithy, Tlepsh. Mother's milk stands for kinship in the Caucasus as well as in Iran, and the loss of mother's milk forced on Sosruquo is a renunciation of a kinship bond, restricted to the son in the Hittite variant.

In sum, the name Toterash (originally *Tw-astr, two-star(s); see the end remark of saga 60) was borrowed into Indo-Iranian lore along with his defeat by the storm god, Proto-Indo-Iranian *swas-aryānām, later *šwas-alānām → Ossetic *Soslan*, Northwest Caucasian *Sosran, Sosruquo*. Apart from these later onomastic borrowings, the Circassian preserves an extremely archaic form of the original myth. The dragon (Toterash) may start out with the storm god's eyes (stars), but he has retained the amorphous state of Hurrian Ubelluri as Toterash's amorphous darkness. The Circassian is also extremely archaic in that it preserves two battles, with Sosruquo (the storm god) losing the first and then winning the second, just as in the Hittite version. We know the dragon or snake to have been associated with life force in non-Indo-European traditions, such as those of Ancient Crete and substratal Greece. Apparently later, within Indo-Iranian, the serpent was reinterpreted both as the thief of the life force and as its source, 'Tvastr' in the Rig-Veda elaborated as "creator," albeit of a vague status, on the basis of a folk etymology of his name, which links it with the Sanskrit root /tak-/ 'to make'. The Hurrian birth of the hero from stone, the painful shoulder of Ubelurri, and the sundering (perhaps the plowing) of heaven and earth are all still preserved by the Circassian. The Hittite helpful role of woman (wife Zaliyanu, mother Setenaya), and the crucial battle scene of the mountain (Zaliyanu, Harama Hill) are also still retained, along with the shift in allegiance (Zaskhapuna's son, Sosruquo's loss of mother's milk). The tragic death of Zaskhapuna's son at the hands of his own father and Sosruquo's apparent murder of a kinsman are also themes the reverberates across the Indo-European world.

The name Totaresh reflects the two starry eyes that play such a crucial role in the fortunes of war and attests to an otherwise unknown Indo-European people of great antiquity and archaic linguistic form between the Tokharians in the east of the Indo-European realm (western China) and the Indo-Iranians in the west (Central Asia). As an archaic and marginal people, they must also have retained the elements seen in the Anatolian tradition and in the Northwest Caucasus. The core of the storm god myth may well have been an ancient common Caucasian theme shared with the Indo-Europeans, who seem to have arisen in this same cultural and linguistic one (Colarusso 1997b). See my end remarks to saga 60 for full comments on the name *Tw-astr.

[1] This is an odd variant of the name Warzameg. It appears in Abaza (sagas 69 and 74).

[2] This is an allusion to Setenaya and to twin sons, otherwise brothers (sagas 2 and 78). This reference is parallel with the Indo-European Divine Twins, (Castor and Pollux, and so on).

[3] Note the allusion to a he-goat here. The Norse god Thor, who was also a preeminent giant killer, had a chariot drawn by goats.

[4] This term refers to a foster child who chooses to remain with his foster parents past the customary age when he is due to return to his natural parents. Such a child brought great honor to his foster parents. The term is / qa-a-n(-a) / 'hor-in-remain(-in)', "the one who remains."

[5] Sana is a magical brew.

[6] Sawseruquo was born from a stone (see sagas 47, 86, and 87).

[7] This is an allusion to normal humans, who are to succeed the Narts (see saga 66.)

Sawseruquo,[1] who abides by us,
Sawseruquo, who is our light,
Whose armor is the shield of the lance,
Whose frontlet is the bright chain mail,
Whose helmet's crest is the thunderbolt,
Whose sword smites from above,
Whose lance head is left embedded in his foe,
When you set out in Nart land to bring back a head,
Tell me now of your wondrous deeds!

Yerey, Lady Setenaya,
Who is the true Lady Setenaya,
Among the matriarchs no one is her equal.
Men do not tell
Of the misfortunes that befall them.
The Narts do not bear their woes to their mothers.

Lady Setenaya grew angry.
"To the people I sent a luckless one.
Whatever be his shame,
It is also the Narts' shame.
If I do not learn of it, then I shall kill myself,
As this blue sky is our God unbetrayable."
And so saying, she held the tempered scissors against her throat.

"Hear then the humiliation which I brought back
When I set forth in Nart land to bring back a head.
This sky was of shifting color.
I stood on Old Dog's Tail Ridge[2] and gazed about.
Then a darkness appeared in my sight.
This vision of darkness I spied first.
'Hayt!' I called out, and I gave chase.
He turned himself
And let me come no closer than his lance's length.
He deemed me unworthy of his lance's head,

So he struck me with its handle instead.
He lifted me from my saddle
Without my swinging the stirrups,
Without my touching the pommel.
The old slag heaps of the Narts' furnaces
He made me plow with my nose.
He forced me to carry the clods on my shoulders.
When he reached out to take my head,
I turned to face him and said:

'For the Narts there is a great feast,
For the Narts there is drinking and dancing.
If you let me return to this feast,
Then to our appointed hill I shall return,
As this blue sky is our God unbetrayable.'
So saying I escaped from his hand."

Lady Setenaya:
"What was his manly speech, what his manly color?"
She asked him.

"A man white of face, with broad wrists is he.
My heart struck my ribs when he walked.
My courage fled at the way he moved.
And the horse on which he sits,
Its head is of heavenly fire.
Its eyes shine like great stars.
It must have been raised in a wild home.
Its like have I never seen."

"This man of such speech, of such manner,
Is Albechquo Totaresh,
My sister's only son.
The head of my luckless lone son
You nearly let him take away," she said.
Lady Setenaya grew angry
And ran to his horse, Little Gray.[3]
"Yerey, Little Gray of the long tail,
Whom no horse can overtake,
I have sent forth among the people
My luckless only son.

If you let shame befall me,
If you let him lose his head,
Then I will make dog food of you,
As this blue sky is our God unbetrayable!"

Then Little Gray complained:
"Yerey, Lady Setenaya,
Who is the true Lady Setenaya,
Among the matriarchs no one is her equal.
By day I run with the fleet deer.
By night I count the stars.
When glory is our lot, no one knows me,
But when I bring home shame, all know me.
With cockscombs and variegated creepers
My manger fill.
To the spring of bulrushes[4]
Lead me to drink.
The old bells of Alaj
Braid into my mane,
And I will bring Totaresh's head,
As this blue sky is our God unbetrayable."

Summoning the dog, Alaj, and the eagle,
Sawseruquo set out
On Little Gray's back
With the sun shining brightly.
Then Little Gray, betrayer of God,
Found a hiding spot behind the hill.
Yerey, Albechquo Totaresh,
Great lone horse rider,
Gazes from the summit.
"This luckless one has betrayed me,"
He said and grew angry.

Little Gray shook his mane
And sprang out from hiding
With the dog
And the eagle.
The wild horse started and reared up.
Totaresh pulled in the bridle,

And in his restraining fury
He ripped out the jaws of his horse.
He tumbled backward over his horse's haunches.
Little Gray descended
Upon the man who was lying there.

"Is it a lame piglet lying here?"
Said Sawseruquo,
And he quickly drew his sword.

"Narts will not beg
On a day like today,
Even if you started the begging,
Setenaya's luckless son,"
Said Totaresh finally.

"If you were to beg, it would be a shame.
The Narts would not abide
The reprieve you have given to me
Or the one I might give to you.
Today is our appointed time,
And to our appointed place we have come,
As this blue sky is our God unbetrayable."
And so saying, Nart Sawseruquo
Cut off the head of Totaresh.

From Hadaghatl'a 1971, vol. 7, no. 685, pp. 241–44; the Circassian text was recorded in America (a West Circassian dialect, close to Chemgwi).

[1] This is the West Circassian form of the name, /sahwsərə́q°a/, whereas the East Circassian one is /sawsrə́q'°a/.

[2] Old Dog's Tail Ridge, /ḥa-ẑ́ɔ-č̍'ʸə/ 'dog-old-tail'.

[3] Little Gray, /šx°a-ẑɔ́-ya/ 'gray-wicked-little'.

[4] Cockscomb, /ataqá-ƛ/ 'rooster-lie'; variegated creeper /qaƛ-wɔ́c/, a type of spreading herb with bright flowers (Russ. vjazel' pëstryj-grass); spring of bulrushes /g°ɔ́λə/ 'a marsh'.

SAGA 25 ✑ *How the Horse of Setenayuquo Sawseruquo Was Killed*

The warrior giants sat in council and deliberated on the best means to kill Sawseruquo. They concluded that as long as his horse was alive, they could not kill him, so they decided to kill his steed first. After many attempts, they had learned that nothing could kill Sawseruquo—not a sword nor any other type of weapon. For a long time they had pondered what to do until at last they decided to send a gnat to see if there was some part of either Sawseruquo or his steed that was vulnerable. The gnat soon found that the two were vulnerable in only one spot: the lowest part of their legs; no other parts were assailable.

Soon thereafter, the giants built a cast iron bridge and heated it until it was scorching hot. Then one day Sawseruquo came to the bridge. His horse refused to go over it, but Sosruquo persisted and forced the horse across. No sooner had it reached the other side than it fell down dead.

From GENEG, 321, taken from V. Kusiko, "About Circassian Poetry," Stavropol Provincial News, no. 2, 11 January 1861.

SAGA 26 ✑ *Lady Nart Sana*

Long ago, in olden times, this earth thundered with the pounding of horses' hooves. In that long-ago age women decorated themselves and sat on their horses. They would instantly saddle their horses, grab their lances and daggers, and ride forth with their menfolk to meet the enemy in battle. The women of that time not only comforted their loving men with their hands but could stand by their sides as well and cut out an enemy's heart with their swift, sharp swords. Still, they were able to harbor great love in their hearts. They were also able to counter the poison of the striking serpent.

The beautiful Nart Sana was one of these women. In her heart, beat great love for a handsome boy whose eyes shone like stars. Once Nart Sana's strong hands brought low both a rider and his horse with a blow from her *hajitsa*. Her silky hair fluttered like red flame in the wind. As the man lay on the earth, Nart Sana bent over from her saddle at his lifeless body and face. When she saw him, a choking cry issued from her mouth, "Oh, withered heart, he is my luckless beloved!"

Nart Sana jumped down from her horse to her luckless lover, whose life she had taken with her own hands. She began to kiss his lips passionately. With the warmth from her strong woman's body, she tried to warm his cool dead one. With her tragic words, she pleaded to start his still heart beating again. But the dead hear nothing. He was deaf to the danger of the battle, to her begging, to her grace. The loving woman gently closed his eyes, the eyes now of a lifeless man lying in a pool of blood.

"My sun has set forever," cried out Nart Sana. With her strong arms, she pulled forth her dagger and plunged it into her breast. The blood from her wound flowed into that coming from her luckless lover. So they lay dead together, Lady Nart Sana and the man she loved.

Where those two dead bodies lay poured forth the medicinal waters of the spring, Nart Sana. Their great love and their boundless courage came out with their blood and was absorbed by the earth, forcing up the medicinal waters. Thenceforth, from the Nart Sana medicinal waters, a heart that was ill would be restored to health. He who drinks of it is renewed with strength, activity, and growth.

From Hadaghatl'a 1971, vol. 7, no. 621, pp. 114–15, in Kabardian East Circassian.

☙ Lady Nart Sana is also known as Lady January (midwinter season), Circ. /ŝ'ʸəλa-g°áaš'a/ 'January, mid.winter-lady', "Lovely Golden Knees," Circ. / dəŝa-k°ač'ʸ-dáaχa / 'golden-knee-beautiful', and as the Forest Mother, Circ. / a-maz(ə)-áh-na / 'the-forest-int-mother', the last being the source of the Greek *Amazon*. The Circassian form is pronounced (amazán), precisely what one finds in Greek (the last vowel is long in both languages)! The Greek form, meaning "without breast(s)," usually considered the origin for this, is a folk etymology. Curiously, by the phonological rules of vowel reduction in Circassian, the same form might be read as coming from / a-maaza-áh-na / 'the moon int mother', perhaps justifying Graves's claim that some saw the Amazons as associated with the moon (Graves 1955, 355 n. 1). Contacts between ancient Northwest Caucasian peoples and Greek colonies, such as Phasis, along the Black Sea would have made the exchange of such a name along with the myth of warrior women quite natural (As-

cherson 1995, 49–88). Women warriors may actually have ridden on the ancient
Eurasian steppe (Davis-Kimball 1997, esp. 336–37; Perry 1986). One might also
note the Greek name for the brother of Medea, Apsyrtos, which is derived from
the Abkhazian self-designation *apswa*. The Abkhaz ethnonym merely means
"mortal" and is derived from * / á-pŝ-wa / 'the-die-one' (Chirikba 1991). The suffix is an old (exclusive) plural now found only with pronouns. Therefore his name
is an unwittingly plural eponymous one, "the Abkhazians."

Saga 27 ◑ *Adif*

Nart Adif's house is still standing on a hill on top of the riverbank of Yinjija to this day. If you look from the village Habaz, you can see it clearly. In
the Narts' era Adif and her husband, Psapeta, lived in that house. Their
story as they describe it is very astonishing.

Adif's husband, Psapeta, would cross over the Yinjija River and drive
back many horses.[1] As Psapeta approached the far bank of the Yinjija, he
would call out to Adif, "Do you hear me?" and she would reply, "Yes, I do!"
because she would always sit, waiting for him to return. From the tower
of their house she would push her white elbow through the tiny open window. Her skin was so white that it shone, and the light from her white
elbow would dispel the darkness of the night. When the mountain valley
grew bright, Psapeta would then drive his stolen horses over Adif's linen
bridge, which was suspended over the deep mountain gorge through
which the river flowed.

Thus they lived, until one night Psapeta had an argument with his wife.

"I am the successful master in this house. I brought everything here. I
drove in a herd of horses every night, but did you ever help?" said the husband.

"You, as a husband, are talking without thinking. You are not supposed
to talk like that to me. It is disgraceful for you to reproach me as though I
am not helping in the household, accusing me of doing nothing while you
brag about the herds of horses that you drive back. If you are famous, then
it is I who made you famous. Try to bring in the horses without my help!"
said Adif.

Psapeta took offense at her words and grew angry with her.

"You still don't know how brave I am. Just see if I cannot drive them in here! I shall go alone, and alone shall I drive them home safely to our yard," he said.

The following night he mounted his horse and departed. He had driven one hundred dapple-gray horses and eight hundred white-tailed horses to the valley. When the horses reached the narrow valley, they grew frightened, and he could not drive the horses onto the linen bridge. Psapeta became alarmed.

"Do you hear me?" he called, but Adif did not reply. A second time he called, "Adif, do you hear me?" Again, there were only the sounds of the river and the horses. Adif would not answer him. When he called a third time, "Adif, dear wife, do you hear me?" she could hear the hopelessness in his voice and she pushed her white elbow through the little open window. The shining light of her arm immediately dispelled the darkness of the night.

Psapeta began to drive the horses across the linen bridge, but when the front of the herd of horses reached the middle of the linen web bridge, Adif remembered his hard voice and harsh words. She pulled back her white elbow. Suddenly all was in darkness above the roaring river. The horses grew frightened and began to push one another off the high bridge. Was he hit by a horse's hoof or pushed by a horse's breast? Who knows? Psapeta too fell into the dark river far below.

The beautiful Adif soon had misgivings about what she had done and once more thrust her arm through the window, lighting all around the river gorge again with her white arm, but she was too late. She could not see anyone on the bridge.

She sent friends to find her husband. They found Psapeta's corpse, which had been carried by the water to an island. From there they brought it home, buried it, and erected a mound over the grave.

Adif went into mourning and wept very hard for her husband. She had not wanted him to die. She had pulled her arm back because she was still angry and had wanted her husband, that bragging, arrogant man, to realize that he could not have done it alone. Matters had not turned out the way she had intended.

Nart Psapeta had not respected his wife, nor had he realized how much she contributed to his efforts. The beautiful Adif had been of great help to him. Offending her had cost him his life.

According to the customs of the Narts, after one year had passed Adif went to his grave and mourned him again. Adif wept bitterly, both because of her husband's terrible death and because of her hard life and her loneliness. Because of her deep grief, she tore at the flesh of her elbow and the blood squirted from it. This blood painted red the banks on both sides of the Yinjija River and the neighboring mountains. She mourned that way for a whole year.

The beautiful Adif was still mourning and kneeling by her husband's grave when Nart Sawseruquo happened upon her. Sawseruquo had long admired this woman whom he now saw weeping alone by the grave. In that very moment Sawseruquo conjured forth a rainstorm.

"Whose grave is this?" he asked her as the raindrops began to fall.

"This is the grave of my husband, Nart Psapeta," she replied.

"Then come here under my cloak. You are getting too wet. And stop hurting yourself so much," he admonished her. He took Adif by the hand, helped her up from the ground, and politely held open his cloak for her. He warmed her hands with warm air from his mouth.

They said very little after that, but then, without their knowing how it happened, Sawseruquo and Adif found themselves joined together as though they were husband and wife. As long as Adif had lived with her husband, she had never enjoyed any embrace such as this one. Adif said, "Sawseruquo, you have aroused all my feelings of love that I never had from the man with whom I lived all my life. He never had any affection for me, neither respect nor feelings of love for me. So, I won't let him lie quietly in his grave, the man who denied me in this life so much love and affection!"

Then she ran out from under the cloak and grabbed a shovel that was lying nearby. "He forced me until now to miss the sweetness of this beautiful universe. I shall dig him up from here and let the dogs eat his body," she said, and she dug three times with a shovel at her late husband's grave. Adif dug three times into the grave, and from her actions there remain to this day three hollow spots. The dirt that she took from the grave became a small hill, which is still there next to the grave.

"Stop! Don't do that," said Sawseruquo, and he took the shovel from her.

So, Nart Psapeta's grave mound is still half dug there on the bank of the Yinjija, where visitors can see it.

That grave and the hill are not so far from the old storage house that was Adif's first home. The old storage house's ceiling is peeling. There is no roof on it anymore, and the stone beams are bare. The inside of the ruin's walls and its warped door frames look as though they were sprayed with blood, for they still have reddish spots on them. The bank on the other side of the mountain valley in front of the old house is reddish. Those reddish colors on the riverbank slopes and those reddish stains on the warped door frames and on the room's walls are believed to be Adif's blood. Between this old storage house and the big house with its tower is one day's walking distance.

From Hadaghatl'a 1970, vol. 5, no. 651, pp. 161–62, in Bzhedukh West Circassian.

  This saga emphasizes the mutual respect between husband and wife that is necessary for domestic tranquillity by illustrating what can happen when egotism prevails in its place. It is an unusual saga in that it contains ritual self-wounding during mourning, used to explain the geographic features and architectural ruins of a locale. Its mundane features are nevertheless explained with truly mythical characters: a crescent moon wife and a hard-soul husband (see n. 1). Sosruquo conjures a storm so as to drive Adif and himself into the intimate confines of a small shelter. This scene is reminiscent of Juno's sending a storm in the *Aeneid* to force Aeneas and Dido to find intimacy in the shelter of a cave [KT].

[1] These names may be analyzed as follows: Adif / ʔa-dəy-f / 'arm-joint-white', "White Elbow" (compare the verb / wə+q°ə+dɔ́y / 'val.enhancer+bend+joint', "to stretch, flex oneself"); Psapeta / psa-pɔ́ta / 'soul-strong; stingy', "strong (but also mean) spirit", Yinjij / yən(a)-ʒʸɔ́ʒʸa / 'giant-shining, smooth (one)' (note Shapsegh / yəna-gʸɔ́gʸa /, with what may be a root for "smooth" or "shining" that shows intensive reduplication).

In Abkhaz versions of this saga the lady is Setenay and her luminescent anatomy is her little finger (see sagas 78, 79, and 80). This Circassian account appears older in that it depicts a woman distinct from Setenaya whose elbow gleams. She might best be interpreted as the crescent moon.

SAGA 28   *Wardana and Chwindizh Dwell in the White-Haired Forest*

Once there were two brothers born of one mother, stalwart Nart men Wardana and Chwindizh.[1] Wardana dwelled in the White-Haired Forest,[2] in a region called Wardanuquo, and Chwindizh dwelled in the region of Pshakhwayisa, around the settlement of Abin.[3] Chwindizh was blind in both eyes, but he possessed seven grown sons. Wardana at first had no sons. He had, therefore, to tend to his cattle himself.

The sons of Chwindizh had gone three times to their uncle, Wardana, to raid his cattle. He had been gentle with them, indulging them in their pranks, but had been careful to take his cattle back before they could reach home.

When Chwindizh learned of it, he grew furious and confronted them: "Why are you pestering him? He is my brother! Stay away from him! He will kill you all. You have gone to his place once each month for the past three months, but I have never heard you driving back any cattle. So what good does it do you?"

"He pursues us and takes the cattle away from us. He does not let us drive them home," said they.

"How does he take them back, away from you?"

"Wardana rides a white horse. At the beginning of our return he rides behind us, keeping pace with us, but after a little while his white horse appears in front of us all, and Wardana leads his cattle off back home."[4]

"If that is how it stands, then do not go to him if you must still rustle cattle. That white horse will be your doom."

But his sons were head busters. They would not listen to their father. The fourth month came, and they set off a fourth time to raid cattle from their uncle, ignoring their father's words. When they started to drive the cattle back, Wardana followed them, seated on his white horse. This time, in fury he overtook the first of his nephews and slew him. After that Wardana overtook another nephew and slew him as well. In this way he overtook each one in turn and slew all seven. At every place where he had killed one, he later had a mound erected.

The hills of the seven brothers, sons of Chwindizh, at the present time still stand in Pshakhwiyisa.

It had been foretold that if a son were born to Wardana, then the blood from that babe, if smeared on Chwindizh's eyes, would restore his sight. At about the same time as the death of Chwindizh's seven sons, a babe was born to Wardana. It lay in a crib, a little boy. Now he was remorseful for the seven slain sons of his older brother, Chwindizh, and being mindful of the prophesy, he went to his own son's crib, took one of the infant's tiny hands, and very gently pricked it so that a few drops of blood appeared. He put the blood in a small vial and brought it to his older brother. He entered the yard of Chwindizh. No one came out to greet him, so he tied his horse to the hitching post himself and went into the main house. "Now, my older brother, I have brought some medicine for you," he said as he smeared a bit of the blood on Chwindizh's eyes. As soon as he had done so, Chwindizh's eyes were healed and he could see again.

"You evil wretch! Can it be that you have left the two of us without a son-sword?"[5] said Chwindizh, for he was mindful of the prophecy and feared that Wardana had killed his own infant son. Chwindizh grabbed a quiver that hung nearby and had belonged to one of his sons. Seeing this, Wardana jumped through an open window, leaped on his horse, and rode home. The other brother, now with his newly healed eyes, ran to the stable, mounted a horse, and took off in pursuit.

When Chwindizh entered his younger brother's yard, Wardana's wife fled in fear and disgrace. Chwindizh ignored her and went into the house, looked around, and saw the crib. When Chwindizh saw that the infant was still alive, his rage turned to joy. "So, as long as one still lives not all is bad," he said. Then he sought out Wardana and found him in the guest house. There the two brothers made peace.

This is a consolidation of two sagas, Hadaghatl'a 1970, vol. 7, no. 650, 167–68, in Bzhedukh West Circassian (mislabeled as Shapsegh); and no. 651, pp. 168–70, in Shapsegh.

◐ I discuss the full significance of these sagas elsewhere (see 1984b). These two sagas are an excellent example of the vital importance of vestigial or marginal material. Only two short tales in the entire seven-volume Circassian corpus refer to Nart Wardana or Wadana. Nevertheless, these two fragments throw light on far-reaching cultural relationships across ancient Eurasia. The "standard" etymology for the Germanic *Wōðanaz (Old English *Wodan*, Old High German *Wuotan*, Norse *Odin*) is to derive it from the root *wōð- 'rage', cognate with Latin *vātēs* 'rage, possession, fury' (Puhvel 1987, 193). As noted by Benveniste (1973, 247), all other forms attested in Indo-European languages that show the suffix *-on- are of the semantic form 'social unit-*on-', that is, "lord of a social unit," with the sole exception of Proto-Germanic *wōðan-az; compare Gothic *kindins* 'chief of the clan' ← *gent-i-n-os, basically, 'lord of the race', Old Icelandic *drottin-*, Old English *dryhten* 'chief of the troops' ← Proto-Germanic *druxti-n-az, Gothic *þiudans* 'lord of the people, chief', Gaullish *Toutonos*, Illyrian *Teutana* ← PIE *tewt-on-os (in historical times this used to denote the tribes themselves) (ibid.: 245–48). Thus the use of a nonsocial term, *wōð-, in *wōðan-az is anomalous.

On one hand, *Wardana*, in its Shapsegh form of *Wadana* (pronounced "Wodéna"), offers a source for the late common Germanic god *Wōðanaz, which has been reworked under Gothic influence from the Germanic "Mercurius" noted by Tacitus in his *Germania* in the first century A.D. Roman interpretation of the Germanic gods. On the other hand, the Goths, with their steppe empire in the early centuries of the Christian era, link up with the Ancient Pontic Iranians (Alans and Sarmatians) and the ancestors of the Circassians, to borrow a hypothetical Iranian *Wardana, which itself would have been cognate with Indo-Aryan Vrddhana, "Giver of Booty," an epithet of the Hindu god Shiva, whose name in turn is an epithet of the Vedic god Rudra. Further, Wardana, like the Germanic Wodan, is fickle, killing all of his nephews but one, and is responsible for raising tumuli over them. In this latter function he assumes responsibility for dead heroes just as Wodan does. His horse, too, like Wodan's (Norse Odin's) Yggdrasil, is the fastest.

His blind brother in his disability not only recalls Wodan's loss of an eye, but also has a name, Old Rook (/ć°andɔ́-ź/ 'rook-old'), which recalls Wodan's brothers, the two ravens (in Norse) Villi and Vé. Wodan cures battle wounds and Wardana cures Old Rook's blindness. Wodan bestows wealth through raiding and looting, and this may lie behind the alternative name of Old Rook, Giver of Old Oxen (/ć°ə-źə-tˤ/ 'ox-old-give') (see Colarusso 1984b for further parallels, and Dillmann 1979 for a study of Odin).

Thus, the two fragments from which this saga is compiled link some of the furthest reaches of the Indo-European world into a religious and historical web.

---

[1] Shapsegh West Circassian /ć°əndɔ́-ź/ 'rook-old' also has a variant, /ć°ə-źə-tˤ/ 'ox-old-give', "give(r) of old oxen." I have taken the latter form to be a distortion driven by folk etymology.

[2] The Circassian has /mázə šḥá-a-tx̌°ə-m ø-ø-x̌a-sɔ́-x̌ˤ/ 'forest head-conn-white-obl (they-)(it-)inside-sit-pl', "they sit in the white-headed forest." Shiva lived in a white forest atop a sacred mountain. Odin had white hair.

[3] These place-names are as follows: Wardanuquo /wardan-ɔ́-q°a/ 'Wardana-his-son', normally a patronymic name, Pshakhwayisa /pˤʁˤʸáax̌°a-yɔ́-s+a/ 'sand-in-sit+in', "situated in sand," and Abin /a-bɔ́n/ 'the-dale, valley(?)'.

[4] There is confusion in both variants that may be of comparative significance. The white horse is said to belong to one of the brothers. If this is incorporated, then it is not clear how Wardana could at first take back his rustled cattle. When Wardana loses his patience with his nephews and flies into a murderous rage, he is said to come up to the last rider, who happens to be on this white horse. He slays him and takes this horse, which is then faster than all the others. So mounted, he cannot be resisted and kills his remaining nephews. I have chosen to motivate the plot by putting Wardana on the fastest horse to begin with, so that his nephews are foiled in their attempts to rustle his cattle.

[5] The words are obscure: /k°awá-nčˤa sá-nčˤa/ 'twig(?)+pred-without knife-without'. The first root is a dialect word for "male offspring" generally. It seems to mean 'branch' in the sense of family lineage.

SAGA 29 ◌ *Warzamegyuquo Yasheruquo's Search for Courage*

There is a proverb: If you don't meet people, you can never find out who is a real man of courage. There are many people who are clever to talk to, but if they meet a hardship, then they are dull. Nart Warzamegyuquo Yasheruquo considered himself a courageous man. To speak exactly, he was a man of courage.

A family decided to betroth their daughter to a man as a wife. In his honor and for that occasion, they were celebrating a seven-day bachelor party. So the bridegroom with his horseman was ready and waiting to take the bride home as soon as the celebration was over.

Nart Yasheruquo was also at that celebration, and this came to his mind. "I shall find out what kind of men these are," he thought. He ran to the bride, grabbed her, took her on his horse, and fled. They tried to catch up to him.

"Boys, quick! Don't let him take the girl away!" They were alarmed and started to follow him, making noise, but when they came out from the courtyard with their horses, he was gone, almost out of view.

When he looked back he thought, "My God, I am losing sight of them. I should not do that." So he pulled on the reins, sat waiting on his horse, and let his pursuers come closer. They were hoping to catch up to him. When Nart Yasheruquo saw, however, that none of the followers had the courage to catch up to him and take the girl from him, he kicked his horse with his boot heels and sped off like the wind, heading for home.

And so they lost him. Not knowing where to go, they could not run on forever. So they all turned back save for one or two riders. The bridegroom did not turn back but continued his search for his bride-to-be until nightfall. Then he rested at the edge of a forest. On the next morning when he awoke, the bridegroom mounted his horse and went to a village. There he recognized the horse of the man whom he could not catch up to the day before. The horse was being led to the river for a bath. He followed the horse to the courtyard where it was led back, and the bridegroom entered the courtyard like a visitor. He told the master his problem. Unexpectedly, it turned out that the master was Nart Yasheruquo.

"Good! You came for the girl. I shall give her back to you," he said, went into the next room, brought the girl out, and gave her back to him. Then he escorted them off and said, "May your road be good!"

From Hadaghatl'a 1968, vol. 1, no. 78, pp. 269–70, in Hatiquoya West Circassian.

SAGA 30 ⌑ *How the Nart Khimish Married and How He Was Killed*

In our land, during the time of the Narts, dwelled both the giants and the little Spe people. Once a little Spe was drifting along on the air current from a giant's nose.

"What are you going to do?" asked the giant.

"I aim to take a stick and strike you," said the little Spe.

Upon hearing this, the giant ran away. The giant was very cowardly.

They tell that Khimish's wife came from the Spe.

Nart Khimish was a hunter. In those times there was another famous hunter from among the Spe. The two men had never met each other, but they claimed that they were friends. Yet they knew each other by name and through intermediaries had agreed to meet someday, but they had not set a definite time and place for their meeting. They admired each other very much, but a very long time passed until they met.

Then one day Khimish decided to set off to see to his counterpart. He took his bow and arrows and departed. He thought, "I shall walk alone slowly and go hunting on the way."

The hunter to whom Khimish was going had made the same decision on the same day, and so he was heading toward Khimish. Khimish had killed a deer and was carrying it. He wanted to rest because he had gone a long way, so he entered a pasture. There was a spring and also a tree. He walked under the shade of the tree and sat down. As he was skinning the animal, a wanderer appeared from the direction in which Khimish had originally been heading.

"I wish you good luck in your work," said the wanderer.

"Thank you. Welcome!" Khimish answered.

Khimish bade the man to take a place in the shade, and so he did. Both men were tired and needed to rest. They were talking and dismembering the animal together. They agreed to roast the meat and eat it at the same place. Now they commenced to ask each other's name and from whither they had come and whence they were going. The visitor asked Khimish, "Where are you going? From what clan are you? And what is your name?"

"I am one of the Narts. My name is Khimish. I am going to the dwarves to see their great hunter," and he told the wanderer that he was on his way to the Spe people. When he had said this, the wanderer replied, "That is very happy news that you are telling me. If you are Khimish, I was also on my way to see you. I am the man whom you mentioned."

At this, both men grew very happy. They both agreed that whoever had walked the longer way should be invited to the other's house. This proved to be the house of the Spe hunter.

So, according to their agreement, the dwarf invited Khimish to his people, and so off they went.

Once there, the Spe told Khimish, "Khimish, don't be lonely. Comfort yourself. Stay here until I come back. You will find somebody who will converse with you. Don't be in a hurry." So he spoke to his guest. Then he mounted his horse and departed.

Since Lady Isp was the master's daughter, she served as the hostess for Khimish, and as such they entered into conversation. Khimish was not a married man. The girl and Khimish were soon talking seriously about marriage.

The girl said, "I'm not going to marry you," she told him, "unless you promise me one thing. There is one phrase that you must never say to me. If you promise not to, then I shall accept your proposal."

"If it is only one phrase that I must never say, then don't hesitate. Ask it of me," said Khimish.

"I'm not telling you how husband and wife should get along. If I don't do what you want, you are allowed to hit me. If I don't fulfill my household duty, you are allowed to do what you want with me. But if you say to me 'little wretch,'[1] I won't accept that one phrase," said the girl.

Nart Khimish smiled and said, "Why should I mention that?" So Isp and Khimish agreed to become husband and wife. So they decided on the time for their marriage, but they did not wait for the man who was off on a journey. Khimish brought Isp back to his house as his wife.

Khimish and Isp lived happily together. Isp became pregnant. The baby in her body was Pataraz. A group of riders entered the yard. These visitors did not want to dally. They wanted Khimish to come with them on their journey. These guests told their intentions to the master, Khimish, that they wanted to be on their way as soon as they had eaten something. So he agreed with their decision.

Khimish was not one of those people who have a passion to stick their noses in the kitchen. He didn't need to tell his wife to cook, as others often did, but when time had passed and still no food appeared, which had never happened before with Isp, Khimish became impatient and went into the kitchen. There he saw that she was not cooking. She had not even put water on the stove. It was Isp's intention to find out what Khimish would say.

"Why haven't you done anything?" asked Khimish. "These guests will not stay. They will leave soon, and I have to go with them on the journey too."

Isp said, "All right, I shall do it right now."

He then went back to his guests and again waited until the time he thought the food should be ready, but still there was nothing. Again he was impatient and went into the kitchen. When he entered, he saw that she hadn't even lit the fire and was still sitting peacefully.

Then he said, "You little wretch! You haven't even lit the fire and you sit there quietly."

At that Isp said, "Now you won't have to wait any longer. Your wish will be fulfilled immediately." The man went away. Food was out and the guests were fed faster than Khimish could saddle his horse. They were ready to go, so they mounted their horses and left with Khimish on the raid.

The group had set off on a distant quest and was gone for a long time. While they were gone, Lady Isp left Khimish's house and returned to her father's, still carrying Pataraz in her belly.

The group had found some livestock and had been driving the herd homeward, when they reached Khimish's house and stopped there to rest.

Khimish asked the visitors to dismount and invited them into the house. As was the custom, they waited for the hostess for a little while, but no one came. So Khimish left the parlor and entered the kitchen. There he did not see the woman whom he had been hoping to see and who should have been there. He went out from the house and asked his neighbors why his kitchen was empty. The neighbors were uncomfortable and did not want to tell him the bad news. Then one lady approached him and said, "Dear

Khimish, if you are worrying about food for your guests, I have already prepared it. If it is time now, we will send it in."

With that offer, Khimish was a little suspicious but not quite sure of what had happened.

"My God! What kind of reason should there be that our neighbor's wife has to cook for us," he wondered. "All right then, send it over," he told the lady.

They brought the serving tables and the guests ate and departed. After the guests left, one of the neighbors approached him and said, "Khimish, there is news in your house. I guess you do not know it."[2]

"I have suspicions, but I am not quite sure. A strange woman had to cook for us today, therefore there must be something wrong," said Nart Khimish.

"But do you have any idea what has happened?" Khimish asked the man who had brought the news.

"None of us knows why, but when you left this courtyard Lady Isp went home too."

When the man said that, Khimish realized on his own what had happened. He remembered what he had promised her and what he had said to her when he was annoyed with her for not cooking for the guests. Then he realized why it had happened.

Khimish thought, "All right then!" and so he decided to live alone, but the neighbors who lived near him were angry with him about something most of the time. Nart Khimish was a handsome man. When the wives of the Narts started to cast their eyes after him, the Narts thought he was not to be trusted with their wives. So they came to discuss whether Khimish should be killed. After a long debate, they decided to kill him. Since Khimish was bulletproof, he could not be shot easily. Therefore, they went to a fortune-teller.

"I will tell you how to kill Khimish," said the fortune-teller. "He likes to play checkers very much. It is his habit to sleep on a chair after the checkers game. So you have to tie him to the chair. If you shoot him while his mother, who raised him, is looking on, then the arrow will kill him. So at that time you should make all kinds of noises, yell, scream. When his mother, who has raised him, hears all that noise, she will be alarmed, for she will suspect tragedy, and she will run toward the noise. Also, Khimish will be awakened, and when he finds that he has been tied to a chair, he will know that something is wrong and will begin to run to his mother.

During the tragic instant when his mother and he see each other, you must shoot him. Then he will be in your hands.

They did just as she told them. He played a game of checkers with one of them and then fell asleep in an oaken chair. Khimish awakened from the loud noise to find that he was tied to the big oaken chair. He then ran out of the room so fast, with the chair still tied to his back, that he struck the upper part of the chair on the door frame and broke it. Khimish ran homeward to his mother, who had raised him. She feared for her son too. As both of them rushed toward each other, an archer who had been set the task and who was standing at the ready shot at Khimish and killed him. That is the manner in which they killed Khimish.

Hadaghat'la 1970, vol. 4, no. 489, pp. 24–28, Bzhedukh West Circassian text.

◌ This saga sets a moral limit on the savagery that the warrior culture can tolerate and sets the stage for the vengeance of Pataraz (saga 31). The killing of Khimish in front of his mother's eyes is a sort of maximal sin, one that amplifies the inevitable savagery of the warrior ethic and places it in opposition to the most tender of bonds, that of mother and child. This sin leads the implacable Pataraz on his quest for vengeance and ultimately to the annihilation of the Narts. The concern that Khimish's mother has for her son is in notable contrast with the indifference that Lady Isp or Spe has for her son Pataraz (see the next saga).

There may also have been an old folk belief that the prowess (invincibility) of a warrior was lost if his (foster) mother was watching when he was attacked (see the next saga, n. 3).

[1] Little wretch is / məɣ°a-c'ɔ́k'°/ 'poor; hungry-little'.
[2] The informer must be a man, because for a woman the tidings would be too sad.

SAGA 31 ◌ *The Ballad of Khimishuquo Pataraz*

Yerey, Pataraz, son of Khimish,
Pataraz was a lone youth with a single heart,
But a man in whose heart lay the valor of a hundred heroes.
He in the womb swore vengeance for his father's blood.

On that same day when Old Khimish
Wed Lady Isp against their wishes,
The old Narts swore vengeance against him.

On that same day when Nart Pataraz
In the belly of Lady Isp was conceived,
Old Khimish was by those Narts cruelly slain.

On that same day Nart Pataraz,
When the Isp lady bore him,
They carried him off despite his mother and nurse
As a fosterling to weigh against a blood price.

For him they decorated his fosterling crib:
Of the maple's hardness were his crib's head and foot,
Of the linden's beauty were his crib's side slats,
Of the doe's back skin was his crib's restraining band.

When his foster nurse laid him down and bound him in his crib,
Pataraz stretched himself and smashed through its head and foot,
Pataraz turned himself and broke off its side slats,
Pataraz raised himself and tore through the restraining band,
Pataraz rose and strode to the great central pillar.
To the Nart sword that hung thereon he stretched out his hands.

His foster mother, being wise, then did divine his destiny:
"This Pataraz will grow into a valiant man,
The old Narts will be left without kin at his hands."
So saying, his foster mother grew frightened,
And in shining Yinjij's[1] high water did throw Pataraz.

The Old Yinjij, a river of many turnings,
Whirled Pataraz about and carried him down,
Where those tending the Nart horses saw him
And from the bright waters lifted him out.

On that same day they took from the herd a colt for him,
A colt from the herd, in every way a *fara*.[2]

For nine years the horsemen trained Pataraz.
On that same day Pataraz mounted his fara and rode off.
On that same day astride it he entered Bars Field.
On that same day Pshimaruquo[3] he did meet there.

"O Lordly Grandfather, whence come you?" said Pataraz.
"From the smithy of Tlepsh come I, my boy,
On that dismal day when I killed Old Khimish,
His thighbone dulled the edge of my Mayi[4] sword.
I set Tlepsh to sharpen it once,
I set him to harden it thrice,
And now I am bringing it home."

"O my Lordly Grandfather, one look do I ask."

"O my boy, one good look I shall grant you."
But when Pshimaruquo turned the sword's edge,
Good fara, a wise horse, took Pataraz aside.
But when Pshimaruquo struck,
When his sword missed its mark,
Good fara, a wise horse, turned back and
To Pshimaruquo's side quickly drew nigh,
And Pataraz wrenched from his hand that sword.
Then in Bars Field did he chase him;
Between two seas and seven times he drove him on.[5]
There did Pataraz strike Pshimaruquo down.

Pataraz to his own lady nurse[6] did return.
"God gave you back to me, my boy,
To your own home you have returned!"
Lady nurse thus spoke to Pataraz,
On that same day she comforted him.

"Lady Mother, to pay a visit to the old Narts is my goal.
Among the Nart wine drinkers shall I enter.
The Nart drinking horn will I take from them,
And there before them will I drain it dry.
There Old Khimish's blood price will I set to them."

"O my boy, to such wine drinking do not go."
So spoke his nurse to Pataraz
And in a bed of thistledown[7] set him to sleep.

The lady went among the Nart wine drinkers:
"For you, Old Narts, this is your eating and drinking feast,
But with the wonder that has come to pass you are ignorant.
With the valor of a hundred heroes my light has returned home.

You, Old Narts, will be left without kin at his hands."
When the nurse to the Narts spoke thus,
On that same day the old Narts came together in council,
On that same day great treachery they together composed:

"On a wild fara we shall set Pataraz,
For water to Old Warp we shall let him lead it.
In Bars Field when he enters there,
'To the fara give the lash,' we shall tell him.
The wild fara will grow angry,
Between two seas it will carry him and down it will throw him.
If it does not throw him and Pataraz turns back,
Old Warp, seven times twisting,
Into seven deltas is divided,
By every delta an army shall we set in place against him.
On that same day they will spear him down," they said.
The Old Narts to the wine drinking invited him.
On that same day the drinking horn of valor they gave
    there to him.
The horn of valor they gave to him and he drained it there.
"You, Nart Pataraz, sit on this fara.
Take it for us to water at the Old Warp.
When you enter Bars Field, to the fara give the lash," they said.

Pataraz sat upon the wild fara.
As he entered Bars Field,
To the fara he gave the lash.
With its hooves he let it plow Bars Field.

As he arrived to Old Warp for water,
From seven deltas seven armies of horsemen emerged.

On that same day seven armies of horsemen he struck down.
Before Pataraz drew nigh to the Narts,
There from the wild fara he dismounted.

When the wild fara arrived with an empty saddle,
The Old Narts toasted each other with drinking horns
    of white wine.
Their weapons and armor as gifts of gladness together they
    exchanged.

Pataraz set to hiding himself with foul skin and foul hair.[8]
Then unnoticed he entered among the Nart wine drinkers.
In the lee of a door he stood and listened to the crowd.

The Old Narts stood over a barrel of white wine.
Of the harvest god they uttered many blasphemies.
Aleg, the leader, told many false stories.
Warzameg, as though true, agreed with them.
Yimis[9] boasted as was his habit.
Sawseruquo composed a hundred evil schemes.
Nart Chadakhstan dreamed of manly deeds.
In all they drove white wine down to the barrel's seething bottom.

Pataraz emerged from behind the door
And crushed the ribs of those who stayed before him
And snapped the spines of those on whom he trod.
He came to the center of the room and turned about.

On that same day Pataraz said to the Old Narts:
"You, Old Narts, stand over the barrel of white wine.
Of the harvest god you utter many blasphemies.
Aleg, the leader, tells many false stories.
Warzameg, as though true, agrees with them.
Yimis boasts as is his habit.
Sawseruquo composes a hundred evil schemes.
Nart Chadakhstan dreams of manly deeds."

Pataraz drew nigh to the barrel:
"If what I am about to say is a lie,
May God make this barrel go dry!
If what I am about to say is the truth,
May God make this barrel overflow!

I had my house built on the mountain where God dwells.
I had my roof covered with the skins of giants.
The bones of giants' thighs are the beams of my house.
And their ribs are my roof's trusses.
My house's floor drinks white wine.
By day I set the giants to thresh my harvest.
They thresh in my yard and make not a sound.
I set them with their bare hands to plow my fields.

By night into a yoke I fasten them.
The hair of my chest stands like the quills of the hedgehog.
I lead shepherds through the evil thickets.
I lead harvesters out, safe from their enemies.
When I arrived between the two seas, I did not turn back,
But with the bright lightning as my bridge I crossed them.
I crossed back to Bars Field, my playground.
Seven times twisting to the Old Warp I did lead the wild fara,
Slipping and sliding he fought against me on the way.
There issued forth from seven deltas seven armies.
On that same day I went seven by seven against the horsemen.
On that same day I speared down a hundred riders on white-tailed
     horses.
On that same day I let the wolves eat the flesh of a hundred white
     chargers.
On that same day I cleaved through a hundred bright breastplates.
On that same day I let the river wash away a hundred white
     chain-mail coats.
On that same day I let a hundred horsemen cry to God.
During my life, Prince Warzameg of the Narts I did meet.
Pshimaruquo was the fiercest among them."

"Where did you find the Nart Pshimaruquo?
You are too young to be Khimish's son," they said to him.

"Pshimaruquo I met there, in Bars Field.
I came at him from the side and wrenched his sword from his hand.
I drove Pshimaruquo back into Bars Field.
Seven times I forced him to run between two seas.
Turning, he lowered his trefoil lance at me.
He cast the smell of burning hair into my nostrils.
He made the sun appear like a hundred shards of light.
He made my legs shake against my will.
And when he struck, he clouded my two eyes.
In all that time I said not a word.
Then I flung Pshimaruquo's lance away to the side.
I drew up behind his horse and struck him,
Knocking him over his horse's head.
On that same day I speared Pshimaruquo down."[10]

When Pataraz had finished speaking,
The white wine barrel welled up and overflowed.

Then Pataraz turned to the old Narts
And the blood price for Old Khimish he told:
"With a sieve bring water for him
And let my savage fara drink its fill.
Across the sky on a ladder must you go.
Gather all the thistledown that lies across Nart land
And on Old Dog's Tail Ridge burn it.
The ash of this down you must collect
And with it fill up the two shoes of Khimish.
Find for me one hundred swift hounds
With heads of black and bodies of white.
On my wagon mount me an axle from the bulrush.[11]
For my portal cut me a solid door from the hawthorn's barbs.[12]
With mosquito blood fill up our father's water barrel,
And stuff his leather food bag with gnat fat.
And melt some butter for me on the point of a spear.
All that is the blood price of Old Khimish.
If you can bring me one virgin,[13]
If you can cover my roof with feathers,
If you can snatch a crow's gallbladder,
I will take these as payment for my father's blood."
On that same day the old Narts sat as one.
On that same day the old Narts wept as one.
Yerey, Pataraz, son of Khimish,
Pataraz, one youth with one heart,
One man in whose heart lay the valor of a hundred heroes,
He in the womb swore vengeance for his father's blood.

*Transcribed in Bzhedukh West Circassian, July 1981, from the original by Kube Shaban,
which I have translated.*

✍ This is a modern account of a saga by one of the most respected Circassian
folk writers. It is faithful to the folkloric canon and appears to be a more elaborate
version of an account recorded by Hadaghatl'a on 5 July 1958, in Shapsegh, as told
by Sh'halakho Ali, born in 1881 in Afipsipa, Adygheya.
    This saga is remarkable in that it lends itself to a simple but dramatic interpre-

tation. The child Pataraz is destined from the womb to wreak vengeance on the Narts for their most heinous of crimes (see saga 30), which, of course, demands the ultimate vengeance, extermination. In effect the child is killed by being washed away. He is reared in a grave mound, growing prodigiously, and his return to his nurse is seen as miraculous. He sets forth and encounters his father's murderer, the Prince of Death, who recognizes his victim's child and attempts to kill him. He comes to the Narts as a resurrected corpse—hence his appearance with "foul skin and foul hair" (see n. 8), unrecognizable as Khimish's son—and presents them with their ineluctable doom in the form of a series of impossible tasks. In a different tale, which nonetheless exhibits many features in common with this one and that of Shebatinuquo, the hero Sawseruquo is reared under the same circumstances and is explicitly called the "Son from Beyond the Grave" (/axratɔ́-qʷaʔa/ 'grave-son'; see the Arabic al ā̊xira 'the hereafter') (Hadagathl'a 1:178). Thus the infant hero is actually killed but is reared by the goddess of the netherworld and permitted to return from the dead. In the details of the saga, the foreordained nature of the drama, the defeat of death, and Pataraz's resurrection and change of appearance, his tale resembles that of Jesus of Nazareth, but he is the inverse of Jesus in that he brings not salvation but destruction. The historical links between this Nart saga and Christianity are worthy of pursuit.

Close parallels with the birth of the hero Indra in the Rig-Veda are also striking (Colarusso 1984b). The abduction of Pataraz and his encounter with the river explain the otherwise enigmatic verses in the Rig-Veda, 4.18.8 (Indra's mother to Indra):

> For no reason of mine did the young woman throw you away.
> For no reason of mine did Kushava [a river] swallow you up.
> For my sake the waters had mercy upon the child.
> For my sake suddenly did Indra stand up.

There has been much speculation as to what this can mean (for example, see O'Flaherty 1981, 142, 144, nn. 14, 15). Little of this is convincing. The verse must be a surviving fragment of an older, coherent tradition, now lost in the surviving Vedic corpus but preserved here. This "ur-myth" is well preserved in the Circassian lore and casts definite light on the relatively obscure Vedic verse. The "young woman" is the foster mother or nurse who casts the infant away to try to save the others (Maruts?). The infant is put in a ravine (the surrounding mountain of Rig-Veda 4.18.6, not necessarily that of Vrtra, contrary to O'Flaherty [1981, 144 n. 11]), to be swept away by storm waters. As he is the infant storm god, the torrent is kind to him and brings him ashore safely, albeit to the abode of the dead. He is reared by the mother of the dead to be returned to the world of the living (compare the Greek, originally Phoenician, Adonis). As a sign of his coming might, he grows prodigiously (a common feature of heroes), breaking all bonds (as he will do when he destroys the "Stifler, Smotherer, Binder," Vrtra), and stands up immediately to claim his rightful weapon, an act affirming his true nature as a hero.

Dumézil (1978, 37–41) discusses this myth in the context of his trifunctional theory of Indo-European society and in the context of Ossetian variants. See also Abaev's (1990b) discussion of Ossetian Batraz on pages 182–98, as well as his etymology for this name (Abaev 1996, 1:240–41), which links it (improbably, in light of the West Circassian forms) with the Turkic-Mongolian *baatyr* 'hero'. This last title is probably of Indo-European origin, as with the Russian *bogatyr* and Persian *bahādur*.

¹ Yinjij / yən-ž'óž'(a) / 'giant-clear, shiny', "large clear glittering river" (in the older Shapsegh version / yən-ǧ'əǧ'óya /); compare / aś°a-ž'óž'(a) / 'chain mail-shining', the name of a god of war; / a-ś°á / may also mean "the skin".

² A fara is a well-bred beautiful, spirited horse used in wars and quests, a thoroughbred warhorse. In the Shapsegh version, this is said to be a *dul-dul*, the Turkic word for a winged horse.

³ "Pshimaruquo" can be etymologized as / pš'ə-mahr-ó-q°a / 'prince-death-his-son', "the Prince of Death" (see saga 3 n. 2), with the stem / mahr / coming from an Indo-European language; compare the English *murder*, *(night)mare*, Latin *mortuis*, Serbian *Mara*, name of a female water sprite, and so on. In a Bzhedukh saga recorded by Hadaghat'la and reported by Dumézil (1978, p. 39), the parents of "(Pshi) Maruquo" avenge themselves on Pataraz. They arrange for him to be showered with arrows while his foster mother is looking on. Her viewing of the attack renders him momentarily vulnerable. I have not included this tale because it seems to play a small role in the vision of Pataraz as I found it among my Circassian colleagues, who generally assume that Pataraz's death is unrecorded. The tale seems merely to transfer the father's death onto the son, even down to the loud commotion that brings each victim running outside to his doom. Therefore this tale would seem to be a late innovation.

⁴ The Bzhedukh version refers to this weapon as / mahyó-sa / literally, 'Mayi-sword'.

⁵ Heroic battles often take place on the shore of a lake or sea. There is a simple tactical reason for this. If one's adversary's horse is superior to one's own, then this advantage is lost when two warriors confront one another on the sand or gravel of a beach.

⁶ The term is / daya-g°áaš'a / , with the second term meaning "lady," as a title of respect, and the first term apparently / dá-ya / 'nut-one of', "nut tree." The use of this term for "nurse" may be linked with the old custom of planting a tree, preferably a walnut, for each child. The nurse may be a personification of the vitality embodied in the nut tree.

⁷ The word is / dahróy / . This is of unclear sense, but possibly a blowing down from a thistle or locust tree.

⁸ The term is / c'ə̀ +ya-ś°ó+ya / 'hair+foul-skin+foul' and is said to be used to describe the rotten condition of a corpse. Though strange, it is a critical line in the poem (see the comments at the end of this saga).

[9] In the Shapsegh version, the character is Prince Asraneh, /psʸə asráhnə/, otherwise unknown in the Nart corpus. This is probably old Turkic *arslan,* "lion."

[10] The Shapsegh version has an intercalated episode here that seems both confused and out of place, since it is not a recapitulation of Pataraz's exploits as depicted earlier in the poem.

> "My great cannon is hauled by eight draft horses.
> I made them draw it to the top of Shawn Mountain to be cleaned there.
> That same day I made them set forty gunpowder charges in it.
> I made them set me in it like a cannonball
> And shot me into Ghud-Ghud, Ghud Fortress.
> I shoved the earth apart for a hundred ells.
> When the enemy army surged toward me,
> I said not a word.
> What I have just told you has little of truth to it!
> If I had crawled into the gun,
> I would have been burned by the powder!
> Who would have pulled the gun to the top of Shawn Mountain?
> But in truth I did have it pulled to the top of Haram Mountain to be cleaned.
> When the old cannon roared,
> I ran under it into its smoke,
> And I leaped into Ghud-Ghud, Ghud Fortress.
> There I pushed the earth aside for a hundred ells.
> When the enemy army surged toward me,
> That same day my sword cut strongly,
> And my bowstring howled like a giant wolf.
> My horse, knowing valor, followed."
> "Poor Pataraz," replied Warzameg, "such words to say over the wine barrel!"
> "If my words are true,
> White wine, surge up to the top!"
> The wine surged up and blew off the barrel's lid!

This seems to be spoken to Warzameg, leader of the Narts, as is evident from Warzameg's reply. Although some scholars have compared this episode to the Trojan War, I prefer to see it as a recent addition to the tale, exhibiting, as it does, modern weaponry.

[11] The word is / šʿʸəmbár/. This is of unclear referent but is a supple marsh plant like a bulrush.

[12] The word is /ḥ̣ameš'k'ʷə́t'/. This is of unclear referent but is a small, thin thorn, perhaps from the hawthorn.

[13] This and the next four lines occur in the Shapsegh version. The demand for one virgin implies promiscuity on the part of the Nart maidens, a theme alluded to by Shebatinuquo (see saga 12 n. 3) in a close parallel to this saga. That it is condemned here is the result of old Christian influences working against women's sexual prerogatives as embodied in the even older paganism of the region.

SAGA 32 ✑ *How the Narts Sought to Reach the Sky*

When Khimishuquo Pataraz demanded his father's blood price from the
Narts, they were unable to fulfill it because it was impossible. After a while
they returned to Pataraz and asked him, "How can we reach the sky?"

> "Throw up the ladder and go out into the sky.
> Stand one upon the other and reach the sky.
> More than that I will not tell you."
> Khimishuquo grew angry with them.
> The Narts looked at each other.
> The Narts asked each other:
> "When we look, we see that
> If we go, we can't reach it.
> What other than the sky is there?"
> Lady Setenaya said to them:
> "A mountain thrusts up into the sky.
> We can see the borders of the sky.
> When the clouds bend low they touch the earth.
> If we stand on it, we can reach the sky."
> They spoke among themselves and grew excited.
> The big Narts stood one upon another.

But they were not able to reach the sky. Then they stacked one upon another people, dwarves, beasts, wide-winged birds and ravens, trees, and
stones; they set one upon another all that they had on sea, sky, and earth.
At the very top they placed Pataraz himself.

When he reached out, he found that he would have been able to touch
the sky if only he had had just one cat's tail left to him!

GENEG, 345–46, West Circassian text recorded in Syria.

✑ Kevin Tuite (personal communication) has suggested that this myth demon-
strates the hero's control over all mundane creation but delineates his ultimate
limit because of his inability to touch the sky, which stands for God.

"I have three whetstones," said Warazamaj.
"They contain magic, like this:
The first sharpens the edge of a sword.
The other brings food to eat.
To obtain the best woman
The third will help you.
To the best of the Narts in courage we will give one.
To the Nart with the best belly we will give the other.
The one left is to him who respects women most.
If one man gets all three, he stands first.
If he does not succeed, then two will go to someone.
If one man does not get two,
The first will be the man who excels in courage."

The Nart *t'hamata* elders agreed on a fixed day to invite all the Narts. Khimishuquo came. His teacher, the shepherd Khamisha,[1] was his companion. Then Warazamaj, t'hamata of the Narts, stood up and showed the first stone.

"I shall give this to him of the Narts who is most courageous," he said.

Then each Nart began to tell his tale of manliness and of marvelous deeds. When Khimishuquo said nothing, Khamisha arose.

"My son Pataraz deserves it.
One hundred enemy horsemen he vanquished single-handed.
No one from the Narts surpasses him in courage,"
Said he to all seated there.

When he had told about that, how Khimishuquo had encountered a hundred enemy horsemen, how he had killed them all, the Nart t'hamatas asked Khimishuquo, "Please tell us how you encountered one hundred horsemen and slew them."

"This was taught to me by my hunting dog. One day as I was returning from a journey, I passed a certain village. From that village there streamed out one hundred dogs and they pursued him. My old dog looked back.

When he saw that the hundred dogs had fevered eyes and sharp teeth, he began to run. The hundred dogs snarled *ghab-ghabgh* behind him as they ran along. Far, far they ran off. I thought, 'They have already eaten him,' but when I looked I saw that my dog looked around. He saw that of the hundred dogs some were still running powerfully, some not so powerfully, and a few could no longer run at all. He saw that they were scattered. Then he turned and killed them one by one, until he had killed them all.

"Thus I thought, 'If you lead the enemy after you, one after the other, in this way you will be able to defeat him.' After this, when I encountered one hundred horsemen, I led them so that they scattered, and then one by one I slew them all."

The Nart t'hamatas stood up and gave to him the first whetstone.

For the second stone the Narts competed as sharply as for the first. Then Khamisha stood up and said:

> "In my son Pataraz
> You will not find a better belly.
> We sat at tables covered with food.
> He sat among us for seven days,
> Not taking a bite into his mouth.
> Among the company of all the Narts
> He was the most energetic.
> He was cheerful, never showing fatigue.
> We grew tired as we ate.
> When we arose from the tables, he touched the food,
> Tasting only the smallest bit.
> Then he arose and left."

And those Narts wondered. "And what did you take?" they asked him. He said to them, "Once when we were traveling along, the Nart t'hamatas sent me to fetch water. I grew worried when I could find no means to carry it. Then I came upon a goatskin bag and went to where a mountain spring gushed forth. I let it flow and flow and more, but the bag would not fill up. I was angry. I was tired. The water reached its limits, but I was unable to keep the bag full.[2] Then I took it, dribbling out, and returned. I let the Nart t'hamatas drink of the water and told them about the nature of the leather bag. 'Look at this!' they said and examined it.

" 'It is human nature not to be satisfied,' they said.

"From that time onward I practiced abstinence with regard to my stomach and accustomed myself so that what little I ate during the day satisfied me."

The Nart t'hamatas arose and gave the second whetstone to Khimishuquo.

A worthy owner for the third whetstone was sought in like manner, and once more Khamisha arose and said,

> "This last stone
> I will not give to a Nart.[3]
> But my son, Pataraz, there is not one of you better with women
>   than he.
> From a journey my superlative son
> At midnight reached his home.
> He found his woman making love with a lone herdsman.
> Taking his burka,[4] he quietly left the house.
> All the cold long night in the courtyard he spent.
> When it dawned, as though he were a true guest,
> My son set the herdsman on his way with care.
> To his woman he returned.
> Jests and jokes spoke he to her
> To force his heart to forget the insult."

And at that the Narts wondered. "How did you do that?" they asked Khimishuquo.

"I shall tell it to you," said Khimishuquo Pataraz. "Once we were traveling and entered a waterless, treeless desert. Long we wandered and were unable to find our way out. Both hunger and thirst began to torment us. Then the t'hamata elders sent us in search of a settlement. In our search we came upon two small earthen huts. A girl and her mother lived in them. But for us there was no other place to stop. They took in our company and fed us and gave us drink. When night fell (we were nineteen horsemen), ten of us barely fit into the larger hut, and nine into the other.

"When I listened to the conversation of the mother and the daughter, as they stood behind the huts, I heard the following:

> "'O my daughter! You are young.
> Much bliss will you come to know.
> Our men have left on a journey.
> How much have we to endure?
> The bliss that shall be shown me tonight
> Might not be my lot again. For that reason
> I shall enter the larger house.'

"Her daughter did not agree and said:

"'Death knows not the difference between youth and age.
Great bliss have you seen already.
Let tonight's great bliss be mine.'

"The two women argued the whole night. When it dawned, we left. Since that time I understood how much women have to endure, and I have trained myself to treat them graciously."

The Nart t'hamatas arose and gave the third precious whetstone to Khimishuquo.

From GENEG, pp. 278–84, an "Adyghe" text transcribed in Syria and close to Chemgwi West Circassian.

⌖ Usually said to be the best and purest of the Narts, Khimishuquo Pataraz is given explicit virtues here. These are Caucasian virtues, relatively untouched by Indo-Iranian or Indo-European influences. The first is courage and cunning in warfare of a guerrilla style. The second is restraint in appetite, a virtue for horse-mounted fighters. The third is tolerance for women's sexual yearnings. The last one ties in with the Northwest Caucasian kinship system, in which relations between husband and wife are formal whereas those between a woman and her brother are close. In such systems (termed "Cherkess-Trobriand," for the Circassians and the Trobriand Islanders where these were first encountered) women enjoy considerable sexual freedom and choice. Implicit also are the Northwest Caucasian virtues of modesty and courtesy: Khimishuquo will not speak of his exploits. His teacher and father, Khamisha, does so in his stead, so that his son must answer the questions of his elders. The award of whetstones recalls the warrior's mark: in Norse a whetstone in Thor's forehead, in India Shiva's moon. A similar mark is borne by Sosruquo's brother-in-law in an Abaza saga (59). This tale is also one of the few where Pataraz's father, usually called Khimish, is said to be a shepherd, thus reaffirming the pedigree in variant 27 of saga 10 (see my comments there) and linking this name to that of Argwana and its variants and to that of Sajemuquo (saga 8).

In contradiction to saga 30, the usual account, Khimish is still alive here. It is unclear which is the original tradition.

---

[1] The patronymic of Pataraz reflects the usual Circassian form of this name, Khimish, / xəmǎš⁽ʸ⁾/. The actual name used for Khimish here, Khamisha, / xaməša /, is archaic and shows links with the Ossetic Hæmyts, /hæməc /. I suggest an original */ hæməč'a /, though

its etymology and source remain opaque (but see Abaev [1996, 4:172–73; 1990a, 247–48], where a Turkic-Mongolian origin is posited).

For the given name itself, most of my informants say / pʻataráz / (with Hadaghat'la noting a rare and anomalous / fataráz /), but the East Circassian forms /bataráz/ and /batráaz/ indicate that the rarer pronunciation / patʻaráz / is closer to that of the original. The Ossetic / bætraʒ / is clearly a borrowing from East Circassian (contra Abaev 1990a, 248–49; 1996, 1:240–41; Dumézil 1978, 34, 36 n. 1) but also points to an old affricate in final position. Thus, the original seems to have been the Proto-Northwest Caucasian */ patʻaráʒ / . I prefer to see in this name a rendering of the Greek *pétros*, with an old suffix, and to attribute the paramount position of this hero, both in Circassian and in Ossetian traditions (Dumézil 1978, 21–49), to his prominence in some ancient North Caucasian form of Christianity.

[2] A water bag made of goatskin is porous and will leak. This apparent fault, however, promotes evaporation, making the water within cool, so that such bags are routinely used in the Caucasus, the Middle East, and South Asia.

[3] This statement is odd because Pataraz is also a Nart.

[4] The burka, /čʺaakʺʻa / in Circassian, is a heavy sheepskin cloak, square at the shoulders.

SAGA 34 ∽ How Pataraz Freed Bearded Nasran, Who Was Chained to the High Mountain

Nart Nasran was a man worthy of praise. He had a keen intelligence and was kindhearted. He always helped Narts who were in need.

At that time humankind was beset with a misery called Paqua. He claimed to be the true god and was always struggling against God. He was always in a fury and would say, "I am God!"[1]

For a long time Paqua paid little heed to the needs of the Narts. Because of his hatred of them, he was always trying to bring disaster on them. In the Nart realm Paqua was considered very dangerous. He could bend oaks as though they were supple twigs. He destroyed the houses of the Narts. He made waves as high as the sky. He made the millet and barley rot in the fields. He split the ground and brought drought to the Narts' land.

"What are you doing?" said the Narts. "Why do you do us such harm? Why have you brought such miserable and bitter cold into our beloved land?"

When Paqua heard that the Narts had been complaining about him, he unleashed a bitter cold gale against them. This destroyed their stoves, and the wind even swept away their ashes and coals, everything that they had, thus leaving the Narts without fire.[2]

The Narts went to Nasran. They asked him, "Our blessed leader, Nasran, what should we do with him who has shown us such misery? We have neither fire nor light and will perish soon."

"Do not worry yourselves! I shall retrieve the fire from that Paqua," said long-bearded Nasran.

Nasran saddled his horse and cinched in the girths. Then he departed for the mountain called the Blessed Peak.[3] Nasran journeyed far and near until he reached the Blessed Peak.

Nasran was not afraid but was seeking a way to ascend the mighty peak. Suddenly he heard a voice like thunder resounding from the top of the mountain, as though someone were talking, and to him it seemed that the sky had split into two. It was Paqua saying, "You, little man! What have you come here to do? If you do not go back, you shall perish at my hands."

"You stand in God's place, and they say you are benevolent," said Nasran, trying to flatter Paqua. "If that is so, then why have you taken fire away from the Narts? Why have you sent bitter cold so that we will freeze to death?"

"If you want to return home, then go! Don't make my head hurt! If you continue in this way," replied Paqua, "I shall not spare that empty, dim-witted head of yours. You, you Narts, don't know what a god is like. You have forgotten me. When you brought in an abundant harvest and were sitting around your three-legged serving tables,[4] I was not among you. You did not offer any of that bountiful harvest to me, your god. When you returned from your quests laden with booty, you all thought yourselves to be mighty heroes, but no one ever shared his gain with me. You[5] are looking for a means of ascending this mountain. In this you are opposing me, God, but today you have come up against one whom you will not vanquish. I shall chain you to the highest peak. I shall hold you prisoner until you die."

Paqua bound Nasran's body all around in chains and then fastened him to the summit of the Blessed Peak. Paqua had an enormous eagle. This ravening beast was greedy for human flesh. The wicked Paqua was enraged and set loose his huge eagle. The eagle's wingspan was so great that it could not fly down in the valleys. When it flew, it blocked out the sun so that the earth became enshrouded in darkness. It flew up and landed on the chest of the mighty Nart Nasran. It tore open his chest with its powerful beak. It drank his heart's blood and pecked at his lungs with its razor-sharp beak. There are many seas and rivers flowing over this world, but there was not a drop of water for Nasran. There are many loudly resounding streams cascading down the mountain valleys, but Nasran is wrapped in chains, unable to get even a glassful, and is dying of thirst. He is encased in the ice of the high mountains, and his arms and legs are squeezed in the viselike grip of the chains. Chained to the Blessed Peak, Nasran roared and moaned, his cries being carried by the winds to the Narts. They were in great distress because of his suffering.[6]

The Narts held a council to discuss how they could save Nasran and bring him safely home. The Narts thought back over past times, trying to remember who had performed heroic and valorous feats, thinking of the youth of such men as Yimis, Arish,[7] and Sawseruquo. They called for them, deeming them to be brave men. They all replied, however, "What would we be able to do?" all of them being afraid of Paqua. "Paqua is mighty and dangerous. You will not be able to overcome him," they said.

Then the Narts thought some more. They decided: "To whomever brings Nasran back we shall give in marriage his daughter and much treasure as his own property."

The Narts waited for a very long time for someone to come forward and say "I shall go," but no one volunteered to go on that dangerous path. Nasran's daughter felt bleak, thinking that no one wanted her enough to risk his life for her.[8]

Finally the Narts decided, "Let us all go together," and off they went.

When the Narts caught sight of the Blessed Peak, they saw that it was sparkling once more with ice. They saw too that Nasran was nailed to the very summit and was suffering great distress. The mountain proved to be strongly fortified, and there was no way to climb it.

Paqua saw that the Narts had come. When he saw them, he unleashed every guardian eagle that he had. These guards came down from the peak. They were not far from the Narts, so they were soon before them. Other eagles dashed about like dancing flames. Their wings made a great noise as they descended from the mountain and flew down into the valleys. They hid the rocks and the grass as does a blizzard. As they flew, the wings of the wicked birds covered the sky, blocking the light of day and bringing on a gloom as dark as midnight.

In that great darkness, the courageous Nart Shebatinuquo lost his horse and could not find it. Many Narts died in the attack there, the survivors huddling together. The living retreated with their heads hanging in despair, for a great blizzard and a bitter cold had entered their land and they no longer had any fire. Paqua had taken the fire of the Narts. "What should we do?" said the Narts. "We have no leader. Our leader is hanging in chains, dying. What will we do, Narts? How will we find shelter? We cannot bring back our fire, nor can we bring back Nasran. What will we do? What plan should we devise? How can we go on living?"

Not knowing what they should do, the Narts were in dire straits. They found no one who would go to save Nasran.

Then Pataraz said, "I shall go. I shall bring back our fire and bring you joy once more. I swear this in the name of the blue sky that stands over us. I shall find our leader Nasran as well, and if I find him alive, I shall bring him back."

Pataraz saddled his horse, which they called Little Black, with its golden saddle, donned his battle garments, and set off as he had in earlier times when he had prepared for a quest.

Now Pataraz reached the Blessed Peak and stopped in the foothills of the mountain. There he commenced his struggle. "Hey, you who bear God's name, who disgraces God! Why are you trembling and hiding in the valley? It is not manly to hide in the valley. Come out here if you want to fight. You have taken the fire and joy from the Narts. You have taken the leader and ruler of the Narts and imprisoned him in steel chains. The Narts have sent me. If you are not afraid, do exactly as I say! Call off your giant blood-thirsty eagle from Nasran and send it down here from the mountain!"

Then the sky grew very dark. This meant that the great eagle had arisen from the mountain. The wings of the wicked bird brought darkness everywhere. The horse on which Pataraz sat grew frightened. "Hey, Little Black, my horse! What has happened to you? Do the wings of the wicked eagle frighten you? Haven't you and I seen many hardships together? Is this the first time that you have seen these wings?" Then he gave Little Black's flank three blows with his riding crop.

The eagle bore down on Pataraz with its steely beak pointed right at him. To the very spot where he stood, that ravening man-eater, hungrier than a wolf, came down from the high mountain. The wings of the wicked bird stirred up a great blizzard. The horse became so frightened that its legs began to buckle.

"What's happening, Little Black? Are you afraid? You were always my true friend and companion. Now don't be frightened and abandon me! Don't be a coward!"

Pataraz laid another lash on Little Black. Thereupon Little Black gave a snort and leaped up into the sky,[9] and they began to fight with the monstrous eagle. They fought for a long time on the ice of the mountain. It was a great ordeal for Pataraz to fight with the wicked bird, but despite this he was finally able to shoot an arrow through one of its wings. When he did this it was as though someone had opened a window; the sun shone through the eagle's wing, and it became light once more. The sun shone on the fields and the mountains, and the whole world became light once again. Again he shot an arrow into the wing of the eagle. In this way Nart Pataraz vanquished Paqua's eagle.

Pataraz ran his lance through the eagle's breast and thereon carried it to the foot of the mountain. He drew out his sword, shining like the sun, and cut off the eagle's head. It was then that Paqua heard the cries of his eagle. Then the Old Black Brigand[10] also heard its death cry. The Old Black Brigand came down from the mountain to do battle with the Nart horseman. Pataraz and the Brigand fought mightily, but finally Pataraz overcame him and beheaded him. With a moan, the Old Black Brigand fell to the ground.

Then the Soul-Taker[11] came to meet Pataraz, but Pataraz was not afraid, for the old Nart woman still lived. Pataraz sent the head of the Soul-Taker flying. With a roar that could deafen, the Soul-Taker fell to the ground. As the Soul-Taker toppled over, his groan made the mountains tremble.

Now smashing all before him came the Fighter. Pataraz was not afraid of him either, and drawing his shining sword he cut off his head as well. Now Pataraz, astride Little Black, galloped up the mountainside. Paqua flung all aside and fled, hoping to save his head.

Casting a shadow on him, the mountain bird flew past above his head.[12]

On that day the Nart Pataraz wrought many great deeds.

Pataraz galloped up to the bound Nart, and with the head of his lance he broke the chains. He set free the leader of the Narts and they returned together.

On that day the good fortune and happiness of the Narts returned. There was great joy all over Nart land. They slaughtered sheep and invited the shepherds to partake thereof. They drank sana, the magic brew, together and no one was excluded.

On that day the Narts drank at a great sana feast. Astride their horses, the Narts performed a round dance[13] and raised up a great song.

The Narts sang the praises of Pataraz. Many Nart herdsmen came from the far mountains to drink sana. Pataraz's mother, who was old, gazed on her son and said, "I reared my son for your sakes."[14] They gave Pataraz the first sana horn. They greeted Pataraz in happiness and honor. They spoke many good and beautiful words about him. They wished him a long life.

With pleasure, Pataraz drank the horn of sana and said, "Now we shall have fire all our lives."

Everyone was filled with joy as they played, ate, and drank. They let the Great Wheel[15] roll down the Eternal Mountain[16] and then they drove it back up again.

They proclaimed Pataraz the best man among all the Narts.

From Hadaghatl'a 1970, vol. 4, no. 534, pp. 152–59, in Bzhedukh West Circassian.

✎ This is one of the Caucasian Prometheus legends (see Olrik 1922, 133–278). Charachidzé (1986) has made a study of such Prometheus tales in the Caucasus. He has studied this saga, or one like it [KT] (pp. 81–82), and has found it a bit too close for his taste to the Greek original, cautioning that Russian literary versions of the Greek myth may have colored the Circassian one. I too was incredulous when I encountered striking parallels between Northwest Caucasian lore and not only Greek but also Norse, Slavic, and Ancient Indic lore. Nevertheless, I have not dismissed these parallels for two reasons: first, most of the bards are simple peasants and are unlikely to have had the benefit of Russian learning in these matters; and second, the details are such as to suggest ancient contacts (Ascherson 1995, chap. 2) rather than cribbing. In support of my second reason, I cite an example that I elicited in 1975 from a young Circassian of Turkey who was studying civil engineering in Vienna, Adnan Saygili (whose Circassian name is Zhazhi Atnan). A nameless hero encounters a one-eyed giant, who traps him and his men when they venture inside a large hollow tree, the giant's lair. Eventually the giant eats two of his comrades (just as with Polyphemus and Odysseus). The nameless hero finally blinds the giant by driving a huge spit into his eye. While the giant is beset with pain, the hero runs from the tree and escapes across a glacier. Meanwhile, the giant throws large stones at him. Saygili had never heard of Odysseus. If this account were a simple act of copying from a Russian collection of Greek lore, even through attenuated secondhand channels, it is unlikely that *The Odyssey*'s roomy cave would have been supplanted by a tree or that the sea which carries the hero to safety would be replaced with a treacherous and slippery glacier. Clearly a common tale has come down both in Greek and in Circassian, with the two cultures situating the adventure in a realm most familiar to each (see saga 52).

This saga has one of the more intriguing villains in it, Paqua, Bzhedukh /pʿáakʾ°a/, apparently a distortion of the older /pʿáak°a/, still used, and from whence evolve by regular sound change the Kabardian and Besleney /páag°a/.

Paqua seems now to refer to a "Tatar," that is, one of the Altaic-speaking, more Mongoloid-looking peoples, who replaced the Iranian-speaking hordes in the Pontic Steppes sometime in the fourth or fifth century A.D. This racial identification may be seen in the name of Paqua's son, /pʿaak°á-q°a tʿatʿar-śáawa/ 'Paqua-son Tatar-lad', "the Tatar lad, Paquason." The meaning of *Paqua* is straightforward: /pʿá-a-k°a/ 'nose-conn-cut short', "the short-nosed one." Perhaps this is an effort to describe a typical Mongoloid physiognomy, common among many of the Altaic-speaking peoples. Certainly the Romans spoke of the Huns in similar terms. However, the notion of a pug-nosed demon may have been older than the incursions of the Altaic peoples and may merely have been applied to them when they were finally encountered.

Lest the reader dismiss this etymology of *Paqua* too quickly, I point out two pieces of supporting evidence, one quite unexpected and startling. First, a meaning of "pug-nosed" would place Paqua in semantic opposition to the hero, Pataraz. The most frequent pronunciation of the latter name (within Shapsegh and Bzhedukh) is /pʿataráz/, meaning "the one with the aquiline (downward-pointing) nose," an ideal of manly beauty still evident in the contemporary Circassian illustrations in Hadaghatla's collection (see, for example, the pictures in tale 534). The analysis is /pʿa-ta-ra-z/ 'nose-down-along-turn' (for this etymology, see GENEG, 205–6). I have argued in saga 33 n. 1 that such a pronunciation and underlying analysis of *Pataraz* is a folk etymology of an older /patʿaráz/, still heard as an alternative pronunciation of the name. The motivation for this folk etymology can now be seen to be the meaning of the name of the archenemy of Pataraz, Paqua.

Second, the analysis of *Paqua* as "the pug-nosed one" finds yet further corroboration in the Germanic languages. Old English had the form /pūka/, and Old Norse a diminutive, *púki*, both meaning a mischievous demon or imp (Weekley 1967, 1165–66). From the Old English form come characters such as Shakespeare's Puck, and the word *pug* is in some way related, with what is for Germanic languages a totally irregular alternation between /k/ and /g/. Weekley thought that *pug* originally meant "dear" and was later applied to short-muzzled dogs or short noses in general. The origin of these Germanic words, as well as the irregular alternation between /k/ and /g/, can be seen in older Circassian, antedating the generalization of /aa/ before /a/ in the following syllable: proto-West Circassian */pʿśk°a/ for Old English *puca* and Old Norse *púki*, and in Proto–East Circassian (ancestor of Kabardian and Besleney) */pśg°a/ for *pug*. The Tatar form of this name is *Puk* (Dumézil 1930, 46–49; Dumézil must be referring either to a Karachay or to a Balkar tale, as these are Altaic-speaking neighbors of the Circassians). Perhaps this name has been reshaped under the influence of the archaic word for "chieftain" or "leader," / buǧ /, but more likely reflects the earlier West Circassian form.

The route for these loans, starting so far away from what is usually envisioned as the Germanic world, is through the Gothic empire. This early Viking-like expansion began in the middle of the fourth century A.D. and was destroyed with the onslaught of Attila a century later (see Olrik 1922, 273–76, for the importance of this route). This empire stretched from the Black Sea to the Baltic (Vernadsky 1943, 120). In fact, Gothic was spoken north of Circassian in one area or another from the second century A.D. (ibid., 114) until the late sixteenth century (Pedersen 1931, 6).

[1] This is a most unusual claim for a man to make. Clearly this story reflects either an ancient religious conflict or an ancient political one, expressed in terms of a conflict between rival pantheons.

Paqua would seem to be an old storm god. In some ways the depredations of Paqua are reminiscent of the general destruction wrought by Vrtra, the archenemy of Indra, the supreme god of the Rig-Veda (Gonda 1960, 55–57). Other parallels with the Indra-Vrtra conflict will be mentioned as they occur in the text.

[2] The popular conception of the Prometheus myth has humans as primordially without fire and Prometheus as ameliorating this barbarous state by bringing fire. Here is a Prometheus myth in which one of the heroes is punished for merely trying to bring back fire, the fire having been stolen from humankind. In fact, the Greek account speaks of Zeus merely "withholding" fire from humankind because of the trickery of Prometheus at a sacrifice (Grimal 1990, 376; Tripp 1970, 499–501; Graves 1955, 1:144). One of the Titans, he fashions humanity from clay and bestows fire on them (Greek for "forethought"; compare Sanskrit *pramantha* 'the fire drill').

[3] The Blessed Peak is Mount Elbruz, the highest peak in the Caucasus chain, in Circassian /ʔ°a-śḥa-máafa / 'ridge-top-blessed', that is, the "Blessed Peak."

As with Paqua, the archenemy of Indra, Vrtra, sits atop a mountain in some of the Vedic hymns (Gonda 1960, 1:55), wherein he has dammed up the waters of the world.

[4] The three-legged tables are the / ʔáana/, which figure prominently in all the Nart feasts.

[5] Oddly, the Circassian here uses the second person plural, / ś°a /. Paqua is being rude to Nasran, so interpreting this as an ancient form of polite address (second-person plurals are often so used in a wide range of languages) is not plausible, nor is it the polite form of address used in Circassian today. This verb form may therefore be a relic of an older form of the tale in which more than one hero was seeking to retrieve the fire from Paqua.

[6] In the Greek accounts, Zeus has an eagle punish Prometheus by eating his liver (Graves 1960, 1:145). Nasran's sufferings, caused by the pressure of his chains and the coldness of the mountain ice, are shared by Prometheus. The ordeal of thirst, however, is reminiscent of the sufferings of Tantalus (Graves 1960, 2:25–26).

[7] *Arish*, /ʔahrə́š⁽ʸ⁾/, has no clear etymology. Perhaps it is a truncated form of the name Yarishqaw, which itself has the variants /yarəš⁽ʸ⁾áq°a(-х̌áaf)/, /yaš⁽ʸ⁾arə́q°a /, /yarəš⁽ʸ⁾q'áw-

x̌áaf / (/ x̌aafa / 'brave'). In Ubykh one finds /yarəč̣ʸxáaw/, /yárašxaw/, and in Abkhaz /yarč̣ʸxáw/, /narǯʸxʸáw/, (see the comments in saga 89). The name seems to denote a hero, originally Circassian, whose exploits are often associated with those of Sawseruquo.

The Circassian forms with the patronymic /-q°a/ 'son' are most likely a reshaping of a Proto–Northwest Caucasian */yarč̣ʿ(ə)q̇ʿáaw/. Very tentatively, one might see here a name connected with the horse of the grave mound (saga 2 n. 9): /yar-č̣ʿə-q̇ʿá-a-w/ 'friend, companion-horse-grave-conn-pred', "companion to the horse of the grave mound." For the element /yar-/ 'friend, companion', note Persian /yār/ with the same sense. The suffix /-a-w(a)/ 'conn-pred' is still productive within Circassian (compare /psa/ 'life, breath, soul', whence /psa-a-wa/ 'life-conn-pred', 'alive').

In the Iranian Ossetic one has the variant Æresxaw, clearly related to the Circassian forms. The variants Saræqcæw, Saræqcaw Dedenæg (from Turkic saryq 'turban' (?) [Abaev 1996, 3:36]) support the Proto-Northwest Caucasian */-č̣ʿ(ə)q̇ʿa-/ as being original, but the initial Saræ- remains obscure (see Miller 1929, 1038 for these names).

[8] This is a good example of the chivalric conduct that often emerges in the Nart sagas, despite their overall exotic character. This is more than mere coincidence. There is a case to be made that the medieval chivalry of Europe originated as an elaboration of the mores of war brought in with Sarmatian and Alanic mercenaries during the late Roman Empire (Littleton and Malcor 1994; Littleton and Thomas 1978; Nickel 1975a, 1975b; Bachrach 1973).

[9] This is an unusual way to begin a fight, particularly as in the next sentence the battle shifts to the more mundane ice of the mountain. Further, since Pataraz defeats the eagle by shooting arrows through its wings, which can readily be done from the ground, it is all the more peculiar that he initiates the battle by leaping into the air with his horse. It would appear that the narrator feels compelled to obey an old tradition that places the beginning of this battle, if not its entirety, in the air. In fact, this aerial combat is a striking parallel with the war habits of the Vedic Indra and his followers (Gonda 1960, 56 n. 9).

Further still, this battle with the eagle monster closely resembles the incident in Heracles' eleventh labor wherein he frees the bound Prometheus after shooting the griffin vulture through the heart (Graves 1955, 2:148–49). Graves states that this episode is a moral fable invented by Aeschylus (152 n. 10). Seen in the light of the present Nart saga, the fable might have been a retelling of a Caucasian tale that must have come to Aeschylus from the Greek colonies on the eastern coast of the Black Sea.

[10] The Old Black Brigand is a member of the rival pantheon headed by Paqua. The next name, Soul Taker (n. 11), supports such a theological interpretation. Again, turning to the Rig-Veda, one has a good case for viewing Indra's enemy Vrtra as the head of a rival pantheon. First, Vrtra is polymorphous (Gonda 1960, 55–56). Second, his name is most often treated as a neuter plural in Vedic verbal inflection (ibid., 55), implying that "Vrtra" is a covering term for a host of entities, all of them obstacles and impediments to the activities of the gods and mankind (Benveniste and Renou 1934, 5ff., 27).

[11] Soul Taker /psa-x̌á-x̌ə/ 'soul-mass-take out', "he who takes the soul out (of the body)"; this would seem to be a god of death from the rival Paqua pantheon. He is remi-

niscent of the Vedic demon Vrtra (Gonda 1960, 56) and the Zoroastrian Angra Mainyu, the spirit of darkness and destruction (Puhvel 1987, 94–116).

His soul is protected by the little old woman who, along with the little old man of the Narts, seems to care for the souls of the dead. Her continued survival here assures the hero that his soul will be tended to by the proper divinity and will not fall prey to the Soul-Snatcher of the rival pantheon.

[12] At first glance this sentence seems enigmatic. The raven (/q°aλa-bzə́wə/ 'crow, raven-bird') hovering over Pataraz is therefore a last relic of an ancient emblem of kingship and the faint echo of an ancient story in which the bird brings the hero the magic brew. This odd sentence, therefore, rather than garbled noise, is a precious relic of a remote period, drawing this Circassian tale into a wider Indo-European context. For the role of helping eagles in Indo-European and Semitic lore, see Knipe (1967).

My informant for this story, Rashid T'haghapsaw, found that it made little sense and preferred to see here the term "mountain bird" rather than "crow, raven." In fact, there are a number of tales in which a hero is aided at a crucial point in his quest by a bird. In a Russian fable (Toporov 1968, 119) a hero, Voron Voronovic, literally "raven ravenson," is brought "living water" so that he may defeat a serpent demon. In the Rig-Veda, Indra is brought the magic brew soma by an eagle, sometimes said to be an incarnation of Indra himself (O'Flaherty 1981, 128–31, 148–51). The counterpart to Indra in the Iranian tradition is the Avestan *Varəθagna* (Vrθrayna), 'Vrθra-slayer' ('Vrthra-slayer'). His name is cognate with one of the epithets of Indra, *vrtrahan* 'Vrtra-slayer'. The second incarnation of this Iranian hero is a bird, the /vaθayna/. Further, within the Iranian tradition, specifically Sassanian, the emperor is depicted as having a bird soaring above him, or as having a crown topped with a bird, usually an eagle. I need hardly mention the prominent role the eagle plays in emblems of kingship, the state, and nobility, starting with Rome and continuing in European heraldry. At least within the Slavic, Iranian, and Indic traditions, one can safely assume the existence of an ancient bird that brought the hero the magic brew at the moment of need. The Roman and European traditions of the bird emblem may be a surviving trace of what was in fact a general Indo-European theme.

[13] The /wə́-ʒ'ə/ 'val-increaser-turn', "to turn round and round," is now performed on foot. The dancers accompany themselves with songs about various heroes. This sentence would seem to indicate that at an earlier period this dance was performed as part of a horseback-riding display or horse ritual.

Kevin Tuite remarks (personal communication): "Round dances like the /wə́ʒ'ə/ are performed on solemn occasions throughout the Caucasus. All the performances I have seen have been on foot, not on horseback. On the other hand, before and after the horse race, which takes place during the midsummer Atengena festival at the mountaintop shrine Iremt-k'alo in Pshavi [northeastern highland Georgia], the participants circle the shrine on horseback." I might add that my Circassian colleagues adamantly insisted that such a horseback dance was well within the riding skills of some of their fellows.

[14] This is close to what Indra's mother says of him after he has returned from slaying Vrtra: "[He was] born to slay Vrtra" (Rig-Veda 8.89.5) (see Colarusso 1984b).

¹⁵ The /ӡʸamahn-šʼaróx / 'jaman-wheel', from Persian /čarx/ 'wheel', is usually depicted as a self-guiding discus (see the Ubykh tales "Soseruquo" [Dumézil 1960, 432–50] and "The Death of Soseruquo" (Saga 88), wherein it is called an iron wheel [Dumézil 1957, 1–4]). The discus is common in both the Greek and the Indic tradition. The meaning of /ӡʸamahn/ is apparently "to strike, striking," but it is not attested outside of this compound. Tʼhaghapsaw states that in this tale a large stone, such as a millstone, is meant, and not a discus. The Narts roll this stone up and down a hill for sport.

¹⁶ Perhaps another name for Mount Elbruz, the Circassian is / y-a-yá-šʼa-ra ?°á-śḥa / 'dir-to-let-pass (of time)-gerund ridge-top', the "Eternal Mountain."

SAGA 35 ☙ Bound Nasran

> O Nart Nasran![1]
> Bearded Nasran!
> Your acts have caused great harm.
> You have ignored God's words.
> You have thwarted his deeds.
> O you, accursed by God!
> O the one who was brought up onto the mountain,
> The eagle flies above you.
> Your dog lies by your side.
> Roaring and thundering he dashes against his chains.
> He is bending the pillar to which he is bound.
> A bird flies over you.
> She alights on the pillar.
> You heart fills with malice.
> You yell, making a great noise.
> You aim at the bird with a stone
> And try to throw it at her,
> But your chains wind more tightly,
> And your pillar sinks deeper into the earth.
> The dog, lying near you,
> Gnaws at your chains,
> Making them thinner.
> They become as thin as gossamer.
> They will soon be gnawed away!

All the early-rising blacksmiths
Down in the smithies are good men.
They strike upon their anvils,
And all your chains are restored,
Exactly as they were before,
Until we unshackle you.
May God keep you bound!
May God kill you at the pillar!

From GENEG, 258–61, in Hatiquoya West Circassian.

⌀ This song exemplifies part of the spectrum of Prometheus figures in the corpus (saga 18, and compare Charachidzé 1986). In this one the bound leader is taken as the evildoer himself. This saga shows the strong influence of the binding of Amirani in Georgian tales, especially in the actions of the blacksmiths. *Amirani* is probably derived from the Persian *Ahriman*, in turn derived from the Avestan *Angra Mainyu*, the Zoroastrian "Evil Spirit."

[1] In Hatiquoya the name Nasran (usually /nasrán/) is Nasiran (/nasərán/), but this seems to be a case of a simple vowel insertion peculiar to this dialect. The interlinear refrain is "wi wi," which I have omitted.

Saga 36 ⌀ *An Old Man Chained to Elbruz*

Legend tells that a giant has been chained to the summit of snowy Elbruz for committing sins of some sort. When he awakens, he asks his guards, "Are rushes still growing on the earth? Are lambs still being born?"

His pitiless guards respond, "Yes, rushes still grow and lambs are still born."

Then the giant grows furious. He breaks his shackles, and the earth then shakes as he moves. His chains give off lightning and a roar like thunder. His heavy breathing is the blizzard's gust. His moaning is the underground drone of a raging river, and his tears are its waters as it emerges into daylight at the foot of Elbruz.

From GENEG, 261–62, by Khan Girey, "Mythology of the Circassian People," collected from the newspaper **Kavkaz,** *no. 86, 1846, p. 172.*

☜ This saga is very close to the Ubykh one, saga 91, especially with regard to the questions that the chained giant asks in the latter: "Do the sheep bring forth lambs? Do the honeybees multiply this year?"

SAGA 37 ☜ *A Cyclops Bound atop Wash'hamakhwa*

Once upon a time, long ago, a giant warrior with only one eye in the middle of his forehead[1] dared to try to learn the secrets of God. He found his way to the gap between two mountain peaks, at the very spot where a huge rock emerged from the earth and a crystal-clear spring issued forth. Immortal God did not tolerate such impudence from a mortal man and chained him to this rock by his neck. Many years passed, so that the warrior grew old and his beard turned as white as the glaciers of Wash'hamakhwa[2] and reached to his knees. His once-proud face grew wrinkled.

To further punish him for his insolence, God sent a bird of prey. This eagle pecks at his heart every day. When the sufferer bends down to drink from the spring, the bird swoops down before him and drinks all the water itself, to the last drop.

This spring has a miraculous power. Whoever drinks of it will live to the end of the world. The time will come when God will grow angry with all the sinful children of Adam and will set the one-eyed giant free from his bonds, set him free from the mountain depths. Woe will betide mankind, for he will avenge his sufferings on humanity!

From GENEG, 262–63, told by Talib Kashezh of Kabarda. Recorded by L. G. Lopatinski, Cbornik materialov po opisaniju mestnostyj i plemen Kavkaza *(Collection of material for the description of the regions and tribes of the Caucasus) (in Russian) (Tbilisi, 1891), 12:38.*

[1] Although it is common knowledge among Circassians and their kin that all giants are Cyclopes, this is the only Circassian saga I know in which this is explicitly stated (see page 52).

[2] In Russian *Oshkhamakho,* East Circassian / ʔ°aśḥa-máax̌°a / 'mountain-blessed', "Elbruz."

SAGA 38 ∽ *How Bearded Nasran Visited Ashamaz*

Oh hehaya bearded Nasran!
Our prince t'hamata is in Nartia.
Our golden beard is in Nartia.
Our snowy beard is in Nartia.
Your beard falls to your waist.
The horse's mane flutters.
Poor old Nasran,
His old reddish coat
Is draped over the back of his horse.
He is dressed in a wolf's fur cloak.
Arrogant Nasran,
He is given the best sheep.
All that is weak they lead out to him.
They saddled a horse for him,
And with his dog and eagle
He crossed Brasa Steppe.[1]
He approached the swollen Indil.
"We shall not cross it!"
He sent for a messenger:
"Bring Ashamaz to me!"
The messenger returned
And sat playing in the ashes of the campfire.
"I considered him a grown Nart,
I see instead a suckling babe!
May God grow angry with you!
You should have thought to kill him!"

From GENEG, 347–49, Hatiquoya West Circassian.

∽ Nasran is seemingly an old figure who has had time to develop a range of char
acteristics denied to younger figures, such as Pataraz. This short song captures the
ambivalent status of this old leader.

[1] This steppe is mentioned in saga 31, where it is called Bars.

My Ashamaz,
My Kyatawon![1]
Whose mother will prosper!
You played knucklebones,
Ashamaz,
And won them from the boys,
Making them cry,
Ashamaz.
"If you are such a great guy,
Why don't you avenge your father's murder?"
One said.
"I'll kill you all," cried he.
"Better to let your mother tell you
Who killed your father,"
Another replied.
Ashamaz returned home in tears to his mother.
"May God show his wrath to the house of the one who made
    you cry!"
Said his mother to Ashamaz.
"I am hungry, Mother.
Please make me some hot porridge,
With plenty of good, melted butter, Mother."
For her son she did prepare
Steaming hot porridge with melted butter.
"Please eat with me, Mother!
If you won't, then I won't eat!
I swear it!"
"I'd like to eat with you, my son,
But it isn't our way
To have the women eat with the men," she replied.
"If you don't sit down with me,
I won't even touch it, O dear Mother!"
So his mother did sit down with him,
At which he seized her hand

And plunged it into the steaming porridge.
"If you don't tell me who killed our father,
I'll boil your hand, O dear Mother!"
"May God curse those
Who put you up to this, my son!
It was bearded Tleguts.[2]
He killed your father, Ashamaz!
He lives beyond the sea.
How can you get there?"
"If you don't tell me
About my father's weapons,
I'll cook your hand off, O dear Mother!"
"Your father's weapons
Lie in a great chest, Ashamaz!
If you pull his bow,
You'll break your back, Ashamaz!"
"If I break my back,
Then I'll prop myself up with poles, O dear Mother."
"If you sling it over your shoulder,
Your back will burst into flames, Ashamaz!"
"If I catch fire,
Then I'll jump into the Meweta,[3] O dear Mother."
"If you lift the sword,
It will spring from your hands
And hew you down, my son!"
"My hand knows how to wield a sword, O dear Mother.
If you don't tell me about my father's horse,
I'll boil your hand off, O dear Mother!"
"A millstone rests against the stable door,
Ashamaz.
The best men in Nartia
Could not handle it,
Ashamaz!"
Ashamaz let go of her hand, went out,
And drew nigh to the stable.
He heaved the millstone aside,
And it rolled away down seven roads.
He put his father's saddle on the horse,
Donned his armor, and took up his weapons.

Then he rode off to the sea.
His horse swam across it.
On the far shore he tracked down bearded Tleguts.
He slew him in combat
And avenged his father's blood.
He set Tleguts's wife on his knees
And returned home with his bride.
Ashamaz!

From tales 21 and 22 of GENEG, 349–58, in Hakuchi and Bzhedukh West Circassian, respectively.

This song reflects the conflict inherent between a young warrior, who must seek to maintain his and his family's honor, and his mother, who persists in seeing him as a child. Ashamaz's methods are peculiarly cruel but perhaps commensurate with his mother's determination to keep him at home. A similar and equally cruel act is portrayed in Georgian folklore, where the protagonist places fresh-baked *khach'ap'uri* (cheese bread) against his mother's breast to make her reveal the name of his father's enemy [KT].

Interestingly, if the Circassian *Yamina* 'not stay inside' is a folk etymology, then *Yamina*, Georgian *Iaman*, and Svan *Yaman* [KT] suggest links with Iranian *Yima* and Sanskrit *Yama*, a god of the dead and the underworld (see saga 3 n. 2), ultimately derived from the Indo-European **yemos* 'twin' (see Puhvel 1987, 284–90). These names would then attest to old and deep influences in the Caucasus from the Iranian world.

[1] Kyatawon / kʸahta-w-á-n / 'sword-strike-inward-inf', "self-striking sword," in Hakuchi, GENEG, 349 n. 1, or in Russian, 350 n. 1 (compare with saga 20).

[2] Tleguts / λa-g°ə́-cʻa / 'leg-zone-hair', "hairy legs." This figure is also known as bearded Yamina, or 'cholera' (see saga 7).

[3] The Meweta is the Sea of Azov, in Classical Greek the *Maiotis*, which derives from the Circassian designation / mə-wə́+t'a / 'not-val-dam.up', "not capable of being dammed up," referring to the large neck of water between the Azov and the Black Sea (see saga 2).

1. About Old Amysh:
   His horn, Old Bzhamey,[1] blares loudly.
   Many of his sheep he drives toward a ravine.
   Old Amysh of the Narts is my suitor.
   Even if he pursues me, I won't marry him!

2. About Khimish:
   The fat bulges on his face.
   Sheep mites crawl on his neck.
   Old Khimish of the Narts is my suitor.
   Even if he pursues me, I won't marry him!

3. About Tlepsh:
   Fire sparks in his hands.
   All he sets his hands to is aflame with sparks.
   Patient Tlepsh of the Narts is my suitor.
   Even if he pursues me, I won't marry him!

4. About Sawseruquo:
   His steed Tkhozhey[2] is slightly lame.
   He himself, made of steel, is master of his weapons.
   Sawseruquo of the Narts is my suitor.
   Even if he pursues me, I won't marry him!

5. About Ashamaz:
   His horse is mighty with a white nose.
   He himself is a courageous warrior.
   Yashemuquo Ashamaz is my suitor.
   If this rider comes for me, then I will go with him.

6. Ashamaz's reply:
   Your daughter, Lady, appears lovable at first glance,
   But seven witches taught her.
   You compose mocking couplets about good men.
   Compose what you will about me,
   I don't want you!

You can't sew good needlework.
Your old breasts dangle like an udder.
You're like an old bitch.
I don't want you!

A Kabardian poem from GENEG, 369.

  It is not clear who Lady Lashyn / λahśə́n/ is. This satire is reminiscent of the banter between Setenaya and Warzameg (see saga 4).

  [1] In the original: /bźa-a-mə-yə́-źə-r/ 'horn-conn-derivational.suffix-the.one.of-old-abs,' "The old one with the horn" (?).

  [2] In the original the hero is /sawsrə́q'°a/ 'Sosruquo', as borrowed by Abaza, and his horse is /tx̌°ə-ź-ay c'ək'°/ 'gray-color.suffix-one little', "Little Gray," with the hero's lameness assigned to his mount instead.

SAGA 41   *Hymn to T'haghalej*

T'haghalej's grain,
Do not blight the millet harvest!
He for whom it is not blighted may offer up praise.
It will be the millet of those offering up praise
Which will endure through time and become a field.
The field will thrive for us a thousand-fold,
And may we thrive with it!

From Shaban 1981b.

  This prayer to the god of the harvest in archaic language remains with the Circassian people to this day. It was recorded in July 1981 by Hisa T'harquakhwa, who felt that the name of the god contained a causative verb, something to the effect: /t̪ha-ɣa-λaǯ˭ʸ/ 'god-cause-abundance (?)'. This name has been borrowed into Abaza (see saga 55), however, in the form /t̪haʕ°aλaǯ˭ʸ/, indicating an original */t̪ha-ɣ°aaλa-ǯ˭ʸ/, so that its sense is 'god-wither(of plants)-inst' (compare /ɣ°ə/ 'dry'). Thus, this is originally a blighting god, and the exhortation that he not blight the fields in this hymn, or /x̌°ax̌°ə/ (also the root for 'to offer praise'), makes perfect sense.

SAGA 42 ◌ *The Shiblawuj, a Round Dance to the God of Lightning*

Yeli, Yeli, do not burn our village,
Yeli, Yeli, do not strike the forest of God's grove,
Yeli, Yeli, prolong our life spans, and then
Yeli, Yeli, together we will drink to the old peaceful one.
Yeli, Yeli, taking hold of one another we dance in a circle.
Yeli, Yeli, we dance around the tree of God's grove.
Yeli, Yeli, you all join in the round dance to lightning.
Yeli, Yeli, those who refuse to enter meet great lightning.
Yeli, Yeli, he throws them into the water of God's grove.
Yeli, Yeli, he drowns those who sink to the bottom.

From Shaban 1981b.

◌ This was a Bzhedukh (West Circassian) hymn by the old men and women to the god of lightning in the form of a round dance, which was of a woodland nature. It did not come down to either the highly conservative Abadzakhs or to the Russians. This hymn has extremely close parallels to the one still used to address the storm god Indra in the dance around "Indra's Tree" in rural India (Colarusso 1984b). In both hymns the libation is referred to as "the peaceful one." The name of the storm god, / šʿəbλa /, is also that for "poisonous snake," suggesting an old cultic iconography. (Among the Iroquoian-speaking Huron or Wendat of northeast North America, the sign for lightning was also a snake.) Hisa T'harquakhwa suggested that the word *Yeli*, / yaλǵ /, was actually an old name for "God" borrowed from an ancient Semitic original, *ele or *eli, assuming that ancient Middle Eastern influence had made its way up along the Black Sea coast. Kevin Tuite (personal communication) remarks that "the refrain 'Yeli, yeli' is almost certainly from the name 'Elia' or 'Ilia,' the prophet Elijah, widely worshiped as a sort of lightning or storm god in the Caucasus and the steppes to the north (for example, Ossetic *Wac-illa* [holy-Ilia])." I have kept the refrain capitalized as an invocational name, since this may be a theonym. One Circassian name for Mount Elbruz is / yaλǵ-p'a / 'Yeli-place', that is, "God's place" or "Elijah's place," which is also known in Circassian as / ʔ°ašḥa-maaɣ°a / 'mountain-blessed', the "blessed or sacred mountain."

THE ABAZA NART CORPUS

Translated by
John Colarusso

with the Assistance of
Michael Elinson
on the Russian Translation

Saga 53 Translated by
W. Sidney Allen

SAGA 43 ❧ *The Time of the Narts*

The Narts dwelled in Nart Sana and in the valleys of the Kubina[1] and Indzhig Rivers. They lived openly and at the same time sought no help. Among them were fortune-tellers who used runner beans, diviners who practiced on shoulder blades, sorcerers, and others. The Narts gathered together in a certain place every year and held games there, horse racing, stone flinging, archery, shooting arrows into a hanging egg, horseback riding, snatching things off the ground while riding a horse—either while staying on the saddle or while hanging from one of the horse's sides—rolling a heavy and sharp iron wheel down the hill (which they called *Harama Toba*) and then rolling it up the hill using one hand covered with a chain-armor glove, dancing on the edge of a large round table while trying not to spill any *bakhsima* (a kind of drink) from a bowl that stood in the center, and other games. That was how they amused themselves.

In the Narts' time, the bravest of the Narts, the carriers of courage as legends witness it, were these: Totrash, Tlepshw, Shebantoquo, Ashamaz, Qanzhoquo, Sasruquo, Badinoquo, Tlabitsa, Bataraz, Awzirmag, and others.[2] Among them the one with compassion for the poor, as legends tell it, was Sasruquo. The legends tell not about a few but about many of his feats, about his resolve and his indulgence, about his concern for people and his struggle.

From M-S, text 1, p. 49. Henceforth all sagas are from this collection by Meremkulov [Meremq'°əλ] *and Salakaja unless otherwise noted.*

❧ This short narration is unique in that it places the Narts geographically near the Kuban and Indzhig Rivers in the Northwest Caucasus, the present home territory of the various Circassian tribes, the Abazas, the Karachays, and the Malkars. The shape of the names (see note 2) reflects the strong North Caucasian influences that have reshaped the Abaza corpus since its original Abkhaz-like form.

[1] The Kubina River is the Kuban, the traditional northern boundary of the Circassians and Abazas.

[2] These names deserve some comments. (I have marked stresses.) "Tótrash" is close to the Ossetian "Tótradz," another form of this name in Abaza being "Tútarash," with the variant "Sótrash." "Tlepshw" shows a rounding of the final fricative peculiar to Abaza. All

the names ending in -(o)quo or -(u)quo show the Circassian and Ubykh patronymic '-(his) son', which has replaced the Abkhaz and Abaza (i)pa. "Shebatinóquo" is West Circassian for "Badinóquo," with "she" meaning "hunter." "Badinoquo" itself is usually "Badanóquo" in Abaza. "Sasrúquo" is probably the original form of this name in Abaza (see Abkhaz "Sas-rúquo") and has been replaced with the East Circassian "Sosrúquo." "Tlabitsa" reveals its Circassian origin by its initial lateral affricate, which means "hairy heels" (sagas 10 and 72). In Abaza this name would have been *Shabitsa, which is unattested. "Bataraz" is close to the Ossetian "Batradz," but both come from an original Proto-Circassian */pat´araʒ/, where the initial unaspirated */p/ has yielded /b/ in Kabardian, /bataraz/. The Abaza form is taken from the Kabardian "Bataraz." Both "Ashamaz" and "Awzirmag" show fos-silized definite articles /a-/. The first is normally "Shamaz" and the second "Urizmay," the latter close to the Ossetic "Uryzmæg." "Uryzmæg" appears in various Circassian dialects as "Warzamayg," "Warzamaj," or "Warzamas" (see saga 2) and must itself come from the form *warza-mǎka, borrowed from an Iranian language other than Ossetian. The name would be an adjective (-mǎka) based on the stem *Hwerg- 'to strangle,' as in several Ger-manic legal terms that have an association with strangling or being hanged, such as Old Norse vargr 'wolf, outlaw', Old English wearg 'monster, outlaw', Modern English worry, and even Hittite hurkel 'outlaw, sex criminal' (see Gerstein 1974, 172). "Qanzhoquo" does not appear again in the Abaza corpus. This saga seems to reflect older variants of these names and therefore older influences.

SAGA 44 ✑ The Burial Ground of the Narts

When people came to the place where the Narts' graves were, they saw corn, wheat, millet, and barley, which surprised them.

What they saw there is the result of the following. When they buried the dead Narts, those who wanted to sowed corn on the surface of the grave, others, millet or barley. Many things came up there and so people took them from there. There they found them again, these seeds. After someone had died they brought the seeds there as a symbol of grief. Don't we, when somebody has died, bring food to the grave? This is the same that the Narts did when one of their number died. When somebody was dying, either someone's brother or relative, somebody from the tribe brought a small portion of wheat seeds as a symbol of grief. In another case, it was millet, in a third, barley or oats. That is how these grains be-came known by people.

From text 25, p. 114.

SAGA 45 ⟡ *The Golden Apple Tree of the Narts*

The golden apple tree of the Narts yielded golden apples. And after they had been harvested, they appeared on the tree again. They say that somebody was stealing these apples from the Narts. So they began to guard this tree. Soon three girls flew down, and when they were picking the golden apples, the Nart guards spotted them and wounded one of them.

Her sisters lifted her up and began to carry her. The Narts followed them by the blood, which was on the road. They realized that this girl lived on an island. Her house was located there, and in order to reach her house one had to swim over the sea.

A youth swam there. Soon he saw her, lying there in a very poor state, and her sisters, who were sitting nearby. So he saw all three of them. They say that she was the most beautiful girl in the world.

He approached them and asked, "What has happened to you?"

They answered, "Our sister was wounded and we cannot cure her. Whoever will find a way to cure her will become her husband."

"I will find a way to cure her. I have one," he said. "Rabbit's milk will cure her," he said. "If you can find rabbit's milk."

"But where we can find rabbit's milk?"

So he found rabbit's milk, cured her, and married her.

From text 29, pp. 118–19.

⟡ This is a short version of the Lady of the Sea, saga 3, in which a beautiful maiden and her sisters who live under or across the sea steal some magical apples while disguised as doves. A youth wounds the youngest and tracks her down by the trail of blood she leaves. He falls in love with her and cures her with her own blood. This narration is unique in its use of rabbit's milk instead of blood. The reference to rabbits links it with the tale of Khmish, the father of mighty Bataraz (saga 74), whose dwarfish enemies ride rabbits.

SAGA 46 ◌ *Satanaya*

Sana, that is her name. There is a fluffy flower that they call Satanaya. That is how she named it. "I am naming you Satanaya," said she. "Sana, Satanaya, like me," so she added her name to it and named it with her name. That is what I have heard. Sosran, Urizmay, Hachmaz, and Acha's son Chamaz (the father of Chwadlazhwiya) are Satanaya's brothers.

There is a place called Nart-Sana. Sana of the Narts lived there. Is that the only place where the Narts used to live? From the Azov Sea up to the Caspian Sea, from one side of these places up to the Volga River and beyond to the far side, that is where the Narts lived. I have heard that they also lived in the Caucasus, on the summits of the Caucasus. The Narts had their own country. They lived as a state. Among the Narts[1] of the world, the territory of the Narts was big.

From text 2, pp. 50, and text 33, p. 133.

◌ Here too Satanaya is the preeminent woman of the sagas, as in the Circassian corpus. This saga links her name not only with that of a flower, usually said to be a rose, but also with the magic brew *sana*. Here the name Nart-sana, which in Circassian saga 26 is linked with Lady Amazan, is also linked to her, showing her syncretistic tendencies. This saga also situates the Narts in the southern Russian steppes and the Caucasus.

The fragment (text 33) offers a unique and obscure inventory of what is, for the Abaza corpus, the first generation of the Narts (see saga 47 n. 1). Also unique is the claim that these Narts are the brothers of Satanaya. Only in saga 48 does Satanaya have a brother, Bataraz. Acha is a relic of an earlier generation in the corpus. This generation is more fully preserved only in the Circassian corpus, with the brothers Pija and Pizighash and Lady Meghazash, the damsel from the sea (saga 3).

[1] This odd locution reflects the original Iranian meaning of the name as "hero." In other words, in its older sense this line is to be read: "Among the heroes of the world, the territory of the Heroes was big."

SAGA 47 ❧ *How Sosruquo Was Born*

Satanaya was very beautiful, and everybody loved her very much, but she did not want to marry, although she was asked many times.

One day Satanaya took her belongings and went to the river to wash them. She descended to the river to wash, and as she was sitting on the riverbank and washing, the Nart shepherd Sosa,[1] happened to drive his cattle to the very same river. And once he saw Satanaya, he recognized her immediately. How could he not? The Nart's heart filled with desire for her. You know what can happen to a warrior once something has settled into his heart. "You who are peerless and the only one in the whole world, what would happen if you, with open eyes, glanced at me?" He was standing on the opposite side of the river, and she was sitting on a large stone, washing her belongings. But how could Satanaya grace him with her glance? "O you peerless one, believe me. Nothing could happen to your beauty if you would just look at me with partly opened eyes." But once she glanced at him, he could not hold back. He was very powerful. And as it happens between man and woman, so it happened between them. "Lady Satanaya! It is coming. I can't hold it!" was what he said, but his sperm missed her and hit the stone on which she was sitting.

When it hit the stone, Satanaya grew angry. She was offended, so she took all her belongings, stood up, and went away. When he saw that his sperm had struck the stone, he called to her, "Hey, Satanaya! You have never yet given birth to anybody. Perhaps this stone could one day be helpful to the Narts. Don't leave the stone here. Take it with you."

Satanaya understood the sense of his words, took the stone, and carried it with her to her home. Nobody created by God knew about that, and she did not tell anybody. She wrapped it in felt and wrapped it again. She warmed the stone and put it under the bed. She watched and watched it, and as time progressed it grew larger and larger. The stone made a strange noise in the night. When she went to bed, she could hear this strange sound. Five months passed, six months passed. "Let me check the stone," she said to herself. And then she decided to bandage it with waxed thread. And in the morning after she got up, she saw that the waxed thread was torn. Again she bandaged it, but the stone grew and the waxed thread broke again. The stone was growing warmer and warmer, and after nine months and nine days, it became scorching hot. From then on the stone grew very hot.

Satanaya confided this affair only to the Nart blacksmith Tlepshw. All night she spent thinking, "Now is the time." She knew how many months and days it took for a human being to be born. The stone began murmuring. "What shall I do with it? If Tlepshw refuses to hide me, nobody else among the Narts will do it. He would respect my request. I'd better go and wake him up before the stone starts to crack open." She said that and went to see Tlepshw when he opened his smithy in the morning. Now that the stone was nine months and nine days old, she came.

"Come in, come in, Satanaya," he said.

"I shall come in, Tlepshw, if you can make me a promise. If you can arrange so that the Narts will not know anything about a certain matter, I would like to ask you to do a favor for me."

After these words, Tlepshw became offended. "O Satanaya. I live in this world only for the sake of the Narts. That is it. You need not fear that."

So then she told him everything about the stone. After she had finished her story, he said, "Go and bring the stone right away! We'll have a look. Go and bring it!"

Satanaya ran right off and soon after brought the stone. Tlepshw looked at the stone. The stone was murmuring. The stone started to burn like fire. Tlepshw's hammer was big, and he himself was also huge. For one day and one night he was hammering on the stone, and at last he cracked it open.[2] When the stone was cleaved in two, Sosruquo fell out. After he fell out from there, Satanaya grew very glad and was happy. She grasped the baby, but he was so hot that he fell from her hands because they could not withstand his heat and dropped to the ground. Then Tlepshw grasped him with tongs above his knees. He lifted Sosruquo and plunged the baby into a barrel of water, where his skin hardened like metal. After he dipped Sosruquo in the barrel, the steam covered the whole smithy and one could not see anything. That was how thick Sosruquo's steam was. So Tlepshw continued to plunge him into the water in this way, first heating him in the fire and then quenching him again, seven times.[3] The baby's knees, however, which he held with the tongs, remained soft like ours. But everything else hardened like steel. That's how he tempered Sosruquo. Satanaya then took the child and returned home.

The main body of this saga is taken from text 6, pp. 52–54.

⊙ This account of the impregnation of Satanaya links the fertility figure to a shepherd, much as Greek Aphrodite was linked to Anchises, the King of Shepherds. The Abaza pregnancy is deflected onto a magical rock, fitting for the warrior offspring Sosruquo, whereas in the Greek myth the offspring of the union was born from a tree, more suitable for a god of male beauty. In one account, text 6, pp. 52–54, the romantic shepherd is swimming toward her when he loses control, and in text 3, p. 50, he shoots his sperm at her because he cannot ford the river. Most accounts in the other corpora justify the shepherd's deflected efforts with this limitation.

[1] This name is taken from text 4, p. 51. It is of Iranian origin, reflecting */šwāsā(nam)/ '(of the) breath(s)', with the nasal indicated by the Ubykh form *Sosna* (Sanskrit *sawāsa-*, English *wheeze*) and serving as the basis for *Sosruquo* and for his evil counterpart *Sosranpa*, both built on *Sosran* ← */šwas-āryānam/ 'breath-Aryans' (gen pl), "Breath of the Aryans." Sosran is either a brother of Satanaya (saga 46) or her son, Sosruquo's brother (saga 65). *Sosruquo* shows the Circassian and Ubykh patronymic form, and *Sosranpa* shows the same for Abaza and Abkhaz. One account, text 5, pp. 51–52, has conflated this shepherd with the dueling suitors Arjkhyaw /arǯʸxʸaw/ (also Abkhaz Narchkhyaw /narčʸxʸaw/ or Ubykh Yarichkhaw /yarəčʸx̣w/) and Quizhwi Arpis /q̄°əž°ə arpəs/) (usually Abkhaz Khozhorpish /x°až°árpəs/ or Ubykh Quazherpish /q°ạżarpə́š/, /q°azarpə́š°/), who fights over the beautiful Gunda. This text is unique in that it links the latter dueler to a Quizhwi family who originated from a village that is now occupied by the Karachay. Their appearance here, however, seems to be a confusion of the traditions.

[2] Text 3 (p. 50) has the fetus forming as an outline on the surface of the stone, insisting repeatedly that Sosruquo was born in some fashion from the stone's surface.

[3] This detail is from text 4, p. 51. This text also equivocates over Sosruquo's parentage, putting forward various opinions on whether Sosa is the father and Satanaya the actual mother or whether she took him from a stone or even whether his real mother died and Satanaya raised him as a foster child. Sosruquo is said to have undergone quenching because he was a weak infant.

She, who is called Lady Satanaya, her name is Satanaya—Sana is her name. And they say "Satanaya" because of this: "I give the name Satanaya to this flower," she said, pointing to the flower Nart Sana. Sana, this was her name. She was a girl among them, a female. It was she who was the Narts' fortune-teller. And all that they did, you see, what shall be, that battle, that which shall happen among the Narts, she foretold. Turning to her first, they would tell her the essence of their own affairs. "Is our affair reasonable or not?" they would say before her. She would point them on the way, and they would stay on that path.

There was among the Narts a boy, her uncle's son. Both were sired by two brothers. She was born by one brother and Bataraz was born by another. (He who was called Bataraz was a very strong man.) Once Bataraz set off to hunt. While on his way, he stopped by to seek the advice of Satanaya.

"You see, I am going to a hunting ground. Will I be lucky or not?" he asked her.

She replied, "I shall not tell you."

"Come on, tell me!" he said.

"No, I won't!" she said.

"Why don't you want to tell me?" he added.

"I won't tell you for this reason. Listen to me!" she said. "There is nobody else among the Narts whom I would choose as my husband. You are the only man whom I like. If you agree to become my husband, I will tell you."

"Oh, I wish an abundance to your house! You were born by one brother. I was born by the other. How may that happen between us?" he said. Then he added, "Everybody will be talking about us so much that we will become gossip for the town. No, that will not happen," he said.

"Bataraz!" she replied. "If you decide to ride sitting backward on an ox, it will seem unusual," she said. "If you do it again tomorrow, if you ride an ox on the streets sitting on him backward again, then they would still see it as something unusual. If you do it again the next day, they would consider that less interesting. And on the following day, they wouldn't even look at you, and nobody would talk about you. So, when they first hear about us, they may begin to gossip," she said. "Maybe they will gossip about us. After a short while they will forget about us, because something more interesting will happen by then. If this is the trouble, then I won't tell you." Having said that, she and Bataraz went in different directions.

They parted, went in different ways, and yet she decided that she would win anyway. So later, after Bataraz had returned from hunting, she went to his wife, Bataraz's wife, and asked her to swear that she would do anything she wished. Bataraz's wife did not expect that she would come to her with such a matter. She came to her with a request to do anything she would ask for. "Don't tell Bataraz that I was here. This is first."

"Good! I won't tell him about that," she said.

"Fine! It is night! Go and put him to bed," she said. She went and put Bataraz to bed and then returned to her.

"So, did you put him to bed?" she asked.

"Yes, I put him to bed," she (Bataraz's wife) said.

"Now take all your clothes off and give them to me," she said. "Now, remember, you give me your word that you will sit here and wait until I come back," she said.

"Agreed! I shall be here," she said. She (Bataraz's wife) did not know that Satanaya would do such a thing.

So that night Satanaya put her clothes on and stepped into the room. Bataraz thought that this was his wife, since she had extinguished the light as she had come in. So, that is how Sosruquo was born. Sosruquo belongs to Bataraz.

He was not born from a rock. And how it happened that he was born from a rock will be explained now. Satanaya went to her sister. "Today," she said, "I went to wash my belongings in the Gum River. After I arrived, my beauty tempted our shepherd. 'O, Satanaya! Mine is coming toward you!' he said, and with these words whatever had erupted from him flew toward me. I evaded it, and 'that stuff' somehow hit the rock and got inside it," she said. "It entered the rock." This was said by her.

Thus she took her sister and showed her the rock. She was pregnant at the time. "Now," she said, "you watch it! What will it turn into?" So she began to come and watch this rock. "Honest to God, it is growing bigger and bigger," she said.

The rock itself did not grow. Nothing happened to it. It was lying as before in the same place.

So she secretly gave birth to Sosruquo. After that she had him hidden. Then she went to the smith and gave him a decisive command. She took him with her, brought him to the rock, and demanded that he break the rock. She forced him to break the rock, and it was as if the baby had come out of there. The smith was witness to that fact, having said it was he who took the baby out of the rock.

She herself afterward candidly explained to the smith what had happened to her. "I am also the witness," said her sister. "I went there twice and thrice and personally saw how the rock grew bigger and bigger."

Thus they provided an alibi for her.

That is how the matter is.

From text 30, pp. 119–21.

๑ This saga takes one side of what seems to have been a debate regarding the origins of Sosruquo, claiming that he was sired by his mother's brother, the mighty Bataraz, and explaining away Bataraz's more usual born-of-the-stone origin as being due to trickery and gullibility. This notion of a natural pregnancy for Sosruquo, with the ruse of a stone, occurs in the Ubykh account of Sosruquo's birth, saga 86. Such "cognitive enhancement" in a myth, a retelling that makes it more coherent, goes back as far as Pindar and his *Olympian Odes* [KT].

Here Satanaya again is equated with Sana.

SAGA 49 ๑ *Satanaya and Tlepshw*

The Narts were a tribe of heroes. They were huge, tall people, and their horses were exuberant alyps or durduls.[1] They were wealthy, and they also had a state. That is how the Narts lived their lives. The place where they made solemn oaths was located at the Psekhuba, which in Adyghey and Abkhaz refers to the city of Pyatigorsk,[2] *pse* 'water', *khuba* 'warm', in the steppe above Gum (in Abaza the name of the river Kuma). Psekhuba was the place of their pledging, so they lived there.

There was a smart woman among them by the name of Satanaya. Satanaya from the tribe of the Narts was not married. Should there befall them any sort of misfortune, the Narts would appeal to the wise maiden Satanaya for advice. And she would set them on the right path.

In the time of the Narts people lived longer. Some lived two hundred years, some three hundred years, and some one hundred years. And so lived Satanaya among them, and she was very beautiful. At the same time there was Tlepshw, who was the blacksmith of the Narts. In the Narts' language, in our language, he was called Tlepshw.

Now Satanaya came to Tlepshw and she saw that he was weary. His anvil was made of wood. His hammer was made of wood. In other words, he was not doing well and was growing very tired. Satanaya sat down and fell to thinking, and soon after she came up with an idea. "If he had such and such an anvil and such and such a hammer, the metal iron he makes would be better." With this idea in mind, she made from wood this thing which everywhere is now known as an anvil. She made it from wood, and she also made a hammer, also from wood, with one side of its head flat and the other side rounded. So she made her hammer's head like this and drilled a hole in the middle.

When hammer and anvil were ready, she waited for Tlepshw to close his smithy and go home. Satanaya then appeared there in the night and threw the hammer and anvil into the smithy. In the morning Tlepshw came back and looked around but could not guess where they had come from. After a bit, he realized this should be an anvil and that a hammer. Using one as a model, he made an iron hammerhead and placed it on the handle, and using another as a model he made an iron anvil. Both the hammer and the anvil were invented with Satanaya's help, but Tlepshw did not know that Satanaya had made them.

The next problem was that Tlepshw grasped the hot iron with his bare hands and burned them. He did not know how to grasp the hot iron! So Satanaya came to Tlepshw and she saw how it was. Then one day she was going to the river to fetch some water, and she saw two sleeping snakes lying one on top of another, neck to neck. They were sleeping on the path Satanaya took whenever she descended to the river. Satanaya looked at them with great surprise, and then she made a model of them from wood. Then, with an awl, she pierced the place where the two necks crossed each other. She took the two sticks up and carried them to Tlepshw.

"Hey, Tlepshw! A miracle, a miracle I've brought you," she said. "Look, your hammer is now made of iron. Your anvil is now made of iron. And you yourself are doing fine now. Now if you had an iron copy of these snakes lying one on top of the other, you could grasp the lower ends with your bare hand, and the upper part would be wider and you could grip hot iron with it."

Tlepshw took the two wooden snakes, looked at them carefully, and made an iron copy of them. So the tongs, which can be used to take hot iron, were made by Tlepshw with Satanaya's advice. He made a model of snakes. So that is how tongs came to be.

From text 7, pp. 54–55.

ⓢ This story expands the theme seen in sagas 4 and 5 of Satanaya's inventive, almost scientific spirit.

¹ An *alyp* seems to be a thoroughbred horse, and a *durdul* is a winged one. Both words are of Turkic origin.

² A resort city in the North Caucasus known for its warm springs.

SAGA 50 ⓢ *Sosruquo's Sword*

Satanaya went away, taking with her the infant Sosruquo. She brought the child up. The child grew up very quickly. One year had passed, and the second year had begun. When Sosruquo turned two years old, they collected many knucklebones for him, and he began to play with them. For one or two months he played with the knucklebones. And one day he said, "Nana, I can hear a sound. I don't know what it could be, but I can hear it. I would like to go there to investigate." This sound was a hammer's sound, Tlepshw's hammer. Satanaya and Tlepshw were neighbors.

"Well, my darling," she said, "your time will come and you will go. It is not your time yet," she said. He begged her for two days. Then, after she stepped out, Sosruquo secretly went to Tlepshw.

Even before this Tlepshw would ask Satanaya, "How is Sosruquo? Is he well? How is he growing up?" Satanaya would answer Tlepshw, "Thus and so, he is growing up well." Now when Sosruquo came to him, Tlepshw stared at him.

"Don't you recognize that I am Sosruquo?"

Tlepshw suddenly recognized him and became very glad to see him. "Come, come, Sosruquo, my boy! Why don't you come more often? Aren't you bored over there?" he asked.

"Our mother¹ will not let me come. Otherwise I would have come."

"She will let you. From now on, come more often!" said Tlepshw.

Now this boy was a true warrior, and he liked to see what was going on around him when he had the desire to do so. Satanaya would always say that he was too small. And in this way she was rearing him.

Tlepshw's forge was big. It was as big as a house. One day Tlepshw said to Sosruquo, "Inflate its bellows if you can." Sosruquo took the bellows' handle. As soon as he pulled on this handle, everything around him, fire, iron, and everything else, was blown away.

"Stop it! Stop it, Sosruquo! It is enough! Enough!" said Tlepshw and stopped him.

One day when he was, as usual, at the forge, three youths came to Tlepshw with a scythe. "Tlepshw! We are fighting over this scythe," they said. "Can you forge from it a sword for us?"

"Yes, I can, but you should try to come to some agreement over it," Tlepshw replied and sent them away.

Early each morning Sosruquo would go to Tlepshw's forge, take his anvil, which stood seven layers deep in the ground, pull it up, and put it in front of the smithy doors. Then Sosruquo would return home.

Tlepshw would come to his smithy in the morning. He would find his anvil taken out and lying in front of his door. Tlepshw was surprised. "Who among those living in this world could ever do that?"

While he was pondering this feat, the three bothers with a scythe came to him once more. All three of them were Narts. They came to him. "Tlepshw, we cannot divide this scythe among us. We ask you to make a sword out of this scythe," they said.

"Why are you arguing about this scythe? What is so important about this scythe?" he asked those three brothers.

"What is in it is important," said the oldest brother. "Here I am the oldest. He is the second, and that one is the youngest. This is our youngest brother's scythe. When we begin to mow, for we are mowers, he is always first. When we have just begun from the head of the row, he is already at its end. Then we think this time we will do it. No, he begins and finishes first. We are constantly fighting over that, and we cannot beat him. Finally we decided to take this scythe away from him and ask you to forge a sword from it."

He looked at the scythe. He liked it. He thought it would make a good sword for Sosruquo. He liked it and said, "Fine, I'll do it, but I warn you that when it turns into a sword, you will be arguing even more. It will be better if I make one sword for each of you, and this scythe you can give to me," he said. He argued with them that he would make one sword for each of them and that the scythe he would retain, to make a sword for Sosruquo. "Go home and come back in three days and your swords will be ready!"

"No! We wish one sword made from this scythe," the eldest replied.

Then Tlepshw said, "If any of you can lift this anvil, I shall make one sword from this scythe. Each of you will have three tries. He who can do it, who can pick it up and put it back into its place, that person will get the sword made of the scythe. Otherwise, I shall keep the scythe and make you fine swords from my own steel."

Sosruquo appeared there. He had come to watch. Sosruquo was a little boy. He was just two years old.

First to try was the oldest. He made a great effort, but he could not move it. Once more he tried, but he could not. Three times he tried and three times he failed.

The second fared no better.

Then the youngest brother tried. He moved it. He tried again. He lifted it a little bit. The third time he tried, he lifted it up to his knee but could not hold it, and it fell down.

After it fell down, Tlepshw asked, "Is the scythe mine now?"

"Yes, it is yours. Let it be for your good!"

"Then I shall make fine swords for you in three days," he said. "And now this scythe is mine. Now you may go! Come back in three days!" he said.

While they were talking, Sosruquo said, "Tlepshw! Let me put this anvil back in its place again." Tlepshw did not know it was he, Sosruquo, who had been taking it out of its place.

Then the oldest brother didn't believe he could do it. "He is a baby," he thought. "Go and suck your mother's breast!" he said.

The middle brother said, "Don't tear up your guts!"

The youngest said, "What a foolish little boy you are!"

When they said these things, Sosruquo became angry, grabbed the anvil, and pushed it eight layers deep into the earth. The anvil itself had only seven layers.

"Fine, fine!" said Tlepshw.

The brothers were also very surprised. "Oh," they said, "we have never seen such a strong warrior among the Narts! We have to tell everybody about him. When the Narts have troubles, he can help. Grow up, Sosruquo!" they said and stroked his head, all three brothers, and left the yard. All three decided, "We must tell the Narts this news."

So they went together and began telling everybody this news. "We saw this small boy at Tlepshw's smithy, Satanaya's son." They came to the Narts' council and told them. Those there were amazed after they heard this news. "Who is he? Where does Satanaya's son come from? Satanaya was never married. She does not have a husband. Where did she get her son from?" They were surprised and talked about her and her son.

There was a witch by the name of Barambukh.[2] They sent a messenger to her. And after she received their message, she went to Satanaya bearing her stick.

"You jumped from a dog's nostrils, you prodigal woman! You such and such! You bearer of an evil spirit. You, giving birth without a husband! You, who disgraced the tribe of the Narts!" she said sitting before Satanaya's place and growing angry.

Satanaya said, "Nina,[3] don't scold me! Instead, you had better talk with me about something good," Satanaya said.

Barambukh learned that Sosruquo had been born from a rock, that was the outcome. She harbored bad intentions in her heart. She realized that Sosruquo would become a mighty warrior.

From supplementary text 1, pp. 170–73.

❧ The infant hero reveals his true nature by tearing the anvil out of seven layers of earth and thrusting it back into eight. Nine are mentioned in saga 55. One is reminded of Dante's nine circles of heaven and hell.

[1] Satanaya is the mother of all the Narts. Her subsequent stigmatization for bearing a child out of wedlock is not consistent with her fertility role elsewhere.

[2] *Barambukh* ends in an old suffix, /-ukh/ ((/-əx̌°/), used in women's names; compare Qaydukh (see saga 60 n. 1, saga 77 n. 2). It originally meant 'woman'; compare Ubykh /x̌a-/ 'you' (an old pronominal index used only to refer to a slave girl). It also plays a role in the formation of the Abkhaz-Abaza word for "woman"; compare Bzyb Abkhaz /pḥ°əššba/ ← */p-x̌°ə-šəmc'a-ba/ 'child-woman-woman-name.suffix', /á-ḥ°ša-k°a/ 'the-women-collective', and in the formation of the Circassian word for "daughter," /px̌°ə/ or /px̌ə/. The remaining stem seems to be *Baram-b-*, based on the Iranian name Baram, and a native suffix /ba/ being either the name suffix or a suffix meaning "great." This suffix might also be a reflex of an old */p/ assimilated in voice to the /m/, so that the original would have been */baram-ə-px̌°/ 'Baram-his-daughter', which is its Circassian form.

Baram occurs in the name of the hero of the Shah Nama, Baram gur. The name reflects the Proto-Iranian *vrthraghna vazra*, cognate with Sanskrit *Vrtra-han vajra* 'Vrtra-slaying lightning bolt', an epithet of the storm god Indra, who killed the serpent demon Vrtra, whose name means "strangler" (Sanskrit *vr-*, English *worr(y)*; Sanskrit *-(t)ra*, English *-er*).

Thus, this witch seems to have an interesting history behind her. She has a parallel in the nurse who betrays the infant Pataraz (saga 31). See also saga 10 n. 5 and saga 64.

³ Hypocoristic term for "grandmother."

SAGA 51 ☙ *How Sosruquo Attended the Council of the Narts*

The Narts were very cruel to one another. They were envious of one another. They disputed among themselves over who was the most courageous. But most of all they hated Sosruquo. They hated him for these reasons. "A rock gave birth to him. He is the son of a rock, illegally born a mere shepherd's son. He will take away our distinction in courage, take away our mark as champions from us." That was what they said, and that was why the Narts did not like Sosruquo.

But Sosruquo loved his people, and he did not do anything for himself. The people's affairs were his fate. Sosruquo had never done anything but help the Narts. Sosruquo became a youth. He would grow up to be a respected man. While still a youth, he decided to ask Satanaya about a meeting that was being held by the Narts.

"So, Satanaya. What have I seen in my life? I don't have a friend. I haven't seen anything yet in this world. I haven't attended a single council of the Narts. And besides, I feel that I don't really know my people, the Narts. I am going, if you permit it, to attend such a meeting. It is impossible for me not to go."

"Wait a minute, my little boy. It is indeed true that they have a meeting on that day, but listen, you are not an adult yet. Many of them will become angry with you. You will make many enemies among them. The Narts are heroic people, but you are just a grown-up boy."

Although she said no, he would not leave her alone about that.

"Well, then," replied Satanaya, "I'll go and ask for their permission. I shall go and I shall ask them if they would agree to let you stay with them. I shall inform you. Wait awhile," said Satanaya and went to the Nart council. And when all of them had gathered together, she entered.

"Come in, come in, Satanaya," they said and invited her graciously. They welcomed her, but Satanaya would not take a seat, although they offered one to her. So they could not make her sit down.

"I came to you with a request," she said. "I have a little boy. All of you know him, he who is called Sosruquo. He is my little boy. Nothing would happen to you if you harbor nothing in your hearts against him. Let him come to the threshold only. Let him learn your customs. Let him find a friend here and become acquainted with your etiquette. Let him be here."

After she had spoken, Totrash thought and replied, "If we began to invite such babies here, then they would take away our Nart places."

"Nothing would happen in the worst case. If you want anything, ask him to bring it and he will bring it. Let him come here, I beg you."

Another Nart stood up and said, "If we were to invite him to whom a rock gave birth, then he would soon start driving us out of here."

"If nothing else, he can clean your horses," she said and asked them one more time.

Yet another stood up and said even more harshly, "It is not possible for him to come here at all. We haven't yet seen his courage; we haven't yet seen his power. He is, so to speak, not yet ready to walk. How can he be seated among us?" he said, objecting.

She turned to go back home, feeling as though a bee had stung her on the head. But as she was about to leave, some of the Narts said, "Nothing indeed would happen. Let him come! We'll see what kind of a man he is."

"Well, even if he comes, let him stay on the far side of the threshold," said those who didn't want him to come at all.

They always held a great feast during their councils. At these feasts they engaged in mock fights with each other. They shot from their bows. They slaughtered cattle. They slaughtered sheep. Besides that, there was an *ayshwa*[1] and they danced on it, on the top of it. They climbed up its three legs, which an ayshwa has, and danced on top.

Now when they had agreed that she could bring Sosruquo, Satanaya returned home.

"So, Mother, did you bring good news?" asked Sosruquo.

"Well, I brought the following. Totrash stood up and said that and that,[2] so be careful with him. Now when you go there be careful. Greet them politely and remain at the door. Then you'll see what they say."

"Well, that's not very good, but we'll see what happens."

He confidently mounted his horse and set off for the council. He arrived, greeted the Narts, and remained standing at the threshold. They looked at him. The boy whom they saw had a beautiful face. He was big. They could tell that he was a hero, a warrior by his build. They invited him in and then brought him to the edge of an ayshwa.[3] So he learned of their affairs. He had seen their council. He had heard their decisions. He had also found himself a friend. And they in turn had seen Sosruquo, but Totrash, Pshey, and Vagwaj were not pleased with him.

"Narts," said Sosruquo on his way out, "there is nothing in this world of which I am afraid, there is nothing in this world which I would like to have, and there is nothing in this world of which I am ashamed. I am not aware either of cowardice or of shame, but there is not and never will be in this world a man from the Narts for whom I would not offer my life protecting him. Narts, tell me why you do not like me! Why do you reject me?"

Pshey turned around and said, "You, Sosruquo, are not from us. That is one thing. Besides that, nobody has ever witnessed your courage. You are just at the beginning of the road, and you have not yet done anything for the Narts. Such people, like you, who have not done anything for the Narts, who are just beginners, we do not invite here, where we hold our councils. Besides, what do you know at all about this world?"

"Narts, although I am at the beginning of the road, there is hardly one place around here with which I am not familiar. There is nothing that I do not know. Today I can challenge anyone here for anything he wishes," said Sosruquo.

"If so, then fine!" They then took the ayshwa and placed a sheep on it. They slaughtered the sheep, and when it was thrown into the cauldron, Pshey shot his arrow into the sky. After the meat was cooked they took it out of the pan, and then his arrow returned, hit the ayshwa, and thrust it into the ground.

"Did you finish your shooting?" they asked Pshey.

"Yes, I did. And now let Sosruquo shoot."

He readied himself and then shot. After he had fired his arrow, Pshey ordered them to slaughter and cook a cow. This they did, and after the meat was ready they ate it. But Sosruquo's arrow had not yet fallen back. And Sosruquo himself sat silently near the ayshwa. Long after, they saw Sosruquo's arrow come back, hit the ayshwa, and thrust it so deep into the ground that nobody could find it. So they concluded that Sosruquo beat them, the Narts, because he was more powerful. That was what they realized.

"Well, you beat us in this, Sosruquo. Now, let us dance!" Totrash jumped on the ayshwa, which was covered with food, and began to dance, but while dancing he stumbled and all the food fell to the ground.

They placed the food on the ayshwa again, and Sosruquo jumped on it.

He finished his dance without even touching the food and then jumped down. After that they gave Sosruquo a present.

"This present belongs to you, Narts. I did not come here for a present. I came here to show you my courage and power," said Sosruquo, and he returned to Satanaya.

"What did you see, my little boy? What did you hear?" Satanaya had *jarsin*, the ability to see from afar, so she knew everything that happened round about.

"O Mama," he said, "I could not find anyone there who could play with me, and I could not find anyone there who could fight me. I have not met such people there." After he said this, Satanaya understood that there was nobody who could beat him.

From text 8, pp. 56–58.

  Trickster figures abound in myths. In the Nart sagas Sosruquo is usually a trickster with evil overtones to his character, reminiscent of the Ossetian Syrdon (see Dumézil's comparison of the Ossetian Syrdon and the Germanic Loki [1948]). This saga, however, sets out the saintlike character of Sosruquo, peculiar to the Abaza corpus. One byproduct of Sosruquo's exaltation is his expansion into the roles that in other traditions are filled by other heroes. The inventory of Narts is thus impoverished in the Abaza tradition.

[1] *Ayshwa* is a Circassian borrowing, / a-y-ś°a / 'the-flat surface-dance', "that upon which one dances," alluding to this famous challenge. The usual Circassian word is / ʔana / .

[2] "That and that" is a common phrase in all the languages of the Northwest Caucasian family and denotes either indifference toward or contempt for something that has been said. Here it expresses Satanaya's contempt for Totrash's words.

[3] There is some confusion between the Circassian form of the eating table, which is round, three-legged, sometimes made of leather, and just big enough for one person and the Abaza form alluded to in this tale. The Abaza variant seems to have been a larger, Arthurian round table, capable of accommodating Sosruquo as well as the rest of the Narts.

One day the Narts set out on a quest. After they had gone some distance, one half of them suggested that Sosruquo join them, and the other half refused. Those who opposed Sosruquo finally won. And soon the troops moved away without him. But Sosruquo guessed that one half of the Narts wanted him to be with them regardless of the other half, and so he decided to follow them.

They traveled far, and soon it grew very cold, witheringly frosty. The cold came on them in the middle of their journey. They had no fire, and without fire they were faring poorly.

Sosruquo appeared before them. "Not all of them want me here, but some do. If some do, I would like to be useful to them," he said to himself, and he came closer to the group and greeted them. He turned to them with a question, "Are you cold? How has it so happened that you are without fire?"

They answered, "It so happens that we cannot find fire around here and we cannot get it. Where can we find it? Where can we go? Nobody can help us. Only you can help us. And if you cannot, we will perish."

When they said this, Sosruquo began his quest for fire. "There may be a chance, so try to hold on until I come back. If there is any kind of fire in this world, I will get it and bring it back to you." Saying this, he rode off on his horse and went far away.

He traveled far, and soon he found himself on a mountain. He glanced down and saw a light. He went toward this light, never taking his eyes off it. It was far even for Sosruquo, but he had an exceptionally good horse. He drew closer and closer to the fire, until he came to an *ayniwzh*, a one-eyed giant, who was lying down before a fire in a cave.

"Live long, Ayniwzh, and be healthy!" said Sosruquo and drew near him. The ayniwzh invited him to sit down and Sosruquo began to look around. Near where Sosruquo was sitting were two men and some sheep inside a huge round rock. Sosruquo guessed that there were people in it, but he did not ask the ayniwzh who were. Soon the ayniwzh started to chat with Sosruquo, and Sosruquo in turn started to think what he could do to avoid raising any suspicion in the ayniwzh.

Soon the ayniwzh grew very sleepy and said, "I had better lie down and have some sleep. Meanwhile, you may stay here. Have a rest, and afterward we shall continue our talk."

Sosruquo agreed to that and remained near the ayniwzh. Soon the ayniwzh fell into a deep sleep. Right after that Sosruquo went up to the rock. He looked through an opening in it. He saw the two men inside and the sheep. He then whispered to them, asking, "Why are you here?"

"He captured us and brought us here. He has already gobbled up our friends. They are gone. And soon our turn will come," they said in misery.

Sosruquo went back to his place. Looking around, he found a huge spit belonging to the ayniwzh. He grabbed it and placed it in the fire. After the spit became scorching hot, he took it out, directed it into the ayniwzh's only eye, and burned it outright on the spot. At that instant the ayniwzh jumped up, but it was too late. The ayniwzh began to roar, rush about, and shatter stones around him. After a while he grew quieter and sat down in his cave in despair, hitting his head against the wall over and over again.

Then the ayniwzh went to his stony sheepfold and began to free all his sheep, stroking each one of them. He was doing that not for the purpose of counting them but to find the two men who were hiding among the sheep. And if he found one of them, he would kill him. That is why he was stroking his sheep.

And when he began doing that, Sosruquo[1] thought, "If he finds us, he will kill us." Then he had an idea. Sosruquo and the men caught two sheep and hung one man between them. The ayniwzh stroked the sheep that was closest to him. The second man did the same. He suspended himself between a pair of sheep and so won his freedom as well. That is how the two men escaped. Sosruquo, meanwhile, took the ayniwzh's fire and returned to his troops.

The ayniwzh grew enraged and said, "I could not find them." So he stumbled off in pursuit, grabbing huge stones and throwing them in the direction of any noise these men made while running away. Whatever happened there, they finally ran away from him, and none of the stones hurt them.[2]

From text 11, pp. 68–70. M-S has two other texts about the return of fire, 9 (pp. 59–62) and 12 [22 sic!] (pp. 70–74). Both are variants of the saga (57) in which Sosruquo tricks a giant who is curious about the hero's habits and eventually slays him, also returning with fire. The return of fire is clearly grafted onto these, and they have been incorporated in saga 57.

ᴐ This saga is one of the Prometheus myths vividly depicted in the Caucasus. The circumstances and even the boon brought back vary enormously, attesting to the antiquity of this theme in the region. This saga is unique, however, in that it is wedded to a striking variant of the Odysseyan tale of Polyphemus, in which Odysseus and his surviving crew escape from the cave of a Cyclopean giant, here an ayniwzh, / a-yn-əž° / 'the-big-evil (one)', Circassian / yənə-ź / 'big-evil (one)'. These giants are commonly thought of as one-eyed, but this is the only Abaza tale that explicitly states this (see saga 37). Here only two of the "crew" survive, and Sosruquo plays the role not only of Prometheus but also of an otiose Odysseus. Links between the Ancient Greek trading cities along the Black Sea coast and the ancestors of the Northwest Caucasian peoples (Ascherson 1995, ch. 2) undoubtedly led to extensive borrowings and influences in the myths of both peoples (see the comments in saga 26 and especially saga 34).

[1] Here the text omits Sosruquo and attributes these thoughts and subsequent actions to the two men. Clearly Sosruquo has entered this myth late and has displaced Odysseus as the clever hero.

[2] I once heard a variant of this tale, told by a young Circassian in Vienna (see the end comments of saga 34). Instead of a cave, the giant's lair was a huge hollow tree. One of the two men blinded the Cyclopean giant with a spit, and then they escaped by clinging to the giant's sheep. They ran across a glacier, and the blinded giant threw stones at them in vain but could not pursue them because he could not negotiate the ice. Sosruquo was absent from the tale.

This young man, Adnan Saygili (Circassian Zhazky Atnan), had heard neither of Cylopes nor of Odysseus nor of Ulysses.

SAGA 53   ᴐ How Sosruquo Brought Back
the Seeds of the Millet

One day Sosruquo said to his mother, Satanaya, "Our mother, please prepare something to eat for me for my trip. I would like to see this world for a while and then I'll come back."

She prepared some food for him, and he, without much trouble, began his trip to see the world, to study new lands and places. But soon after he had set off, the Narts received a letter from the god of the harvest, T'haghadlej.

"I have grown old and helpless. I have no strength anymore. I kept your millet seeds as long as I could. You had better keep these seeds near yourself. Take care of them! Be careful with them! You know how many times the ayniwzhes have tried to steal them. But they couldn't get them from me. They may steal them from you after I pass away."

Thus he gave his will to the Narts. He also gave them a wineskin full of real millet seeds. And this millet had a special quality. By using just one seed one could prepare a whole cauldron of beer. That's how strong this millet seed was. T'haghadlej gave it to the Narts. The Narts held a meeting and decided to build a copper barn and ask the strongest of the Narts to take care of it.

In that ancient time, an ayniwzh lived at the edge of the world. Nobody from the Narts could ever reach his house. He had long coveted these seeds. Nobody in the world had ever been able to defeat him. T'haghadlej was aware of that. When he gave out these seeds from his hands, this ayniwzh realized that now he could steal them. He could not have stolen them from T'haghadlej.

When the ayniwzh became aware of that, he did not reveal it for a week. He did not reveal himself to the Narts. The ayniwzh hid himself, and when a week had passed, on one of the nights when it became dark, he came to their barn, killed the caretaker, cut the barn in half, stole the seed, and ran away. In the morning when the Narts awoke and got together on the street, they began to say to one another, "What was it last night? What a strong noise! As if the sky fell down!" Didn't they know that this powerful noise had erupted when their barn was destroyed by the ayniwzh? But soon everybody knew that he who had guarded the barn had been killed, that there were no seeds in the barn anymore, and that their barn was destroyed. The Narts called a meeting.

At this meeting they realized that their seeds had been stolen by the ayniwzh. Helpless were they! Didn't they know where this ayniwzh lived? They came to Satanaya and said, "This is what happened to us, Satanaya. Those millet seeds which T'haghadlej had guarded and then given to us, this is what has happened to them. The caretaker was killed and those seeds are stolen now. And where the ayniwzh lives, where his house is, we do not know," they said and asked her to give them advice.

Satanaya said, "You think of Satanaya only when your affairs go badly.

When everything goes well, you do not know Satanaya. When you become helpless, nobody but Satanaya can help you." That is what she said to them.

"Well, even so, do not let us die from hunger! Do not destroy our tribe! It cannot be that you would not tell us! If you really know something, tell us! We live here only for your sake, Satanaya."

"I shall tell you," she said. "If you have somebody who will dare to go there, I will tell you where he lives. His place is such: If you have a man who can cover a long way without stopping, from sunrise to sunset, then you may have these seeds again. Should you not have such a man among you, you will never again have these seeds."

"How far is it? We do not know who can reach such a remote place," said the Narts.

Pshey said, "I swear here, with the name of God, one can destroy his feet and be forever boneless after such a trip."

Another Nart stood up and said, "Well, if you can, then go. If you cannot, do not go. But that is the place where he lives."

While they were discussing it, Satanaya turned around and went home. When Sosruquo returned home from the Laba River, he saw that the Narts were holding a meeting. As he passed by, he thought, "What might be the reason?" He soon met one of the Nart boys at the edge of the village. When he asked him what kind of meeting was going on, the boy replied that their seeds had been stolen, that an ayniwzh had stolen them, and that he had killed the guard. "These are the reasons the Narts are holding a meeting, and they are now looking for a man who would go there, to the abode of the ayniwzh."

Sosruquo said nothing. He went straight home. He arrived home and had something to eat. "Mother, please help me get ready for a long trip! Tell me where this ayniwzh lives, and send me to him!" That is what he said.

"Why do you need it, my boy? You will not be able to reach his place. Nobody can reach his place."

"I am not talking about that, Mother. Just tell me where it is and the rest, whether I will make it or not, leave with me," said Sosruquo.

"Forget about that, my dear boy! There is no need for you to go there."

"The Nart man does not renounce his words. You must tell me. It is impossible for you not to tell me. I am a Nart. I am a man," said Sosruquo. "And if a man from the Narts has made a decision, he will not renounce it."

"Then, my boy," she said, "if you think you can make it, you must over-come sixty mountains on your way, from sunrise until the sun reaches late morning.[1] From late morning until midday, you will cross sixty rivers. From midday until sunset, you will cross three big seas. When you cross these three seas, you will see the place in which the sun sets, in a big val-ley. You should go up to its edge, and as soon as you reach there, you will see a fort where he lives. Now think about that again, whether you can go or not."

"Mother, from sunrise to midmorning is one step for me. From mid-morning until midday the bridle on my horse may get just a bit loose. And I hope I won't have to hit my horse at all until the very evening."

"Sosruquo, whatever or whomever you encounter on your way, either an animal who lives in the forest or water or a man, do not hurt him. On the contrary, if he needs help, help him." That is what Satanaya advised Sosruquo. "Now go! And good luck!" she said, and Sosruquo set off.

He went out and he crossed sixty mountains, sixty large rivers, and three seas. In the evening, when the sun was ready to set, he saw the picture Sa-tanaya told him about, and he stepped up to the edge of the valley. A woman from the Narts happened to live with the ayniwzh who had stolen the millet seeds from the Narts. He had stolen this woman a long time ago. After he had brought the seeds to his place, he forced this woman to stand guard. Every God's day he forced her to look around.

The ayniwzh had a fort. The fort was of such a nature that neither horse nor man could get inside it. The fort was very high and surrounded by barbed wire, and it was flat on top. Nobody but pigeons, birds, and the ayni-wzh himself could get inside. That was the kind of abode this ayniwzh had.

As Sosruquo rode into this land, it was the time when the ayniwzh was preparing to plow his land and sow the millet seeds. His lookout, this woman, climbed the watchtower from where she used to scan the sur-roundings. She looked around and soon saw a rider. She looked more closely. If this rider encountered a mountain on his way, he climbed it. If he met a forest, he jumped over it. If he faced a ravine, he jumped over it as well. If he saw a river, his horse and he himself together drank all the water out of it. There were a lot of fruit trees along the way, so Sosruquo ate apples and pears as he traveled. He also ate grass and plane-tree nuts. Deeper and deeper he penetrated into the ayniwzh's land. This woman quickly turned around and went to tell the ayniwzh.

"A lone horseman is coming, and I do not like the manner of his riding."

"Go and look again! Try to notice what kind of water he drinks, what kind of fruits he eats, the way he prefers to go, and the road he follows," he said and forced her to return to the tower.

"He drinks clean and foul water. He eats sour and sweet fruits. He jumps over mountains and ravines. That is how he travels. His horse moves by air. That is how it is," she said, returning and telling him again.

"Oh, I do not like the way he travels! He is not like the others who have tried to come here before. His manner bodes not well," said the ayniwzh and began thinking. "Well, I think nothing really bad can happen after all. Ninety-nine heads are placed on ninety-nine stakes. You, woman, know about that. His head will make one hundred. My double-edged sword, which hangs on the gates, will not let him in. As soon as he enters, it will cut off his head. And you, woman, right after that, go there and place it on one of the stakes! I am going to plow my land," he said and took a jar with the seeds of the millet, straddled his horse, rode off, and climbed the mountain.

Soon Sosruquo approached the gates. He bore a sword, which Tlepshw had made for him. It was neither long nor short, but of medium length. He drew closer to the gates. A sword was hanging on the gates. Not even a fly could pass it. He pulled a hair from his horse's tail and threw it. No, it could not get through. Then he said to his sword, "O sword made by Tlepshw during ten days and ten nights! You, Tlepshw's sword, if you fail to beat this unknown sword, it will be an honor neither for Tlepshw nor for me, Sosruquo, for whom you were made. Let all power gather in you!" he said.

Tlepshw's sword withstood the blows of the ayniwzh's sword. Sosruquo smashed this sword and entered the fort. As he entered, he met the woman. He peered closely at her. "You are from the Narts. Who is living here?" he asked.

"What do you need from him who lives here? What do you want? You must be a Nart man. What did you come here for? Do not ask who is living here, but better turn around and go home," she said.

"Oh, no, I am a Nart man and I need to see him who lives here."

"Well, he is not here right now. He has stepped out somewhere."

"Well, I shall wait. Tell me how you happen to be here," asked Sosruquo.

"That is what happened with me. That is how I came here," she said. "And ever since I have no chance to return home. I am a woman. I am a Nart," she said.

"Well, that is good. I am a Nart as well. Now, can you tell me, does he have the Narts' seeds, the Narts' millet? Tell me the truth!"

"Yes, he brought it, and right now, as we talk, he is plowing his land. And he has all these seeds with him, but you had better not go," said the woman.

"What is the best way to reach the top of the fort?" Sosruquo asked her.

"There is none. Nobody is able to climb this fort, neither horse nor man."

"You had better stop talking like that," said Sosruquo. His horse was gray. "Hey, Gray! If you fail to jump to the top of the fort, you should not have been my horse at all," he said. He struck Gray, and his horse, in an instant, jumped to the top. While there, Sosruquo saw on the other side the ayniwzh plowing his land, and the jar with seeds was standing on an oak stump. And tied to it with a long rope was the ayniwzh, plowing.

Sosruquo [rode to that distant field in a flash and quietly crept up to that oak stump. Then he] grabbed the jar with seeds and ran away. So he started on his way home. He rode and rode and rode.

The ayniwzh soon realized what had happened. "Oh, son of a dog!" he said. "He has taken the millet seeds and is returning home." He unharnessed his horse, came back home, had a rest, had dinner, then saddled his horse and began chasing him.

Sosruquo had not yet covered one-third of his way when the ayniwzh caught him and rammed him with his horse's chest. Sosruquo and the jar of seeds were knocked to the side.

"Hey, you, Nart, son of a dog!" he said and grabbed the jar of seeds and galloped away.

Sosruquo stood up, cleaned himself off, caught his horse, and began to chase the ayniwzh. Sosruquo was of steel. The ayniwzh had hit him and had thought that Sosruquo was killed, but Sosruquo was chasing him again.

When the ayniwzh came home he began to boast, "Ha, ha, this milk-sucker Nart wanted to take the millet seeds away from me!"

Sosruquo waited until the ayniwzh had started to plow again, and then he entered his yard.

"Did I not warn you? Go home! Go home! He will not leave you alone," she said.

"No, he left me alone. He thought I was dead. Now, you can do a favor for me. When he returns home, start to weep and ask him where his soul is hidden."

"Good!" said the Nart woman.

Sosruquo left the yard and hid himself somewhere. The ayniwzh had plowed as much land as he could and returned home in the evening.

When he returned home, she prepared dinner for him and said, "You sometimes go out and do not come back for two or even three months. When you go plowing you stay there a week, and I am alone for days, sitting here and talking to the trees. Tell me please, where is your soul kept?"

"And then you will tell it to Sosruquo, the milk-sucker," said the ayniwzh.

"You have killed him, haven't you? Besides, what do I need this Nart for? You, ayniwzh, are my Nart and my husband. Whether he is a Nart or somebody else, I do not need him at all. I live in this world only for you. I have no business with him."

"Well, in that case, my soul is in this door."

The next morning the ayniwzh went out to plow again. While he was out, his woman painted the door with golden paint. She decorated it and made it very beautiful.

The ayniwzh returned home in the evening. "Oh, why did you do that? Why did you spend so much time?" he said.

"Come on! Look how nice it is now! I shall make it even better. There is nothing else in this world, save only your soul, to be taken care of. You will see how much nicer I will decorate your soul tomorrow."

The ayniwzh laughed. "Oh, no! I fooled you. My soul is not here," he said. There was a stump in his yard. "This stump is my soul, my death. Inside it is my soul," he said.

"Oh, how unfortunate I am! Why did you lie to me? Is there not enough grief in my life? Had you told me that your soul is here, this stump would not be standing here half broken." She started to decorate the stump the very next morning. Soon she made it very beautiful. When the ayniwzh came back home in the evening, he found a nicely decorated stump.

"What have you done to it?" said the ayniwzh. "Now, I trust you, and I am sure that you are candid with me, but again I lied to you, and now I shall tell you the real truth. I shall tell you in truth where my soul is hidden. Nobody in this world has yet been there. Myself, I was there only once. Only once I had a chance and went to see where it is. I haven't been there twice. There is nobody in this world who would dare to go there. Now you will know where it is," he said.

"Oh, why did you torture me? What would have happened if you had told me that before?"

"In that land, in that place a woman has a horse that does not have a match in the whole world. There is a mare in her herd, my steed's mother. She is destined to foal twice. When she foaled the first time, she gave birth to my horse. She will foal one more time, and the next horse she will give birth to is my death.[2] There is not a single man in this world who would dare to go there," he said.

"Who in that case can reach this place? How can I reach this land if I need to? How would I find it?"

"If you want, you can go. If not, don't go, but that is the place where my soul is. That is where it is," he said and left to plow.

Soon after he left, Sosruquo returned. "So, did he tell you anything?"

"Yes, he did." She related what the ayniwzh had said to her.

"That is good. Now, I shall go, and sooner or later I will come back. And now I go. I shall not come back without it."

"Hey, wait a minute, Sosruquo!" (for now she realized that he was Sosruquo). "What about the millet's seeds? If he sows all of them, what will you take back with you?"

"Do not worry! I have already finished with the land that he is now plowing." Sosruquo had prayed to Allah for whatever needed to be done. "Oh, Allah, freeze his land so that he cannot do anything with it!" The next moment all his land became frozen and the ayniwzh set off for home.

"As long as I am away from here, he will not be able to plow his land," he said and rode off.

He had one gourd of *khampal*, a kind of mush made from corn or wheat flour, and a piece of meat in his bag. He set off on his gray horse. His trip seemed endless. Finally, he grew tired and found himself in a remote forest, where not even a single bird could be seen. As soon as he left this forest, he encountered a very skinny wolf, very helpless. All his ribs could be counted.

"How are you, Sosruquo?" the wolf said. "Oh, my God, look at me! I am dying of hunger. Can you feed me anything?" he asked Sosruquo.

So Sosruquo gave him his khampal and piece of meat.

"Thank you very much, Sosruquo! I wish you good luck on your trip. Should you be in trouble, I will help you as best I can," said the wolf, and he took the khampal and meat and ran off into the forest.

When he had passed this forest, Sosruquo entered a land that stood by a sea. Suddenly a wave came ashore and a fish washed up. Sosruquo rode past it, but then he recalled his mother's advice. He turned back and threw this fish back into the sea.

The fish swum about and said, "Good luck, Sosruquo! Should you be in trouble, either at the beginning or at the end of the day, call me! I will help you." Then it swam off into the sea.

After the fish, he heard a noise in the air. He saw one eagle trying to eat another. "One eagle is eating another! What could this be?" He drew forth one of his arrows, shot it at the attacking eagle, and killed him. The other eagle dropped from the sky and alighted on Sosruquo's head.

"Sosruquo," said the eagle, "all my brothers to whom my mother gave birth have been eaten by this eagle. I was the last one in this world. He would have eaten me had you not saved me. If you become helpless, call me! I will come back," and he flew away.

After all of these, he came to the land of the old woman who had a herd of mares. The whole land was divided into parts. One part was protected by wolves. Beyond that was a part protected by eagles. All the wolves and eagles were under her rule. They lived in accordance with her law. Now he went among them, and they began to fight him. They would not let him enter their lands. He turned around and retreated into the forest, where he proceeded to kill a bear and a lion. Then he hung their carcasses on both sides of his horse and galloped forth on his horse through their lands. The wolves and eagles attacked him, and each time they bit, they bit into the flesh of the killed animals instead of him and his horse. He finally made it and entered the land of that old woman.

He saw her lying in the sun on one of her hills. He stealthily approached her, grabbed her breast, and sucked on it for a little while. After that, he hid himself on the other side of the hill.

Soon the old woman awoke and opened her eyes. She stood up, looked down at her breast, and began swearing. Her old breast was in milk. "Oh, dogs! Damn you! May you live only until tomorrow! May you become blind and may your heart be damned! And may your dreams be damned also! Who did it? Oh, if only one of my eyes could see him!"

Sosruquo waited for a while, and then he appeared before her. "Let your eyes be better than ever, your heart nicer, and your lifetime longer! It was I who sucked your breast," he said and came closer to the old woman.

She had to adopt him.[3] She made him her son, and then she took him with her and asked, "Why do you always follow me? How did you come here? No one before has had the luck to come into my land. Tell me, why did you come here?" she said.

"Well, I came here to ask for cattle," he said.

"But are my cattle better than yours? There is none that is better than yours. And besides, I do not have cattle to give away. My real wealth is the three horses," she said. "Three days and three nights I shall let you pasture them, and if you can drive them back unhurt and alive, I will give you a present, some cattle, which I do have for such an occasion. And you can choose any kind you want."

"Fine," he said. Then on the first night he took all her horses into the steppe. He took them into the steppe and at first had no problem taking care of them. By sunrise, however, all the horses had run away into the forest and disappeared. There was a huge stump in this forest. Sosruquo leaned on this stump and began to think of what to do.

Suddenly he heard a voice, "Hey, what are you thinking about? Why is your soul in deep grief, Sosruquo?" It was the wolf.

"The problem, Wolf, is that I was to guard the horses of the old woman, and now all the horses have run away. I cannot find any of them and do not know what to do."

"Well, that is not good. Calm down! Stay here and wait for me!" He ran away and soon drove all the horses out of the forest.

Soon morning arrived. "So, do you have all the horses here? Let us count them." He counted. All the horses were there.

"Now you can drive them home," said Wolf, and he went back into the forest.

Sosruquo drove all the horses back home. The old woman was waiting for him.

"Did you bring all of them home?"

"Yes, all of them."

The old woman considered that a miracle. She counted them, and all of them were there. "Well, now you can rest. You have won this time, my boy," she said.

The next night she counted her horses again and again let Sosruquo lead them out. He watched over them until sunrise, and when the sun had risen all the horses jumped from the ground and flew into the sky. Sosruquo leaned against a stump again and grew despondent. Suddenly an eagle landed nearby.

"What are you thinking about, Sosruquo?"

"Ill luck has befallen me," answered Sosruquo, and he told the eagle what had happened to him.

"Have a rest, Sosruquo. I shall soon bring all of them back to you." The eagle flew away, and in the early morning he drove all the horses back to him. "Now count them to be sure that all of them are here."

He counted. "All of them are here." He drove the whole herd back to the old woman.

She counted them and said, "Well, you have won again, two times in a row. Now you can rest," she said.

And on the third night things went similarly. At the end of the third night, at dawn, all the horses plunged into the sea. He went and stood near the stump. The fish jumped out of the sea and crawled near him.

"What is the matter, Sosruquo? What have you done?"

"I am sad because of what has happened to me. While I was guarding the horses, they plunged into the sea and disappeared. Now what will happen to me?"

"Do not worry, Sosruquo. Sit here quietly. I shall bring them back," said the fish.

The mare that Sosruquo had come for had foaled the night before and given birth to a small foal, exactly as the ayniwzh had predicted. Sosruquo counted all the horses coming out of the sea, and there was one more in the herd. He looked again and saw the foal among them.

The fish said, "The old woman will offer you everything you wish for your work. Ask for this newborn stallion. Tell the old woman that you need nothing but this stallion, and do not take anything but him. No horse in this world can beat him. He has a brother. The ayniwzh owns him, but this one is much better. No other horse in this world is like him." That is what the fish told Sosruquo, and Sosruquo now knew what to do.

He brought all the horses back home.

"Well, you beat me again. Three nights in a row you have won. Take a good look and choose among them whichever you wish," said the old woman. "There are many good horses among them."

"I do not really know which to choose. While I was working I noticed that a foal was born. He will be a good price for my work. I do not want anything else. Give him to me," said Sosruquo.

She could not refuse. The stallion was caught, and Sosruquo took him and with him set off for home.

His own horse was running as fast as he could, and yet the stallion was walking quietly. They traveled for one day and one night. In the morning Sosruquo said, "Well, now I shall have a rest and my horse will have a rest, so that we can eat a little bit."

After he dismounted he said, "My gray ran as fast as he could, and this stallion just ambled. He will probably become an excellent horse."

As soon as Sosruquo had spoken, the foal spoke to him. "Hey, Sosruquo!

You probably do not know it, but I am a good horse already," said the young stallion. "You can take the saddle off him and put it on me. But the stallion we are going to is my brother. He sucked milk three times and the ayniwzh grabbed him away. I also sucked just three times, so we are equal. We have the same strength. We have the same endurance. Should I suck one more time, this horse would not be equal to me," said the stallion.

"But we have already traveled two days and two nights. How could I bring you back and make you suck your mother's breast one more time?"

"While you are resting, I shall turn back, touch my mother's nipple a fourth time, and return to you."

"Fine, you can go," said Sosruquo, and he began to hobble his gray. After he finished, he turned around and saw that the stallion was still there. "Why did you not go?" Sosruquo asked.

"I went, sucked, and returned. Now you can saddle me and we can go."

Sosruquo took the saddle off his gray horse and put it on the stallion's back. He grabbed his gray horse by the bridle, and together they all set out. The stallion was ambling along while his gray was galloping as fast as he could. Soon the gray gave up. He could not keep the pace, and he started to stumble. Sosruquo turned around, looked at his horse, and began to cry. He felt sorry for him. At the same time he thought, "If the stallion sees that I am crying, he will think that I love my horse more than I love him."

"Hey, Gray," shouted Sosruquo. "If I leave you here, the wolves will gobble you up. If I don't leave you, I will lose you. You are too slow. Best of all, you should know that I was very much pleased with you." He took his bow, shot an arrow into his gray, and killed him. He then set out and went, went and went, and soon he reached the ayniwzh's land.

"O Allah, please make everything peaceful around here! Let today be a nice warm, quiet day!" As soon as he prayed, the ice covering the land melted and everything around it flourished and grew beautiful.

"Oh, look how sunny it is today!" said the ayniwzh. "I'll take a look to see if my land is ready to be plowed. Give me something to eat!"

The Narts' daughter gave him some food. He took the jar with seeds, saddled his horse, and went out to plow.

Sosruquo also went there, and as soon as the ayniwzh hung the jar on a branch, he grabbed it and ran away. He also took the Nart woman with him. Soon the ayniwzh realized what had happened and spied Sosruquo in the distance. He realized that Sosruquo was riding a different horse. Sosruquo was riding very slowly, taking his time. The ayniwzh forgot about his supper and his rest. He quickly saddled his horse and began to chase Sosruquo. He began to beat his horse. He beat him so hard that he almost killed him. Soon the ayniwzh drew near Sosruquo.

"O lazy you! You have let him nearly overtake me," said Sosruquo to his horse.

"Do not be afraid, Sosruquo," answered his horse. "He will not overtake me. Do not worry."

Could the ayniwzh's horse not keep up the pace? "Hey, my younger brother!" he said. "We are brothers, aren't we? Do not let him kill me. The one who rides me is killing me. Don't you see? Let me overtake you."

"If we are brothers, then soar upward and throw him down from your back. Why are you carrying him?"

And the horse soared upward into the sky and turned over. The ayniwzh fell off. The horse came back down and kicked the ayniwzh in the head and killed him. The horse then returned to his mother.

Sosruquo, riding his horse with the Narts' daughter and the seeds of millet, returned to his village. At the end of the village he met Qhabizh-Chkun,[4] who pastured their goats. The woman Sosruquo was carrying with him was nice, and Qhabizh-Chkun was a good man. He was tending the goats.

"Salam aleykum, Qhabizh-Chkun," he said and approached him.

"Aleykum salam, Sosruquo! Where is your present,[5] Sosruquo?"

"I give you this woman as my present," said Sosruquo (the man was not married), and he gave Qhabizh-Chkun the Narts' daughter. He brought the millet seeds, returned them to the Narts, and went back home to his mother, Satanaya.

The Narts sowed these seeds and harvested the millet. They invited Satanaya and asked her to say the prayer, the *khokh*. That is how Sosruquo brought the Narts their millet seeds.

From text 8, pp. 75–87.

∽ This variant combines the Prometheus theme with that of a youth helping animals in distress, a wolf, an eagle or a raven, and a fish, and being helped by them in return to overcome a witch. The latter theme is common in Russian folk tales and is probably a late borrowing into the Caucasus. The motif of the ogre's soul in a special place, this time in a box nine mountains away, also occurs in some Georgian folklore [KT].

[1] The Abaza divide the morning, /qʷˈ°əšləqˈ°/, into two periods. From dawn to midmorning is "small *kushluk*," and from midmorning to noon is "great kushluk."

[2] The notion that one's death, soul, or vulnerable spiritual power resides somewhere quite apart from one's body is odd. It seems to be confined to this saga. That the giant's death should take the form of a swift horse, in fact, the swiftest horse, is reminiscent of the Circassian tales of Wardana or Wadan and of Odin's horse Sleipnir in Norse myth.

[3] Fosterage was practiced in the North Caucasus. A man could become a fictive child to a woman by grabbing her breast and pretending to suck at it, regardless of whether he was older than she was or whether he took her breast surreptitiously or by force. Blood feuds were sometimes ended by a furtive and desperate act of such symbolic suckling.

[4] Qhabizh-Chkun is literally / q̇á-bəž̍ʸ(ə) č̍ʸkʷᵒən / or / q̇á-bž̍ʸə č̍ʸkʷᵒən / 'head-seven (?) child / youth', "seven-headed youth." The canonical word for "seven" is / bž̍ə /, with a retroflexed fricative due to the influence of the initial labial stop. Hence the form / bəž̍ʸə / in the name must be old, whether it meant "seven" or not. If my reading is correct, this suggests an old polycephalous figure.[5] Qhabizh-Chkun's reference to a gift is enigmatic. Perhaps those who remained behind had the right to demand some part of the booty of a returning warrior. Qhabizh-Chkun recurs in sagas 69 and 72.

SAGA 54 ⚬ *Shardan*

In the time of the Narts, there was a man of short stature named Shardan.

The millet was ripe, but the Narts did not know how to harvest it, how to mow it.

"Go," said Nart Sosruquo, "and bring Shardan. Shardan will tell us how we should mow the millet."

They went and brought Shardan, but he could not climb over the threshold of the Narts' door. Eventually he somehow managed to climb up, stumble, and fall down into the room.

"O, sons of idiots! You could kill yourself here!" he said.

"Here he is. Shardan! We brought you to solve this problem." When he had fallen, the Narts, who were seated, began to laugh at him. He was insulted, but he said nothing.

"They laugh at me," he said to himself.

"We do not know how to mow our millet."

"I shall not tell you!" he said. He stomped out and returned home.

Sosruquo said, "Go and eavesdrop on him! He will walk along and talk to himself." One of the Narts rose and went out to follow him. He overheard Shardan talking to himself.

"Oh, tribe of stupid people, born by a bitch! They do not know that one has to make iron scorching hot, bend it so that it is shaped like a chicken's comb, then sharpen it, and only then begin to mow."

The Nart returned. "By God, I am back!"

"What did he say?"

"He said, 'Don't they know that first one should make the iron scorching hot, bend it, shape it like a chicken's comb, sharpen it, and then mow?' That is what he said."

It did not take the Narts long to do all this. Soon they had fashioned a sickle and had begun to mow.

From text 26, p. 115.

  This tale depicts a sort of dwarf or gnome, who, though wise, is the object of the Narts' ridicule. It closely parallels Circassian saga 16, in which the water sprite Lady Isp assumes the role of the knowledgeable dwarf. Only in saga 74 are such small people depicted again.

SAGA 55   *How Sosruquo Brought Sana to the Narts*

Every year, on top of Mount Elbruz, the "blessed mountain," the gods used to meet. And the gods who used to meet there were these: Psat'ha, the god of life; Mazit'ha, the god of the forest; Amish, the god of cattle; T'ha'wolej, the god of plenty; and also Sozresh and Tlepshw. They used to meet and drink sana. O sana, which is sweet and strong and gives you power, the drink of the gods! And every year at sana-drinking time, the gods used to invite as a guest the man who stood before the people in strength and manliness. And the reason they used to invite him was so that he would repeat to the people how the gods made him their guest and how they gave him sana to drink. And the mortal whom the gods made their guest was considered fortunate in the land of the Narts.

Well, as the gods were drinking while sitting together thus, their leader, Psat'ha, stood up. "Who is it from among the Narts to whom we shall give our sana to drink this year? Who is it who stands before the Narts in manliness?" he asked.

"It is Nasran of the big beard, the leader of the Narts, to whom we shall give our sana to drink," said Sozresh.

"No, no, it is Shaway the son of Qanja, the huntsman of the Narts," said Mazit'ha.

"I prefer old Gworgwoni, the swineherd of the Narts," said Amish, the god of cattle.

"It is Khmish, the plowman of the Narts, to whom we shall give our sana to drink," said T'ha'wolej.

After them all, Tlepshw stood up and spoke thus: "O gods, someone has been born on the earth. When they speak the name of that one who has been born, all those of whom you have made mention here just now rise to their feet. Listen, O gods! A true man has appeared in the country of the Narts. He is still a child, but until now no man has emerged from among the Narts with strength such as his. He pulled up my anvil, which was set in seven layers of earth, and thrust it back into nine layers of earth."

The gods were afraid and asked Tlepshw, "Who is he?"

"Sosruquo is his name," said Tlepshw. "It is he who deserves our sana."

"Bring the man here!" Psat'ha ordered Tlepshw. And Tlepshw, the god of the smiths, went and brought Sosruquo to the place of the gods.

"Try our sana, my boy," said the leader. "You are the one who stands before the Narts in courage and strength. The people who are on the earth do not have sana like this." Having said this, the leader handed the horn full of sana to Sosruquo. Immediately Sosruquo drained the horn, his heart grew glad, and the world appeared brighter to him. "Aha, now go to the earth and tell all the people what our sana is like," said Psat'ha. But although the gods spoke thus, Sosruquo remained where he was, standing. He marveled infinitely at the sana. He began to see the earth as more beautiful and his strength as increasing.

"O gods, if it is possible, give me yet another hornful. What marvelous sana this is!"

"It will not be possible, we cannot change our custom; it is a single horn that we give mortals to drink," said the leader.

Tlepshw loved Sosruquo. Being pleased with him, he spoke thus: "We will give him yet another horn to drink. He deserves it. He will tell the people even better than the others how our sana is."

"We will give him another horn to drink," said T'ha'wolej. "We will do as you wish. But if we change our custom, will the god of the gods forgive us?"[1]

"He will forgive us," said all the gods.

After that, the jester god of the forest took the horn and approached the barrel holding the sana. And Sosruquo followed him and went near the barrel. Mazit'ha said, "This barrel belongs to the great god. And our sana is in it."

"What a marvelous barrel it is," said Sosruquo.

"The marvel is not the barrel," said T'ha'wolej, entering their conversation. "It is what adheres to the bottom of the barrel that is marvelous. It is the seed of the sana. And it is my strength that causes the sana to ripen."

When Sosruquo heard these things, he went to the barrel, and while pretending to look at it, he seized the barrel, threw it down Mount Elbruz, and caused it to fall to the plain. "Not just one man, but let all the people drink the sana of the gods!" When the barrel reached the plain, it broke, and the sweet sana overflowed like water and descended to the land of the Narts. And when the seed, which adhered to the bottom of the barrel, entered the earth, it immediately grew and increased. When the people saw the sana plant with its sweet bunches, they did not know what to do with it and brought the bunches to the wise Satanaya.

Just at that moment Sosruquo returned. The strong sana that he had drunk had greatly increased his strength. "It is this from which the gods extract their wonderful drink. Today they gave it to me to drink on top of Elbruz."

Satanaya immediately attended to the matter. She put the bunches in a barrel, and on the lid she placed the Abra stone.[2] Before a year had passed, the sana had matured and fermented, and it even threw off the lid on which the Abra stone sat. When the Narts drank the sana, it made them feel pleased with the world. Thanks to Sosruquo, the sana of the gods came into the possession of the people.

From Allen 1965, 19–20: 159–72. I have done some minor editing, since Allen's translation is literal.

◌ This marvelous saga is a version of the Prometheus myth that was collected in Turkey by the late W. Sidney Allen, who also translated it. It is unique in the entire corpora for the detail it gives regarding the old pagan pantheon.

[1] This is a unique reference to a supreme deity, who otherwise remains an enigma.

[2] The Abra stone is a borrowing from an Indo-Iranian language, in which *abra* meant "heaven." So this is the heavenly or divine boulder, perhaps a term used for a meteorite that, if of the usual nickel-iron composition, would have been the heaviest stone known.

SAGA 56 ∽ *Sosruquo and the Blind Ayniwzh*

The Nart Sosruquo loved to travel. When on a trip courage was called for, whether in war or in fighting, he always tried to display it. Being of this frame of mind, one day he decided to attack one of the more remote and wild lands and to plunder it. He called up all his vassals for this reason and ordered them to ready themselves. There were fifteen vassal horsemen altogether. All fifteen riders prepared themselves very quickly: saddles, weapons, horses, and food for the long trip. They were ready in a moment. To carry heavy stuff, they took an additional five packhorses with them and soon departed on the long journey.

On their way, they found themselves in a deserted land, a lost land. There was no place where a man could live, nothing but rocks, trees, mountains, canyons, and forest game. There was no cleared land, no plowed land, no land for hay, and no meadows. They met nothing but forests, mountains, and mountaintops, shelter only for wild animals and birds. Slowly, with Sosruquo ahead of them, they moved along a treacherous road until they came upon a huge boulder with a hole in it. Sosruquo passed this rock first, and then the rest of his vassals passed it in pairs. If you looked at the protruding top of this rock closely, you would see it was not wide and only about two *qu'lach* around;[1] a rider could reach around it with his lash.

"Where did this rock with a hole come from? How does it happen to be here in the middle of the road?" Sosruquo asked himself.

"What is it supposed to mean?" his men asked him.

That is what Sosruquo was thinking about. "Is it indeed a rock or something else? Until I know what this rock means I will not go any farther," he said after he had passed the rock and halted.

"I will have a rest," he said to his men. "I will stop here for a while, and you can go farther. Do not slow down. I will soon catch up to you. Somewhere in a proper place you can have a rest," said Sosruquo, thus giving his friends advice. His companions departed and Sosruquo dismounted. He pulled his dagger and approached the rock with the hole in it, which they had just passed. With the sharp tip of the knife he began to pick away at it. Clay, small stones, sand, and the rest, which were covering the rock, he picked off. When he had cleaned the rock entirely and carefully, he gazed at it. It turned out to be not a rock but a bone, a half-rotten bone covered with clay, small stones, sand, and such. When Sosruquo saw this, he grew even more amazed. "What a miracle! Where has this bone come from? What a huge animal it must have been to have a bone this large!" While he stood in this manner and gazed at the bone in wonder, the earth suddenly gave a mighty shake. The bone moved from its place. In a moment a huge ayniwzh appeared near Sosruquo. He had a face that could stop a heart, without two eyes. He appeared as a large cloud covering the whole world.

"Hey, you, Sosruquo, whose feet trample the earth! Why don't you live alone, neither dead nor alive?" said he. He bent down and in an instant lifted a huge rock, which he threw at Sosruquo, but Sosruquo dodged it. The rock, as though it had fallen into a marsh, sunk deep into the ground and could no longer be seen where it had hit the ground.

After Sosruquo had stepped aside from the rock, he had seen that the ayniwzh was blind. He became calm and pulled his spirits together. "Stop it, stop it, you unfortunate one! Stop it, don't bend yourself one inch! Not only for a blind ayniwzh but also for many ayniwzhes with two eyes have I prepared a regrettable fate.[2] You will be better off if you stop doing that."

Once the ayniwzh realized that the rock he had thrown had missed Sosruquo, he became very frightened and began to behave differently. "O Sosruquo, I have made a mistake. I beg your pardon, Sosruquo. I lost my mind and did what I should not have done. Let all the misfortunes prepared in this life for you fall on my stupid head! Forgive me, please!" he said.

"Well, I forgive you this time, but move just a bit and your soul will suffer the same fate as your eyes have suffered. As with them, I will rip your soul out of your body," Sosruquo said.

"I have heard you, and should I disobey, do whatever you want with me."

"Let us talk peacefully in that case. I am going to ask you about something, and I expect you to answer all questions without a lie."

"Ask me! Speak! I am listening," said the blind ayniwzh.

"What is this rock with the hole which is lying on this false path?"

"This is my bone. It has a hole, an opening in my pelvis."

"How, in that case, did it become embedded in this road?" asked Sosruquo.

"When I died, I was buried here. One hundred and sixty years have passed since my death. All my bones have scattered all over. They were taken away by water and wind. Dust, sand, small stones, slowly covered this bone. And that is how this bone with a hole in the middle became embedded in the ground. Everything was covered. Only one hole remained untouched."

"That is forgivable, but what is this land all about? I cannot see any clean, flat land. Who is living here?"

"Well, that is true. There is nothing here, as you said just now. Besides wild animals, birds, and we ayniwzhes, nobody is living here. We were seven brothers. Two of us are still alive, but the other five, including me, are dead. This land totally belongs to us and is under our rule. Not a single man who entered this land has returned home alive. Know that Sosruquo and leave. Do not encounter my live brothers!"

"That is not a good way to talk. Do not threaten me and do not worry about me! You would do better to tell me how you manage to live here. What do you eat? Whence do you obtain milk or porridge and such?"

"I will show you our porridge,"[3] said he. Then he bent down and lifted a lump of earth, close to a wagon in size, and began to squeeze it. Wheat began to fall from this lump. "That is how we obtain our porridge. It comes from this plowing land itself." The ayniwzh bent down again. In an instant he had lifted a huge stone and had begun to squeeze it. Soon he squeezed milk from it. "That is how we get milk. If we want to have meat, all game in this forest belongs to us. That is how we live. Unlike you, we have no need to plow the land, to harvest hay, to look after cattle," said he and then disappeared.

Sosruquo did not know what had happened and so remained standing on the same spot, looking around. And then, being very surprised at what he had seen, he went to join his group.

From text 10, part 1, pp. 62–64, with part 2 (pp. 64–68) forming a portion of saga 58.

✍ This and saga 58 have the unusual themes of a blind giant. This saga is unique, however, in its depiction of a giant as a cloudlike being, hovering between the worlds of life and death. The discovery of a huge bone or skull in both sagas reminds one of the prescientific finds of fossil dinosaurs which inspired awe and puzzlement, and it is likely that this theme, unique to this saga, has a similar source, since the rocks in the Caucasus are fossiliferous.

Sosruquo's cohorts are not vassals in a medieval feudal sense; instead they are subordinate members of a war band. The giant in this saga and in saga 58 resembles the Titans of Greek lore, as in Hesiod's *Works and Days*, wherein presocial, preagricultural people live naturally off the land [KT] Kevin Tuite (personal communication) thinks this theme may be a circum-Pontic one of great antiquity.

[1] Qu'lach /qʼ°laǯʸ/, translated as Russian *obxvat,* "girth."

[2] Here, uniquely, giants are explicitly said to have two eyes, and not one (contrast this with saga 52).

[3] The Abaza term is /basta/ "pasta," but in the Caucasus "pasta" refers to corn mush.

SAGA 57 ᐧ *Sosruquo and the Inquisitive Ayniwzh*

Sosruquo's men had ridden off on a raid with him and had paused to rest in a desolate land while he lingered behind to study a huge bone, which all thought was a rock. His group was resting in the shadow of a huge tree, waiting for him. Seeing Sosruquo returning, they grew glad and began to prepare wood and fire in order to make dinner. But it turned out that they had lost their flint. They began to search. They searched through all their things but could not find the flint, as if it had fallen into the ground. The air had turned cold and a wind had picked up. A blizzard seemed to be coming, and they had no warm clothing. Many began to suffer. When Sosruquo was told that the flint had disappeared and when he saw that a blizzard was coming, he said, "So we have no flint anymore. Then I shall go and get fire. You stay here and wait for me. Stay as warm as you can. Do not despair!" He took aim at a star and shot an arrow into it. A piece chipped off and fell to earth. "This will keep you warm until I return," he said, then taking one companion he departed to find and bring back fire.

Sosruquo and his companion traveled for two days and two nights, but they could not find a sign of fire. At the end of the third night, while sitting on top of a mountain and looking around, they saw light coming from the bottom of a ravine. Having seen that, they grew very glad, and during that night they watched the source of light. After sunrise they lost the light, but they could see the smoke. Sosruquo left his companion to watch the horses, and he himself descended into the ravine.[1] By constantly watching the source of smoke, he soon approached a cave from which the smoke was coming. The cave's door was open, and Sosruquo without hesitation entered. The cave was wide. Twenty riders could have entered it easily. In the middle he saw a bonfire as huge as a mountain. Near the fire, as huge as a mountain, there was a big ayniwzh, asleep. He was larger than the largest ayniwzh that Sosruquo had ever seen. He was sleeping with a terrible snoring and whistling. Two huge clubs were lying near him.

Sosruquo drew his dagger, bent over the ayniwzh, and picked up a large charred brand by piercing it with the tip of his dagger. With the charred brand in hand, he turned and set off on his horse, back to his companion. But a small piece of coal had broken off and fallen on the ayniwzh's beard. When his beard burned off, the ayniwzh awoke, shook his head, and counted his firebrands. One was missing.

"That is no good. It seems that the Narts have stolen one of my firebrands." He immediately set off after Sosruquo, saying to himself, "Ah, you Narts' child! Narts' milk-sucker! Where are you carrying my fire? You must have thought that it would be easy to get away from me."

Suddenly the earth began to quake and shake. Sosruquo guessed what was the matter. He tightened his horse's bridle, prepared his weapons, and got ready to meet the ayniwzh. As soon as the ayniwzh, the earthshaker, arrived, he said, "Hey! Sosruquo, Sosruquo! Is it you who is stealing my fire?"

"Yes," said Sosruquo. "Of course I took your firebrand. I came to take it away from you."

The ayniwzh hurled a club.

Sosruquo stepped aside, and the club, missing him, plunged into the ground up to its handle. The ayniwzh grew angry, and he threw another club that he held in his left hand. Again Sosruquo evaded it, and the club sank into the ground.

Sosruquo then made a move as if to throw one of these clubs and said, "So what! What do you have now to beat me with? I am not Sosruquo. I am his cook. You are lucky you have not met Sosruquo himself, then you would be dead by now. I myself, his cook, with Sosruquo's help will cut off your head right away," he said.

The ayniwzh's heart filled with fear. There was a change in his face, and he began to shake and murmur. "Please don't!" said the ayniwzh. "Don't kill me! I mistakenly took you for Sosruquo. We have nothing to share, have we? So let me take my clubs."

"No way! You will not take them. Do not move from the place where you stand now!"

The ayniwzh grew more frightened from having seen how Sosruquo grew more arrogant. The ayniwzh no longer had his weapons, so to get them back he changed his voice. Sosruquo, realizing this, continued to be stern. He behaved like a lion before the ayniwzh.

"Turn around right away and go the same way you came!" said Sosruquo.

"Well, I shall go, but before I do can you tell me about some of Sosruquo's games, please?" said the ayniwzh.

"What do you need Sosruquo's games for?"

"Well, I would like to check whether I can play the same games. Everyone says his games are very interesting. I ask you again. Tell me about them or show them to me!"

"Well, when Sosruquo is bored he throws a stone up a very high and steep mountain, like this one, and he plays with the stone, hitting it with his forehead while the stone is rolling back, trying to get it back to the mountain's top."

"Wait a minute! I can do the same," said the ayniwzh, and he lifted a huge boulder. He threw this boulder up to the top of a steep hill and began to push the boulder with his forehead as it rolled down, driving it back to the top.

When Sosruquo saw that he thought, "What a strong forehead he has! It should be difficult to cut it. No, I wouldn't beat him if I tried to do this. I have to think of something else."

"Sosruquo is very smart. What a fine game it is indeed," said the ayniwzh. "Tell me about something else, I ask you!" said the ayniwzh.

And Sosruquo said, "He has another game like this. He loves to bathe in a cauldron of boiling milk."

"I will try that as well," said the ayniwzh. And he took three round stones, put them on the ground, picked out two or three carts of coal, and dumped them between the stones. He found a huge cauldron and placed it on the stones. He picked up a large boulder, and by squeezing it he soon squeezed out a cauldron full of milk. He took the brand Sosruquo was holding and started a fire. He placed the fire under the pile of coal, and blowing on it he started a huge blaze. When the milk began to boil, he plunged down into the cauldron. The ayniwzh was resting on the surface of the boiling milk and was enjoying himself.

"Oh, what a pleasure it is! It makes all my bones very soft," said the ayniwzh.

Sosruquo became very surprised. "What is the way to kill him? Even the boiling milk cannot boil him."

The ayniwzh soon climbed out of the cauldron. "Sosruquo is smart indeed. He found an extremely good way to warm up the bones. Can you tell me now about his third amusement?" said the ayniwzh.

And Sosruquo began to narrate another story. "Once when he was freezing from the cold, his brothers set a plow on fire and made it scorching hot. Sosruquo stood nearby with his mouth open. They grabbed the plow with big tongs and placed it into Sosruquo's mouth. After that Sosruquo began to chew the scorching-hot plow and then spat it out. And when his brothers asked him, 'Hey, Sosruquo, how did you like it?' He answered, 'That's not bad when it's cold outside; it makes one's heart a bit warmer.'"

"Do you think that I cannot do that? Would I not be able to cool it off?"

he said. So he brought his huge plow. Then he seized the cauldron, poured the boiling milk away, and set the cauldron aside. He placed the plow on the fire and began to blow on the coals. When the plow was red hot, he stuffed it into his mouth and began to chew it. When it had cooled he spat it out.

"Ah, how fine a way to warm up! Tell me of Sosruquo's fourth game!" asked the ayniwzh.

Sosruquo began to think. "Here it is!!"

"Sosruquo enters the place where all three seas meet each other. He stands at the spot on the bottom, so that only his head can be seen. He does not eat anything for three days and three nights. For four days and four nights he stands in water. He makes the sea freeze, and then gathers all his powers and lifts out the whole sea as ice, icebergs. He takes it out on his shoulders. Can you do that?"

"Would I not be able to do the same?!" said the ayniwzh and plunged into the sea.

Sosruquo began to pray, "O God! Please freeze the sea today!"

As soon as he said so, the ayniwzh became frozen in the sea. He was paralyzed up to his neck.

"Now make an effort to get out."

The ayniwzh gave a mighty heave and rose out of the sea together with the ice.

"Now you see? You said I would not come out of the sea, but I made it. Tell me now what else Sosruquo does!"

At first Sosruquo did not know what to say, but then a simple idea came to him. "Sometimes Sosruquo throws himself flat on the ground and asks somebody to ride a horse on his back."

"That is nothing," said the ayniwzh and threw himself flat on the ground. "Get your horse and ride him on my back!"

Sosruquo thought, "Now, finally, I have found a way to get rid of him. O God! Gather all my strength into my sword!" Then he struck his horse. As he rode onto the ayniwzh's back, he drew close to his left shoulder blade and hit the ayniwzh's neck with his sword, just where it joined the shoulder. He jumped off his back right away.

"Now listen! Your death is from Sosruquo's hands. I am Sosruquo."

The ayniwzh began to roar as loudly as he could. His head pulled him in one direction. He thrashed in convulsions, twitching all over. Sosruquo stepped aside and watched.

"Oh, how painfully have you cheated me," said the ayniwzh. "Otherwise I would show you how to strike a really good blow. If you were born to be a man, come closer and charge me one more time."

"No. To hit twice is not my rule. I think one hit was enough for you."

The ayniwzh made the ground quake like a thunderstorm. His blood flowed from his arteries like a fountain and hit the sky, making such a noise as a river in flood time.

"Had I been smarter, I would have recognized that you might be Sos-ruquo. Although you could not beat me with your power, you beat me with your intellect," the giant said. "Now, can you bring here my sword, which is hanging on the cave wall, above my bed? And in order not to torture me, hit me with this sword and cut out my entrails," the giant said.

But if Sosruquo had touched this sword with his hand, it would have killed him. The giant had hoped that even in death he could have tricked Sosruquo and killed him in turn. But would Sosruquo, being so smart, not know about it? He had a smart head. He did not touch this sword with his hands at all. He found a pair of tongs hanging in the cave, grabbed the sword with them, and brought it to the river. When the giant saw that Sos-ruquo was carrying the sword with tongs, he lost any doubt that before him was the real Sosruquo.

Then the dying giant said to Sosruquo, "Take all my innards and tie them around one of the trees. Then all the people will know that you have truly killed me."

"So be it! I will gratify your last wish," said Sosruquo, and then he hit him with his own sword and cut his stomach open. He grabbed the innards with the tongs and tied them around a tree.[2] Then he returned to his com-panion. He told him all that had happened and brought him to see the body of the giant.

They cut off the ayniwzh's head. Although they intended to take it with them, they could not manage to put it on their horses, so heavy was it, so they decided to cut off one ear. Laden with the huge ear, Sosruquo and his companion rode back to their fellows. They found them suffering in great cold, in darkness and misery. They used the brand of the giant ayniwzh to light a fire. In this way the men and horses were saved and they all returned to their homes. Later, after they had returned home, they peeled off the skin of the ear and made strips from it. These strips were used in making five saddles.

From text 10, part 2, pp. 64–68; text 9, pp. 59–62; and text 11 [12 sic!], pp. 70–74.

◌ In text 9 Sosruquo is said to be the eldest of seven Nart brothers (see comments in sagas 59 and 60). In this account he refers to the ayniwzh as "Dada," the hypocoristic term for "grandfather." In an inversion of Sosruquo's characteristic marginalization, the remaining six brothers feel spurned at the end and take offense when they realize that Sosruquo has engaged in a great feat without their participation.

In text 12, a young Sosruquo, typically outcast, is spurned by a troop of elder Narts under the leadership of Nasran as they set out to raid the Chints, Isps, and Marakunts, all of whom are said to have states.

While on the trail, they are smitten by a severe blizzard and are dying for lack of fire, since a giant has stolen all fire from the world. Sosruquo's mother clairvoyantly sees their predicament and sends him to help. The freezing Narts acknowledge their injustice toward him and beg for his help. He then proceeds to bring fire. Sosruquo masquerades as his own shepherd, revealing himself to the ayniwzh only at the end. The giant swallows molten lead rather than a red-hot plow.

Like sagas 52 and 77, this is one of the Prometheus tales from the Caucasus. This one is reminiscent of the Cyclops in the cave (see saga 52 n. 2).

[1] This otiose companion is a shadow of the second man in the encounter with the Cyclopean giant, saga 52. The tradition preserves an Odyssean tale of the return of fire, and this variant involves an inquisitive giant.

[2] There is a late-winter custom in the North Caucasus, widely observed among the Ossetians, neighbors of the Kabardians, of tying ribbons around the trunks of trees in sacred groves. Women and children are forbidden to enter the groves at this time. Perhaps these ribbons, the entrails, represent the death of the giant and the coming of spring's warmth.

SAGA 58 ◌ *Sosruquo and the Giant's Skull*

Sosruquo was riding along together with his warriors. They rode and rode until at last they halted somewhere for the night. There they came upon a huge skull. Sosruquo looked at it with surprise. "We are the biggest people in the world, but that one, whose skull this was, must have been huge," he said.

It grew dark. They moved aside a bit and sat down. Sosruquo returned to the skull. He prayed for God to bring the owner of this skull back to life but to keep him blind, so that he could ask him just a few questions.

God brought him back to life and set him on his feet but left him blind. That one who had just been resurrected was huge, but he did not have any eyes. Sosruquo himself was big, but this one was even bigger.

Then Sosruquo asked this, "Oh my God, if you are this big, then how long did people live in your time?"

"I died when I was five hundred years old. I died in the middle of my life. In my time people lived one thousand years. I died when I was five hundred."

Then Sosruquo asked again, "If you were so big, what did you eat to keep you alive?"

The man took a bunch of huge rocks in his hands and began to squeeze them. Sosruquo had his jar ready. When he began to squeeze the rocks, Sosruquo put his jar under them and filled it.

"Have you seen it?" asked the giant.

"Oh yes," answered Sosruquo. "But how did you prepare this?" asked Sosruquo.

"That is how we used it. We just licked it once and it was enough for us until next time," he said.

Sosruquo wanted to know just that and he said, "O God! Please turn him into dust again!" and he returned to dust. And Sosruquo returned to his warriors, holding a jar in his hands. From then on his troops were alive only because they licked this.

From text 14, p. 88.

∽ Again, one is reminded of an encounter with a large fossil skull (saga 56). This tale suggests some vague memory of a narcotic, perhaps used by warrior bands.

SAGA 59 ∽ *Sosruquo and Six Men*

Sosruquo set out on a quest.
Far away he went and did not return.
He brought sorrow to his wife's heart.
At last, she called her brother.

She and her brother waited for Sosruquo.
But Sosruquo did not come; he had disappeared.
Both hearts were now in distress.
Both had sorrow in their eyes.
They yearned for his return.
Sosruquo had been far away, but he was now on his way home.
He had been plundering seashores.
Five months had passed and he was returning.
As he came he overcame mountains.
He traversed the Nibna Forest.
As he came he stepped to the edge of the forest.
He was going and he saw a miracle.
Right before him an enormous horse's skull fell.
The horse's skull turned into dust.
Six men appeared from it.
They appeared with all their belongings.
All six spread around instantly.
For an instant Sosruquo was confused.
But then he began to chase them.
He brought all six of them together,
And he began to drive them.
He drove them to the place of the horse's skull.
He lined all of them up in a row
And began to question each of them in turn.
The first said, "I am a marksman.
With my arrow I can cut off a bird's head.
With my arrow I can cut the blade of a knife in half."
The second stood up and said,
"My eyes see perfectly.
Sharp-Eyed. That's what people call me."
The third stood up and said,
"Sharp Ear, that's what people call me.
I can hear all possible sounds."
The fourth stood up and said,
"I carry the whole burden of this group.
The Heavy Burden Carrier I am called."
The fifth stood up and said,
"Skillful Carpenter people call me.
I can build a house in a second."

The sixth, "I am a skinner.
I flay the skin from animals that they kill.
Then I salt the flesh and dry it."
Sosruquo then said,
"Wonderful! Let it be good!
Now how did all of you get together?" he asked.
"All of us were born in one village.
Every year we hunt in these places.
Whatever we kill we divide in equal parts for everybody.
Everything is common for all of us,
And whatever we do we do together.
Each of us does whatever he can."
"Well, let it be good!
Now, where did that horse's skull come from, this I ask?"
"Today we were caught in a heavy rain.
It began to make us wet.
There was no good in our getting wet in the rain.
The sharp-eyed one saw the horse's skull.
'There is a big bone,' he said.
And all six of us ran to the horse's skull.
And all of us sat inside the skull.
Soon a huge man approached it.
He pushed a stick into the bone's opening.
He lifted the horse's skull and set off on his journey.
And all six of us inside the skull were frightened.
He turned this skull on his stick.
He played with the stick as he traveled.
At last he grew angry about something and threw it away.
The bone flew, flew, and at last fell down.
It turned into dust, as you witnessed.
And all six of us, like worms, ran away in different directions."
"Well, let that also be good!
What kind of a man was he, this I ask?"
"This man was very big, huge.
His height was about three times the distance between one's
     widespread arms.
His neck one could embrace twice.
The pupils of his eyes were as big as a head.
His eyes were as red as fire.

And when he walked, the ground under him shook.
Two big clubs were hanging on him."
"Well, let that too be good!
When he carried you, what was he talking about, this I ask?"
"'This skull is a part of my horse's corpse.
You remain a great sadness for my heart.
It is time to break you to pieces.'
He was talking like that and the skull was this bone.
'Sosruquo's *alyp*[1] will be carrying me.
I will take the alyp of Sosruquo.'
He said that and threw the bone away."
"Well, let that be good as well!
Hey, Sharp-Eyed! Here is my command to you.
Look in the direction of Injig-Chkun![2]
Look through the whole length of the valley!
Look carefully and let it be a dove![3]
All, whatever you can see, tell me about!"
The sharp-eyed one looked at him and said,
"I have looked through the valley, its total length.
I can see the fort belonging to Sosruquo.
In this fort there are two persons.
A man and a woman sit there.
Both of them are sitting behind a table."
Hearing that, a change came over Sosruquo.
Both his eyes darkened.
"Who is sitting near my wife?
Who is it? Who, without fear, is sitting with her?"
Sharp-Eyed's words had struck very close to Sosruquo's heart.
He had changed greatly because of them.
"Hey, Sharp-Eyed! Look again, immediately!
Look at both of them!
How are they in their appearance?
Look at them and tell me everything in detail!"
"The woman has dark hair.
Her body color is beautiful.
With highly arched eyebrows.
She herself has black eyes.
With a straight and beautiful nose.
With hair long and dark.

That is how she appears to me.
Of this fellow who is sitting with her, I shall say this.
As if he is her copy he is standing close to her.
Without any defects he very much resembles her.
On his forehead I can see a mark in the form of a half-moon."[4]
When Sosruquo heard all that,
At once the anger left his heart.
He knew that this was his wife's brother.
Sosruquo gave a command to the sharp listener:
"Those two who have been seen by him,
What are they talking about?
Listen to them and tell me their words!"
The sharp listener listened attentively.
"They are obeying Sosruquo's advice.
They think about Sosruquo constantly.
'He has not returned yet,' they say.
'Where is he?
If he were alive, he would have returned by now.'"
"Well, let it be good!
Hey, you watcher with sharp eyes! Come here!
Have a look on this path! Look along it!"
The sharp-eyed watcher looked closely.
He looked along the whole length of the path.
At last he said this:
"A huge man is sitting on the path.
The man who is sitting is exactly the same one who threw
    the horse's bone."
"Well, let it be good!
Sharp Ear, now you have a good try to hear whatever you can."
The sharp ear listened and said:
"'Sosruquo is not here. He did not come.
He should have returned by this path.
As soon as he appeared, I would have taken the alyp away
    from him.'
He is talking like that with himself and he is sitting on the path."
"Well, let it be good!
I shall go in his direction.
You should go in the same direction.
We will go together until we see him.

As soon as we see him, you will stop.
I shall go directly to him.
As soon as I reach him, he and I will jump on each other
With our hot heads out front.
We will strike each other mightily.
When I grow weak, I will shout.
'Hey, let us gather our strength together,' I will say.
Once you hear that, you, the marksman,
Shoot your arrow in our direction.
Aim at his ankle and shoot!"
Everybody agreed to this.
Sosruquo set off on his way.
He rode until at last he came upon that man.
Both jumped on each other at once.
Both forced each other to spin like a top.
Sosruquo began to lose his strength.
"Hey, let us get our strength together!" he said.
The marksman shot his arrow out,
And it struck this man on the ankle.
He fell to his knees.
But he did not fall to the ground; he rose again.
He stood on one foot then.
His other leg was hanging.
Red blood flowed out of him.
Red blood wet the ground.
The ground turned into red mud.
They both trampled the red clay under their feet.
In the red clay they fought.
Soon the man began to feel nausea.
His foot started to tremble.
Sosruquo shoved with all his strength,
And like a ninepin the man went down.
Sosruquo sat on him.
Sosruquo called the group.
"Hey hunters! Come here quickly!"
All the hunters came down.
And he began to command them.
"Hey you, Heavy Burden Carrier!
Give me the chain quickly!⁵

Tie both his legs tightly!
Band him quickly, quickly!"
He said that to the heavy burden carrier.
With a heavy chain he tied both his legs tightly.
"Well done!" said Sosruquo.
"Hey, Carpenter! Give me quickly a split tree and put both
    his hands in between!"
The carpenter took both hands and put them into a split in a tree.
"Well done!" said Sosruquo.
Sosruquo climbed down from this man.
The giant man was very angry.
He was lying on the ground and was gnashing his teeth.
He was lying on the ground in a fury and was bleeding.
And scarlet blood flowed like a rivulet.
Sosruquo gave this command.
"Hey, Skinner! Right away, quickly, take enough skin from
    his back for seven belts!
And dry it and make each of us one belt!"
The skinner worked swiftly.
"Well done!" said Sosruquo.
He gave a command to the sharp-eyed one:
"Have a look for where his house is!"
"Now I can see his house.
His house is at the bottom of an abyss.
Inside his house I can see a big cauldron and a trunk.
A huge ax is there.
A spit is hanging on the wall.
There is a heavy chain with a bull hanging from it.
Also a deer's thigh hangs there.
The chest is filled with silver and gold."
"Well done!" said Sosruquo.
"Let us go to his house!"
They left the giant where he was lying.
Sosruquo took the two clubs with him.
And together with the entire group he set off on his way.
Soon they reached the giant's house.
After great difficulty, they broke open the chest.
They took silver and gold from there.
Sosruquo took a golden earring for himself.

The rest he gave away to the hunters.
Sosruquo freed the hunters.
They gladly went to their homes.
And he gave his wife his golden earring
And to his brother-in-law a belt of the giant's skin.
These he gave as gifts when he returned to them.
The giant was eaten by the earth on which he lay.[6]

From text 16, pp. 90–96.

⌖ This saga is one of the few tales in which treasure is mentioned. As in saga 57, the image of the river of blood from the wounded giant is repeated. The six men may have originally been Sosruquo's brothers, since he is said to have been one of seven in text 9, part of saga 57, and perhaps to have killed his own brother in text 15, part of saga 60. It must be remembered that although Sosruquo is the one hundredth brother of the Nart war band, he is always marginal. This marginality is canonically attributed to his bastard status as the son of a rock and sometimes to his lowly paternity; he is the son of a herdsman and therefore not from the warrior caste. Sosruquo may have originated at an earlier period in a separate blood lineage, a family that fell outside the war band's kinship bonds.

This myth is especially rich in parallels with various far-flung Indo-European traditions. Some of these may reflect older common Pontic themes (Colarusso 1997b), but most are probably traces of ancient contacts between Northwest Caucasians and various Indo-European bands as they passed through the Pontic Steppe in what is now the Ukraine and southern Russia.

[1] An alyp is a marvelous warhorse.

[2] The name is / yən-ʒʸəgʸ-č'ʸk'°ən / 'big-shining-youth', Russian Indzhigov.

[3] This obscure reference to a dove relates to Sosruquo's wife, who seems to be derived from the myth of the golden apples and the lady of the sea (sagas 2 and 45).

[4] The mark of a half-moon has parallels in the Hindu iconography of the god Shiva, where a half-moon is depicted just above the head of the god and is one of the marks of Shiva with which the god is born. The halo surrounding the Irish hero Cuchulainn is said to be a "warrior's moon" (Gaelic luān lāith) (see Puhvel 1987, 185). It is also reminiscent of the whetstone that remained stuck in the brow of the Norse god Thor after he had fought the giant Hrungnir, perhaps lending to this preeminent giant-slaying god a permanent warrior's moon as a mark of his function and prowess in dealing with these monstrous adversaries.

[5] Here is another Norse parallel with the binding of the monstrous wolf, Fenrir, brother of Loki who is the trickster and tormenter of the gods. In the Norse saga, the binder is the god Tyr, who loses a hand in Fenrir's jaws when he places it in his mouth as a surety of the

gods' good intentions. In this tale an inversion has taken place. It is not the binder but the monstrous giant that loses an extremity, and, in keeping with an inversion, the extremity is not a hand but a foot.

⁶ This odd, somewhat grim demise links this giant with the one with which Herakles wrestled, Antaeus, who was invulnerable as long as he stayed in touch with his mother, Gaia, the earth. This giant is also an "earth giant" and returns to his source at death.

SAGA 60 ☙ *Sosruquo and Sotrash*

As legends say, Sosruquo of the Narts was the son of Sos. Sos was the cowherd of the Narts. That is why all the Narts called Sosruquo Tuma.[1] They considered it a source of shame to call him brother. But because of the great courage that Sosruquo possessed, because of his frightening and attention-grabbing qualities,[2] all the Narts, when they saw him, showed him great honor and respect. Although they showed him their respect to his face, behind his back they were seeking ways to kill him, to get rid of him. Finally the Narts agreed among themselves to extend to Sosruquo an invitation and then kill him. They invited him to a wedding feast where he could show his strength. They were sure that Sotrash would be there too and become jealous of the young Nart's strength.[3]

Sosruquo went to the Narts who had invited him. He was there for a long time and returned very sad and tired. His mother, Satanaya,[4] having seen him, did not like the way he looked. She suspected that something had happened to him and began to question him:

> "My adopted child, my Sosruquo,
> Sosruquo, light of my eyes,
> My Sosruquo who is like the lightning.
> What did they say yesterday, they, who invited you?
> What did you see? What have they done! What did they say?"
> "Oh, like my soul, Satanaya, my mother!
> Don't intervene in a man's affairs! Don't ask!
> A woman does not ask about a man's affairs.
> There is no answer due a woman."

"That you will not say what happened I shall not accept.
If you refuse my plea, you are not my son."
"Well, if you insist, then I will tell you what happened to me.
It is a shame and a great insult.
The Narts invited me yesterday to a wedding feast.
They introduced me into the circle of the Narts.
The Nart elders were sitting there.
'Go play with the horses!' they said there.
I stepped into the center of a huge circle.
I shouted loudly the sounds of thunder.[5]
I showed them my courage there.
They presented to me the hero's cup.
Afterward the Narts gave me signs of high esteem.
Then I quietly descended into the old Aryq.[6]
I went far until at last I reached evil Aryq's end,
Beset with mist and cloud.
Something black saw I in front of me.
I called that black, whom I had seen,
But he heeded neither my voice nor me.
I started to chase him—could not catch him.
I turned back then but did not go far.
He turned about and spied me.
His eyes shone like two stars,
Eyes in size like the morning star.
He called to me and I heard him.
A great curse he hurled at me,
Like a sword hurled against me.
He pursued me and caught me.
This rider was a horseman of the Narts,
One of those I saw among the Narts.
He carried a long, unbreakable lance,
With which he goaded my horse along, beating on its back.
Then he put it against my ribs.[7]
He set my arse on the ground.
He furrowed the sky with me, lifting me like a felt ball.
He tossed me about the way he might some feathers.
He seized me again and set me to the ground.
He forced me to plow the Narts' ground.

He forced me with my shoulder to make seven furrows.
I sweated like two plowing oxen.
Then he forced me to vomit three times.
All the breast milk that I have drunk
He made me vomit out my nose.
He covered my mustache in dust.
At last he grabbed his sword.
He prepared to cut my head off, and I began to beg,
'O you, the Narts' fearless horseman,
Don't kill me lest you are never free of my blood.
Give me just one day—tomorrow—as a reprieve!
Harama Summit will suffice for our resumption.'
I decided to be shrewd and I begged him about it.
He listened to my request and so I have returned to you."
"Hey, Sosruquo! Like my eyes!
Sinewy Sosruquo, iron-eyed!
That was Albayk's son, Sotrash,
The only rider of whom we are afraid.
The horse under him has a deer's head.
Its head hangs in the sky.[8]
They were nine brothers.
That is their number.
Eight of their heads have I made you fetch already.
Sotrash is the ninth.
It is necessary that he go the way of his brothers.
Force the smiths to make little bells.
Not few, but many.
Then tie them to the tail of your horse.[9]
Arrive on time as you have agreed on.
As soon as you see him, rush upon him!
His horse will become scared and will bolt.
If you are God's adopted son, he will give him to you."

Sotrash stood on the mountain.
Sosruquo stood and waited.
He was wrapped in a black cloud.[10]
Sosruquo jumped onto the summit.
The clangor frightened Sotrash's horse and it bolted.
Sotrash became angry and struck his horse on its muzzle.

Then he pulled his horse's jaw backward and tore it off.
He pulled the bridle up through its ears,
And he himself fell down on his back.
Sosruquo dismounted and sat down on him.
"Hey, sinewy man with iron eyes!
A rider made of steel, Sosruquo!
I granted you a reprieve yesterday.
Today grant me a reprieve likewise!"
"You grant me a reprieve, then I grant you a reprieve.
So we shall be staying here on the Narts' mountain forever."

Sosruquo had hardened his sword.
Sosruquo cut off the Nart's head.
Sosruquo returned and brought his head home.

"O my little boy, my light, how have you been?
What have you seen? What have you said? How did you
    come back?"
"I went there; I saw; and I conquered.[11]
Sotrash's head I have brought to you."
"You did the unseemly and returned to me."
"Whose fault is it? You said 'bring it,' and so I brought it.
Now if you say 'carry it back,' I will carry it back.
To attach the head again, that is your problem."
"I have no need of Sotrash's head.
I do not want to hear about it or see it.
Go and give it to Sotrash's mother!
Show her the head of her last son!"

Sosruquo went to Sotrash's mother.
He threw the head into her lap.
"Oh, you horseman's plague, the cowherd's son!
Never were you Satanaya's son.
You have brought grief to me, you stray dog.
You have eaten me. Let wolves eat your flesh!"
She jumped to her feet and hurled a spit at him.
It utterly shattered her door frame.

"Steel is my blood. I am steel alloy. I am Sosruquo of the Narts.
You yourselves made a miracle. Whose fault is it now?
Your miracle has come back to defeat you."[12]

From text 15 (unnumbered in the original), pp. 89–90; text 20, pp. 103–6; text 21, pp. 106–9.

❧ I have given the unaltered text 21 as a specimen of Abaza at the end of this section. See the comments in saga 23 for a detailed discussion of the possible parallels between the sagas of Totrash / Tutarash / Sotrash and the Hittite myth of the storm god Zaskhapuna.

Text 15 deviates from the others in that it depicts the villain as an uncle of Satanaya, but then it has Sosruquo returning from battle and showing his adversary's head to Satanaya as 'your(.feminine)-son his-head' (/ bə-pá yə-q̄á /). At this, Satanaya flies into a rage at Sosruquo and wounds him in the Achilles tendon (echoes of that famous Greek's heel!) with her scissors, rather than Sotrash's mother trying to do so with a spit that shatters only a door frame. I suspect that as garbled as it is, this account preserves an older theme of fratricide and the consequent spurning of Sosruquo by his (step)mother Satanaya. This would explain the animosity between these two, frequently seen in the Ubykh corpus. It may also explain the variant name Sotrash, possibly reinforcing a link of kinship with Sosruquo, both originally the sons of Sos. This tale also asserts that Sosruquo was one of eight brothers, (one of seven in text 9 [see saga 57] and one of six men in text 16, saga 59), whereas the other variants assert that Totrash / Sotrash was one of nine, eight of whom have already been killed. The actual wounding of Sosruquo in the ankle is echoed in his epithet Lame Sosruquo.

The name of the villain, Totrash, but here Tutarash (showing a Circassian influence), or Sotrash, may be the most interesting name in the entire Abaza corpus and deserves some discussion.

In the Rig-Veda of ancient India, written in Vedic Sanskrit, Tvastr is an enigmatic figure who is killed by the hero Indra and who may have been Indra's father. Within Vedic scholarship the significance of this figure remains obscure and his name opaque. As Totraz, Totyradz (Ossetic), Totaresh (Circassian), Totrash, Tutarash (Abaza), Totrash (Abkhaz), and Tutaresh (Ubykh) this name, however, is continued from an Iranian source in the Nart sagas, with suffixes *-(d)z* or *-esh / -ash*. Its immediate source cannot be Ossetic, because the expected Ossetic development of a Proto-Indo-Iranian (the branch of Indo-European from which both Sanskrit and Iranian languages, such as Ossetic, are descended) *twastr* would be *Tosra(dz)*; compare Proto-Indo-Iranian *wasti* 'woman', Iron Ossetic *us*, Digoron Ossetic *uosæ* (Bielmeier 1977, 41). The first syllable, *to-*, shows the expected Iranian development of *twa-*; compare Proto-Indo-Iranian *hwaha* 'sister', Iron Ossetic *xo*, whereas the Circassian form, Tawtaresh, is automatically from *twataresh* and shows a more conservative development, as with the Proto-Indo-Iranian *hwahar* 'id.', Digoron Ossetic *x°æræ* (ibid., 40). The compound nature of the name is evident from the variant Sotrash in myth 91, with *so-* from Proto-Indo-Iranian *šwas-a-* 'breath, life' (Proto-Indo-European *kwes-* → English *wheeze*), as seen in the Ossetic Soslan from *šwas-alānām-* 'breath-(of the) Alans', Abaza Sosran(pa) (saga 61), Circassian Sosr(uquo). Thus, this myth offers striking evidence that the name of this ancient figure was a compound, Tva-str, and that this form was continued down to the present through an Ossetic-like language of the western Eurasian steppes.

Further, text 20 and the following one give striking and unique evidence concerning the meaning of the name. In the present one the eyes of this figure, Totrash, Tutarash, are seen as two stars, shining like the morning star. In the next text this figure, called Sotrash, has an inchoate dark form, like the night. The head of his horse, which is that of a deer (see n. 5 of saga 91), "hangs in the sky," further attesting to the rider's original celestial nature.

The interpretation of this figure is now as startling as it is simple. The original name is to be read as an ancient Indo-European, *Tw-astr* 'two-star', with a form for 'two' that is classically peripheral, and hence oldest Indo-European in that it shows a form for 'two' with *t* and the form for 'star' with the original *a*-coloring laryngeal consonant in vocalic position. More central or familiar Indo-European languages, such as Sanskrit and those of the Iranian branch, would have gone back to forms such as *dwo-* for 'two' and *ster-* for 'star', so that the name would have been *Dwoster*. Therefore Tvastr cannot be Indo-Iranian because one would have expected Sanskrit *Dvastar* or Iranian *Dostar*. The older, marginal languages, however, show tendencies toward voicelessness, as with the Germanic *two, Armenian *erku* ← *tku* ← *tgö* ← *two*, or Sikel (ancient Sicily) *rutilos* and Ausonian (eastern ancient Italy) *Rutulos*, both based on the root for 'red', or Illyrian (ancient Croatia) *metu* 'middle' and Messapian (at the heel of ancient Italy) *mess-(ap-)* ← *metya-(ap-)* 'between-waters', both from ← *medh-yo-*, or Pelasgian (early settlers of Greece) *Korinthos* ← *ghor-ent-os*, based on the root for 'city, enclosed area for the horde'.

Twastr thus falls naturally into this set of forms from peripheral and therefore very old Indo-European languages. It therefore must be a borrowing from a lost "first-wave" Indo-European language of inner Eurasia, "Twastrian." The only first-wave language directly attested from this region is Tokharian. Its form for 'two' is *wu* ← *twu* and that for 'star' is *s'cirye* ← *ster-yo-*, so that the name would have been *Wus'cir* if the source language had been Tokharian. The figure himself may have been a syncretistic stellar god (the morning and evening stars), combining the iconography of the Divine Twins, Castor and Pollux, and their congeners. In the Nart corpora this figure is supremely ferocious and mighty and can be defeated only by the guile of a hero who is one or two generations younger than he. He may have been an earlier hypostasis of the Divine Twins, perhaps even their father. If so, then outside Indo-Iranian and Twastrian, his role as father of these Divine Twins was usurped by the Indo-European sky god *Dyews → Sanskrit Dyaus, Greek Zeus, Latin Iu(piter), Old Norse Týr, English Tues(day), Irish (Dag)dae, Hittite šiu-š, who may have been opposed to him as day to night, and his eyes have become the twins themselves, who perpetuate their celestial origins in their names in Greek (Kastor and Polydeukes) and in Latin (Castor and Pollux) but who retain the important equine aspect of Tvastr in their hippomorphic forms in Sanskrit (Ashvins 'two horses') and in the invading Germanic Saxon leaders (Horsa 'horse' and Hengist 'nimblest').

My point about Twastrian is that some such language had to exist simply because the sort of discontinuity that is found between Indo-Iranian and Tokharian in the eastern reaches of the Indo-European expansion simply does not come into existence unless there is a major geographic barrier (not the case on the Eurasian steppe) or intervening material, Indo-European or otherwise. Such a language would have been absorbed by an expanding group, and Indo-Iranian was an expanding group if ever there was one. Such lost material should show traces, such as place-names or toponyms, non-Indo-European words in the distinctive vocabulary of Indo-Iranian, and Indo-European words that lack Indo-Iranian features within Indo-Iranian itself. All Indo-European branches show both non-Indo-European and anomalous Indo-European words as part of their "signature" vocabularies, for example, Germanic dog, non-Indo-European, and folk Indo-European, but of unknown provenance, since Indo-European *wol-(es)k- should yield Germanic *wol(is)x-, as in Old English Wælisc, W(e)alh, Modern English Welsh(man).

The name *Tw-astr was borrowed into Indo-Iranian along with the overthrow of this earlier god by his successor, the Indo-Iranian storm god Indra, the allusions to him preserving the mythic representation of a cultic struggle. Thus we can see in this one name direct proof of the existence in ancient Central Asia of an otherwise unknown Indo-European people of great antiquity and archaic linguistic form. If the Nart sagas had yielded no other insight than this, their study would be well worth the effort.

---

[1] In Abaza /təwma/ 'hybrid, cross-breed, hodgepodge'.

[2] Here the Russian (p. 244) reads: "Because of his usefulness and the good things that he did. . . ." This is one of several euphemistic renderings in the Russian translations of this corpus.

[3] In text 20 Tutarash (Totrash, Sotrash) is attending a wedding feast and is amusing the

guests by shoving a large boulder under a gate with his toe and then extracting it with his finger. Sosruquo passes by, stops for a drink, and performs the same feat, but he uses his toe both to wedge the boulder under the gate and to extract it. Tutarash grows jealous and sets off to murder Sosruquo, who has already resumed his journey.

[4] Text 15, "Lame Sosruquo," uniquely refers to his mother as Sataniya.

[5] This feature survives from the much older storm-god form of this hero (see n. 10).

[6] The Aryq is the gorge of a river. As with the other languages of the family, the Abaza suffix /-ž°/ can mean "evil" as well as "old," so this gorge is a forbidding place.

[7] Text 15 has the villain, here unnamed, lift Sosruquo out of his saddle by placing a pronged lance under his armpits.

[8] Many of the Iranian or Scythian burials of southern Siberia have revealed horse head-dresses sporting reindeer antlers (Raevskij 1985). This myth now offers an interpretation of the cultic lore underlying these otherwise enigmatic trappings. The reference to this deer's head hanging in the sky is a remnant of the original celestial nature of Sotrash / To-trash, as is the amorphous black form in which Sosruquo first encounters him (for a horse mask with antlers, see Rice 1957, plate 11). The reference to nine brothers in the next line also suggests a possible celestial referent, such as a constellation.

[9] In text 15 the bells are attached to a shaggy, coarse woolen garment called a *gwabanayk* (/g°abanak‍ʸ/).

[10] As with his thunder (n. 5), this is an old legacy of Sosruquo's origin as a storm god.

[11] With such an echo of Caesar's *veni, vidi, vici* (Abaza /s-ʔá-ca-z, s-bá-č'°ə, sɔ́-r-q̄-y-a-t'/ 'I-there-go-past.part, I-see-exhaustively, properly, I-their-head(s)-go-on-past', all old-looking forms), it is tempting to see here, as well as in the Latin, an ancient and widespread warrior's formulaic declaration of victory. Note the plural reference to "their heads" in the third Abaza verb, suggesting the formulaic nature of this utterance, which is otherwise at odds with the single enemy of this story.

[12] The "you" (plural) here seems to refer to the Narts or perhaps even the listeners. The quizzical ending is the bard's way of denouncing the catastrophic consequences of pursuing the warrior ethic to its conclusion. This warrior ethic is still very much alive in the Caucasus, as its recent tragic history has once again shown.

SAGA 61 ✑ *Sosruquo and Sosranpa*

I

> Sosruquo brought out his *alyp*.
> He saddled him with a copper saddle.
> All his weapons he hung on himself.
> He mounted his alyp and set out on a journey.
> Sosruquo was galloping and galloping.
> The sky and earth grew close together.
> A cloud pressed down on the earth.
> There was no rustling, just stillness.
> Nowhere was there a sound, just silence.
> Sosruquo was peering through the cloud.
> Ahead of him a horseman with a pointed helmet came galloping.
> He was riding, drinking the lightning.
> Both horsemen passed each other and greeted each other.
> Then they continued on their ways for another ten paces.
> Then both horsemen turned around.
> And at the same time they attacked each other.
> They fought using their clubs, urging their horses against one
>   another.
> In this battle Sosruquo was like a lion.
> He pulled the horseman out of his saddle
> And flung him down.
> Into shards of stone his shoulder shattered.
> And darkness covered him.
> Sosruquo climbed on him
> And put his sword[1] to his throat.
> "O Marja![2] Don't kill me, I beg of you!
> My warm blood will not gratify your heart."
> Sosruquo began to waver.
> "Stand up, you animal! I set you free.
> Go into the world again! I am freeing you."
> Having said that, Sosruquo rose off him.
> And having put his sword back into its scabbard,
> He stepped away from him.

II

The horseman stood up and shook himself.
And with fervor he again attacked Sosruquo.
They were once again fighting.
Clods of earth flew from under their feet.
Pebbles, like birds, flew above them.
Dust covered the whole sky above them.
The steam coming from them turned into clouds.
The ground was crying out because of them.
Fire was coming from them.
Sosruquo was fighting, attacking straight on.
No other means did he use.
He relied solely on his power.
The horseman fought very skillfully.
The horseman tripped Sosruquo.
He threw Sosruquo onto his back.
"Oh, yes! Now God has given him to me.
I was shrewd and I am once more on my feet."
Sosruquo drew together his strength.
But in vain, for he had erred.
"Give me a chance to stand up, I beg you!
He who becomes weaker the third time, let him then perish."
"Thunder and lightning, man!
You are already weaker than I am,
And you are already dead.
You were stupid and foolish,
Allowing me to stand up the first time."
Then Sosruquo grew furious.
He tried to pull his sword out but could not.
But the knife hidden under his sword he did pull out.
And he thrust this knife into the foe
Who was sitting on him,
So that he fell down.
"It is a pity that you have bitten me in vain.
Let my blood be a symbol of your lifelong shame!"
Having said that, the horseman with the pointed helmet died.

III

Their two horses were standing peacefully together.
They stood near one another, looking one upon the other.
They listened to the words of their masters.
They had been gazing on the deeds of their masters
As if they had wanted to discern which of them would win.
Both were standing like brothers.
Sosruquo drew close to the horses.
He drove both of them over to the dead man.
He turned the dead man on his back.
He pushed against his back and bent him.
Then he bound him over the horse's back with a rawhide rope
And covered him with a coat that had been tied there.
Then Sosruquo slowly continued on his way.
He wondered about the man he had killed.
"Who was he and whose was he?" Sosruquo did not know.
Some time passed in this way.
Then he chanced upon an old goatherd
Tending his flock.
"Salam aleykum, goatherd, may your herd grow!"
"Aleykum salam, Guest, may everything be good for you!
Welcome, welcome to us, good man!"
"I came indeed with a request to you."
"Tell me, and I shall always do whatever I can."
"I shall show a dead man to you.
Will you become scared?
I want to know who he is."
Sosruquo opened the coat.
He showed the dead to the goatherd.
"Oh, my God! My boy, I know him.
Let the life of the one who killed him be long,
For he has made happy all the people around!
This is Sosranpa[3] the bloodsucker.[4]
A great villain, people called him.
He lived his life in spite, only mean deeds did he do.
He tanned many human skins for his coat.
He trampled all under his feet.
He stopped the mouths of all.
He made all eat bowls of dung.

He was born in the neighboring village.
It is not far away.
What I have wished for so long has finally come to pass.
Be healthy and may your old age be happy!"
"I shall carry the dead man to his home.
Good-bye, until I see you again!"
The goatherd was gazing down and thinking.
He was pondering what to give him for such good news.
"For the joy you have brought me,
I shall give to you my goats.
May you be happy and rich with them!
If you accept, I wish that you be my guest.
I wish that you try my salted porridge.
If you refuse, I will be offended."
"I accept," said Sosruquo.
And they both went toward the village.
They soon came upon an old woman.
His wife, the old woman, prepared corn mush.
She also prepared *ashij,* curds and cheese in oil.
The ashij was hot, so hot that Sosruquo could not eat it.
Seeing that, the old woman began to fuss about.
"You, just like Sosruquo, rush straight ahead.
Sosruquo does everything like that.
He grows tired because he is not smart.
You also are not smart.
You plunge your hand deep into the hot ashij!
Start from the edge, my dear, whom I love!
Meanwhile, it will cool so that you may eat the middle."
Hearing that, Sosruquo smiled.
He recalled how the dead man had thrown him down.
They had a drink and some food, and then Sosruquo set out again.
He traveled far, and at last he entered the dead man's village.
He found his house and came into the backyard.
Some people who were in the yard took his corpse.
They carried him into the guest house.
His relatives gathered and began to mourn.
"Oh, we shall know who killed him," they said.
Sosruquo then stood up and said,
"I killed him myself.

And I brought him to you.
Whoever wishes to avenge his blood, leave the yard!
I am setting off for my home!"
The other villagers grew happy at what Sosruquo had done.
They gathered together and appointed three men.
These ran after Sosruquo and invited him to return with them.
The whole village feasted Sosruquo.
They proclaimed him forever their son.
A whole herd of cattle they gave him as a present.
Sosruquo began to drive the cattle.
The whole herd of cattle he drove along.
He was driving it to the goatherd as a gift to him.
He was driving it along, and at last he came to him.
The goatherd welcomed Sosruquo to him.
He was his guest.
Feasting and games were prepared for him.
Then Sosruquo set off for his home.
He was riding, and soon he reached the site of his recent battle.
Sosruquo stopped in his tracks.
He was remembering all his past deeds.
He stood, listening and looking around.
He was standing in the melted cloud.
He heard some sounds to the left of him.
Sosruquo rode toward these sounds.
He looked and saw a throng of people.
He drew closer.
They were trying to erect a huge stone.
They saw Sosruquo and recognized him immediately.
They all said to him,
"Sosranpa's village thanks you, Sosruquo.
Live a long life, Sosruquo, and be healthy!
You have shown your courage here!
You earned all these praises.
We all are erecting a monument to you.
The village of Sosranpa sent us here to do this.
We do this in your honor."
Sosruquo bade them farewell and went on his way.

From text 19 (marked 20 and mistitled), pp. 98–103.

◌ This tale closely parallels the preceding one, with Sosranpa taking the role of Totrash / Sotrash. Here Sosruquo is guileless, whereas Sosranpa is treacherous. The delivery of the dead man to his kin is far less dramatic than in the preceding saga, with the themes of mourning and revenge not elaborated on.

[1] The word / psaḥ°a / is an old one, not known to most speakers, and appears to be based on / ps-aḥ°a / 'to die-sword', from the Proto-Abkhaz-Abaza * / pś-ax̌°a /. It refers to the long Caucasian dagger, now known by its Turkic name, *kinjal*.

[2] A term of address, showing respect and obeisance.

[3] Sosranpa may in fact be the original name of Sosruquo, showing the Abkhaz-Abaza patronymic -*pa* in place of the Circassian -*uquo*. This Abaza doublet, Sosranpa, son of Sosran, a brother of Satanaya (see saga 46 and n. 1 of saga 47), preserves the original evil trickster quality of this hero as well as his demonic storm aspects. He would be Sosruquo's cousin. The moral transformation of this hero carried out under his Circassian name is made absolute by the defeat of the evil Sosranpa at the hands of the good Sosruquo in a historical and mythical irony.

[4] The Northwest Caucasian peoples have vampirelike figures as part of their inventory of supernatural beings, but this reference to such a villain is unique among the Nart corpora.

SAGA 62 ◌ *Qaydukh of the Narts*

She who was called Qaydukh[1] of the Narts was a very beautiful woman. She was a wise woman too. Qaydukh's husband was called Psabida.[2] Raiding against his enemies and robbing them was his means of life and his custom. He was stealing, robbing. He was very courageous. That is what Psabida did for his livelihood.

In their time were the tribes of the Chints and the Marakwa,[3] who were his enemies. He attacked them. Although they lived far away from him, his lands had a common border with theirs, so he raided them and robbed them. He drove away their cattle, their mares, their sheep, and their bulls. He drove away everything he could and all that they had. He fought with them and defeated them. So that is how Psabida lived, near the Injig River. He lived near the river Injig.

When Psabida set off, he had to cross the river. It was very big. He made a linen bridge, and whenever he had the need to cross the river he stretched his bridge out, and after he had crossed the river he rolled it up. So that is how he crossed this river when he was returning from his raids with mares, cattle, and other booty. He used this bridge only at night. It was not possible to use it in the daytime.

When he was returning home at night, his wife, Qaydukh, put her diamond ring out the window, and thus its light helped him cross the river. If it had not been so bright, the darkness would not have allowed him to drive the cattle and horses over the bridge. They would have been scared. So thanks to this light, she actually helped him cross the bridge. Psabida did not know about any of this. That is how they lived for a while.

Psabida was very courageous, and yet he was very boastful. After his return from another raid, he usually said to Qaydukh, "Is there among the Narts a man who is like me? There is not and will not be among them a man such as I." After he returned from a raid, he used to brag before his wife, saying that he was the only one with such a courageous character. Qaydukh was wise, but she disagreed with that.

Some time passed since these events, and at last she said, "What is it, Psabida? I have heard that there is Sosruquo, a great warrior, and someone named Badanoquo, also a great warrior. Although I have not seen them, I have heard about them. You too have probably heard about them, haven't you? And they have done much greater heroic deeds than you have. So there are real men among the Narts these days besides you. A real Nart does not praise himself. What is the purpose of praising yourself?" The conversation turned into an argument from this point on.

"No!" he said. "There is no one greater than I!"

Then she replied, "Let's not talk about that. All that you do, all that you bring home is really due to me. It is I who does it. I am doing it while I sit at home! You can't do anything without my help!"

"How come?" he retorted. "You don't come with me on my raids, and I cannot see or feel your help at all. So tell me how is it possible that all I bring home is indeed, according to you, done by you."

"No," she said. "You wouldn't be able to drive the cattle without my help. It is I who helps you. Although you think that you do it, it is I who accomplishes that. Without my eyes, without my power, you would not be able to do anything."

So they argued about that. In the heat of the argument she said, "It may be true that it is you who drives them home, but you will see whether you can do anything without my help."

"You will see," he replied. "I will drive them home without you anyway."

"No, you can't!" she said.

"You will see that I will drive them myself. All that you have said will be a lie," he said. So he grabbed his horse, saddled it, and set off on his way.

He set off in the night. He wore a coat made by Qaydukh and shoes made by Qaydukh. She was the woman who did all that for him. She is the woman. If not for her, he could not have done those things for himself. She was a wonderful craftswoman. The saddle on his horse was also made by her. She also took care of his horse when he rested at home after another raid. Qaydukh zealously looked after him, tended to him. She was glad to take care of Psabida's horse. Psabida's horse loved her more than Psabida did himself. It also understood everything she told him. That is how much Psabida's horse loved her.

Now, when Psabida set off on his way, his horse became aware that its master had quarreled with his wife. (This horse was smart.) Every time Psabida left his place for the land of the Chints, the two would travel a long way. On all past occasions when Psabida reached the crossroads, he would talk to his horse. "Follow the road on which we will have luck!" He would pat it on its neck and say these words, and the horse usually chose the road where they indeed were lucky.

That night, after husband and wife had had their quarrel, Psabida and his horse reached the crossroads. The horse stopped. As soon as it stopped, Psabida said, "Hey, you! Come on! Go ahead!" The horse would not budge. Then he hit the horse hard. At this the horse moved in the direction in which the reins were pulling, so that the horse set out on the wrong way, a way that it had hitherto avoided, a way chosen this time by the man and not by the horse. The man in turn thought that the horse had chosen the right path as usual.

So after a long time he assumed that they had reached the land of the Chints. But when they crossed over onto this land, a severe blizzard began to howl and it grew very cold. His felt cloak would not keep him warm and his horse could not help him either. The saddle under him became loose, and his shoes would not keep his feet warm. He became helpless. He could neither start a fire nor hide himself anywhere. He was freezing and in big trouble.

Then soon after the frost, a terrible heat wave hit him, so terrible that no one could stand it. Again his felt cloak did not protect him. He wanted to drink and looked for a spring or pond, but whenever he found one it would turn to mud. Besides, he was stricken with hunger, but when he tried to eat his food, his mouth was too dry. He became completely helpless and exhausted. He did not know what to do. If he returned home now, it would be a great shame before Qaydukh. So he suffered this misfortune and left the land of the Chints.

From there he entered the land of the Isps.[4] The Isps themselves are undersized, dwarfish people. Their buffaloes, horses, and cows are out in the steppes both day and night. When he approached them, he rounded up all the horses and drove them to the road. Then he did the same with the buffaloes and cows. But when he had gathered all of them together on the road, his horse refused to move. He began to beat his horse, all day and all night until the blood appeared on its ribs and until he had finally broken all of its ribs.

"Kill me! Do whatever you want!" said the horse. It placed its legs wide apart and would not budge. Psabida beat it until he grew tired.

"What has happened to you? What are you doing?" said Psabida. "Although we may have had an argument, her heart is still watching us. Don't you know that with her heart she, Qaydukh, is here?" When the horse heard her name, it began to move again and continued on its way.

He and his horse followed all the horses, buffaloes, and cows that he had rounded up. They traveled for many days and nights. At last the Isps realized that their cattle had been stolen, that they had lost all their livestock, that a Nart had rustled their herds. They gathered into a powerful band and set out after him. But since he was far away, they could not immediately overtake him. They still had not caught up with him when he reached the banks of the Injig. He approached the river. As soon as he had started to cross the linen bridge hanging over it, he heard the sounds of the pursuing war band. It was night. As soon as he heard the sounds of his pursuers, he stopped and looked behind him. How many of them were there? He realized his danger, and so he began to herd the buffaloes, mares, and cows tightly together and drive them to the linen bridge.

Since he was two or three days late in returning, Qaydukh had begun to worry and her heart had grown softer toward him. "This is no good. I have hurt him enough. I tried to freeze him to death and then I set a great heat upon him. By now he must be very tired." Having said that, she put her arm out the window of the tower she was in and with her ring illumined the whole area around the bridge.

When it became light, Psabida grew very glad and began to drive all his booty across the bridge. When they had reached the middle of the bridge, however, her heart felt doubt again. "He may reproach me again," she thought as she saw him and withdrew her arm into the room. The bridge was plunged into darkness, and all the mares and cattle fell from it into the

Injig River, taking Psabida with them. The waters whirled him about. He was unable to escape the waves and drowned.

Qaydukh looked around and could not find him. He had been on the bridge when she illumined it, but he was no longer there. "This is no good," she said. She lived atop a precipice in a fortress that now bears her name, and in the morning she looked out with binoculars and saw that the waters had carried him all the way to the village of Bibakart (now El'bur-gan). She could see him floating in his felt cloak among the small islands, where he had washed up against a tree. She recognized him in his cloak, drowned and washed up against the tree. What could she do now? She descended, went to the village, pulled him from the water, and carried him back up to her fortress, Qaydukh. To the best of her ability she buried him. She dug out the ground and hid him, buried him. (He was, after all, her husband. How could her heart not be a bit sad?)

For three days and three nights she mourned him, as custom dictates. As she was sitting on the shore weeping for him, a rider, Sosruquo, passed on the opposite side of the Injig. This horseman heard her crying and stopped to look around. "Oh, my God! She has no one with her, and this lonely, weeping woman seems to be in great sorrow. I must learn what is the matter with her." Saying this, he plunged into the river while still on horseback, and he and his steed swam across it. He approached Qaydukh and greeted her as he was supposed to, as custom dictates.

"O woman!" he said. "Why are you crying? What has wounded your heart? Look at me! Nobody is around here. You are alone. What has befallen you? Why do you grieve?" Sosruquo loved the Narts very much. He was ready to give away his soul or head for a child, for an old man, or for any man of the Narts. That was the kind of man he was, unlike anybody else. When Sosruquo did anything good, he did it only for the sake of the Narts. He loved the Nart people more than he loved himself. That is how great Sosruquo's heart was.

"I am Qaydukh, and I have lost my husband," she said and proceeded to tell him of her woe. "All this is true, but the most surprising thing is how you managed to swim across the river. It is not possible for anyone other than a Nart man to swim across this river at this place. How did you do it?" she asked.

"It wasn't I who swam across it. It was my horse," said Sosruquo.

When he answered her in this way, she was reminded of the words and character of her husband, of her argument with him, of his bragging, of his words that there was nobody among the Narts who was stronger than he. "This one doesn't even praise himself," she said to herself. She liked him for this. The main feat he did he attributed to his horse. He did not count his courage. Besides, she liked his words. "Wonderful, and so may it be!" she replied.

Now after she had told him about all her problems, he said farewell to her. "I must be on my way now. When I return, I shall visit you. So may it be!" he said, mounted his horse, and set off again.

He was on his way once more. He swam across the river and set off. Qaydukh was amazed. She watched carefully how he crossed the river. "And for that, my husband praised himself. Only one night I refused to help him, and he could not cross this river. He and his horse were drowned. This is a Nart man. My husband was a Nart man. Yet this one does not claim that it was he who crossed the river. He said that it was possible thanks to his horse. When he wanted to be on this side, he crossed the river. When he wanted to be on the other side, he did it again. I shall test him one more time," she said to herself. "I shall find out what the limit of his courage may be. Make it so, Allah, that the goddess of water, Gwasha,[5] floods this valley with water! Let it rain everywhere! Let a severe blizzard begin right now! O Allah! Make these things come to pass now!" she beseeched God. A severe blizzard began. The goddess Gwasha brought water, drawing together two or three more rivers to join the Injig. The whole valley soon filled with water.

When this happened, Sosruquo thought, "Something might befall that lonely woman whom I just left. She cannot help herself. This strong frost will kill her. I must postpone my quest for the time being." Having said that, he turned back and began to ride in her direction.

Qaydukh watched him in amazement. She had wanted to test his courage, but now the river had two or three times the volume of water that it had when he crossed it earlier. She wanted to see whether he could cross it again.

Once more, without visible effort, he crossed the river just as he had the first two times. Then the sun disappeared and it grew dark. He swam the river and stepped onto the opposite shore.

"O Sosruquo! When you crossed this river the first time, it was almost unbelievable. But how did you manage to do it this time!" she asked.

"I have already told you. It is not I who swam over it, but my horse," he replied.

"No," she said, "my late husband, Psabida, often said that there is nobody among the Narts who would be equal to him in courage and strength. But only once I refused to help him, only one night did I fail to help him, and he could not cross this river. He drowned. Over there he is buried," she said. "It is he for whom I mourn. You crossed this river several times when it was a big river and even when it became two or three times greater. You stopped your travels and out of concern for me turned around. He was not a true man. He often lied to me. You, though, are a real Nart man. All he said to me were falsehoods. He lied to me until his last moments. I shall dig him up and throw his corpse off this cliff," and having said that she rushed over to his grave.

"No!" said Sosruquo. "Be calm, Qaydukh! All this is unnecessary. It is no good, Qaydukh. There is reason for restraining yourself. Listen! There were times when you had a hard time living together. It is true that Psabida loved no one but himself. But your revenge is useless now. Once you did not help him, and he, being unable to cross the river, drowned. You have had enough problems with him. You have worried enough with his grave. Now you are alone, and you should not work so much ever again. He was also a human being, so leave him in peace. The world will not turn upside down, neither will he appear alive once again. But it is true that he loved his own head only. All the rest about him in the world he did not love."

"But he said that I was the only one whom he loved in this world," replied Qaydukh.

"If that was true, what he said to you, then let us see what happens with his grave where he is now lying," said Sosruquo.

The earth around the grave was soon covered with blossoms and grass. The whole world grew green, calm, and beautiful, but his grave alone remained as it had been—barren and black.

"You see," said Sosruquo, "of all else in the world, he loved only himself. He did not love you at all. He lived with you just for pleasure. You were not important to him at all. That is the reality of it all," he said. "Now think about it!"

It was still raining a bit. Where should she go? Sosruquo had a felt cloak, and together they took shelter under it, hiding themselves away and chatting. What should he do with her? So he married her.

Sosruquo married Qaydukh. That is the legend of Qaydukh, and that is how it was with her husband, Psabida.

From text 31, pp. 121–28.

⌾ This saga and the next one present one of the two women in the Abaza corpus who rival Satanaya in their qualities, if not in the abundance of their lore. Qaydukh is primarily a sorceress whose properties have been largely subsumed by the fertility figure Satanaya. Unlike Satanaya, however, she is of Sosruquo's generation and becomes his consort. This alone is probably the reason that she has survived in the corpus and has not been completely absorbed by the image of Satanaya. The woman in the next saga is the nameless warrior maiden of the forest (see saga 74), who is a congener of the Circassian Forest Mother, Amazan. There are strong convergences between Qaydukh and this maiden of the forest: both live in remote castles, both have the magical power to create storms or great cold, and in both sagas there is a body buried by a river. Qaydukh's saga, however, is one of the eventual fulfillments of love and trust, whereas that of the forest maiden is one of the eventual betrayals of love and trust. The two sagas are inverses of one another.

¹ This figure is cognate with Adif, "White Elbow," of the Circassian corpus. In the Abkhaz corpus Satanaya has taken over even this tale. The name Qaydukh may be of mixed Iranian-Abaza origin: / qay-dəw-x̌° / 'magician-great-woman' (saga 77 n. 2). The first morpheme, / qay /, may reflect Iranian *Kay (Us)*, cognate with Sanskrit *Kavya (Ushanas)* (see Dumézil 1986, 12–15), the name of a figure who was preeminently a sorcerer, the first magus. The second morpheme, / dew /, is Abkhaz-Abaza for 'big, great'. The third, / x̌° /, is an old root for 'woman' (see saga 50 n. 2). Such an etymology for her name would suit her attributes well.

The story of Qaydukh is one of domestic fairness and marital ideals. It offers a paradigm for women's critical contribution to men's success, even in warring and raiding, from the linen bridge her husband uses to cross a chasm to her guiding light, which he uses to find his way home. Although in this saga her husband, Psabida, made this bridge, in the Circassian accounts this bridge is of his wife's making and can even be depicted as being the long sleeve of her gown. Her husband is a cruel figure exemplifying the crudeness that the male temperament and the obligation of warring may induce. His brutishness contrasts with the valor of Sosruquo, who stands for the grace to which the male should aspire despite his role as a warrior.

² This name appears to be Kabardian (East Circassian) and means "hard life," / psabəda / 'life-hard, difficult'.

³ It is unclear whether these people, traditional enemies in the Nart corpora, may have had any historical origins. The second name seems to mean "killers": / mara-k'°a / 'death-agent', with the agentival suffix being Circassian even though this name is absent from the Circassian corpus

⁴ In the Circassian corpus the Isp or Spe are the tribe from which Bataraz's mother comes. In the Abaza corpus (saga 74) her tribe is that of the Marakwa. In this saga the Spe and the Marakwas seem to be conflated.

⁵ *Gwasha* simply means "lady" in Circassian.

SAGA 63 ☙ *Qaydukh Fortress*

Psabida of the Narts lived in Qaydukh Fortress. His guest house was located there, whereas now this is Kubanskaya. During morning tea, the tea was sent there still hot, and that which he had to eat as his dinner also was sent there not cooled. It was a place where they had their dinner. Their guests and such sat there.

Psabida of the Narts was like this. He went to the Kalmyks[1] and drove back horses. He drove these horses, but there was no bridge in Qaydukh. It was only a linen bridge there. He drove them onto this bridge as he was returning. His wife lit the surrounding area with her ring. And under her ring's light all the horses passed over the linen bridge. Always, by the time of his return, as soon as he climbed down from his horse, she had prepared food in advance and would have it waiting for him.

"How does she know when I am returning?" he said. "If I never say what I am going to do, then her fortune-telling will prove false." So saying, he pretended to set out on his way, but he turned back soon after and hid himself somewhere. While he was hiding somewhere, she tossed her beans.[2] Nothing happened.

"Something has stopped him," she said, and so she turned from her fortune-telling for a while. Later she tossed the beans again. "Now he is on his way back." Again she prepared dinner and met him with a ready meal.

"Ah," he said. "Why are you so excited?"

"I do not know what happened to you this time, but your signs are so unpleasant," she said.

"Anything could have happened," he said. "In this case, your beans were false. Your fortune-telling told a lie to you."

"They are not false! They are not false, my beans!" she said. "It is you who are lying."

At this point they disagreed. They stood back from each other and began to argue.

"It is thanks to me that you bring horses home."

"How come? What do you mean by 'thanks to me'?" he said.

"It is I who does it," she said.

"No. It is not due to you," he said.

"Yes, thanks to me," she said. "Let us see whether you can do it yourself!"

They grew angry with each other. They had infuriated each other.

Once he returned with rustled mares when it was shiny and rainy. She did not use her ring to cast light. The linen bridge grew shaky and he, together with the horses, fell into the water. That redness which we have in the neighborhood of Haghuntquaya[3] is exactly this indeed. That red which is lying there is blood. So she ruined him or killed him.

She killed him in that place. Then a year passed, and on the anniversary of his death she, claiming to be a man, set off to look for a wife. She found a woman, brought her home, and married her. They lived together for three years. And that woman whom she had married did not have a chance to realize that she was not a man. She did not tell her. They lived together for three years.

Then she decided to move. Sosruquo wooed her and said, "Either I'll go to you or you come to me."

"In that case," she said, "this will not do. How come you can't find somebody for my girlfriend?" she asked him. So she herself found a man for the woman whom she had married. Then she married Sosruquo and they lived together.

From text 22, pp. 110–11.

◌ This saga is a garbled account of Qaydukh. In the canonical form of the tale (saga 62), the wife is Qaydukh, but here her name remains only that of the castle. The wicked, boastful husband was originally Psabida, but in other texts he is Sosruquo, in his typical syncretistic fashion, has taken over his role and suffers Psabida's fate, the price paid for overextending himself as a mythic hero. Sosruquo attempts to test Qaydukh's clairvoyant powers, noting that she failed to foresee his own illegitimate birth. Qaydukh herself is in a transitional stage of being assimilated by Satanaya, as Sosruquo's allusion to his illegitimate birth indicates. Most interesting in this version is the allusion to a lesbian marriage, which has been distorted by the excuse that the new wife did not know the gender of her "husband." This "lesbian" marriage emphasizes the role reversals of which Qaydukh is capable (see also sagas 27 and 74), rather than suggesting overt homosexual practices. Recent finds from Scythian burials in the steppes of Inner Asia have revealed skeletons of women dressed in armor (Davis-Kimball 1997; Rolle 1980, 86–91), proving that such women warriors were more than mere myth.

[1] The Kalmyks are a remnant of the Mongol hordes. They live northeast of the Caucasus in their own republic, just to the west of Astrakhan. They are predominantly Buddhists.

² Scattering beans and then divining the future from their pattern was a favored means of fortune-telling in the Caucasus.

³ Now the village of Aliberduko in Karachai-Cherkessia.

SAGA 64 ◌ *The Doom of Sosruquo*

The Narts hated Sosruquo because of his great courage and his kind heart, because he had compassion for poor people and cared about them. They also hated him because he was the winner in all events. He beat all the Narts, all the heroes. They hated Sosruquo and were looking for an opportunity to kill him.

In the meantime, they could show only their disrespect, for despite all their attempts, they could not do anything to him. They laughed at him because he was the cowherd's son. Because they taunted him, Sosruquo did not leave the Narts in peace. They could not do anything against him despite their fervent wishes.

One day the Narts held a meeting among themselves. They made a pact with the ayniwzhes. They summoned a great group of ayniwzhes and asked them to gather on a certain day to kill Sosruquo. Then they went to the old sorceress, Barambukh. "If you show us the way to kill Sosruquo, there is nothing in this world we would not give to you," they promised her. This old sorceress could prepare any poison draft, and she herself could become a dog, a pig, or such. Then the Narts called a great council and invited Sosruquo.

Sosruquo was ready to go to the Nart council, and Satanaya became aware of his intentions. Satanaya was a fortune-teller who used beans, and she soon divined the Narts' intentions and their promises to that old lady sorceress. "My little boy! The Narts are plotting against you with the help of magic. Whatever you see on your way, do not pick it up!" She knew he would not return from there if he chose to go.

Few people in this world knew that Sosruquo's knees were not hardened. Only he knew about that, Tlepshw knew, and Satanaya knew. Now, he told Satanaya that he was going there, that he had been invited, that he chose to go, and that they had called him.

"Forget it, my little boy! Don't go! There is no return for you."

"No, I cannot. My heart tells me to go. He who does not obey his heart's dictates is not a man. A real Narts' man, once he has prepared himself to go, will not cancel his decision. I shall go. I cannot not go," he said.

She asked him many times. He refused.

"This way of yours is bloody. Don't go!"

"Oh!" he said. "How long does one live, anyway? One day you will die. Should you live a long time, you will still die anyway. My heart told me to go. I cannot not go. I will not live forever, anyway. If nothing else, let this fact be known about me. I will not retreat from my decision."

"If so, go, my little boy! My little boy, there is a plot against you that uses magic. On your way you will see many things. It may be some wonderful gold. It may be a diamond. It may be anything. You'll see many transformations. Whatever you meet, don't look at it, don't talk to it, don't pick up anything, and don't touch anything. Now go there, my little boy!"

"Fine," he said. "I won't touch anything." He promised her that he would not touch anything and departed. He rode along, Sosruquo did, and soon he saw a pair of boots[1] made of well-treated leather and a pair of boots made of raw leather fighting each other under a big tree, under a big pear tree. They were fighting for this tree. Once, when the raw-leather boots climbed the tree, it began blossoming. Then the boots made of well-treated leather pushed them off the tree, and the tree began to wither. Once again they fought, and once again the raw-leather shoes were on the tree and the tree bloomed, and yet again the other pair of boots pushed them off and the tree withered. "What a miracle!" he said as he passed them and rode on.

He rode on and saw a rope tied into knots lying directly on the road. He did not want to pick this rope up. After all, Satanaya had told him not to. When he passed that rope, it suddenly untied itself. He turned back and saw again that this rope was tied into knots. "What a miracle! When I pass it, it loosens itself. When I look back it ties itself into knots!"

He passed it and rode on. Soon he saw two horns lying in the road. One was full of beer and the other was empty. The empty horn was begging the full one to give it some beer. The full one refused. "What a miracle!" he said and rode on.

He went farther and saw a golden lash lying in the road. He passed it as well. Then he met a golden hat. "Here is a golden hat! There is a golden lash!" He had resolutely passed by all those strange and beautiful things, but with the last one he said, "How can a person resist taking one of those things?" He bent down, took the golden hat, put it on his head, and moved on again.

After he had ridden a little way, his horse said to him, "Hey, Sosruquo! Don't you remember what Satanaya said? She said, 'Don't touch anything!'"

"Hey, you good for nothing," he said and hit him hard with his lash. "What are you afraid of? What have we not done in our lives? What have our eyes not seen? Is that your loyalty? What are you afraid of? My death is in my knees. If my knees are not facing to the rear, there is nothing in this world I will be afraid of.[2] What if the Narts know that my knees are not hardened? They might hit them, cut off my knees, and thus kill me. Does your heart tell you that? As to you, your legs will be strong and swift as long as you stay off a beach. Don't be afraid of anything!"

He looked. There was no longer any golden hat on his head. That witch, Barambukh, had turned herself into a golden lash, a golden hat. He looked—the hat was gone.

"Oh! My hat is gone!" he said.

"Now, you see what that golden hat has done to you? Whatever was to have happened to you happened. Now you see for yourself the truth of your mother's words!" the horse said.

"Nothing will happen," he said, and he traveled on as if nothing had happened. Thus he reached the village.

A woman who had never been married lived there. When Sosruquo came by on his way, she was waiting for him. "Will Sosruquo stop at my house?" she said to herself. First he passed her house, but then he turned around and started coming back. "O God! Will he pass my place again without even stopping here for a while?" she asked herself. Sosruquo rode past her many times without stopping, so she left the yard and went back into her house. It was then that he halted.

"This day is growing a little bit dark. I'll have my rest here," he said and entered her yard. He dismounted and tied his horse to the tethering post. At the threshold a dog was lying on the ground, a pregnant bitch. It was impossible to enter the house without stepping over her. So after he had tied his horse to the tethering rail, he stepped over the dog. At this the puppies in the bitch's womb began to bark. He was very surprised.

He entered the house. An old man and an old woman were sitting there. He greeted them. When the old woman tried to talk, fire came out of her mouth. When the old man tried to talk, snakes came out of his mouth. He was astonished to see that.

He entered the next room. A young woman was lying there, sleeping. He looked at her attentively. She was a beautiful woman. She was of marriageable age. He gazed at her again, and trying not to awaken her, he put his hand on her right shoulder. Can one hold a fire? That is how strongly he was burned. He put his hand on her left shoulder. He felt as if he had put his hand on a piece of ice. While he was looking at her she awoke.

"Oh! How sweetly did I sleep!" she said. She saw Sosruquo standing nearby. She jumped up right away. "Sit! Sit down, Sosruquo! What brought you here? Sit down! Sit down!" she said.

"No!" he said. "I saw a miracle on my way, so I cannot sit down until I know what kind of miracle it is."

"Well, when on a trip one usually sees many wonderful things, but you sit down first. Let us see and discuss what was so miraculous in what you met," she said.

"When on my way I saw wonderful things. Soon after I departed, I met two pairs of boots fighting each other under a pear tree. One pair was made of well-treated leather. The other was of raw leather. That pear tree was almost dead. When the raw-leather boots were winning and they climbed the tree, that tree began to blossom. When the well-treated leather boots were winning and they threw the raw-leather boots down from the tree, that tree withered. That is what I saw."

"That is one. What else did you see?"

"I passed them, and then I saw a rope tied in knots, lying on the road. I found it tied in knots, but when I passed it, it became a plain rope without knots, lying in the road. When I turned back, it again had tied itself into knots."

"That is two. What else did you see?"

"Two horns. One was full with drink and the other was empty. The empty horn asked the full horn to give some liquid to him, but I saw that the full horn refused to share. I could not understand anything. They were not living horns, were they?"

"What else did you see?"

"On my way I saw a golden lash lying in the road. I did not pick it up. I passed it and picked up a golden hat and put it on my head. While I was riding and talking about this and that, the golden hat disappeared. That is how it was!"

"What else did you see?"

"Now, when I was passing this house, I stopped in at the yard. Nobody was there. Only a dog was lying near the threshold asleep there, a pregnant bitch. I stepped over her and heard the puppies in her womb begin to bark at me. That dog did not recognize me, but her puppies began to bark at me."

"What else did you see?"

"An old man and an old woman are in this house. When the old woman begins to talk, sparks fly out of her mouth. When the old man begins to talk, everything he says turns into snakes crawling out of his mouth."

"What else did you see?"

"I did not want to wake you up, so I put my hand on your right shoulder and burned my hand. When I put my hand on your left shoulder, I felt intolerable cold. Why did that happen?"

"I shall tell you why. When you decided to come here, your mother was very upset about that. You have chosen a bad way. Your mother was not happy about that. Those boots made of well-treated leather, which you saw, were those people who think the whole world belongs to them. And the boots made of raw leather represented simple people. These and those will fight each other some time in the future, and when that happens, the simple people will take the life of the whole world into their hands. They will win.

"That which you saw in the form of a rope lying in the road—when it straightened it meant that your way is straight. When you turned back, you see, it again tied itself into knots. It resembles your mother's heart. From time to time it catches fire, becoming tied into little knots. The way you have chosen is no good. Your mother's heart is squeezed into little knots.

"The horns that you have met were a sign that a sated man will never understand the needs of a hungry man. The sated man will not understand that a hungry man is hungry indeed.

"The golden hat that you saw was that which will kill you. The golden lash was also the one that will kill you, but when you passed it without picking it up, it turned into the golden hat. It appeared again ahead of you. You picked it up there and put it on your head. When it had heard enough about your affairs, your weaknesses, and the rest, it disappeared, didn't it?"

"Yes, it disappeared."

"This is what will kill you. Now you have reached the end of your way. That golden hat now knows all your weaknesses.

"As to that dog which was lying asleep, a man will come after us, and he will be smarter than we who live in the world. The time will come when this man will come as a baby. That time will come.

"As to that old man and that old woman, they are my father and mother. My elder sister was married without their permission, and they gave their word to curse her forever. They swore but could not keep their oath. They forgave her. Now, because they could not keep their word, sparks are coming out of her mouth and snakes from his. They broke their oath.

"When you went on your way, I thought, 'How much time has passed? Why did Sosruquo not stop at my house just one time?' I was burning, I wanted you so much. That is why my right shoulder was hot. When you turned back and passed by a second time without stopping at my house, my heart grew cold. That is why my left shoulder was cold. Both times your acts went straight to my heart, and with the last one my heart turned cold."

As soon as she said this, a wind began to blow. It became very windy. Crows began to fly down and gather above the house. Their beaks were covered in blood. Crowing, they flew around the roof. Then they took some hay from the roof and flew away.

"Don't go there! Turn back and go home! They are waiting for you. They have already prepared that with which they will kill you. Don't go there, I ask you!" said the girl.

"A real Nart man does not heed signs that others see. He never turns back," he said, and without listening to her, he set off on his way.

And there, when he arrived at Harama Toba,[3] a great throng of Narts had assembled. They were holding a feast. Nearby they had set all the ayniwzhes, and these awaited their chance.

The Narts began their games. First, they began to wrestle. Sosruquo beat them all. He beat them in horse riding as well. In other games he was stronger. They decided to throw a *djin-charkh*[4] at him. He hit it with his forehead and turned it back. Then he hit it with his chest and turned it back. He hit it with his foot and turned it back. He beat them in everything.

But did Barambukh, the witch, sit on his head as a golden hat in vain? "Oh, these Narts were never smart," she said. "You cannot kill him. You cannot kill Sosruquo, whatever you do. But his knees are not hardened. Their skin is soft," she said. "Tell him to hit the djin-charkh with his knees. He cannot refuse. It would go against his courage to refuse." They grew glad at her words.

"O Sosruquo! You have beaten us in everything. You have won our prize. It is yours. Now at last, can you turn back this djin-charkh with your knees?" they asked. He considered it undignified to refuse.

They threw the djin-charkh (very sharp was that djin-charkh), and after he hit it with his knees, the djin-charkh wounded both of them. Sosruquo fell down on the ground. His horse broke the tethering rope, ran down to him, and said, "Lie down on my back!" He lay on his horse's back and grabbed his mane. The Narts did not have a horse that could compete against Sosruquo's horse. The Narts grew very glad, and all the ayniwzhes, with their clubs, with their bows, all together with their warriors, ran after him to catch him.

"Hold my mane more strongly," said his horse. "If I begin to fly, you will fall off my back." His horse's legs had a secret. He had talked about it when the golden hat had been on his head. Barambukh knew that his horse's legs would be hurt if it went on a beach, especially one made of stone shingle.[5] "Drive them to the sea, to the sea!" screamed Barambukh after them.

The horde of ayniwzhes and Narts chased Sosruquo and his horse but could not overtake them. Soon they drove them to the shore of the Azov Sea. They drove them to the shore, and Barambukh said this: "The Narts could not understand anything. This horse's legs will grow weak on the beach shingle." And by driving the two of them closer and closer to the beach, they cut off all other possible paths, so they did not give the two of them a chance to go any way other than the shore of the Azov Sea. His horse had no choice but to turn to the seashore, but once it stepped on the shingle its legs grew weak, and it fell down. When it fell down there it said, "Now I am good for nothing. Kill me. Take my skin, and you can fight them for a short while. Get inside my skin, you man, and fight them! Now kill me!" his horse begged him.

He cut the horse's throat, flayed him, and got inside its skin, and for three days and three nights he struggled with the army of giants. And when he ran out of arrows, the Narts came closer to him and began to strike him with their swords. Both warriors and ayniwzhes began to strike him with their swords, but they could not even scratch him. He was as hard as steel, so they could not even scratch him. Whatever they tried, they could not do anything to him.

"Who wants to drink the hero's, the superman's blood? Who wishes to try to eat his flesh? Come here!" they said and called all of the wild animals and birds.

Soon all of the wild forest animals and birds gathered together. The first to speak was the wolf.

"I will not drink his blood or eat his flesh. When Sosruquo was alive he did not eat the flesh of wild animals. He gave it away to poor people and birds."

"I am giving away one-seventh of my power to the wolf. I give him my neck," said Sosruquo. That is why the wolf became so powerful and courageous. Had Sosruquo said "I am giving away all my power," it would not be possible to beat the wolf at all.

[Other animals came, and each refused to harm Sosruquo. To each he gave a part of his might. To the hare he gave his speed; to the eagle, his keen sight; to the fox, his cunning; to the deer, his surefootedness; and to the fish, his hard skin.]

Finally a small quail flew up and said, "I will not drink this hero's blood, and I will not eat his flesh."

Sosruquo asked the gods who lived on the summit of Wiriwsh Yiqimghwa,[6] "Please make it so that when the quail flaps its wings, it will make the same sound as my lash does, so that all its enemies will be afraid of it." So it happened.

Then, when his enemies realized that they could not kill him, they buried him under the ground so that he could not get out, and above him they erected a great burial mound. [So Sosruquo still lives to this day under the earth.]

From text 14, pp. 112–14, and supplementary text 2, pp. 173–79.

☙ Sosruquo meets his end through his vulnerable spot, much as Achilles and Siegfried met theirs, the first through his famously vulnerable heel, the second through a soft patch on his back. When Siegfried bathed in the dragon's blood to harden himself, a leaf fell on him and so kept a small spot of his skin untreated. Sosruquo's end, however, is conflated with the dismemberment and underground retreat of a fertility god, much like the Egyptian Osiris or the Greek Dionysos. The pertinent original, text 14, speaks only of the wolf and the quail. I have supplemented this list with material from Ubykh and from the sagas where animals are helped (2 and 53).

I suspect that originally Sosruquo was the preeminent warrior of steel and a storm god, much like the Vedic Indra, whereas the underground fertility theme was subsumed from another god whose identity is utterly lost.

---

[1] The term / g°anč'rəq'° / refers to the soleless, soft-leather knee boots of the Caucasian horseman; it resembles a leather knee sock and is bound by straps at the ankle and the top of the calf.

[2] This odd phrase may mean that as long as he can see his knees, that is, as long as they are at the front, which of course they would always be, he can guard them. Sosruquo seems to exhibit a hero's tragic hubris here; he knows what his enemies may do but refuses to take heed of his own counsel. One should also note the custom observed at warriors' funerals, in particular that of the late American president John F. Kennedy, of leading the horse in a procession with the dead man's boots in the stirrups but facing backward.

[3] This place-name is / ḥarama taw-ba / 'Harama Tau-name suffix', with a Kipchak Tur-

kic word for "mountain," *tau*. This is Sosruquo's chosen site of rejoined battle after a chivalric time out (see saga 60).

[4] A djin-charkh is a discus. Its name is from the Arabic *jinn*, here meaning "magical," and Persian *charkh*, "wheel."

[5] This odd detail about the seashore and its hazards for a warhorse may lie behind the common theme of a hero fighting a mortal duel by a body of water, seen in the Arthurian romance as well as the Nart sagas. A beach is the hardest place to fight a duel on horseback. It can prove either the ultimate skill of the hero or his undoing. It nullifies any advantage that a mounted warrior has against foot soldiers.

[6] Wiriwsh Yiqimghwa is / wərə́šʿ-yə-q̇ə́-mʕºa / 'Russian-their-head-road / pass' and seems to mean something like "guiding headland of the Russians." In his note (p. 327), Meremkulov remarks that an earlier form of this name was / wərə́m-yə-q̇ə́-mʕºa / 'Romans-their-head-road / pass'. Mount Elbruz is the tallest mountain in the Caucasus (in all of Europe, for that matter) and can be seen from vast distances. For millennia it would have served conquerors well as a landmark. The name Elbruz is of Iranian origin, as can be seen from the variant Elburz, used for a mountain range in Iran.

SAGA 65 ❧ Sosran of the Narts

There were many other Narts in the time of Sosruquo. One was Sosran. Some say that he was Sosruquo's uncle, the brother of Satanaya and the father of the wicked Sosranpa. Others say that he was Sosruquo's brother.

"Is there a man better than I am?" Sosran once asked himself and then set out on a long journey. He rode along until he encountered a man who sat with a huge rod and fished. He went to meet this man, who was fishing, and stood near him like a little bird. That is how big this man was, although Sosran had thought to himself, "Who is bigger and better than I?"

Sosran approached him, and this man said, "Where have you been, you lovely fellow?" he said.

"'Are there around here people, anybody, who are better than I?' That is what I am thinking to myself as I am journeying now," said Sosran to that man.

After Sosran had spoken thus, the man replied, "Go and visit my mother! It is not far away from here. I shall soon come back and we shall have a chat: 'Who is the better man,' they say."

He rode along the way in which the man had pointed. When he reached the place where the man had directed him, he happened to find the mother at home.

"Where are you going? Who are you?" she said.

And as an answer he replied, "This and that, your son said, and told me to come here."

"Oh, unlucky me! Oh, you should not have come! My son will not leave you alive," she said. "There is no way that he should see you," she said, so she hid him.

When her son returned, he asked, "Where is that man whom I sent here?"

"I saw nobody here," she answered.

"How come you didn't see him? I sent him here not long ago."

"I said I didn't see anyone here," she said and gave him his dinner. While he was eating, she set Sosran free. "Go in the direction where your head is turned to! Go wherever you want! Go away from my yard!" she said.

She let him go, and he, being scared, ran as far as he could go, but when her son realized that Sosran was running off, he began to chase him. Meanwhile, Sosran met another man who was walking from the opposite direction. He had only one arm and one eye. He came upon Sosran as he was running.

"What is the matter with you? What is the matter?" he asked Sosran.

"He who is coming here will catch me and kill me. That is why I am running," he said.

He who had been walking put Sosran into his mouth, they say. He put him into his mouth and closed it, they say.

"In this direction a man was running," said the first man and pointed in the direction where he thought Sosran had been running. "Haven't you seen him?" he said and drew closer.

"He passed me and ran off in that direction," said the second man and pointed in the direction with his arm. The first man ran on. When he had disappeared, the second man took Sosran out of his mouth. "What has happened to you? Why is he chasing you?" That is what he asked.

"Well, I rode out with the intention of finding out whether there is a man who is as good as I am. That is what I said to myself, and he began to chase me. He began to chase me because I said that," said Sosran.

"Do not say that anymore," said he who had hidden him in his mouth. "The reason that I lost one of my arms and the reason that I lost one of my eyes are that I once pronounced the very same words," he said. "He who plucked out one of my eyes and pulled off one of my arms is a shepherd. Henceforth, do not say those words anymore! There are a lot of people like you and me. I also said those words about myself. There are a lot of people who are bigger than we are. Do not say that anymore! Now, go any way you want," he said and let Sosran go.

From text 18, pp. 97–98; fragment 17, p. 97; and fragment 33, p. 133.

SAGA 66 ✍ *The Nanny Goat of the Narts*

Toward Qaseyhabl (now the village of Kabez), there is a ruin called Qaydukh, where the Adzghara is located, this being a dam on the Zelenchuk River. It was built in ancient times, when the Narts lived there, when big people lived, those people who built it. No one has dwelled there again.

Two people like those of today were on a journey. They came to this place and saw that the owner had goats of a very large size. His nanny goats were as big as cows. They drew near the giant: "Hello! Hello! Long life to you!" Then all of a sudden they said, "Give us one of your nanny goats!"

He looked on them. They were small in size, as we are now. "If I gave her to you, you wouldn't be able to carry her. I'll go and ask my mother what to do." Having said that, he went toward his house. His mother was still alive. "Some tiny people have come to us," he said, "and have asked me to give them a nanny goat. If I give her to them, they won't be able to carry her."

"They will catch her," she said. "If they have appeared here, then our lives have come to an end. There will be no offshoots from our tribe. We ourselves will not live much longer. After us, they will come. They are small, but they will be skillful. Give the nanny goat to them."

He came back. "Catch her!" he said.

When he said "catch her," one of them looked into his bag, took out a rope, swung back his arm, and threw it on the nanny goat. When they had thrown the rope on the goat, the goat began to run and dragged both of them a long way. But they soon caught her and choked her. They caught her, trussed up her legs, and prepared to kill her. Then they slashed her throat. The giant was following and had observed all this. Then he returned to his mother.

The house they lived in was located not far away. "What did they do?" she asked him.

"By God, they took out a rope, threw it on the nanny goat, and pushed her on the ground. Then they bound all four of her legs and cut her throat," he said. "That's how it was."

"I have already told you," she said. "From now on they will live in this world. Although they are not very powerful, they are very skillful."

From text 28, pp. 117–18.

✎ This is one of two myths that depict the Narts as prehuman giants, the other one being the Ubykh saga 90, and one of the few that speak of their end as a race. This fragment still has the prophetess Qaydukh situated in her fortress, but now it centers on the end of the Narts and the coming of modern humans, people of normal size. Through the use of magic, she prophetically tells her son of their imminent ascendancy.

Tales recounting the demise of the giants or of the dwarves through the retribution of God include a giant nanny goat to warn of impending disaster (Dumézil 1978, 344–51).

SAGA 67 ✎ *Badan and Badanoquo of the Narts*

Badan of the Narts was one of those who were always giving advice to the Narts. Badan had a son. This son's name was Badanoquo.[1] Badanoquo loved his father very much. His father had only this one son, and he in turn loved him very much.

Some time passed, and then there came Badan's time to die, when Badan became so weak that he could not water a cow, when he could no longer work, and his mind became abnormal. The Narts gathered at a meeting to decide his fate. They usually threw an old man into an abyss. When Badan became worthless, they gave Badanoquo this advice.

"Your father is an old man. He is worthless. His life is over. Take him into the mountains and throw him over a cliff. You know this is our custom," they said.

So he had no choice but to throw him from a cliff. What could he do?

How could he respond? He could not ignore their decision, even though he loved his father very much. They threw old people into the abyss like that. They prepared a basket to fit someone, placed him or her in the basket, and then threw it down into an abyss. Now, Badanoquo had no other choice than to do this.

They used a two-wheeled bullock cart in that time. They had such a cart, an *arba*. So Badanoquo took his arba, made a basket, placed Badan in the basket, put it onto the arba, and began to wheel him toward the mountain where there was a cliff from which he could hurl him into an abyss. He carried him there, and Badanoquo began to weep for his father from sorrow. But it did not matter how long he would weep. He still had no choice but to throw him into the abyss. So he did it. He threw him into the abyss.

There was a bushy tree on top of this cliff, on the very edge of this cliff. So he fell into the abyss, but the handle of the basket clung to this little tree. When Badan remained hanging on this bushy tree, Badanoquo had no choice but to get on all fours, crawl to this tree, and try to push him, Badan, down into the abyss. He crawled down to this tree, and when he was ready to push, his father began to laugh. When he burst into laughter, Badanoquo, the son, asked his father, "O my father! You are about to die now. I am going to throw you into the abyss. What gives your heart such delight?"

"I am laughing, my son, because now, at this moment when you are about to throw me into the abyss, I am wondering what your heart will feel when the time comes for a boy born to you to throw you into this abyss," he replied.

When he said this, Badanoquo felt so surprised that his heart ached. "Then," he said, "you, my father, you are speaking the truth. If there is any way on this earth, then let your heart never know feelings of insult until your very last day. There may be times when you are hungry, but you have sired me. I am giving you an oath that I will care for you until you die," he said.

"My boy, if you can do it, that would be good," he said, and the son, reaching an understanding with his father, took him off the edge of the abyss and carried him into a place where no man had walked before. Only the father and son knew about this place. He brought him into a big cave so that he need have no fear of frost or rain.

Badanoquo returned and told everyone that he had thrown his father into the abyss. The Narts whom he told never again mentioned Badan's name. Now, Badan's son visited his father every week and brought him something each time: food and clothes. If his clothes needed washing, he took them home with him and returned them to his father the next time. When he needed food, Badanoquo knew the right day and would visit him once a week. Thus, he took care of his father.

Four, five, six, many years passed. During these years the Narts did not see any rain and their land became very dry. A drought came upon their land so that they no longer had anything to harvest. One year they had no crops at all. Two years, three years—there was no rain. In addition, their trees withered and bore no fruit. They did not know what to do. They had some reserves, but they soon finished them. A great hunger struck them. That was their plight.

Badanoquo gathered his last reserves of millet, and since there was too little to thresh, he prepared hampals[2] for his father and carried these to him. His way lay along a river's bank, and he saw people near this place where his father was hiding. He came to the cave one day and saw that an apple and a pear tree were drifting down the river. "This is a miracle!" he said. "Where did this apple and pear tree come from? We Narts no longer have either apples or pears. All of our trees have died, so that we can no longer find trees and seeds to plant new trees." He was astonished to see the trees and determined to take their seeds for planting. He caught the trees, pulled them out of the water, and placed some apples and pears in his pockets. Then he went to his father, Badan.

When he reached his father, he gave him everything he had brought, including the apples and pears. This time he had not brought for him the same food that he usually brought.

Badan said, "Hey, my boy! Why haven't you brought me the same kind of food that you usually do? I can even see unthreshed grains in the hampal. Am I a trouble to you?" he said. "What has happened with you Narts?"

"I did not want to tell you, Father. Our Narts are suffering a great drought and famine. That is what has befallen us. We have no food. Since the great drought, we have no fruit. That is what has befallen us. I scraped together every grain that I could find, but if I tried to thresh it, I would have almost none left. That is why I prepared it in the husk. That is what has befallen us," he said.

"Then where did these apples and pears come from?" he asked.

"These apples and pears were drifting down the river, so I thought that I would take them to you. Then I would use their seeds after you have eaten their flesh. When I saw them floating, I pulled them out and brought them to you."

"Hey, my boy! That is no good. Is there anybody among the Narts other than myself who can help in these dire times? If not, then heed me. Go back home, my son," he said, "and plow again all the land where the silo stood, all the land where the millet's threshing floor lies, and all the plots of land used by the Narts to grow millet. You will see what will happen. Then," he said, "never take anything that you find floating in water. It will never prove useful. On your way home, look attentively at the forest through which you will pass. Apple trees and pear trees are growing there in a certain place. Some apples and pears will probably still be there. Pick some apples and pears and take them home. You Narts will find them useful for seeds."

"So be it!" said Badanoquo, turned around, and went back home. He returned home, but on the second day he went to Badan again and said, "There are no bulls among our cattle. There are no rams among our sheep. They have grown dry and can no longer sire offspring, of which there are very few left. Only females are left in our herds. We have no more bulls or rams."

"Drive all the sheep," said Badan, "where the villagers would drive them before and make a sheepfold there."

Badanoqouo agreed and returned home. The next morning he plowed all the fields and roads where millet was either grown or carried. The Narts looked at him with wonder. "Where is he going to find seeds for sowing?" Next he plowed all the barnyards and threshing floors where millet had been stored or threshed. He did not miss even a single place where he thought farmyards might have existed earlier. And in those places where people had once brought their sheep, he brought all the sheep herds into a single sheepfold. He went to that place which before had been used as a mating grounds, and there he erected a sheepfold and therein kept his sheep. Soon all his ewes began to give birth to two to five lambs. There were rams among them. And millet sprung forth of an unusually high-yielding kind, so that again they had a millet crop. The Narts harvested their crops so that they had an abundance of millet that year, and their herds began to grow again with all the sheep that they had acquired.

Now the Narts began to wonder, "How could Badanoquo, being so young and ignorant, do what he has done? How could that have happened? We must figure this out." So they summoned him. "Badanoquo," they said, "you plowed, but we did not see you sow. Perhaps you did it in secret. We do not know. Where did you get the seeds? How has all this been possible at all? Also, all the sheep gave birth even though there were no rams. In olden times, after mating, our sheep would yield one or two lambs. Now they yield from two to five. What a miracle! You must tell us. If you refuse, we will kill you." After this warning, he did not have much choice. What could he do?

"I shall tell you the truth," he said. "I shall tell you what I did. I shall tell you my affairs, whether they were right or wrong. But before I do, I ask you to swear that you will not punish me. If you refuse, then do whatever you will with me. I shall not tell you anything!"

The Narts conferred and then said, "We want to know what you have done. Why should we kill you or punish you?" They offered their vows before him and gave him their true word that even if he had done what nobody on earth had ever done and was in some way guilty because of these deeds, they would not say anything.

When they gave him this vow, he began his story about his father, and he told them all that had happened. The Narts then conferred again and decided, "We have had the custom of throwing all old people down into the abyss. Let all old people, even if they can no longer work, live to their natural ends! Henceforth we shall not throw old people into the abyss. Go and bring your father here!" they said.

Badanoquo went and brought his father, and together with the other Narts he received Badan with great honor and joy. They had plenty of millet seeds and many fruit seeds, so that since that time they have always had seeds for grain and trees. Their lives began anew. That was how useful Badan was to the Narts back then, and since then they never again have thrown old people into the abyss.

From text 35, pp. 135–39.

◌ Badanoquo was the preeminent hunter of the Narts, known in Circassian as She Badanoquo, / ša banadaq°a / , Hunter Badanoquo. Although his exploits are generally confined to a few tales in any one corpus, they suffice to paint a picture of a mighty hero. The present tale is unique in that his father, Badan, appears. It is also an example of a theme with wide distribution, that of the child sparing the aged parent out of empathy, and in this case, by learning that the parent is not so useless after all.

Tales in which the elderly are disposed of once they are deemed useless are nearly universal. The presence of this tale in the Caucasus, however, is interesting for there are few places on earth where elders enjoy greater respect and veneration than in those mountains. So, it is hardly credible that this tale depicts an earlier ethic of the region. Rather, it must articulate and reinforce the sense of inherent worth attributed to the aged members of the community while holding at bay any disgruntlement with them that might arise from their infirmity and limited productivity.

¹ Ubykh (saga 86) preserves the form Bardanoquo, / bardanaq°a /, so that the original name of the father must have been *Bardana. This closely resembles the name of Satanaya's consort, Wardana. Both may have the same Iranian source, with the first coming from an Iranian dialect where *w- has yielded *v- or even *b-. Wardana does enter several tales in which he is saved by his son, whose name may be Sosruquo, Pataraz, or Badanoquo. This tale suggests that the original son is the hunter Bardanoquo.

² A hampal / ḥamp'al / is a flat cake made of grain which is sometimes boiled.

SAGA 68 ⊙ *Badanoquo of the Narts*

Badanoquo from the Narts carried home a woman as his wife.¹ The woman he brought was very strong. She was stronger than he. Badanoquo knew that. They lived together, and one day Badanoquo went hunting. He departed and did not come back for two or three nights. This woman grabbed a cow by her leg, pulled her over the fence, gave her water to drink, and then pulled her back again and put her in her place. Badanoquo did not know about that.

When Badanoquo embarked on one journey, he came upon a tiny man, one like us. When he found him, he thrust him into the back of his boot and brought him home. He came home, dismounted, stretched his leg out, and said to his wife to pull off his boot. She pulled off his boot and the small man fell out.

When the little man fell out of there, he hit her hard in the head and she took offense at her husband. She felt offended, and Badanoquo's wife said to her husband, "May you suffer as many diseases as the number of those who are stronger than you!"

"Who is stronger than I in this world? Honest to God, I shall find out who he is," Badanoquo said and so mounted his horse and departed on his way. He set out, and on his way he met one man who held a huge log on three fingers.

"Salam aleykum!" said the man.

"Waleykum salam!" said Badanoquo.

"Where are you going?"

"In that direction."

"This is the road you should follow at this propitious hour," the man said, and he bade him farewell. The man whom Badanoquo had just met was his wife's brother.

After that he met another man. This one could hit the ground with his toes, dig it up, sow seeds, and plow with his toenails. So he met this man, they talked, and then this man also bade him farewell, having showed him which way to go.

Farther on, in a forest, he saw a little hut. His wife had five bothers, two of whom he had already met and three of whom were hunting. Their mother was at home when he came to their house, to this hut. His wife's mother saw him, and she recognized her son-in-law and invited him into the house.

The brothers and their dogs were not home, so she invited him in, offered to him the windowsill to sit on, and covered him, Badanoquo, Badanoquo of the Narts, with her thimble. Soon those three hunters came back and the other two came back, the one who plowed and the one who played with huge logs. All five brothers met each other again.

"Where is this human smell coming from?" they said. This smell touched everybody, whoever entered the house. They felt that there was a human in their house. Their dogs were shaking the whole world, so hard did they bark.

Then their mother told them, "This is your brother-in-law. Do not make such a noise. He is a human, and the human scent you smell is coming from him. Now lock up your dogs and I shall show him to you," she said.

They locked up their dogs and he, the husband of their sister, appeared to them, the same one who marched out on a trip to find out whether there was anybody else in the world stronger than he was. He came out from under the thimble when she told him to do so. He stepped out and they were glad to see him. There he was given the honors that the best guest deserves. There he learned that there are stronger people in the world than he.

From text 34, pp 133–34

  ❧ It is a peculiarity of the Abaza corpus to have several tales in which haughty Narts are tested or humbled by their encounters with giants (see sagas 59 and 65).

---

[1] Marriage was by abduction, usually by a prearranged mock abduction.

The Narts set out for plunder. As they set off to go looting, an old man who lived there in the same village joined them. When they had traveled a great distance, this old man grew weary and could no longer ride his horse, so he was left behind. He could not keep up with the others.

When his daughter came upon the old man sitting sadly, she asked him, "Our father, why are you so sad?"

He replied, "The Narts set off to find booty and I could not keep up with them."

"I shall go in your place," she said.

"Go, go, your father's soul!" he said.

She dressed herself as a man and followed the Narts. Soon she overtook them and joined them when nobody saw her.

In the morning one of the Narts said that there was a woman among them. He could distinguish women from men by their odor. They were ascending the summit of one of the mountains.

"When we reach the top of this mountain," he said, "let all of us take off our hats."

She drew near the man who could tell who was a man and who was a woman by odor and said to him, "Wait a second!" And while on their way up the mountain, she pushed him into a cave and closed it with a big rock. Then she climbed the mountain, and that man was left in the cave under the mountain.

There was a shabby, uncouth youth, Qhabizh,[1] among the Narts; he was the youngest among them but was very courageous. When he stormed a fort, he killed all who were there and broke down the gates so that Narts could return home laden with booty.

On the way home, when they reached the place where she had entombed the Nart, she released him from his cave. "If you say anything, it will be the death of you," she said. "Don't say anything!" She pulled him out of there. And when she arrived back, the Narts had already started to divide their goods. Sosruquo demanded the biggest part.

When he was asked why, he answered that he had done more bold deeds than anybody else had.

Qhabizh did not agree with that. "Where is your courage? I cannot see it. I am courageous," he said. Another one, Wazarmis,[2] said that he himself was courageous and not anybody else.

When they said those words, Sosruquo sat down on an iron bench and pushed against it with his back until it broke into pieces.

Qhabizh stood up and said, "Hey, Sosruquo! Our mother had many cows and she fed you sour milk. That is why your butt became so fat. That is why you managed to break it!"

When he said that, Sosruquo grew angry and hit an iron rod with his head and bent it.

"Hey, Sosruquo! Our father has many sheep. He must have fed you their heads. That is why your head became so strong and you bent it," he said.

"So what do you want now?" asked Sosruquo.

"I ask for this: Let us take a cauldron and put a little cold water in it. The water will not rise when a liar strikes the cauldron, but it will rise when one who speaks the truth strikes it. That is what I wish," said Qhabizh.

"Let us begin!"

They prepared a cauldron and set it in place.

"Sosruquo! You are older. Hit it!" they said.

He hit it, but the water did not rise. Then Wazarmis hit it, and again the water did not rise. When Qhabizh hit it, however, the water started to boil, and soon rose to the brim. Qhabizh possessed real courage.

After the cauldron was filled with water, Sosruquo kicked it with his toe and sent it flying into the clouds,[3] sending it over the mountaintops.

From text 23, pp. 111–12.

◌ This saga is another tale depicting a woman warrior, but before anything of significance can be told about her, the tale shifts to the theme of the uncouth but valorous youth and the cauldron. This cauldron or barrel of the Narts was a sort of horn of plenty that filled up or boiled over only in the presence of a true hero. Littleton and Malcor (1994) have argued that this is related to Amonga's cauldron of the Ossetic tradition and to the Holy Grail of the Arthurian cycle.

The youth, Qhabizh, may have originally been identical with the warrior woman, hence the conflation of the two themes. He appears as a shepherd in saga 53 and as the companion to the Old Child in saga 72.

---

[1] This curious, rough youth's name means "seven heads," / q̇a-bəž̓ /. Polycephalous figures abound in Hindu iconography (though not in the earlier Vedic one) and seem to characterize the pagan Slavic gods. Perhaps the Iranian material, which lay between the Slavic

and Hindu worlds, also had polycephalous figures, of which Qhabizh is an Iranian relic preserved outside his original Indo-European home (see saga 53).

[2] In the Circassian corpus, Wazarmis is the leader of the Narts (see also saga 74), the name being variously by dialect / warzamag^y /, / warzamaʒ^y /, / warzamas /. The Abaza has / wazarmis /.

[3] The term / pstḥ°a / can refer to mist, clouds, or storm clouds. This word may show an elusive cognate for 'water' * / psə /: Abkhaz / á-pstḥ°a / 'the-cloud', Circassian / psə / 'water' and / tx̌°ər(əm)ba / 'foam', but contrast Abkhaz-Abaza / ʒə / 'water', Ubykh / bzə́ / 'water', West Circassian / pca / 'fish', that is, 'water one', from * / pəʒə́ /, / pəʒá / (Colarusso 1994d, p. 24, §82).

SAGA 70 ◌ *The Dream of Ayniwzh, Nana's Son*

In ancient times there was nobody in the whole world except the Narts and the ayniwzhes. These two were enemies. The ayniwzhes were summoned by Ayniwzh Nana, the old woman who the ayniwzhes thought was the woman who began their tribe. Her son had had a dream.

"Nana! I had a dream last night," he said.

"What kind of a dream was it?"

"Our father was lying in bed. I was sitting near his bed and looking at him. The first time I looked at him he grew very small. Then I looked at him and he became totally white. As I looked at him a third time, all his teeth fell out. That is how I saw our father," he said.

"All dreams can be explained by Satanaya, that Satanaya who begot the Narts, their mother. They have one great woman with the name of Satanaya. If she cannot explain this dream, then I will not be able to give you an answer about this dream either. I have no way to answer you. Go to Satanaya of the Narts! If you tell her your dream, she will give you an answer," she said.

"Nana, how can I go to the Narts?" he replied. "We and the Narts are enemies. As soon as they see me, they will kill me."

"They will not kill you for this reason. An envoy cannot be killed or held hostage," she said. "'I was sent by Ayniwzh Nana to see Satanaya of the Narts in order to tell her something.' If you say these words, nobody will kill you. You will be their guest."

So he set off to visit the Narts. Soon, however, while on his way to them, he was attacked and stopped by their lookouts. He said to them the following: "I come to you with business. Do not stop me! I was sent by Ayniwzh Nana to see Satanaya in order to tell her something."

Upon hearing this, they sent one of their number to Satanaya to report what he had said.

"Ayniwzh Nana has sent someone to see you. What do you want us to do with him?"

"Do not hold him! Release him! Honor him with the utmost respect as our best guest," she said. "I do not have time for him tonight, so bring him here soon after sunrise."

They killed an ox for him. They killed four cows for him. They showed him great honor and respect. They gave him every pleasure that the best guest could have been given. In the morning, at sunrise, she said to them, "Bring him here!" and so they led him to her.

"What do you want?" she said.

"Ayniwzh Nana sent me here. I had a dream that she cannot explain. She could not give me an answer. 'Satanaya of the Narts will be able to give you an answer. I know that for sure,' she said and sent me here. That is why I have come."

"Well, tell me your dream," Satanaya said.

He began to narrate it again. "Our father was in his bed. That is how I saw him in my dream. I am gazing upon him, and as I do so he is growing smaller and smaller," he said. "Again as I gazed at him, he turned the whitest of white. As I gazed on him again, all his teeth fell out."

"Now, this is what I would tell your Ayniwzh Nana," Satanaya replied. "In the coming time people will come to possess a great deal of knowledge. They will be educated, but they themselves will become very small in stature. They will not grow, yet they will turn gray. They will be children, and yet all their teeth will turn loose. They will know a great deal, but they will suffer terrible toothaches. Those are the sorts of people who will soon come after us. That is what your dream means, and that is what you should tell Ayniwzh Nana," she said to him.

He promptly returned to Ayniwzh Nana and told her what Satanaya had said. When he had told her that, she began to speak with these words on her tongue, "If such people are to come after us—" and then she fell down with a heart attack. Her heart was broken.

That is the legend of Ayniwzh Nana.

From text 27, pp. 116–17.

&, Here again is a tale foretelling the coming of normal humans (see saga 66).
The shock of the prophecy is too much for the grandmother of the giants.

SAGA 71 &, *Tataruquo Shaway*

Sosruquo had been away on a quest. As he was returning home, he looked
around and saw a horseman riding behind him.

"Salam aleykum, son of the Narts!" said the horseman as he came
abreast with Sosruquo.

"Waleykum salam!" replied Sosruquo. He scrutinized the rider. He was
a young man. They rode on together.

"O son of the Narts, choose a shorter way! Make it shorter!" he said, but
Sosruquo gave no response to that. They continued until they came to a
crossroads, and again he spoke. "O son of the Narts, one of these ways is
a near farness and the other a far nearness. Which way do you choose to
follow?" Again Sosruquo refused to answer. "Then good day to you, Nart!
My way is this one," he said. He struck his horse and rode away.

Sosruquo, son of the Narts, returned home and dismounted. He saw
that his wife was sitting in her room. His daughter, Nawgrash,[1] came up
to him and shook her head. His glance was gloomy as well, and he himself
was sad.

"Today," he said, "my gaze is gloomy because of the following. I met a
young fellow and he said to me, 'Son of the Narts! Salam aleykum,' and I
returned his greeting. We were riding along and he said to me, 'O son of
the Narts, make our way shorter, will you?' We rode farther until we came
to a crossroads with the paths diverging. 'O son of the Narts,' he said. 'This
is a near farness and that a far nearness. Hey, son of the Narts, may your
day be good, but this is my way.' Having said that, we parted and he rode
off. What sort of riddle did he say? I could not understand it."

Nawgrash burst into laughter, and Sosruquo asked her, "Why do you
laugh, you who jumped out of a bitch's nose?"

"Oh, Daddy," she said, "how come you did not understand what he said?
When he said 'make our way shorter,' he wanted you to tell an interesting
story and so continue your trip. By 'this is a near farness' he meant that this
way would be a long way for you to go, although the road itself is good.

By 'that far nearness' he meant that this road is bad," she said. "What did he look like?" she asked.

"I swear by God that he was poorly dressed and did not impress me at all," replied Sosruquo.

She remembered him and was henceforth especially attentive to all poorly dressed, unattractive poor people. At this time a young fellow stopped by their backyard with a bag over his shoulder.

"Approach, young man!" she said.

He touched his mouth to show that he was mute, without a tongue.

"Even if you are mute, come here!" she replied.

At this moment Sosruquo came out of the house. "This daughter, whose house is perishing, gives away everything, all our possessions, to strangers, to bums. You are giving away everything to them and they will eat it all," he said.

"Daddy!" she said. "Don't say that! It is a sin. He is but a poor man," she said and led him into the house and into her courting room. "Have a seat," she said. She showed him a chair and made him sit down. She seated him, and he pointed to an old, violinlike instrument hanging on the wall, a pkhyartsa,[2] thereby offering to play it. She stood up, took down the pkhyartsa, and gave it to him. He, the mute, took it and began to play it. He played so well that even the birds began to dance.

"Oh, my God!" she said, astounded by his skillful playing of the pkhyartsa. She stood up, walked around the whole room, and then sat down again.

The music that he brought forth from the pkhyartsa said, "Oh, my God, how lovely she would be if she were not lame."

As soon as she heard that, she took off her clogs and shook out of the heel three millet grains. She then stood up and walked a bit.

"Oh, my God!" sang the pkhyartsa again. "I swear with my father, if only the hearth wall were not curved. If not for that, how beautiful she would be!"

Her eyes were slightly crossed and she said, to him, "You! Even if the hearth wall is curved, smoke is passing along it smoothly."

"I wish I knew her bride-price," sang the pkhyartsa.

She undid her hair, showed it to him, and said, "If you can drive here as many cattle as I have hairs, then I am yours."

He put aside the pkhyartsa and spoke for the first time. "I am adding my two kisses to that sum. Give me your hand!"

"If you begin talking, then I shall give you my hand," she said.

But he feigned muteness again.

"No, you are not mute," she replied. "A mute man cannot do all this. You are the one I have been looking for. Tell me! Who are you?"

He signed "No!" and attempted to leave.

"No!" she cried and blocked the door with her body. "I shall not let you leave. Tell me who you are, and then I shall let you leave."

He began to speak and said, "If you truly want to know, then know that I came here for only one reason, to see you."

"Who are you?"

"I am the youth whom your father met the other day. He must have told you of that. It was I who overtook him."

"So, do you agree to my conditions?" she asked him.

"Yes, I do. Now, give me your hand," he said and took her hand in his. "Henceforth, you belong to me. All good fortune to you." He then slipped away after holding her hand for only a moment.

He left their yard and then bode his time until Sosruquo and Nasran were ready to embark on another raid. When word reached him of the impending quest, he followed them. He decided to join the quest. At first he rode behind them, but he soon overtook them.

"Good day, sons of the Narts! May your affairs prosper!" he said.

The two looked at him. He seemed a young fellow, very young. "Good day, little boy, beloved of Allah!" they replied.

He ceded to them the right side of the road and took the left, acknowledging his junior status by doing this. They resumed their way.

After a bit they said, "What is on your mind, young fellow? What is in your heart? Where are you going?"

"I have no special plans," he replied. "I am going nowhere. I am just following you."

"It is good that you follow us, but we Narts will not stay here. The place where we are going is far away. You are young, still a child. You will not make it. It would be better for you not to start emulating us. You will perish because of us. It would be better for you to return home."

"No," he said. "Nothing will go wrong. I shall be your page. Even if I cannot be of much direct help to you, at least I can saddle your horses for you. I shall hold them for you when you mount, hobble them for you, and I shall cook for you."

"If you had been listening well, you would understand that we are not staying in this land. We are traveling far away, to such places where you cannot reach."

"Whether I can get there or not is something you must leave up to me," he replied.

"Very well, join us!" they said and set off on their way.

Where they stopped to rest, Tataruquo would tend to their horses. When they dismounted, he unsaddled their horses. When needed, he saddled them again. Thus they traveled, all the time keeping an eye on him but never asking who he was. Finally, when they reached the lodge that was their destination, they said, "Good fellow! We shall return soon. In the meantime, make a fire in the fireplace."

"As you wish! I shall do that."

He did as they asked, and as the evening passed and midnight approached, he prepared food for them. At dawn they returned, very tired, but did not see the young man. "Come here! Come here!" the two called.

"I am here," he said, appearing from behind the lodge. He served them their dinner and bade them to eat and drink. Then he readied their beds. He took their horses, brought them to a pasture, and set them to rest. He returned to the lodge only later in the morning.

"As God is our witness, our affairs are not going well. We must go there again tonight," they said. That evening they left again and at dawn returned a second time, even more tired than before. On the third evening this young page decided to follow.

"Hey! What are you up to, good fellow?" they said when they discovered what he was doing.

"Tonight is my turn," he replied. "Return to your beds and rest! I shall go tonight."

"Go if you will!" they replied and showed him their goal, a land rich in mares that lay across a nearby sea.

This young fellow bent himself down, set to the task, set across the sea, and returned driving all the horses before him across the water while his two masters slept. Both sons of the Narts were awakened by the thunder of the herd and jumped from their beds, frightened. One looked out and could not see the earth for the horses.

"Oh, my God! We are doomed," they both said. They saw their page among the horses and called to him, "Drive them farther on! This is not our land anymore, so drive them farther on!" And so he continued to drive all of the mares back to his home.

They arose with the sun and set off after him. By afternoon they came upon the herd and saw that all the mares were already marked. On their left side, in the place for a brand, one could see the trace of his lash. Where he had hit each horse, a large blister had formed. At the mere sound of his voice the mares galloped ahead. The two joined him, but when he stopped, the horses did too, and the two of them were unable to drive them on without him.

In this way they had covered most of their return when they came upon the spot where he had joined up with them.

"Now we have come to the place where we first met," he said. "All the best to you! May Allah bless you both! With your leave, I shall go my way." And he set off in a different direction, leaving the mares.

Sosruquo, son of the Narts, said, "Hey, dear fellow! You are a mere youth. All these mares that you have caught and driven here do not belong to us, but as your masters you must give us our share. You must divide the herd into three parts."

"No," he replied, "I do not want a share. If I need horses, I shall find them myself. Because of your good company, I give all of the horses to you. All of the horses are yours. May they bring you good luck!" he said and turned to leave.

Nasran then said, "We cannot accept that. Take your share!"

"So," he said, "you are willing to give me a part?"

"Yes, we are," replied Nasran.

"Are you giving it to me from your hearts?" he asked.

"Yes, from our hearts," they both replied.

He then took out his rope and put it on a brindled stallion that was among the mares. "I do not need anything other than him. I am pleased with him," he said.

"Then everything is all right with us," they replied.

The youth set off with his horse.

A little later Sosruquo said, "Hey, Nasran!"

"What?" the other answered.

"Who was that youth who was with us? Who is he? Where did he come from?" asked Sosruquo.

"By God, I do not know, but he belongs to the Narts as we do. I give my word before God that I shall not let him go," said Nasran.

"Go!" said Sosruquo. "Go quickly, Nasran! Find out who he is and bring word back to me!"

Nasran set off and eventually caught sight of the youth. "Hey! Hey, you! Please stop, won't you?" he called.

The youth turned and said, "What has happened?"

"You know what happened," answered Nasran as he caught up with him. "There is no place or affair where the advice or word of the Narts is not important. The same goes for our courage, but we have lost our courage. Who are you? What tribe are you from?" he asked the youth.

"I am Tataruquo Shaway, the page boy, the Tatar's son. All that is in the past," he said. "Now, Nasran, I shall confide in you if you can keep a secret."

"Of course! I won't tell anything to anybody," Nasran replied.

"I need nothing save for one thing," he said. "I need Sosruquo's daughter, whose name is Nawgrash."

"Oh, yes, yes," replied Nasran.

"I am going to give this little horse as a present to her, but only after I have ridden him once on a raid. Now, wait for me for a little while," said the youth as he took off his shirt and made to put on his felt cloak. His shirt was bloody as well as his undershirt. "Give this to Nawgrash," he said.

Nasran took the bloody shirt and put it in his bag. He brought his horse close to that of the youth and whispered in his ear, "Good luck!" and then rode off. As he left, he thought, "Harsh is the man to whom I return. How should I explain it to him? What should I say?" he asked himself. Finally he decided, "If he is so, then so be it. If I fail to explain matters to him, then I shall go to his wife and tell her everything. Somehow his wife and I together will calm him down . . . if he agrees with us."

"Who is he?" asked Sosruquo. "May the fire in his hearth die out!"

"'I am Tataruquo Shaway,' that is what he told me," replied Nasran. "The Tatar's son, the page."

"May the fire in his hearth die out! Who is he, this Tatar's son, Shaway?" asked Sosruquo again. "Who is he?"

They were astonished because he was so young.

They returned home with the mares. They put them in the stables. Thence they allotted everyone a certain number of mares. Nasran took a spotted horse and led it to his own stable. Then he took the bloody shirt and went to see Sosruquo's wife. He met her and told her all that had happened. Nawgrash was also there.

"Is he as courageous as you have just described?" she asked.

"Yes. If you wish, invite him. I promised to give my sister to him," Nasran replied.[3] "If she refuses, then that is her prerogative. So do as you please, but I suggest that you persuade him to visit."

"Agreed! This is not hard. We shall invite him," they said.

"Now then, take this shirt. It is his," said Nasran, and he took it from his bag and handed it to them.

Nawgrash took it and looked at it. "I swear by my God that I shall not wash this shirt until the blood wears off on its own." She then undressed herself and put the shirt on.

"He also sent you, as a gift, this horse 'with apples.'[4] Do with it as you please. But he needs it. You must give it back to him for one night, whereon he will ride it on a raid. It is all wonderful if true," replied Nasran.

"I shall take this horse with apples," Nawgrash said.

Later her father began to grow cross and asked her, "What are you up to here?"

"Oh, how unhappy I am, how poor!" she replied.

"Do not worry!" Sosruquo's kinsmen replied. "We shall demand a bride-price that he will never be able to pay in his whole life."

"If this is so, then fine," he replied.

Earlier the youth had departed from Nasran, saying, "If you need me, I will be in such and such a place."

Then they sent a messenger to him. "Hey, you! Good man, Tataruquo Shaway! We will be talking about your affairs," said the messenger. "Come to us!"

Thence the messenger went to Nasran. By asking people round about, he managed to find him. When he reached Nasran he dismounted and said, "Our future son-in-law is coming. He will take his bride one way or the other, so let us give her to him with all honor."

"We will give her to him only under these conditions," replied Nasran. "Tell him that we shall erect gates. If he can, from dawn to dusk, drive every horse through these gates, then we shall accept this as a bride-price and she will be his. That is what they say. 'If between dawn and dusk he can drive all the horses through these gates, then she is his.'"

When the youth arrived, he heard about the bride-price. He went up to Nasran and said, "Let me shake your hand! If I cannot do this, then let her remain with you. Your daughter is yours. But if I succeed, then your daughter is mine.[5] I agree to your conditions," he said and shook Nasran's hand and asked for one thing. "Please go and tell Nawgrash to let me have for one night only the horse with apples which I have asked about before."

Nasran went and said to Nawgrash that she must keep her promise, about the horse that Nasran had mentioned before.

"Is that how it is?" asked Nawgrash.

"Yes," he replied, "that is how it is."

"Wonderful! Bring the horse to me! Bring him here and place him before me!" she said.

He brought the horse before her.

The youth arrived before her. "Now, keep your promise!" he said to her.

"This horse with apples is not more important than you," she said, "but you must swear to bring him back in exactly the same condition as he is now. Without your word, I shall not give him to you. Even though you yourself gave him to me, I have nurtured him with my own hands. That is why I shall not give him to you unless you swear to bring him back just as he is now."

"What can I do about it?" he replied. "I gave him to you. What does it matter what I do with him? How are you related to him?" he argued and swayed her mind so that she gave him the horse.

He mounted it and rode off. Soon he found many horses and began to drive as many as he could. On and on he drove them until he reached Gwal Dew.[6] He then dismounted and looked at the horse with apples. Its ears were not sweaty. He drove the horses again at dawn. Once more he dismounted and checked his horse's ears. Again there was no sweat.

"What kind of man am I to promise to give back such a horse?" he asked himself. He began to ride him along the shore of the lake. He forced the horse to jump over the water, and as it was in midair over the water, he slammed both legs against the sides of the horse, breaking all its ribs. He did this because he felt insulted. He unsaddled the horse and left it in the water. He then went back, mounted his piebald horse, and returned him.

He drove all the mares back. Between dawn and dusk he drove them all through a gate that they had erected. Then he gave them to the villagers. "I give them to you as a gift," he said.

When Nawgrash saw him she said, "Where is my horse, you oath breaker?"

"Your horse was not a horse that could carry a man for an entire night. If he had been a good horse, he would have brought me back here," he said. "You were right to worry."

"Where is he? Where did you put him? I shall go and find his carcass. I shall go and bring his carcass back here," she said.

"Of course, go!" he said. "He lies in that lake."

She took people with her. When they reached the lake, they found the horse and pulled it out of the water. She drove him back and nursed him. After a long time he recovered and became the best horse among all those of the Narts.

They gave her to him. He married her, he who is called Shaway, the Tatar's son.

From text 37 (mislabeled in the original as 32), pp. 156–64.

◌ In the chivalric society depicted in the Northwest Caucasian Nart sagas, warriors were similar to medieval European knights, even to the extent of having young men who waited on them as pages. In Circassian such a page was called a shawa, / śaawa /. In some sagas it seems to have meant "warrior." This tale, a curious blend of the romantic and tender with the brutal and cruel, centers on a Tatar youth whose name is Shaway, perhaps from the Circassian / śawa-y(a) / 'page-one', "the pagelike one." He is the archetypal page boy (servant to a warrior, but not his foster son, as was often the case among European feudal pages). This tale also reflects Northwest Caucasian attitudes toward many of the Turkic nomads of the steppes. They were seen as valiant and skilled horsemen, but also as crude and cruel. Further, it introduces a motif that reappears in sagas 72 and 74: the youth who proves his heroic nature by outriding his companions into dangerous or unknown territory. This overreaching horseman is a tangible form of the mythic imperative that the true hero transcends all measures of normal attainment and is thereby imbued not only with superhuman strength and valor but also with a whiff of social offensiveness and transgression.

This saga also provides a glimpse of courting behavior within a maiden's room. The Circassians, Abazas, and their kin assigned a room to unmarried daughters, where they could receive suitors. The room was theirs, but they seem nevertheless to have been subject to parental oversight and were expected to follow certain rules of conduct.

[1] The name Nawgrash is Circassian, / na-g°-ra-ɣ⃐ / 'eye-zone-inst-wide', "wide around the eyes," and may allude to her being cross-eyed or perhaps of Mongoloid countenance. This name is borne by the son of Tlepshw, the smith of the Narts, in the Circassian corpus.

[2] The term / px̌ʸarca /, "violinlike instrument," seems to derive from the arched bridge over which the strings were mounted and the angle thus formed by the strings across this bridge (compare / px̌ʸa-ca-ra / 'corner-go-inf', "to drive someone into a corner," and hence / px̌ʸa-r-ca / "angle-by-going"). This instrument is thus contrasted with stringed instruments in which the bridge was flat.

[3] Nasran speaks here as though he were Sosruquo's son and Nawgrash's brother. Henceforth in this tale Nasran effectively replaces Sosruquo. A woman's brother often assumed the duty of finding her a husband. In the Circassian corpus, Nasran is of the same generation as Warzamas and even takes his place in some of the tales.

[4] A spotted horse.

[5] Here Nasran is addressed as though he were the father of Nawgrash.

[6] Gwal Dew / g°al dəw / 'lake big', "Big Lake," perhaps the Sea of Azov. The word / g°al / may be of Turkic origin; compare Turkic *kül* 'lake'.

Chwadlazhwiya[1] and Qhabizh Chkwin[2] played a game of knucklebones on the ice. Young Qhabizh won all of Chwadlazhwiya's knucklebones.

"Give me another chance!" he said.

But Qhabizh refused, and so Chwadlazhwiya started to hit him.

"Instead of hitting me, you would do better to kill the man who murdered your father," Qhabizh Chkwin said to him.

"Tell me who killed my father! I shall give you my dice made of deer bone. I'll let you keep all of my knucklebones. I'll give you everything!" said Chwadlazhwiya.

"I won't tell you!" said Qhabizh. "Ask your mother to tell you!"

"My mother won't tell me. You tell!"

"Your mother will tell you if you do as I say," he replied. "You must make her prepare some hot corn mush for you. Go home and start to complain about your stomach. Tell her that it hurts. Ask her to prepare hot corn mush for you. After she does that, tell her that you will not taste it until she tastes it first. When she goes to taste it, grab her arm and thrust her hand into the porridge. Say to her, 'Until you tell me who killed my father, I shall not let you take your hand out of the mush.' That is what you should say and do."

Chwadlazhwiya returned home and did just as Qhabizh had said. When he stuck his mother's hand in the hot mush, she said, "Who told you to do this? O God, do not let him live his full span! I'll tell you all when you grow up. What are you doing? Pull my arm out of the mush right now!" she protested. But he would not relent until she cried, "Tlabitsa[3] the Lame killed your father!" Only then did he let go of her arm.

"They say to me that you are too young. Over there, where the *abra*[4] stone is standing before the door, in that shed is your father's horse," she said. "His weapons are in a black chest. If you decide to open it, his weapons may set fire to the whole house. They say that fire comes out of his weapons. And nobody can even come close to his horse. He eats only what we throw at him through the window of his stable. Is he suitable for you? Will you be able to ride him? Will you even be able to mount him? An abra stone is lying before him as well, before his stable," she said.

Chwadlazhwiya went to the stable and kicked the abra stone with his knee, knocking it away from the door. They say that that horse was sleeping when Chwadlazhwiya entered the shed. He grabbed a nearby iron club and jumped on the horse's back. The horse grew frightened when he realized how strong this new rider was. The horse did everything possible to try to throw him off. He reared up, but the rider held on to his mane and hit him on the head with the club. Then the horse began to speak and said, "Oh, Heaven, if you are a rider, then I am your steed!"

So he led the horse out and mounted him again. Then he rode up to his mother and said, "Prepare food for me! I go to avenge my father." Then he took his father's weapons and set off on his horse to kill Tlabitsa the Lame.

While on his way, it happened that his father's brothers, Sosran and Sosruquo,[5] also decided to set off on a quest, saying, "We shall drive back all of Tlabitsa's cattle." A little farther along, they looked ahead and saw smoke coming from some grass in the distance. "Who is he, born of a dog, who in a manly way precedes us and spreads all this smoke?" Sosruquo sent Sosran to see. When he rode ahead he saw a child sitting near a small fire, warming his meat and eating it.

"Who are you?" Sosran asked him.

"After a man becomes poor, many people no longer recognize him. You have no need of me. Whoever I am, he is me. Don't bother me!" he replied.

Sosran returned and told Sosruquo. "He answered that way? Who is he? What kind of talk is that?" So his uncles rode up to him together, and then they recognized that he was their nephew. "May your way be hard! How did you come to be here? Where are you going?"

"Where am I going? I am going to avenge my father's blood," he replied.

"That would be fine when the time is right for you, when you are grown. Then we would tell you. May Allah punish your mother for letting you mount this horse and come here," they said and began to curse his mother.

"It is none of my mother's fault. I came here on my own," he said.

So they took him with them and continued on their way. Soon they came to the pasture where the horses and all the cattle of Tlabitsa the Lame grazed. They hid themselves nearby to rest and then settled down and went to sleep. Sosran placed the boy at his feet, saying, "Lie down at my feet!"

But after Sosran had fallen asleep, the boy quietly stood up, mounted his *durdul*,[6] galloped off to the pasture where Tlabitsa's herds were grazing, and began to drive them off. Two guards were standing by the livestock. The boy killed one and said to the other, "Tell all of your grief! Return home and tell Tlabitsa the Lame that all his horses have been stolen!"

He drove all the mares back with him. When Tlabitsa's people saw so many horses moving, they thought they were being attacked by a huge army and fled, not realizing that these were horses alone.

The boy returned to the camp of his uncles, hobbled his own horse, and set him out to graze. Then he lay down in the same spot to sleep.

His uncles awoke and looked at the herd. They quickly realized that they were just horses, just mares, but they lay there, and each wondered to himself who had driven them there.

"I drove them here," bragged Sosran.

"No, it was I who drove them here," countered Sosruquo.

They boy just lay there quietly and listened to their bragging. They decided that no matter who might have driven them there now, they themselves would drive them back home.

Later in the night the boy decided to return to the pasture. This time he went to two shepherds guarding cattle. He killed one of them but only gouged out the other's eye. "Go! You will be the herald of grief. Go and tell Tlabitsa the Lame that we are driving all his cattle away!"

He returned to his own camp and gave all the cattle to his uncles. Then he set out a third time. There, where his cattle were supposed to be, was Tlabitsa himself. The two met.

"You, born by a dog! So it is you who have driven off all my herds. You have left me with nothing on which to put my brand," he said.

"It is you who was born by a dog!" Chwadlazhwiya replied. "Yes, it is I who have stolen them, but I came here to fight. I need your head, not your herd. I came here to take your head back with me."

Tlabitsa was astonished that such a youth was speaking in this way to him, an old man. "So be it! Let us fight!" he replied.

They put a black felt cloak on the ground. One stood on one side, the other on the other side at the opposite end. There they began to fight with their swords. They fought for some time, until Tlabitsa began to grow tired and to find the fight hard.

"Hey, fellow! I am one day older than you, you see," he said. "Leave me alone!"

"I agree," the youth replied and stepped back.

"Seat me on my horse and send me home," he begged. "You see, I am no good for anything anymore."

The youth sat him on his horse and let him go. As soon as Tlabitsa returned home, he touched his wife's skin. With God's will he suddenly returned to normal, healthy and unharmed, as good as the day he was born.

He touched her skin and turned once more into a healthy and whole warrior. Then he returned to Chwadlazhwiya.

He returned and again became badly wounded as they fought standing against one another. The old man said, "Give me your sword! I shall go and sharpen both mine and yours, and then I shall bring them back. Let me go!" he implored once more.

Chwadlazhwiya gave his sword to the old man and let him go so he could sharpen their swords and bring them back. Tlabitsa made his own sword very sharp but blunted that of Chwadlazhwiya. Then he brought them back. The youth could do nothing with the blunted sword. Tlabitsa subdued him, tied him to his horse's tail, and dragged him back to his home. There, near his backyard, was a pile of horse dung. He flung Chwadlazhwiya into this pile and then entered his house and told his wife, "I have vanquished my enemy and brought him here. He is lying in the horse dung, still tied to my horse's tail."

"I shall take a look," she said. "I shall gaze on this enemy with whom you have fought for three days. I would like to see him." She took a pair of elevated wooden clogs and walked out on them to see her husband's enemy. She reached the dunghill and saw a child. His soul was hardly in his body, and he lay there near death. She felt a pang of shame in her heart. She was so outraged by what she saw that she took off her high clogs and threw them on the ground hard so that they broke into pieces. She went back home barefoot, she felt so angry.[7]

"Was it that child with whom you fought, whom you have brought here, and of whom you have made an enemy?" she scolded.

"Even though he is a child, he is made of evil power," he retorted. "What do you know about him?"

Now a woman who grazed the geese of the village passed by after her grazing and saw the child on her way back.[8] She picked up the child, wrapped him in her skirt, and carried him home. She brought the poor unfortunate lad to her home. She nursed him with warm milk mixed with fresh goose fat. She rubbed him with goose fat. Soon the child began to feel better. He became healthy again and began to crawl. When he had begun to move, he said to her, "Carry me to the door of Tlabitsa the Lame and leave me there on the threshold!"

"Oh, you poor boy! You can't even walk. If I leave you there, he will kill you for sure as soon as he sees you. When you begin to walk again, then you can try to do something."

"No! I will not have enough patience to wait that long. Take me now and leave me there," he said. "Set me there!"

The old woman put him on her back, carried him to Tlabitsa's house, and set him down on the threshold. Then she returned home.

He crawled over the threshold and crept into the house, where he struck against something.

Tlabitsa heard the sound and jumped up. "It is my enemy coming back," he said.

"Hah! He whom you called your enemy, that poor child who is now dead," said his wife scornfully, "how could he come here?" Thus she shamed her husband.

Chwadlazhwiya kept crawling until he drew near the hand of Tlabitsa's wife. He knew that if he could touch her skin, he would become strong once more. The instant he touched her hand, the boy jumped to his feet. His enemy was lying in bed with his own weapons and those of Chwadlazhwiya's father hanging on the wall over him. Tlabitsa sat up, lit a lamp, and saw his enemy. The child seized his father's sword, hit Tlabitsa on the head, and then cut his head off.

"You no longer have a husband," he said to Tlabitsa's wife. "He who was your husband is now gone. I shall not harm you. Just tell me where his jewels are! Tell me!" he said to her.

"I shall give you his jewels," she replied. "I shall not leave them here. I shall go wherever you go." She took all the gold and other jewels and put them in a cart.

So, Chwadlazhwiya took all the jewels and gold, the wife, and Tlabitsa's head and set off for home.

He journeyed for one whole year. As he was returning home and drew near his village, he saw a little boy eating candy. As this child ate he also began to weep. This was a small shepherd boy who was grazing a few sheep at the edge of the village.

"You, little boy!" he said. "You eat and weep at the same time!"

"I do so because I once had a friend whose name was Chwadlazhwiya," he said. "Today they gave a commemorative feast in his honor, and then they gave me these candies. I eat them because they are tasty, but when I begin to think of him I begin to weep."

"Tell me! If you saw Chwadlazhwiya now, would you recognize him?"

"Of course, I would recognize him," replied the shepherd boy.

"Then why don't you recognize me? I am Chwadlazhwiya," he said.

"You are not Chwadlazhwiya," replied the shepherd boy.

"Oh, it is really I. Go and tell my father's brothers, Sosran and Sosruquo! Tell my mother that Chwadlazhwiya has returned!"

The boy ran off, shouting and swinging his hat as he ran, "Hey! Hey! Chwadlazhwiya has returned!"

"What is the matter with you?" people asked.

"Chwadlazhwiya is back! That is what!" he shouted.

"We don't believe it," the people replied.

"Let us go! I shall show you where he is now," he offered.

They came to Tlabitsa's wife, seated on the cart, and they came to him, Chwadlazhwiya.

"Now, this is the head of Tlabitsa the Lame. These are his jewels, all that he had. In these bags is his gold. Here is his wife. I brought her to you as a gift. Take whatever you want!" he said.

"If you stick his head on a stake before your house, your mother will be satisfied when she sees it," they said. "May she live forever! And this one, she is your own wife now."

The rest they divided and took away, and they carried Chwadlazhwiya to his mother's house.

From text 38, pp. 164–69.

◐ This saga, like the following one and the Circassian saga 39, tells the adventure of a youth who sets off to learn the fate of his missing father and by doing so attains heroic manhood. It offers a vivid example of the smothering mother, a well-meaning woman who will not willingly acquiesce in her child's ambitions (see sagas 39, 74, and 90) until forced to do so. Like the young hero in the following tale, this youth is really nameless, Chwadlazhwiya being an epithet.]

[1] The name Chwadlazhwiya is based on an assimilated form of Circassian, /č'aaλa/, with the Abaza suffix for "old" and the Circassian suffix for "the one of," thus: / č'ºaλa-ž°ə-ya / 'child-old-one', "the child who is old." This is an account of how he behaves in the story as an avenging adult. A peculiarity of this term for "child" is that it can denote a human male that ranges in age from an infant to a grown youth. The term / č'ºk'ºən /, by contrast, can mean only "a small child."

[2] The name Qhabizh Chkwin seems to be / q̇a-bəž' č'ºk'ºən / 'heads-seven child' or 'starts-seven child', meaning "the one who started seven events," perhaps referring to six other tales that are now lost in which he served as the instigator. The name may also imply an earlier imagery of polycephaly (see saga 53 n. 4 and saga 63 n. 1).

[3] Tlabitsa is Circassian for "hairy heels," /λabó-cʰa / 'heel-hair', which was used of animals; this nickname suggests a monstrous or bestial quality to the villain (see saga 10 and a variant of this name in saga 39).

⁴ *Abra* is a borrowing from an Indo-Iranian language in which it meant "heaven." So this is a heavenly or divine boulder, perhaps a term used for a meteorite that, if of the usual nickel-iron composition, would have been the heaviest stone known (see saga 55).

⁵ Here Sosran, Sosruquo's father, is of the same generation (contrast with saga 69).

⁶ The mythical winged horse.

⁷ In the hierarchical Abaza society and in those of their kinsmen, women of rank wore platform shoes with pillars at the ball of the foot and at the heel. To go barefoot was a great disgrace, and only a slave or a prisoner of war would do so. Tlabitsa's wife is so outraged by her husband and his foul deeds against a mere child that she symbolically renounces her status by smashing her shoes. She will affirm this renunciation by going willingly with Chwadlazhwiya as his captive. Merely to touch her hand is to be rejuvenated, and as a life-giving woman she is a fit wife for a hero.

⁸ This can be taken metaphorically as meaning that the child hero was nearly dead when found by the goose lady. Alternatively, it could be read literally, that the child was indeed killed and then resurrected by the old goose herder. This reading finds support in the comment by Tlabitsa's wife about the impossibility of the dead child's returning. Further, in Circassian sagas this old woman, sometimes with her husband, an old man, serves as the guardian of souls and is responsible for resurrecting a youthful hero, rearing him in a grave mound until he can leave to avenge his father. Chwadlazhwiya, therefore, is a resurrected hero much like She Batinuquo (see sagas 9 and 10).

SAGA 73 ☙ *Nasran and Shamaz*

Nasran and Shamaz set off on a quest for plunder. They set off and soon returned with a herd of mares as their booty. On their way back, Nasran rode ahead of Shamaz, with Shamaz following in his tracks. Thus they rode and soon met a horseman.

"Salam aleykum! May your affairs prosper!" said Nasran.

"Waleykum salam!" he replied to Nasran, but when this rider approached Shamaz farther on, he grabbed him, pulled him off his horse, and tied him up, you see, and began to gallop off. He rode his horse all that day and all the next.

Nasran meanwhile looked around. "No, the mares have not returned yet," he thought. "They must have run away in different directions." The mares had not returned and he did not know what to do. So he rode back and came to the place where Shamaz should have been. Shamaz's horse was mingling with the other horses, its saddle empty. Shamaz was not to be seen anywhere. He rushed here and there but could not see him anywhere. He could not find him at all.

Nasran returned home and drove all the horses along with him. He had lost his companion; Shamaz had disappeared. When he returned, Shamaz's wife asked him what had happened, but he answered, "I don't know what happened to us."

"It cannot be that you know nothing of his whereabouts. This is something you should know," she said.

But how could he tell her that which he did not know?

So she went away harboring the conviction that Nasran was hiding something. "It is impossible for him to know nothing of where he went, how he disappeared," she said to herself.

Now at this time Shamaz's wife was pregnant. She soon gave birth to a son. In time Shamaz's son grew into an adolescent. As he matured, he came to rely more and more on his strength. One time he casually pushed somebody.

"Hey, you scoundrel!" that man said. "Instead of testing your strength on me, you would do better to find out where your father is. Why don't you know who your father's kidnapper is?"

When he heard this, he was offended and returned home. He began to pester his mother. "How did my father perish? How did he die? How did he disappear? Where is he?"

She replied, "I don't know anything. Go and ask the one who lost him!"

But he continued to pester her, and she said once more, "Go and ask Nasran! It is he who lost him. They were together on a raid when your father disappeared."

So he went to Nasran. "O Nasran, do whatever you want," he said, "but tell me where my father is! Show me where he perished! Show me where you lost my father!"

"May the tongue of the one who told you about this dry out!" replied Nasran. "Let us go!" He mounted his horse and set off. Soon they reached the spot and he said, "Here it was. I was ahead of the herd of mares, and he was behind it. I thought that he was following me, but then something baffling happened. The herd of mares dropped back behind me, and when I went back to them, I found his horse with an empty saddle, wandering among them. I understood immediately that something was wrong. I rushed about but could not find him. But a horseman did pass by just before this happened."

Then they rode home, and the youth went to his mother. "Thus he told me, and more than he told me I cannot know," he said to his mother. "I cannot live the same life as I did before until I know where my father is or how he could have disappeared. Where could he be now? I cannot allow people in our village to reproach me every day because of this. I do not want to live here any longer," he said, packed his belongings, and set off on his way.

This lad set upon his travels and went a great distance. When he was far from his village, he chanced to look around and saw a horseman riding up to him.

"Salam aleykum," he said as he approached. He was also a youth.

"Waleykum salam!" replied Shamaz's son.

"What is afoot, my good fellow? Where have you been?" asked the stranger.

"I shall tell you the reason for my journey," Shamaz's son replied. "May Allah be good to me! When I was in my mother's womb, my father disappeared while he was on a raid. Now my heart cannot find peace, and I have set out on my quest to learn any word I can about my father's fate."

"Well," he said, "such things may happen. May Allah bring good news to you of your father! If this is the matter, then let us set off together!" And he joined him on his quest. Soon they arrived at a small village and dismounted. The stranger invited Shamaz's son into a guest house.

"Now, good fellow," he said, "rest for three days, and perhaps Allah will send us some good news about your father. Wait here for me for three days. I shall return before three days have passed," and he set off.

The son of Shamaz remained in the guest house. Every day his hosts brought him clean clothes. Each day the clothes were different. Each day the food was different. These things were by order of the mysterious youth.

After three days had passed, the youth returned, and both of them set off once more on their quest. They traveled together, and soon they entered a marvelously beautiful region. It was so beautiful that one could not help but admire it. As soon as they crossed over into it, the strange youth said, "This, my dear friend, is my land."

There they dismounted, and the stranger arranged for them to rest for one whole month. When a month had passed, the mysterious youth said, "Now let us go! I shall lead you to one more place." Having said that, they set off and he took the son of Shamaz to a seashore. There he stopped and said, "You see, I have enemies. I am now going to visit them. You stay here and wait for me. At midnight, when the 'show' begins, set fire to this stack of hay, so," he said, pointing to a pile of hay nearby.

"Good! I shall do as you say," replied Shamaz's son.

So the stranger set off to visit his enemies. When he arrived in their land, he began to fight with them. They retreated into the sea. If someone could light the hay for him, then the light from that fire would blind his enemies and he would have them in his power. So far, he had not been able to find a good helper.

This time the son of Shamaz helped him and he was victorious. He returned from the sea. He wanted his helper to know who his enemies had been, and so the stranger said, "Know, you, good youth, that I have avenged my blood and returned home. They have paid for the blood they spilled and I have come back. Tuzumbiy," he said, "there were seven brothers and they were called Tuzumbiy. These seven brothers and my father became enemies. They killed him. No one else was able to join me and help me fulfill my revenge except you. May Allah be pleased with you! Only two of the seven were still alive. I just encountered both of them exactly as I had planned. If not for your help, they would have seized me and not let me go. You were an immense help to me. I have killed them. Now let us return home!" Saying this, they set off for home.

Once more they came to the lovely land of the stranger. "Young lad, now tell me your problem! What is the matter?" asked the stranger.

"Well, my problem is my missing father. I have told you about him already," replied the son of Shamaz.

"Do you know of the Narts?" the stranger asked.

"I am one of them," he replied.

"Whose son are you?" the stranger asked.

"I am the son of Shamaz," he replied.

"Splendid! If the Narts still want you back!" he said. The stranger then sat down and began to write a letter.

"If you wish to take back the Narts' son, the son of Shamaz, then be aware that he is still alive. You can come and bring for him so much gold. Come, dignified fathers! Narts, come!" he wrote.

He sent the letter. They read it. It was written so forthrightly that they had to respond to it by going there. They assembled all the Narts, any one of them who considered himself a man, and set off on their way. They asked along the way and scouted the road until they came to the stranger's land and crossed over into it. Soon they came upon him.

"Narts! You have come! You made it!" the stranger said. "You have done well to come here. Tomorrow we shall talk with you."

"Agreed!" replied the Narts.

In the morning, as the young stranger had said, they gathered. They came from near and far. Shamaz, the father of the lad who had been searching for him, also came. The young stranger brought him as well. He sat them all down on pillows filled with chicken down. He gathered all of them together at his invitation and sat them all on one side.

Now, the Narts could not recognize Shamaz, their lost brother, because he had a long beard, reaching down to his waist, that had turned white. They could not recognize Shamaz's son either, because many years had passed since he had left. He had grown to manhood, with a beard and a mustache. They say that he sat beside his own father and did not recognize him.

"Now, Narts," said the young stranger, "I wish to fight with you. I have the urge to do combat with you. Whoever trusts in his strength, let him step forward. If you best me, then you can take your brother back. You can take your fellow. But if you fail to best me, then all of you Narts will stay here."

They agreed to this. Very few people could best the Narts. They turned to their youngest and said, "Now, you go and fight!" He went up against the stranger and was bested. Then they turned to another and sent him against the stranger, but he too was bested. And so the combat proceeded.

Nasran and Shamaz's son, Shamazuquo, were among the group. Shamaz's son turned to the man with the long white beard and said, "Hey, my father! If only Shamaz were with me today. Oh, if only Shamaz were near me today!"

Shamaz knew all the Narts and recognized them all, but he could not recognize this youth, his own son.

By the time he had finished saying this, the young stranger had bested nearly all the Narts. He stood up and departed from them with great dignity. The stranger who had beaten the Narts had left, but as they stood awaiting his return, a fine girl came to them. She was so beautiful that no one on earth resembled her. She came before them and said, "Allow me to explain my affair to you."

"Tell us!" they replied.

"My father," she said, "my father's friends together with my father were the enemies of the Tuzumbiys. In their struggle, they killed five of the Tuzumbiy brothers, but two of them survived. They killed my father.

They mortally wounded him when I was still a little girl. My father's dying words to me were, 'My daughter, you must avenge me.' That is what he said to me. 'Do as I say! In the womb of Shamaz's wife is one who, together with you, will avenge my blood. No one but he can do it.' Those were his last words.

"The one called Shamaz sits here, among you," she said. "He is that old man. Next to him sits his own son, who set out to find him."

Shamaz and Nasran[1] jumped up at the same time and embraced one another. Then Shamazuquo arose and embraced his father.

"Now, Narts!" she continued. "If you like me, then I consent to be your bride.[2] If you do not like me, then I shall give all my belongings and cattle to you. Return the way you came! It is your choice what you do. Decide now, and it will be as you say. Take Shamaz and Nasran with you and you yourselves return home! I myself shall go with this young fellow as his bride. If you do not like that, then I shall stay here alone and you may return home."

No one had realized that the young stranger was a woman, not even the son of Shamaz. Then Shamaz stood up and said, "If this person, who took care of me for so many years, does not come home with me as a daughter-in-law, then I shall beat my own son."

So Shamaz brought her home as his daughter-in-law. Her belongings and everything else she left there. She returned home with the Narts as a bride. That is how it was.

From text 32, pp. 128–33.

↻ This story has a surprising twist that ties it in with sagas 63 and 74. Nasran and Shamaz belong to an older generation of the Narts. The nameless son of Shamaz, whom I have dubbed Shamazuquo, wins a glorious but equally nameless bride. The identities of the "transsexual" bride and of her enemies, the Tuzumbiy clan, are quite unclear. She resembles the warrior woman of the next saga, as well as Lady Amazan, or Lady Nart Sana in saga 26 (Circassian).

[1] This line, to which I have added Shamaz's son, Shamazuquo, suggests that Nasran is in fact the son of Shamaz, whereas in the Circassian corpus, where they are slightly more prominent, they are clearly coevals.

[2] This line suggests that she is offering herself to all of them as their joint bride. This is not as odd as it sounds if one sees in this nameless warrior beauty a junior version of Satanaya, who stands as mother and often consort to all the Narts. This offer is quickly reinterpreted in more ordinary terms as being directed at the hero, the son of Shamaz.

The Nart called Khmish was a very mean man. He relied only on his own strength, on his own courage, and that is why he never asked anyone from the Narts to join him on his raids. His tale runs as follows.

In that time there were many animals. In that time also there were many forests around and few people. The world was very big. Khmish lived by hunting. He was not afraid of the Narts when he met them. He neither feared them nor bothered them, and they in their turn knew him and tried not to annoy him. Should the people he met be Chints or Marakwa, traditional enemies of the Narts, he would encounter them alone, relying only on his own strength.

So one day Khmish set off to hunt alone. On this hunt he soon came to a forest where he had never hunted before. He roamed for one day, two days. There was much game in the forests in that ancient time, but this time he encountered neither deer nor aurochs nor any other animal. He roamed for several days, and one morning, to his surprise, in the bright early morning, he came upon a meadow in the forest and suddenly heard dogs barking. He turned his head in the direction of their barking and wondered, "A prodigy indeed! This place has not known man's footsteps before. Where are these hounds coming from?" As he pondered their noise and peered into the woods, a stag jumped out into the glade and rushed toward him. There was indeed a man in the forest because his arrow suddenly shot past the deer and past the tree near where Khmish was sitting on his horse. The stag ran toward Khmish, and he was about to shoot it himself when he thought, "Why should I shoot him now? He himself is coming to me. When he is closer, then I shall shoot him." So, you see, he lowered his bow.

When the stag was still not close enough for him to shoot, there emerged from the woods in just the spot where the stag had jumped out a man riding on a rabbit. The deer bolted to one side, and Khmish galloped out on his horse toward the man on the rabbit, but both rider and rabbit skipped underneath the belly of his horse. Then the stag suddenly fell down. The man jumped down from his rabbit, ran over to it, and slit its throat. Khmish wheeled about on his horse and rode over to the man who had finished killing the deer. Khmish asked him, "What a wonder! Did the deer fall down because he was frightened? Did a gust of wind knock him down? What happened to him?"

But the man did not answer. Khmish did not like that, but he said, "I wish for you to feast on whatever you find."

"Let us go together! I shall offer you the young meat to eat," he said. "Be my guest." He was from the Marakwa tribe. Soon his two companions came out and joined him. Now there were three Marakwas. All three of them knew that he was Khmish. They had hated him all their lives and had seen themselves as his enemy.

"All right!" said Khmish. Khmish could not refuse an invitation. He said, "I never refuse to eat bread and salt." Meanwhile the first man had already dressed the stag's carcass. He tied it to his rabbit. Those who had come later, the friends of the first Marakwa, then left and Khmish went with them.

Khmish, the two who arrived later, and the one who had killed the stag set off for the house of the deer killer. Soon they reached his house. The Marakwa hunter dismounted and opened the door. "Come in, Khmish!" he said. Khmish dismounted and with great difficulty crawled through the low door. When he entered the house, however, he found it big and light inside. He liked the house.

That day they fed him and treated him as a best guest. Then he was allowed to rest, and Khmish slept soundly. The Marakwa hunter had a very beautiful daughter. Even though she was short, she was already a teenage girl. She was very beautiful.

The rider who had invited Khmish gave an order to his daughter and a further invitation to Khmish. "I go now, but I shall be back in three days. You, Khmish, rest here until I return! And you, my dear, entertain him, give him enough food, and take care of him!" He said this loudly so that Khmish would also hear it. Then he mounted his rabbit and rode off.

Khmish grew to like this girl during these three days, her character, her manner, and everything else about her. He himself was not married and neither was she. Finally he said, "Hey, dear girl, I have fallen in love with you during these three days. Be my wife!"

At first the rabbit rider's daughter felt insulted, but then she started to think, and she realized that she too liked his character, his face, and his words. She liked his words. "Well," she said, "if you are speaking seriously, then I shall marry you. But I would like to know your sincerity for sure. My conditions are as follows. I am short in this world, but for you I will be tall. I am also big for a family, but if ever you call me short, deliberately or accidentally, as soon as you have uttered that word, then it will be the end of our life together. It will be at an end! I am telling you this as the only truth."

In his turn he spoke seriously to her, "As long as I am alive, I will never say that word, and it will not even be in my thoughts."

"Then I agree," she replied.

Soon the rabbit rider returned and found that Khmish had married his daughter. He then set off to gather his friends. They met to plan a way of killing Khmish. They decided to kill him by deception. They would lure him into an open field and kill him there. There was no one among them, you see, who could fight him openly. They all knew his courage.

Some time passed. One year went by. After that one year, his short wife became pregnant and her time for delivery drew near. At this time those same three Marakwas came into his yard and greeted him. "Khmish! We are going to travel. We want to see how other people live, to hunt a bit, and then return. Will you join us?"

Khmish did not even discuss the matter with his wife. Rather he sent one of the Marakwas into the house, instructing him, "Go in and tell her to prepare food for me for this long trip."

The Marakwa went in and told her what her husband had demanded. She replied, "It will take me a moment." He went back out to Khmish, who was readying his horse for the trip.

When Khmish finished with his horse, his food was not yet ready, and so he again sent the Marakwa to his wife. "Just a minute! I'll do it. I'll set everything into his bag," she said.

When after a while his food still was not ready, Khmish himself went to her and said, "What are you doing here so long, my dear, short wife?"

That is what he said. He was not supposed to have said that, as they had agreed before. She had made a strong vow no longer to be his wife if he ever spoke like that. The time for her delivery was near and she said, "Well, well, it's almost ready. It took me a little bit longer. Now it's ready. Here you have it. Take it!" and she put the food in his bag. Soon thereafter she gave birth to a son, and they named him Bataraz.

Meanwhile Khmish traveled with his companions for about a month. After this time, they turned to head back home when they came upon a large valley. They decided, "We'll have a rest here. We'll feed our horses here, and we ourselves will rest here a bit." Thus they spoke and dismounted. When he dismounted, Khmish heard a scream from that valley, an awful scream in the middle of the day, in the late morning. "Whose voice is that?" he asked and sent two Marakwas to find out. The Marakwas went to see and an ayniwzh saw them. It pulled a big tree out of the ground and began to chase them. It could not catch them but threw the tree at one of them and broke his leg. The other one ran back. Khmish saw all this. "Oh, this is no good, to kill our companions!" he said. He jumped to his feet and grabbed his sword. Khmish and the ayniwzh took positions against each other and began to fight. They fought for a long time until they both grew tired as the Marakwas watched. With his last strength, Khmish killed the ayniwzh and won. After this fight, his sword was blunt and he himself was exhausted. When the remaining Marakwas realized this, they crept up on him from behind and murdered Khmish. He tried to resist but could do little with a blunt sword. Khmish perished there.

Now Khmish's wife was ready to deliver. She planned to abandon her baby and return to her parents. Khmish had broken his word, violated their agreement. The Narts were glad that she bore a son. They named him Bataraz and were full of joy, but his mother wanted to abandon him and return to her parents. She refused him her breast. The Narts gathered when they realized what was happening and begged her to feed him. He was an unusually beautiful baby. The Narts knew that he would become somebody special. They held a discussion about him and decided that he would grow up to be a great warrior. "At the least he will probably be of help to us in some way," said the Narts. So they gathered about and began to beseech her to stay. Old men and women came to this gathering. "Don't abandon him. Bring him up for us. After he has learned something, then you may return if by that time you still wish to!" they entreated her. She refused to do as they asked.

"No! After I leave him, I won't give him my breast. Nut juice is similar to my breast milk. Squeeze the juice out of nuts and feed him with this juice. It is even stronger than mother's milk," she said. So after offering this advice, she left for her parents.

The Narts once again gathered because they had learned of Khmish's death. The Marakwas were afraid only of Khmish. "If they realize that Khmish's son still lives on the earth, they will say that when he is grown he will avenge his father's blood. So they will try to kill the baby. It would be better to raise the baby secretly." They decided to give him to a woman to raise. The first woman summoned said that she had no place to hide him. Two others were suggested. They both declined as well. But one wise old woman did not have children of her own. They summoned her to their council and said to her, "We live on this world only for your sake. We tend to your hay, your dress, your food—everything is our responsibility. For this reason you will take this child and rear him until he is an adult."

The old woman glanced at the child and said, "Fine, I agree." Thus she spoke and took the child, Bataraz. She took him, and the Narts made a cradle for him. He was laid in the cradle. One day passed. Two days passed. Three days passed. Special restraining belts made of deerskin had been put in the crib. These belts resembled buffalo hide. No one knows what happened to the child, whether he was frightened or something else, but he strained with all his might, broke all the belts, and fell out of the cradle. The old woman looked at him lying on the floor and thought this very unusual. She went out and brought her neighbor, another old woman, back to her house. "I shall show you a great wonder. Look here where he is lying and look at what he did, at what he broke!" she said to her and showed her the belts.

Her neighbor happened to be a wise old woman and said, "Don't tell anyone else what you have just shown me! He will become the warrior of all warriors, of all Narts. He will not remain small much longer. A year from now he will become a man. Whatever a normal child gains in one month, he gains in one day. Whatever someone gains in two months, he gains in two days."

So very soon Batarez had grown out of his cradle and was nearing manhood. At the time when he began to go out on the streets, Wazarmis's wife happened to give birth to a girl. Wazarmis's daughter was beautiful. Wazarmis once said, "When Bataraz becomes an adult, I would not mind having him, Khmish's son, as my son-in-law." The Narts were the sort of people who usually kept their word. They also turned their words into reality. Bataraz knew what he had said, Wazarmis's daughter knew, and Wazarmis himself knew because he had made the remark! So as the two grew up, each day they became closer to one another, and each day he grew closer to being a real man.

One day Bataraz said, "Oh, my God! Mother, I want to go out from the yard for a short while. I want to be with other boys. I want just to look around, just to walk a bit on the street."

"Forget that, my little boy! That is not good. When your time comes, I will tell you," said his stepmother.

Several more days passed. During that time he secretly made a bow and some arrows. Now he began to shoot down birds on the wing, to shoot and kill flying crows. That is how skillful and courageous he had become. "Mother," he said, "don't you see what I have done? I have shot down birds.

I have shot down flying crows. I have even shot down flies. I shall go and hunt for a while."

"No, my child! It is not your time yet. When your time has come, I will tell you myself," she said.

"You will see yourself whether my time has come or not. Let's go!" he said.

"No, it is not your time yet," she said. "This shooting and killing of birds can be done by women as well. Even crows and any other birds! But you try to flush out some deer, and then go after one and try to catch it with your bare hands."

"Let's go! You'll see!" he said.

"That is no good. He just will not leave me in peace," she said to herself. So she decided to take him to find deer. They approached a ravine, and suddenly a deer jumped out. He began to chase it, grabbed it by the legs, and returned, carrying the deer under his arm like a lamb.

"Well, I can see that you have grown up," she said. "You are ready now."

When he caught the deer he was only two years old, but he had grown to resemble a man of marrying age. During these two years Wazarmis had not forgotten his word, those first ones. He was an honest man. Whatever he promised he would fulfill. That was the kind of man he was.

One day he said, "It strikes me that I want to look around a little, to hunt a bit," and so he set off on an adventure. He set off and soon came to a mountain range that he had to cross. "There will probably be more to overcome," he said. Indeed, he had to overcome six more.

When he had crossed the seventh range, he saw a huge herd of mares grazing in a valley below. "Oh, my God! Who is the owner of this herd?" They seemed like a miracle to him. "I shall go closer and have a better look," he said. When he was among the horses, a huge ayniwzh appeared out of nowhere.

"O you! Born of a dog!" he said. "Where did you come from in this world, you who have appeared among my possessions? What kind of Nart are you to appear here? The likes of you I have not seen since I was born," he said. He seized Wazarmis, tied him up, and brought him back to his house, which was surrounded by a moat. There he kept him for one week, two weeks, and then he said to him, "Wazarmis, I shall not kill you nor do any violence to you. Instead I shall tell you how it will be. You will remain here and serve as herdsman to my horses until the day you die. You have no other choice. If you try to run away, then as soon as you are caught you will be killed." Thus he spoke to Wazarmis and so made him his herdsman.

So Wazarmis became a herdsman. Some time passed. Two years passed. A third was almost over. Wazarmis did not have anyone around to shave him, to wash his things. The ayniwzh was busy with his own affairs. He tended to his affairs, his house, and his moat, but from time to time he kept watch on Wazarmis. All day and all night Wazarmis oversaw the grazing of the herd. The ayniwzh brought food to him so that Wazarmis was always among the horses. He became unrecognizable.

In the meantime Bataraz was going to be married. The Narts gathered together. Only Wazarmis was absent. When Wazarmis had been captured, his horse escaped and ran away, back to the Narts. The Narts realized that Wazarmis had not been killed but was captured, tied up, but they understood that no one would rescue Wazarmis. So they married his daughter to Bataraz without Wazarmis' presence. For three days and three nights they held games. They held a big feast, and they showed Bataraz every honor as required by etiquette. Soon the feast was over and all the participants dispersed.

That night, when they went to bed, Bataraz's new wife let out a sorrowful sigh. When he heard that, Bataraz said, "What is the matter? Do you need any worldly thing? Why did you sigh so sorrowfully? Do you need anything or feel the want of anything? Do you not like the way you were treated? Or maybe you do not like the style of life that you now will live? What is happening with you?"

"Yes," she replied, "if I do not sigh with sorrow, then who will sigh for me? You came to me nicely and my life is good. Everything is all right. But although everything is good, my father is tied up. He is a captive. So, if I do not sigh with grief, who will?"

Bataraz said nothing but stood up, dressed himself, took his bag and saddle, and thrust the bridle behind his waist belt. Then he stepped out and went to the old woman who had reared him. He came to her and said, "Mother, I need your advice. Tell me where the ayniwzh lives. Tell me how I can find him—the ayniwzh who captured Wazarmis. Give me your advice and I shall soon bring Wazarmis back home."

"O my little boy!" she replied. "You won't make it. There is no one among the Narts who would be able to bring him back home. The Narts do not have a horse that could reach that place."

"No, do not mistake me. I am not asking that because I do not want to go. I am asking you that because I am going there. So please give me your advice. Just tell me how I can reach that place," he said. "The rest of it, how to bring him back, is my business."

"Now, listen, my little boy! Your horse will not get you there," she replied. "Besides, I do not know the way to him who captured Wazarmis. And no one among us would know. When Wazarmis was captured, his horse ran away and returned. No one among the Narts, besides me, knows the secret of where this horse is now kept. I have hidden him. In a certain valley, in a cave, where not a single sunbeam can penetrate, the horse lies. During the day the horse hides there. In the evening, after sunset, he comes out from the cave and grazes until morning. Before sunrise he returns to the cave. Thus has he spent these past years[1] without seeing the sun. Since Wazarmis was captured, the sun could not warm his horse. He is in a certain valley. You probably will not be able to catch this horse," she said. "But if you catch him, then saddle him, hit him in the neck, and turn him loose. This horse will go on his own to the right place. Do not try to turn him from his way, no matter where he goes.

"If you can catch Wazarmis's horse, then you will catch him in this way. His horse has trampled a path. You will see a big birch tree along this path to his pasture. This path will pass under this birch tree. It then proceeds toward the pasture, where he is grazing. When he is finished, he returns and passes under that tree again, on his way back to the cave. Climb this birch tree, and when he is passing under it, jump on him when he least expects it. In this way you will catch him," she said. "Jump on him, hit him on the neck, let him go, and he will run and will carry you directly there. Nobody from the Narts knows the way."

"That is fine. Do not be frightened for me, my mother!" he said, and with a saddle on one of his shoulders and the bridle in his waist belt, he set off on his way. After a time, he came upon the path and followed it to a valley, where he saw the birch tree of which the old woman had spoken. He approached the tree and waited for evening. When it grew dark, he climbed into one of its branches. The horse had to pass under him on its way to pasture.

Soon the horse emerged from a nearby wood and passed under the tree. Just then he jumped down on his back. The horse became frightened and reared up. Bataraz squeezed him powerfully between his legs and the horse calmed down. Then the horse began to speak, "If you are indeed a real man, then I shall serve you as a horse. I swear before you on your Narts' gray rock[2] that I shall be worthy of you, that I shall not shame you. Just stop squeezing my ribs!"

Bataraz dismounted, stroked the horse, put the bridle on him, and saddled him. Then he mounted him and said, "Go!" and let the horse run free.

Soon they crossed one mountain range, then a second, and then seven more.³ The horse ran on by himself, and where it went Bataraz did not know. Soon he saw a large herd of horses, the mares of the ayniwzh. He saw them, as well as someone among them. He drew near him, stopped before him, and greeted him, but he did not realize that this man was Wazarmis. His beard had become very long, his hair was long and unkempt, and he himself was thin and helpless. When Bataraz drew near this bedraggled man, the horse would no longer obey him and instead put his head on the man's shoulder. Wazarmis gazed at the horse and stroked is head. Then tears began to fall from his eyes.

"Greetings, good old man! Why are you crying? What do you know about this horse?" Bataraz asked Wazarmis.

"Good lad," he replied. "You know nothing of this horse, but when I was free—today I am feeble—but when I was free, we wrought many wonderful deeds together, this horse and I, in the land of the Narts. That is why my tears flow."

"Wazarmis, is that you?" asked Bataraz.

"I am the one to whom this horse belongs," replied Wazarmis.

"This is not the time to dispute that. Your horse agrees with you," said Bataraz. "I have come to take you back."

"Good youth," he replied, "you cannot take me away from here. Nobody in the world can vanquish the ayniwzh who captured me. It would be better for you if you went away immediately. It is probably God's will that I am here. I will probably die here. There is no chance that I can escape. As soon as I move, he will catch me again."

"No, Wazarmis," he said, "I did not come to take you away in secret. I came to take you away openly."

"If you indeed have such plans, then I shall pray for your success. His place is that house which you can see from here, and that moat which you can see. Be careful! Approach him carefully! May Allah help you in your efforts! May Allah bless you!"

"Do not move from this spot, Wazarmis. Tomorrow, at the same time, I shall return. Be patient, Wazarmis, and wait for me!"

He struck the horse and jumped over the ayniwzh's wall. He forded the moat and on the other side saw a long awning. It was a beautiful, warm day, and the ayniwzh lay under this awning, asleep. He had three heads. A beautiful young woman was walking around him and brushing off flies.⁴ He slept. When an ayniwzh sleeps, he sleeps for seven days and seven nights, then he is awake for the same amount of time. That is what people say about them.

"What is going on, woman? Who are you and how did you happen to get here?" he asked her. The ayniwzh slept on, lying on the ground.

"I am his slave," she replied. "I am human, of the race born of woman. This one brought me here and now uses me as a flyswatter. When he falls asleep, he sleeps for seven days and seven nights. He has already slept for four days and four nights. He has three more to go. Leave! He will not let you live. This place has become my home. I have turned into nobody. You leave! Do not let him kill you!"

"No!" he said. "I did not come here to be scared and to run away without killing him." He then drew his sword and struck the ayniwzh, cutting off two of his heads at once. This left one head.

"Aah!" said the ayniwzh and jumped up. "Hey, you Nart!" he cried. "I have never struck a sleeping Nart. I never fought them when they were sleeping. Your courage, Nart, is in killing sleepers. To one who is awake you won't even try to come close. If you are a real man, strike me once more!"

Bataraz knew that if he hit the ayniwzh one more time, all three heads would grow back. But Bataraz was insulted, so he struck him again. At once the ayniwzh grew his three heads back. With all his heads restored, the ayniwzh let out a scream and grabbed Bataraz. They began to struggle and push one another in different directions. They began fighting in the early morning and fought until evening. Then Bataraz grew truly angry, and he struck the ayniwzh's sword and shattered it. With his sword broken, the ayniwzh was left with nothing in his hands. Then Bataraz began to slash him and finally cut his three heads off. He killed the ayniwzh and took the young woman with him. He came back and took Wazarmis as well, so that they all returned home together.

On their way home, when they were crossing one of the mountain ranges, Bataraz asked Wazarmis, "Wazarmis, you have been so long in captivity that your daughter married. Tell me what you would do to him who married her when you get home."

"Before you and before all other Narts, I will take her to the place of execution, where I will cut her head off," he said. "And I will do the same to that one who married her without my permission."[5]

Bataraz made no comment. This marriage had been Wazarmis's will, and that is why Bataraz had married her. He said not a word. They returned home.

When they returned, all the Narts were gladdened. They arranged a great feast. For ten days and ten nights they killed animals, danced, and held games. There Wazarmis learned that his daughter had married Bataraz. Bataraz's wife had delivered a baby girl. She was already two years old. [Wazarmis was pleased and for once forgot his word.]

But Bataraz's family life unfolded this way. Bataraz's daughter fell ill and died. He mourned for one month. During this month, his wife also grew ill and died. The two losses doubled his sadness, and he spent a whole year in mourning. He was distressed and could not marry anyone else again. All the Narts pitied him. His grief was a great anguish for them.[6]

One day he said, "It does me no good to sit and do nothing for such a long time. I cannot live the rest of my life without having joy again." So he readied himself and set off on a quest. On his way, soon after he had set out, a young and handsome youth overtook him. Well dressed and well armed, he did not even greet Bataraz. He silently joined him and together they continued. They had to cross a river that was in their way. When they reached its banks, Bataraz's horse stopped and began to drink. The youth's horse also began to drink. Up to this point, Bataraz had not said a word, but now he was determined to say something.

"Hey, good fellow, do you not know that bad manners cause needless insult?" he said to the youth. He did not like the youth's behavior.

"Oh!" replied the youth, and without another word he drew his sword. But Bataraz reacted swiftly, drew his sword, and struck him first, dealing him a wound from which he could not recover. Only then did the youth begin to talk.

"O Bataraz," he said. "I began this quest, traveled many places. I wanted to see you, to join you and do something good in my life. Now you have slain me. I set out on this quest only because of you, to see you."

He had good intentions, but before he had said these words he had drawn his sword and had wanted to kill Bataraz. Judge for yourself what sort of good intentions these were. Nobody in this world would have known what this young fellow had in mind. As he lay dying, the youth said, "Hey, Bataraz! Don't make me go far away! Don't carry me far away! Bury me somewhere here on the river's bank! The water will avenge me. The wind will avenge me. The vengeance for my death is not a complicated matter."

As requested, Bataraz buried him on the river's shore. Bataraz, feeling depressed, turned back and returned to his village. When he returned, he told what had happened. He walked among the Narts and asked the wise old ones what the fellow's last words could have meant. Then he made a vow to himself, saying, "That youth in his last moments had said that his name was Quayda. 'Quayda is my name,' said this fellow. When I asked him where he had come from, all he said was 'Quayda is my name.' That was all he said at the moment of his death. I swear that I shall discover the meaning of his last words. I will not return until I know."

He readied himself and set off again on his way. He traveled one day, two days. Soon he saw three horsemen galloping ahead of him. He overtook them. They happened to be three Nart brothers: Batoquo,[7] Sosruquo, and Shaway. All three were great warriors. "Salam aleykum!" he said.

"Waleykum salam!" they responded.

"Are you on a long quest?" he asked.

"Yes, we want to see the world a bit," they said. "Not only we, but you too are on a long quest." So all four continued on their way together. They rode for fourteen days and nights. Then Sosruquo said, "That is enough. We have traveled quite a long way. Let us rest! We shall explore the surrounding area and then turn back and return home."

When Sosruquo said that, Bataraz spoke: "We are a lazy bunch! Our kids usually reach these places, play here for fun, and then return home. If this is as far as you had planned to come, why did you plan this journey at all?"

After he said these words, they set off again, and again they rode for fourteen days and nights. They entered a wood with beautiful trees, with resting places, with high, thick grass. As they came into the heart of the forest, Batoquo said, "Now we have a place to rest, and water is nearby that seems good. There is plenty of food for our horses around here. The grass is thick and juicy. Let us halt here!" That is what Batoquo said.

"Ah, you slackers!" said Bataraz. "Our Nart elders bring their horses here to graze for one night, and then in the morning they take them back home. If you were planning to go only this far, why did you set off at all?"

Once again they set off farther. Again for fourteen days and nights they journeyed along their way, and when they reached another good place, Shaway said, "This is far enough. We can't go any farther. We have journeyed enough. What we have covered is enough!"

"This may be enough for you," replied Bataraz, "but I cannot stop here. May all go well with you!" he said. He left them and continued on his way. He covered a great distance, and in that faraway place a handsome horseman overtook him much as Quayda had done.

"Salam aleykum!" said this horseman.

"Waleykum salam!" replied Bataraz. "Good fellow, how fast you are!"

"Yes," he said, "but I am also very tired. For a long time I have searched for my brother. A long time has passed since I began."

"I have seen many things and have heard many things," said Bataraz. "If you tell me more about him, then I will tell you what I know if it may be of interest to you."

"Quayda is his name," he said. "For one with the name Bataraz he has a beautiful sister as a gift. She is a warrior girl—his sister, that is. His sister used to say, 'My fate is he whose name is Bataraz.' That is what she would always say. She was about to be married when her brother said to her, 'If such a one exists at all in this world, then I will find him for you.' That is what he said. My brother set off on this quest and has not returned since. I cannot find him. I have grown weary in my search, but I cannot find him."

"No, I have not met anyone like him," Bataraz lied. "By the way, where does his sister live?" Bataraz now knew that Quayda had been seeking him on behalf of his sister. Now Bataraz understood.

"Well, if you do not know, then I shall go farther with you," said the fellow and continued his journey with Bataraz until they came to a certain spot. "Do you see that mountain over there?" he asked. "When you reach it, where it stands in the heart of the forest, then you will see her dwelling place. You will enter a beautiful land. You will see where she lives. You will see her house."

But when Bataraz looked about, he could see only low hills. When he turned to the handsome young man, he found that he had vanished. Then he said to his horse, "Qara!⁸ Let's go!" He struck him with his riding crop, and the horse took off until they came to a mountain in the heart of the forest. You see, it was easy for his horse. He found the mountain with ease.

The place that the youth had foretold was indeed beautiful. It was a lovely world with high grass and beautiful blossoms. He stopped on one of the low hills at the mountain's foot. Then he decided, "I shall rest for a while. My horse will also rest for a bit. After sunset I shall have a look at those houses which are standing there." He dismounted and stood there, but as soon as he had dismounted a huge cloud rolled across the sky. It started to rain. The whole world became covered with clouds. He grew very sleepy. He placed his felt cloak on the ground and fell asleep on it. He slept one whole day and night, and still it rained. He slept for the next day and night, and then for the third day and night. All the time it rained without stopping. His horse stood near him. On the fourth day it stopped raining and the clouds disappeared. Once again the day was beautiful.

"Hey, wake up, Bataraz!" said a well-armed and well-dressed rider who had happened by and who was trying to wake him.

"Oh, how sweetly I slept!" Bataraz said.

"Yes, you have been sleeping, good fellow," said the rider. "Now it is time to rise." He drew near Bataraz and asked him to join him. Bataraz took up his saddle and felt cloak. He saddled his horse and followed the rider. They rode together, and soon they reached the place that he had seen from the low hill. They entered this land together.

"Dismount, Bataraz!" said the one who had brought him.

Bataraz dismounted. The rider then took Bataraz's horse into the stable, came back out, and locked it.

"Follow me!" said the rider, who stood in front of Bataraz and then led him into the house. The house was beautiful indeed, and the one who had invited him in sat down.

"Now, Bataraz," said his host, "I shall probably roam until midnight. I may not return until tomorrow. Until I return, you must not go outside no matter what happens. If you leave, things will go badly for you. Until midnight, do not go outside whatever may happen—war, misfortune—do not leave this place. If you leave this place, there will be no salvation for you." The rider closed the door, left, and roamed who knows where.

Bataraz awaited his return. He walked about the house until midnight. He lay down. "Why can't I leave this place? What would happen to me?" he thought as he lay in bed. Soon he fell asleep. While he slept the whole house filled with fog, so that nothing could be seen.

"Hey, Bataraz!" someone yelled as he came into the house "Are you in here? What are you up to?"

Bataraz awoke. "Who is entering? It must be the same man."

The rider entered and suddenly began to fight with Bataraz in the dark. It was very dark in the house. They fought until sunrise, when they both grew weary. When Bataraz realized that he was not defeating the rider, he gathered all his might and grabbed his adversary, lifted him, and threw him on the floor. He tied the rider up.

"So, Bataraz, I gave a vow that I would marry only he who could vanquish me. You have vanquished me. If you are a man, I am a woman. Untie me and help me up! I am a woman," said the rider.

Bataraz untied her and helped her stand. She took off her man's attire and stood before him as a woman. Then she dressed herself in women's garments in a moment. If there ever was a beautiful woman in this world, it was she. They came together as one, and he married her.

He took her as his bride and they began to live together. One year passed and Bataraz began to feel homesick. Often he thought about his home. She understood his mood. "Yes, Bataraz, I have not seen you so sad before," she said. "You have always been in a good mood. You must miss your home. We agreed that if you wished, you could visit your home, your relatives. If you wish to return after that, then come back. If not, then you may stay there. It is your choice. I give you your choice. Go there and return to me soon!"

"No, if I go alone, there will be blood," he said. "I want to see my home again. If I go, why can't we go together?"

"No," she replied. "I cannot go there, and I shall tell you why. Some time ago my brother went to search for you. Until now I have heard nothing of his fate. I know neither where he might be nor whether he is still alive. Until I receive word of my brother, I cannot leave this place. So I cannot go with you."

"Well, if that is the case, then I also cannot go there. I have no mother, father, or wife there. Most of all I miss the land itself. If not that, then, well . . . that's enough," he said and fell silent.

"Let us walk a bit, and perhaps a fresh breeze will cool off your heart," she said, and they set off walking together.

There was a river not far from her place. Their walk took them near its bank, where they decided to rest and to gaze on the water. As they sat down, Bataraz noticed a grave on the river's bank.[9] He saw it, and as he looked at it he recalled Quayda's words. She noticed his gaze and asked him why he was looking so pensively at the grave.

"Just because it is nearby, that is why I am looking at it. I am also looking at the things around it. My eyes are looking all around this place," he said.

They grew silent. Before she could speak again a strong wind began to blow, whipping up big waves in the river. One of these crashed on the grave on the bank and washed the corpse of a man out of it. Once again a wave crashed on the bank and slid back into the river. Bataraz gave a bitter laugh. He recalled Quayda's words of vengeance and began laughing bitterly.

"Why are you laughing?" she asked him.

"I laugh merely because I want to laugh," he said.

"Oh, no!" she replied. She did not believe him, did not believe his excuse. She would not leave him alone.

"Then," he said, "I shall tell you, woman, why I laughed, but before I do you must swear that you shall not condemn me for my reasons, that you shall not become my enemy—no matter who is involved, your brother, father, or mother—whoever in the world it may be," he said.

"I had only one brother," she said. "Until today I knew nothing about his fate, even though I traveled far looking for him in the guise of a young man. Even if your account touches on him, I swear that I shall not become your enemy. I swear upon our gray rock." Thus, she gave him her word. She made a vow.

"If so, then sit down," he said. He sat her down and told her everything that had happened with her brother, that he had perished at Bataraz's hands. "That is why I laugh. His last words were, 'The wind will avenge me. The water will avenge me.' That is what he said as he was dying. That is why I was gazing on this grave and why, after his words came back to me, I began to laugh." She gave a great sigh and then he said, "You see now why I did not tell you before."

"No," she said, "I sigh so sadly not because of you but because of my brother. He was a very good brother, a very kind brother. But you are the best, the most darling one among all who live in this world. You are better for me than my father, mother, or brother, and that is why I hold nothing against you."

They grew calm again, but despite her words she began to nurse a grudge against him. "How can I live with the killer of my brother? When I can, I shall kill him," she thought. So she reassured him at the same time that she felt a deep hurt. She harbored grief in her heart.

They lived together peacefully for about one more month, until it came that Bataraz said, "I shall walk around for a bit. I shall look around for a while, hunt a bit." He armed himself and went out. When he was gone, she quickly dressed herself in men's clothing, put on her armor and weapons, and set off, as she had so often before, as a warrior. She began to track him until she finally came upon him in the heart of the forest.

"Hey, Bataraz, good man!" she called. "Do you really think that you can leave here alive? Was it not Allah who sent you to me?" she said, and thereupon she cast a great darkness over the earth and called down first ice, then fire, and then rain. They began to fight. "Do you still hope to return? Your skeleton will stay here. Crows will devour your flesh. There is no way that you will go back," she yelled at him.

So they fought for a long time until Bataraz found his real power and threw his adversary to the ground, you see, and tied him up. He was just about to cut off his enemy's head when she cried, "Don't kill me! I am a woman. Don't kill me! I did not keep my vow. I did not keep my word. You are not guilty. Now I give another vow. Believe me! Henceforth until I die, I shall not repeat this. We shall live together as we lived before. Don't kill me!"

"I cannot trust you anymore, you who do not keep your word, " he said. "It does not matter how many vows you make again. Stay as you are now. Since you begged, I shall not kill you. Henceforth, our happiness will never be one that we share. Return to your house and live there as you wish. Henceforth, bother me no more!" He set her loose. Then Bataraz turned about and rode back to his own land.

From text 36, pp. 139–56. For a similar Kabardian tale, see Dumézil (1978, 290–92).

๑ This lengthy account relates the stories of Khmish and his son, Bataraz (see saga 48). Usually the former is a tale of treachery and murder, and the latter is one of implacable vengeance. In this rendering, however, Bataraz embarks on two quests. The first is the rescue of his father-in-law, Wazarmis (see sagas 43 and 49), a variant of the motif of rescuing the father, which occurs frequently among the Nart corpora. The second is a quest into the unknown reaches of a magical forest, Bataraz's overreaching heroic prowess having led him beyond what his companions could endure (see sagas 71 and 72). There, like his father, he encounters both little people (see saga 54) and the nameless forest maiden, an Amazon-like woman warrior (see saga 27) who can appear as a young man on horseback. She bears some resemblance to Qaydukh, both in her person and in her surroundings (see saga 62). Their love, however, is a story of betrayal and the loss of trust. It is a mythic inverse of the story of Qaydukh.

The penchant of the present woman warrior for fighting and wrestling is also attributed to Gunda the Beautiful in saga 83 (Abkhaz). This suggests that Lady Nart Sana, Amazan, Qaydukh, Gunda, and the present nameless maiden may have a common source. That some of these women shine also suggests links to Lady Adif (saga 28), whose name means "White Elbow" and whose image therefore calls forth the crescent moon.

[1] The text reads "for all its life," ignoring the fact that the horse was out and around bearing Wazarmis on his quests. This slip is crucial, for it suggests that this is the underground horse used to rescue a hero who appears in a number of sagas, a horse of the grave. The hero in need of a rescue is therefore actually dead and must be brought back from the land of the dead. The lovely valley with its multitude of horses harks back to the original Indo-European vision of the afterworld (Puhvel 1987, 138–39), clearly preserved in Ancient Greek myths.

[2] The gray rock is a unique reference to what must be an *abra* stone, or a "stone of

heaven" (see sagas 55 n. 2, and 72 n. 4). If such a stone were an iron-nickel meteorite, then its appearance would be gray.

³ Wazarmis crossed only seven mountain ranges, not the nine referred to here.

⁴ The three-headed giant combines the features of Hades (Pluto) and the demonic dog Cerberus. The maiden fly swatter is an echo of Hades' wife, Persephone.

⁵ Despite this ominous threat, and despite Bataraz's breach of protocol in marrying Wazarmis's daughter without his permission, no retribution is visited on the young couple by Wazarmis, perhaps because they have fulfilled his wishes. Therefore, I have added a sentence in brackets for the sake of narrative cohesion, noting his forgiveness.

⁶ This is the only account in any of the corpora in which Bataraz has a family, suggesting, as does their dying off, that this rescue tale originally belonged to some other hero, most likely Badanoquo, as attested in the Circassian corpus. The rescuer would then have married the maiden flyswatter, who here simply drops from the story after her liberation.

⁷ "Batoquo" may be a form of "Badanoquo" drawn from a dialect of West Circassian because it shows an original / -t- / . Otherwise, this name is unknown.

⁸ "Qara" is Turkic for "black." If this is a horse of the grave, it is only fitting that he should be dark, one that has not seen the light. Underground horses are found in other sagas, such as sagas 11 (Circassian) and 90 (Ubykh).

⁹ The grave on the riverbank, with a couple nearby, occurs in the saga of Qaydukh as well (62), where its function, however, is different there. In "Qaydukh Fortress" it is the woman who seeks vengeance against the corpse, and not the corpse who brings vengeance on the man. The grave in Qaydukh's saga brings the couple together. Here it destroys their union.

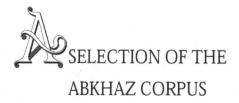

SELECTION OF THE ABKHAZ CORPUS

Sagas 75–84 Translated by
B. George Hewitt and
Zaira Khiba Hewitt
and Edited by
John Colarusso

Saga 85 Translated by
John Colarusso

Without the sun she gives warmth,
Without the moon she gives light,
Princess Satanay!
Click-click go her heels
As she passes by.
She walks the Kuban's banks,
Mother of a hundred sons,
Princess Satanay.

She plucks a thousand flax stalks
And winds them around her.
A huge bare beech she beholds.
One kick and over it goes.
She tears it out,
Turns it this way and that.
She trims its branches
And fashions a spindle,
Then lays it across her knee.
A huge rock she beholds.
One poke for a hole
And she has pierced it
As her spindle's weight.
What a whirring as she spins!
What a clatter as she weaves!
What a thumping as she scrubs!
In one day, she spins;
She weaves; she scrubs
The clothes of her hundred sons.
No, not in one day,
For this is her constant task,
Standing in the Kuban.

Once the whir of her spinning
And the thumping of her scrubbing

Rang as she walked Kuban's banks,
When, weary, she paused.
She took off her clothes.
Naked as when she was born
On the bank she stood.
The cold air cooled her body,
White as fresh cheese
And bright as amber,
Shining like a living sun.
To cool her soft skin
She slipped into the water.

She surfaced and looked about.
On the far bank, in the shade,
She beheld the Narts' cattle
Huddled and stamping. "Well, well,
My sons' cattle," she murmured
And was very glad.
But looking closer she noticed
Something among the cattle.
A tree? No, too small for that.
A rock? No, for that too big.
The beasts rubbed their horns on it,
Scratched off swarming flies from it.
"Ah, Old Zart, the Narts' herdsman
It must be!" she decided
And she gave a shout,
Which awoke the Narts' herdsman.
His brows, blowing in the breeze,
Shot up to his scalp.
Amazed, with wide eyes
He beheld something standing
Shining brighter than the sun,
Lighting up both banks

"Heavens! What is this, at noon
Brighter than the sun
And blinding me so?" said he.
He arose and walked through the herd

Rubbing his eyes with his hands.
He stopped and peered once more.
Princess Satanay,
Lovely in the cold Kuban!
The poor herdsman grew wild.
His blood could be heard to boil.
He felt himself on fire.
His sore soul hurt his heart.
Now, though awake,
He grew dumb and still.
At first, confused,
He tried to stay calm,
But he, such a lady's man,
Was no longer master of himself.

The Princess stood on the bank,
Shining. He called out, "Hello!
Was that you shouting, my lady?
Was it to me that you called?
Why be coy? Let us love!"
The Princess had not plagued him.
Many nights and many days
She had longingly dreamed of him.
Now hearing him, she answered,
"Yes it was I
Who dared hail you
But cannot from here say why.
Come across and I will tell."
Hearing this, the heart of Old Zart
Trembled in his chest.

"What shall I do? Here's a flood.
If I enter, I will drown.
If I enter, I will die.
But for you, what would I not do?
But for me, my soul is still dear."
"Damn you for a bitch's son!
I've lowered myself to you.
I might have guessed your answer!"

The Princess, glowing hot and bright,
Turned her back on him, swam off.

The herdsman looked after her.

His wrath stirred, his anger grew.
"Did I dream or was it she?
If not a dream, then I am ashamed!"
Then into the wild Kuban he dived,
Almost tore himself asunder.
In vain the Kuban spat him back.
His soul grew wilder still.
He seized his staff and dared again,
But the wretched waters swept on,
Spat him out once more.
But the waters could not dampen him.
Fearless he set his strength,
And with staff in hand dived in once more,
But again the river won.

The Princess, dressed and ready,
On her bank stood spinning yarn,
Glancing at him now and then.
"Poor fellow!" she thought.
"Would the water bear him off,
Him, who is as good as dead?"

What should the proud herdsman do,
Stranded on Kuban's far shore?
It was like a nightmare.
And he called to her,
"Ah! Too wide! What can I do?
Ah! Too wide! What shall I do?
One thing I shall say: Listen!
Tie up your glorious hair!
Tidy your fine skirt!
Show me your fair neck!
And show me your face!"

"So that is it!" she said.
She turned full to him,

Struck a pose. What a pose!
Without the sun she gave warmth,
Without the moon she gave light,
Standing there on the shore.

With raging heart,
With boiling blood,
Wordless, a moment he stood.
Then, with all his might,
"So, across, across!" he cried
A cloud-dark arrow he hurled.
Like lightning it flashed.
Like thunder it shook the earth.
Like mist it enveloped all.

Princess Satanay, until now fearless,
Darted to and fro and
By a rock threw herself down.
The arrow flew true to the rock
And stamped a man's visage on it.
Then in a twinkling
The mist had lifted
And silence had fallen.

Princess Satanay emerged
And saw where the arrow had struck.
Look! A man's face, clearly drawn!
Knowing this for a wonder,
She would cut it out, take it.
The herdsman had seen all.
"If you would learn what this means,
You must ask Aynar[1] the smith."
"O Mother, what shall I do?
Where shall I go?
I thought I could do all
A woman can.
Oh, poor Old Zart!
How can I release your wonder?"
"Oh, bright Princess Satanay,
Take it to Aynar the smith!

His right hand holds the hammer.
His left hand holds the tongs.
His right foot works the bellows.
He lacks neither strength nor wisdom.
He will raise the face for you."

Off went Princess Satanay,
Came back with Aynar the smith;
Showed him the visage.
He kneeled by the rock,
Hammered at the thing,
Prepared to chisel it out.
Three days and nights he worked.
Princess Satanay stood by.
On the third night he freed it
And gave it to the Princess,
And he said to her,
"Clasp this under your right arm,
And nine months hence a warrior
Will be born. At that moment
Your neighbor's mare will give birth
To a steed none will mount and live.
No steed will be so mighty.
Now you must do this:
Before the Narts' new brother
Comes into the world,
Let no one go near this steed.
When the Narts' brother is born,
He will know what he must do."

Princess Satanay agreed.
With the face under her arm
She went; kept it for nine months
In the warmth of her fair skin,
Neither showed it nor spoke of it
And waited for the day.

[Modified from The Elek Book of Oriental Verse, ed. Keith Bosley (London: Penguin, 1979), pp. 176–81, taken from Inal-Ipa et al. 1962, saga 3, pp. 24–33, trans. B. George Hewitt and Zaira Khiba Hewitt, 1981, ed. John Colarusso.]

¹ The name Aynar is etymologically / a-yna-r / 'the-big-part', "the Great One," and is the same as that used elsewhere for the giants, Circassian / yənə(-ź)/, Abaza / a-ynə́(-ź°)/, Ubykh / yənə́(-ž°)/. It may also be the source of "Indra" in the Rig-Veda and of the goddess Innara of Hittite myth.

The question is where does the name Indra come from. A generally accepted etymology is to see it as a reflex of PIE *ə₂n-(ə)r-, see the Greek *anḗr* (Lincoln 1981, 97 and n. 4), the Sabine *Nerō* 'strong' (a personal name), the Umbrian *nerus*, and the Old Irish *nert* (Pisani 1947, 147, 302). Gonda (1960, 60 n. 35), however, expresses skepticism over the etymologies of this name, including this one. In fact, PIE *ə₂n-(ə)r- is attested in Indo-Iranian and it shows no *i*-development from the cluster *ə₂n-; see the Vedic *nrtama* 'most manly' (an epithet of Indra), the Sanskrit *nā́*, *nár-am* (accusative) 'man, hero', the Avestan *nar-*, *nərə-(gara-)* (Pisani 1947, 147, §302), and the Ossetic *nart* (Benveniste 1959, 37 and n. l). Both the phonological shape of "Indra" and its meanings within and without Indo-Aryan are best explained if a Circassian etymology is assumed.

"Indra," with an intrusive -*d*-, that is, **inra*, has a transparent etymology within Proto-Circassian. The original would have been **/yənə-ø-ra/* 'huge-be-ger', "the one who is huge," that is, "the gigantic one," with a variant **/yəna-ø-ra/* or **/yənə-a-ø-r(a)/*, the latter: 'huge-he-be-ger', preserved in this name of the Abkhaz Nart god of the forge, / a-ynar / 'the-gigantic one'. This form is probably of Pontic origin (the phylum from which Northwest Caucasian and Indo-European are descended [Colarusso 1997b, 170, §70]). This form is reflected in Indo-Iranian as an epithet of anyone huge, hero or demon, whence Vedic *Indra*, a heroic god, Avestan *indra*, a gigantic demon; perhaps here we should also include the Hittite goddess Inara (/ inra / [?]), based on the root *innar(a)-* 'strong, virile', which shows a wide development within Hittite (Benveniste and Renou 1934, 184–87).

SAGA 76 ✑ *The Birth of the Valiant Sasruquo*

When her month began to draw near, Lady Satanay busily prepared the clothing of her little son who was about to be born. She wove for him a cherkesska made of wool, which came from a sheep on which there was not a single black hair. When she wove it, when she noisily beat at the front of her loom, the Narts' castle shuddered violently. That which was to be woven she wove, washed in the river, and pounded to soften it. Five times she took it down to the shores of the Kuban to wash it. When she laid the cherkesska material, washed and white as a flower, on the stony bank, the people stood and stared at it, asking themselves, "What is it?"

One day in the morning, when she had thus prepared the material from which the cherkesska, shirt, and hat would come, she set her hand to the task of cutting and sewing them. Lady Satanay, who had woven and sewn on a single day the clothes of her ninety-nine sons, would she really have spent so much time on the clothes of her baby? But because the manner of the baby's birth was to be something wonderful, her thoughts were many. She was so engrossed in her work that she did not notice when midday approached. Having sewn her son's clothes, she was sorting them, one by one, and gaily singing over them. Without spending further time on it, however, she elegantly sewed and hung up Sasruquo's suit of clothes.

Lady Satanaya did not deem it fitting to use for Sasruquo the cradle she had used to rear her other sons. On the evening before Sasruquo's birth, quickly, with her best foot forward, Lady Satanay secretly went to Aynar the smith.

"Smith Aynar, my good man, you know, and no one other than you knows, what I'm like. Give me the help of your strength. If I don't obtain a certain something, I'm lost!"

"What is the matter, my dear lady? How on earth can you speak with a sorrowing heart? Surely you of all the women on the earth have every reason to rejoice. If anything has upset you, the smith Aynar will not spare his arms. He'll not spare his hammer. If it is a question of his anvil, it stands ready. The flame of the hunting god shoots forth from his bellows. What desire have you conceived, my lady? I am asking."

"I want a cradle by tomorrow. But that cradle must not be like any other cradle, just as he who is to lie in it is not like any other man. That cradle must be made of molten iron. It must rock to and fro on its own, but he who is lying in it must not hear its sound."

"Fine, I shall then try to make a cradle that is like that," said Aynar the smith. "But what can I do? You have set the finishing date too utterly close. The making of such a cradle is not easy. That which is hardest is the melting of the iron. You cannot melt that iron with bellows and fire."

"Begin then! I'll see what you are able to do," said Lady Satanay, turning away, but before she could take a step, she spun around and said, "Smith Aynar, what you just said to me pleased me, but I fear that you have forgotten something."

"No, your lady, Aynar the smith does not so easily forget anything as a rule," he replied.

"So it may be, but why did you not ask about the length, width, and height of the cradle that you are to make?" said Lady Satanay.

"Ah, my lady Satanay," cried the smith, "the Narts' brother who is about to be born will not be like any other Nart. The manner of his birth will not be like anyone else's. His manliness will not be like that of any other Nart. For those reasons the cradle must not be made like any other. Its length, width, and height must also not be like those of any other cradle that man has yet seen. Since this is so, before he, the baby, is born, why should we talk about what size his cradle will be? If anyone hears that we are talking about it, it will certainly make the people laugh at us, saying, 'What's all this? Some people, before their brother has been born, are breaking in a foal for him, which itself has not yet been born.' If you wish to place this matter in my hands, then leave it to me. You will then see what I am capable of," said Aynar the smith.

"Fine," replied Lady Satanay. "It is not that I have no faith in your golden hand. Not only I but also the enemies of the Narts have already looked upon it with amazement. But, Smith Aynar, I wanted to say to you one other thing."

"Whenever has it happened, Lady Satanay, that I do not listen to what you say?"

"You are now setting to work with your smith craft to make my cradle. Night and day your forge will be aglow. The air issuing from your bellows will again and again wash over this meadow like a dry wind. The people will again and again hear the blows of your hammer like claps of thunder. 'What is it? Are we suffering a drought?' the people will ask one another. Under these circumstances, when my sons, the Narts, come, having returned from their exploits, they will repeatedly ply you with questions, perhaps seizing you and even striking you, saying, 'What is this, Aynar the smith, in which you are engaged?' Then what will you say to them? 'Your little brother, the one hundredth, is about to be born. I am making a cradle for him.' Will you say this? In that case, if they say to me, 'Mother of ours, where did you bring the child from?' how shall I tell them? Let the child be born. Let them see the child. Until that time, I do not want to reveal one word about it."

"Ah, don't be afraid of anything, Lady Satanay. Aynar the smith, just as he knows the art of the smithy, knows also the way to keep a secret. I shall begin my smith's work, but there is not a man who will hear any noise from me. No dry wind will issue from my bellows. The sound of my hammer will not escape from the smithy. The steel will be as malleable as wax in my hand," said Aynar the smith.

Lady Satanay, having calmed her heart, set off for home.

Throughout that night, until the coming of dawn, there was a great snowstorm. Hail fell on the roofs with a constant drumming. Thunder and lightning had no respite. Yet all the people who lived in that Nart village were sleeping that night with tranquil hearts. But two people did not allow their eyes to close. They were Lady Satanay and Smith Aynar. Lady Satanay was unable to sleep. Many were her thoughts. She was waiting and saying over and over to herself, "When will the baby's soul enter him?"

That woman had borne ninety-nine sons, but she had not known so much worry and anxiety. When they were born, she had not worried so much about them, trembled so much for them. Had she been as she was now, she would never have sent them away to trusted friends for their up-bringing either.[1] She bore her ninety-nine sons at home, but she took them all to different places to be reared. Lady Satanay looked on the baby who was to be born that night completely differently from the way she looked on the others. Even though he was not yet born, she loved him so much that far from sending him away anywhere, she could not bear the thought that someone might stretch out his hand and touch him. As she lay at home that night, tormented and restless, Lady Satanay pondered what name she should give her little son. Who on earth knows how many names she mulled over, but at last she settled on one. It was Sasruquo.

As for Aynar the smith, throughout the night he was engaged in the art of being a smith, moving around his bellows and his blazing forge, drawing out the hot iron on his anvil, making flames shoot forth from his hammer. He was fashioning the cradle for the babe who was about to be born.

When day began to dawn, the storm abated. Before the sun cast its first ray of light across the range of mountains, the women in Lady Satanay's bedroom began to rush about, saying, "The child has been born! The child has been born!" The women neighbors who had been outside rushed in. Lo, there was the child! But what good could they be to him when no hand could be stretched out to hold him? His body was red like a firebrand. His skin and flesh were hotter than fire. The women tried this and that but could not manage to pick him up. The women spoke among themselves and hit on the idea of wetting the baby's throat. Quickly one woman offered the babe her breast, but she could not bear his heat, and shrieking "I'm burned! I'm burned!" she rushed out the door. They fetched another nurse, but the same thing happened to her, So it went with a third one and a fourth. This was a miracle. The women, not understanding what they were doing, gathered around the baby in a circle and regarded the wonder of what they saw. He had to be left lying where he was, but he did not cry. He lay silently, as though waiting for something.

When the babe was born that night, as the neighboring women stood about the room fussing, some people came and brought news to Lady Satanay. "Nearby a mare has given birth to a foal, but it is unlike other foals. It neighs and paws the earth wonderfully. It lets no one approach it but has killed a few who have drawn near. We are frightened lest it inflict on us a great defeat some day. Alas, what should we do, our lady?"

"It is to be guarded. It is to be raised. It was born together with my son, who is like no other son. No other foal like that one will ever be born! Know that apart from that foal, no other is worthy of my new son! Do not kill it, but keep guard over it instead!" So saying, she sent them away.

Then Lady Satanay turned around, stood among the gathered women, and addressed them thus, "Let this child whose birth came about unlike that of any other have the name Sasruquo! Why are you all standing around? Call the smith Aynar! Aynar the smith knows what he must do."

At once they sent someone to Smith Aynar. Smith Aynar, as though he had been sitting at the ready, in a flash appeared standing at the door of the room where the baby had been born. Then he entered and peered at the baby.

"Narts! May God multiply your name!" So saying, he took out his tongs, opened them, gripped the babe between them, and lifted him. Then he rushed outside with the child and thus carried him back to his smithy. There, the molten steel was glowing in its cauldron, seething. There Smith Aynar held out his tongs with the child in them and plunged the babe into the seething mass of steel. He plunged the child into the cauldron in the morning and, lo, it was midday and the child was splashing about and frolicking in the glowing metal, as though swimming in warm water. Then Aynar the smith concluded, "He's already had enough if he's ever going to have enough," and withdrew the child with his tongs. On both sides, at the tips of his shoulder blades where the child had been held between the tongs, the skin remained untempered. Just as Aynar the smith was lifting the babe out of the molten steel with his tongs, Baby Sasruquo suddenly called out, "Mother! I'm hungry! Hungry!"

Smith Aynar quickly snatched an iron bowl, dipped it into the molten steel, causing the surface to ripple, and brought it up to the baby's lips. The baby, as though he were ravenously hungry, began to swallow the molten steel, gulp after gulp. Smith Aynar drew up three bowls. Three bowls the baby drank. Then Smith Aynar stooped to the fire and scooped up a shovelful of burning embers. These he poured down the baby's throat. The baby ate them with a crunching and clunking noise. When he had thus finished drinking and eating, the baby called out from within the smithy, "Mother! I'm tired! Tired!"

Lady Satanay, who up to that point had busied herself around the forge, clutched the child to her bosom and returned to her home. When she picked him up, she was astonished, for until that time he had been as red as fire, hotter than fire, but now he was neither cold nor hot. He had the temperature of an ordinary person.

When she entered the bedroom with him, he said, "Mother, where are you going to lay me down? I don't see my cradle."

"Even before you were born we made your cradle. They will bring it this instant," said Lady Satanay. She took him and laid him on her bed. Then she hurriedly sent someone to Aynar the smith's to fetch the cradle.

But the man she had sent quickly returned, almost collapsing and with sweat pouring off him. "My lady, Satanay, I pulled and pulled on the cradle, but I could not move it from the spot where it stood."

"Alas, you rotten soul! How could this happen to you thus?" So saying, she sent someone else and called after him, "In the twinkling of an eye the cradle must be here!" But he too returned, having been unable to budge the cradle.

"Alas, you stinking soul, is there no more bone in you than in a snail that you can't lift the child's cradle?" said Lady Satanay, and with her heart nearly bursting, she summoned another.

But at that instant the child's voice was heard behind her, saying, "Mother, leave them alone! Leave them alone! They cannot do it. What are you arguing with them about? I shall go. I shall bring the cradle. If I go out, I will stretch my legs a bit."

Then Lady Satanay looked, and the child, Sasruquo, had opened the door wide and was standing on the threshold, elegantly dressed in his cherkesska and shirt. He had on his tight, light boots, and his silken hat hung from his shoulder.

"Oh, my dear, my dear! Don't even think of such a thing! Don't give any one the excuse to say to us, 'When the Narts gained a brother, they didn't gain a cradle.' The one who will fetch the cradle is sure to come soon." But before she had finished saying this, Sasruquo had already split the yard in two. He was making his way across with a baby's uncertain gait, not visible in the mass of green grass. Lady Satanay set off after him, thinking to herself, "Now I'll grab him by the arm and stop him." But do what she might, she couldn't catch up with him. As she was about to come up to him and overtake him, Sasruquo drew up to his cradle and stopped, suddenly and unexpectedly. Then in a flash he lunged at his cradle, climbed into it, and lay down quietly. As soon as he lay down in it, the cradle began to rock to and fro all on its own.

From Inal-Ipa et al. 1962, saga 4, pp. 34–43.

✑ The close and formative bond between Sasruquo and the smith is reminiscent of the one between the Celtic hero Setanta, known as Cúchulainn, and the smith Culann (Delaney 1994, 99ff.). For the Abkhazian cult of iron and the smith, see Ardzinba (1988).

[1] Because the verb / a-təy-rá / 'to sell' is used for fosterage, many of the neighbors of the Abkhaz slandered them by characterizing the custom of fosterage as the selling of children into slavery.

SAGA 77 ✑ *How Sasruquo Plucked Down a Star*

Standing still was not for the Narts. They used to journey about, roaming the seas and mountains, hunting, always in search of fame.

Very early one day, the ninety-nine Narts arose all together. They had prepared their armor, clothing, and food for the journey earlier. Their horses were in the yard, which was enclosed by a drystone wall. The Narts bustled around among them and fitted on them their bridles and reins. They groomed them and led them down to Kuban's standing water, washed them, rubbed them down, and cooled them with cold water. Then the Narts brought them back, fitted out and saddled, and tied them to the tethering pole.

The brothers ate and drank. Their mother, Lady Satanay, came and stood among them. She gave a blessing and a benediction to her sons. "May you set out on a happy road, my dear ones!" The ninety-nine sons stood up together and seized their whips. Nart Siyt[1] mounted first. Following him, all the others mounted by rank. When Nart Siyt brandished his whip with a crack, all around heard it as if it were the sound of thunder. He shot out of the yard like a bullet. As one, all the others followed him. You could hear the sound of their horses, as though the sky were grinding corn, until they were far away in the distance.

The great yard of the Narts, which until then had been merrily full of people, was empty and deserted. Only the solitary figure of Sasruquo was seen standing in the middle of the field. He was standing holding his horse, Bzow, by the bridle. His brow was wrinkled with sadness, and he gazed after his brothers as they rode off side by side into the distance. His brothers had not told him on which day they were going. They had not told him where they were going. When they arose, he too arose, poor thing, groomed his horse, bathed it, and saddled it. But no one had said to him, "Let's eat!" When they took up their whips, he too took up his, but no one said to him, "Go and mount up!" They had set off all together, having struck up the Narts' song, but they had not had a thought for Sasruquo. Off they rode like the wind. Off they went to perform heroic deeds and gain fame. Sasruquo remained alone, with his arms folded. He stood in the yard, unmoving, as though he had been transfixed like a target. Had they left him to take the calves to pasture? Had they left him to frighten off the jays? While his brothers were still in view he did not move, but when they disappeared he spun about and shouted "Mother!" so loudly that his voice reached Lady Satanay.

"I am here, am I not, darling? What do you want?"

"Mother, all my brothers have left. They have set out to gain fame. They neither left me to tend the house nor invited me along, saying, 'Come along with us!' Why? What has happened? What's the matter with me?"

"Nothing at all is wrong with you, my pet, my darling Sasruquo. They are your elders. How could they have said to you 'Come along with us'? You must go on your own to the place where your brothers have gone," she said to him.

Without asking for his mother to repeat her words, Sasruquo quickly mounted Bzow and struck him a cracking blow with the whip. Without your being able to tell whither he was going or from whence he came, he shot out of the yard.

As the sun was just reaching its highest and hottest point, Sasruquo caught up with his brothers.

"Hey, may game await you!" he called to them.

But not a single one looked over his shoulder at him. They continued on their way just as before. Sasruquo followed along in the rear as they rode forward a while. Then Siyt suddenly turned about and said, "Where are you from? Who are you, you who trail after us like this?"

"*Uuuhh,* what's all this 'Who am I?' Am I not your brother?" answered Sasruquo.

"We brothers are all here. Apart from those who are here, we recognize no others," said Khmish.

"Get away from us, you bastard!" they said in unison. "Is it fit for the great Narts to go in search of fame accompanied by a bastard? Be gone from us, bastard! Be gone!"

What was Sasruquo to do? He turned back with his head bent low to his chest. He returned home, in gloomy thought the whole way. Calmly he rode into the yard, dismounted, and sat down.

"There, there, my son! Why have you returned? What happened to you?" Lady Satanay asked him.

"Nothing at all has happened to me, Mother. When I was setting off I forgot that I was supposed to take food for the journey. I haven't had any breakfast yet. I'm hungry. You must prepare something to eat for me," said Sasruquo.

"This instant, my darling, this instant, only what would you like to eat?" replied Lady Satanay.

"Make me maize porridge with cheese, Mother, maize porridge with cheese!"

Lady Satanay quickly set to and made him thick maize porridge with cheese. She placed it on the serving table with steam rising from it and then set the table before him.

"Mother, come here! Sit down beside me and let us eat together!" said Sasruquo. Lady Satanay took a portion and sat down beside her son.

Just as she was about to take hold of a spoon to eat the porridge, Sasruquo seized her hand and plunged it into the scalding mass and held it there.

"Right now you must tell me just whose son I really am!" he cried.

"What are you saying, my dearest? Are you not brother to the Narts?" cried Lady Satanay.

"'You're a bastard,' the Narts said to me. 'We would be shamed at having you in our company. We'll be disgraced, won't we?' they said to me and sent me away. I'll not release your hand until you tell me who my real father is," said Sasruquo as he held fast to his mother's hand.

"What can you mean, my dearest? You are brother to the Narts and better than they," she cried.

"It doesn't matter if I am better or worse. The question is, who is my real father?" said Sasruquo growing even angrier. "I must learn who my real father is, from whence I have come."

"Oh, may you witness these Narts, who have angered you and who have deemed you unworthy, helpless and lost without your aid!" was her curse on her other sons. "You, my dearest, were not born from my stomach. You sprang from a rock. You came into being through divine will. If you ask Aynar the smith, he will tell you that I speak the truth."

Before she could finish her word, he released her hand. He mounted his horse with more speed and spirit than he had ever shown before, and with a thunderous shout to Bzow, he shot out of the gate.

Lady Satanay, from where she stood in the yard peering after her son, looked up at the sky and uttered these magical words, words that would be fulfilled: "You sons who have torn the heart of my darling little son, before you reach your destination, let foul weather befall you so that it rains worse than any rain before, so that the wind blows worse than it has ever blown before, with hail falling harder than hail has ever fallen before, with snow falling deeper than any snow has fallen before! Let you find yourselves with no one to save your souls but Sasruquo!"

Bzow, never faltering, moved onward, without a drink of water, with no wind holding him back. As he crossed fields and plains, he moved alone and dark like a raven. As he crossed the face of a mountain or the rocks of a ravine, he sprang nimbly like a mountain goat. The track of the ninety-nine ran clearly along. There was no fear of losing their trail.

Sasruquo rode on for two days and two nights. Just as he was saying to himself "I'm about to overtake them," lo, he began to lose their trail, for he had come to a horrible barren mountain. The weather was horrible. A terrible wind shattered boulders and hurled them down. A great mass of snow was blowing on the mountain face, and in its foothills lay black fog in a thick blanket. Sasruquo looked about and then rode on into the barren region, saying to himself, "How will I find my brothers?" The snow howled and then suddenly ceased. Suddenly the sky brightened. Soon it was as bright and clear as glass. It began to freeze. It froze so hard that you would ask, "Will it split the earth itself?"

Sasruquo rode onward. Nothing held him back. He peered ahead and there he saw his brothers in the midst of the barrenness.

In what a state they were! The intense cold had made them huddle together so closely that one hat would have covered all! They were starting to perish; their teeth were chattering. The icicles that hung from their beards reached to the ground, so that they could not move and help themselves. They were perishing.

Sasruquo rode up to them and said, "Hey, wretches! What's happened to you?"

"Sasruquo, Sasruquo! You are both our brother and our better. We are dying, wretches that we are! Help us!" they begged him.

"I am here. Fear not!" Sasruquo replied, and hope came back into their hearts. Sasruquo then turned and peered into the sky. The sky was glowing and clear with the light of evening and the stars had begun to appear, filling the sky with their sparkling. Sasruquo shot his lead-weighted arrow at the brightest star. It began to fall from the sky, still glowing, and landed in the midst of his brothers. The Narts, whose teeth had frozen together, gathered around the star.

"This will keep you warm until I return," said Sasruquo and rode off. He rode to the peak of a mountain and looked about. Far below in a distant valley he saw that a long, black plume of smoke was rising. He smote his horse a cracking blow and set off for the spot where he had seen the smoke. As soon as he reached the spot, what a sight he beheld! A monstrous giant was sprawled there, with his head and feet intertwined. He had a roaring fire going, big enough to warm an army, and a great pile of firewood lay nearby. He lay there, curled up around the fire.

Sasruquo urged his frightened horse closer, using his whip as a prod. He drew near the giant's side but could not jump over his bulk to get to the fire itself. Then he said to Bzow, "Put down your hoof as lightly as the paw of a squirrel! May my weight on your back be like that of a feather! He stole forward until he came to one of the giant's ears. He rode into the ear hole and came out the other side and so came to the fire. He seized the biggest brand, turned about, and set off. Just as he was about to ride out of the giant's ear, an ember fell from the brand and landed in the mass of hair growing in the ear. The hair sizzled for an instant and then caught fire.

The giant awoke with a start. "What's going on? Who has burned me?" When he raised his hand to his ear, it touched the tail of Sasruquo's horse, even though Bzow had already begun to run off.

"Alas, you miserable Abkhaz! Where has it all brought you?" he said as he raised Sasruquo and his horse as one and set them on the palm of his hand. "Who are you?"

"I am Sasruquo's footman, if it please you!" replied Sasruquo.

"Aha! Now I've got you in my clutches. Come, tell me, you miserable Abkhaz! What's all this about a certain Sasruquo, who they say has risen

among you? They say that from the day he was born he has been per-
forming heroic deeds the likes of which no man before has ever performed. Is this true? Tell me then of his heroic deeds!"

"Sasruquo's deeds of heroism are many. How should I, poor wretch,
know what they all are?" So spoke Sasruquo. He understood immediately
that this giant was not going to let him go easily. He was greatly distressed
for his brothers as well. If he could not get back to them soon, they would
all die. Somehow he had to kill this giant, but how?

"If that is what you really want, then I shall give you some examples of
his deeds," said Sasruquo, who had fallen into dire straits.

"Very well," replied the giant.

"Sasruquo would climb the great rock called Qaydog[2] with a boulder
the size of a house and set it on the summit. He would balance it so that
it would fall at the slightest touch. Then he would leave me standing beside it. Sasruquo would then descend. When I gave it a push and it plunged
downward, Sasruquo would butt it with his forehead and shatter it. This is
how Sasruquo scratches his head."

"If wretched Sasruquo can do this, then why can't I?" said the giant.
They went to the great rock Qaydog. There the giant balanced a boulder
the size of a house atop the rock and set the wretched Abkhaz next to it.
Then the giant descended and shouted to Sasruquo, "Fine!" Sasruquo gave
the boulder a shove, and it hurtled down toward the giant's head. The giant
butted the rock with his forehead and shattered it into myriad pieces.

"Ah, that is an excellent head scratcher!" said the giant.

When Sasruquo saw that the cursed giant was unscathed, he grew frus-
trated, but what could he do?

"What else does Sasruquo do by way of heroic deeds?" asked the giant.

"Well, Sasruquo also does as follows. He goes about and gathers enough
scraps of iron to fill a cauldron. Then he sets the cauldron over a fire big
enough to melt the iron by noon of the same day. Then after it has all
melted and grown hot enough to begin to boil, he pours the whole con-
tents of the cauldron into his mouth and swallows it. This was how Sasruquo warms his heart."

"If wretched Sasruquo can do this, then why can't I?" said the giant. So
he went about gathering scraps of iron. He then set them in a cauldron
and placed it over his fire, the one big enough to warm an army. The pieces
of iron grew red hot and began to melt. Then before long they began to
seethe and boil. At this point the giant seized the cauldron in his hands and
placed it to his lips. Then gulp after gulp, he swallowed the whole mass!

"Hey, that valiant Sasruquo knows a good way to warm the heart, as you can see!" yelled the giant. "*Wah,* lovely! Lovely!" he said and rubbed his chest. Sasruquo was amazed to see that even this could not finish off the giant. What was he to do, poor wretch?

"Now, little horseman, tell me what else your prince does by way of an act of prowess!" commanded the giant.

"He has even further acts of prowess. One of these takes place in winter, at its depth, when the frost is coldest. Sasruquo goes and stands in still water up to his neck for seven days and seven nights. The water begins to freeze. He does not stir until he is frozen from neck to toe. When all the water is frozen, Sasruquo gives a mighty heave, shatters the ice, and comes out. This is his way of cooling off."

"If wretched Sasruquo can do this, then why can't I?" said the giant. So they went toward the mountain where the great cold had trapped his brothers. The giant found a lake and stood in it up to his neck.

At that moment, from where she was standing, Lady Satanay knew that Sasruquo was in dire straits. Did she not, after all, have the power to see all things? She rose from her chair and cast a spell, "With frost worse than frost may the giant freeze, in still water from neck to toe, and let my son achieve his goal!" As she said this, the ice began to crystallize until the giant was frozen fast. For seven days and seven nights the giant and Sasruquo waited. Then Sasruquo said, "Now move!"

The giant put all his might into his effort. The ice crackled and began to shatter as the giant began to pull himself free.

"Ah, wait! Wait! Sasruquo used to wait eight days, if I remember correctly. That is how he does it. Wait one more day!" said Sasruquo, hiding his desperation as best he could.

The giant agreed.

Valiant Sasruquo speedily set off and found some haystacks. He gathered them up and took them back to where the giant stood in the ice. Then he spread the hay over the water that still lay thinly on the surface. The ice grew harder and harder. After the eighth day and night had passed, Sasruquo said, "Now move!"

The giant heaved mightily, but the ice and hay had frozen together, and try as he might, the giant could not budge.

"Woe is me! You have beaten me with a foul and clever trick. If only I weren't stuck so!" moaned the giant. "You have tricked me. You are Sasruquo!"

"It is true. You are not wrong. It is Sasruquo himself who stands before you, you evil giant!" Having said this, Sasruquo drew his sword and stepped up to the giant to cut off his head.

"Hey, Sasruquo! Don't set your mind to beheading me with that puny little knife of yours. You won't be able so much as to nick a vein, you wretched Abkhaz. Go over there! Do you see where my sword is lying? Of course you won't be able to lift it. Content yourself with merely drawing it from its scabbard. Then drag it onto the ice and point it toward me. It will behead me on its own. I will tell you one more thing. Listen to me, Sasruquo! You are still young and a strapping fellow. But many trials and hardships lie before you. If you use your own guile and my strength, then together there will be no man who can defeat you. So, after you behead me, a thick vein will protrude. Take half of it for a belt for Lady Satanay, the most beautiful and intelligent woman on earth. Tie what is left around your own waist as a belt. Then see what sort of man you become!"

Without waiting to hear another word, Sasruquo went to where the giant's sword lay. With all his strength he managed to unsheathe it. He dragged it to the ice and pointed it at the giant. The sword flew across the ice and sundered the giant's head from its neck, as though the two had never been joined. Black blood welled up from the stump, and in its midst wiggled a large vein.

"Wait a moment," thought Sasruquo. "When was it that this evil giant ever did anyone a favor? Something evil must lurk here still." He carefully drew the vein out using the tip of his sword and carried it to a large beech tree that stood nearby. He carefully took the vein in his hands and tied it around the trunk. Instantly the trunk was sliced in two as though riven by a great sword!

"Ha! May the gods of the smithy roast you in their fires!" said Sasruquo. Then he again took the vein with his sword, hurled it to the ground, and this time cut it into tiny pieces. In this way he was done with the giant.

He went back to the fire and drew forth the largest brand. With ease, he mounted his horse. Poor Bzow was afraid of the brand and sped along like a falcon level with the ground. Gripping the brand, Sasruquo hurtled onward, glowing like a falling star. For him the rugged mountains were like smooth plains. For him the great rivers were like mere streams.

When he reached the spot where he had left his brothers, he found them still huddled around the star. The star itself was growing cold, and darkness was beginning to appear on its surface. What little life had returned to the poor wretches with its warmth was beginning to fade again, and they began to shudder with cold.

"Hey, poor souls! Have no fear! Fearless brothers of mine, I have brought you a real fire," said Sasruquo as he leaped down from his horse.

He stood beside them holding the firebrand, but, alas, to what end? There was not a log or twig with which to build a fire. All about him was barren mountain covered in snow. There was not even a single stunted tree!

"Take out your cartridges, each one of you, and chop them into small pieces, poor souls!" Sasruquo cried out.

They blew on their hands and took out their cartridges as they had been told. Then they drew their sharp swords and chopped them up like pine needles. With these, Sasruquo lit a huge fire, big enough for an army. Then he turned about, crossed over to the far side of a nearby river, and there slew a buck. Then he crossed back to the near side and slew a wild goat. Then he descended the mountainside and slew a roe deer. Then he ascended the mountainside and slew a mountain goat. On every path stood a pole from which his kills were hung. Over every rock his arrows whistled. He cooked the flesh of the game until it was tender. He made his brothers sit huddled together and slurp up the juice of the cooking meat. Then he fed them. He joked with them. When the life had flowed back into all of his brothers, they mounted their horses as one. They rode home singing with joy in their hearts, not at all like men who had met with failure.

From that day onward, the Narts, both young and old, began to set Sasruquo at their head. But what did it avail him? Because they feared him, they still spoke of him as unworthy. Behind his back they still called him bastard. They envied him and hated him because he was their better.

From Inal-Ipa et al. 1962, saga 21, pp. 173–85.

✍ This saga, a variant of saga 57, is one of the Prometheus myths of the Caucasus (see also sagas 34, 35, and 36).

---

[1] *Siyt* / səyt / is pronounced like *seat* and perhaps, if it is a borrowing from Circassian, means "(one who) gives knives," / sa-əy-t / 'knife-dir-give'.

[2] The name Qaydog is obviously related to "Qaydukh" (saga 50 n. 2; saga 62 n. 1), where / -əx° / means "woman," whereas here / -ag° / is a suffix for "place," thus: / q'ay-d-ag° / 'sorcerer-great-place'.

Far away, on a mountain's summit, stood the Ayirgs' palace.[1] That palace was made from the bones of birds. The mountain atop which it sat soared high above all others, and the palace, embedded in its summit, rose higher still. The winds, the rays of the sun, and the clouds were all that could reach that palace. No living thing had the power to reach it. This was because the palace looked out on and was surrounded by nothing but rocks and sheer cliffs. It was hard to see because it was always changing color. In bad weather, when clouds settled about, it took on the form of a cloud. When the sky was bright, it would look like the bright sky. That was the palace of the Ayirgs' only daughter. Here she lived; her beauty and her fine shape were impossible to describe. She did not grow old. She always looked as fresh as the day she was born, and her beauty in no way faded with the years. Like the spring, she always bloomed and blossomed.

Two men without peer, each of whom knew nothing of the other, heard about this maiden at the same time. One was Sasruquo, the other Narjkhyaw.[2] And one day both of them set out at the same time to win the hand of this maiden. Sasruquo rode along on his own, as did Narjkhyaw. Both of them knew that there was no way to win such a maiden other than to perform a deed of heroism the likes of which had never been seen before. Neither knew what might lie before him, but both were determined to stop at nothing, whatever they might meet.

No one knows how far they traveled, but the two of them came upon one another in a barren place. At first they rushed at each other and jousted, and then they drew their swords to duel, but before long each recognized the heroic valor of the other and ceased to do battle. Then they set off together and traveled along, getting to know one another and exploring the countryside. Soon they drew near the maiden's palace.

They reached the foot of a great rock face and drew up beside it. On the summit above them something shone forth like the morning star. Suddenly the clouds at the summit scattered and the palace shone forth in all its glory. Then they knew that they had reached the place that they had been seeking with their hearts' courage. They knew that whenever the maiden's brothers returned from a quest, she would light their way by sticking her little finger out a window of the palace. The light given off was like that of the sun. When her brothers saw that, they would be over-joyed and ride home into their yard singing a song. And as fate would have it, just as these two had drawn up by the rock, the maiden's brothers were returning from a quest and were singing a song as they entered their yard.

Sasruquo said, "Her brothers have gone in. We won't get a better chance than now."

"That is so," replied Narjkhyaw, "but how can we reach the summit?"

They looked about and realized that they would have to climb the rock. They saw the prints of horses' hooves ascending the rock face but none at all coming down. They understood that others before them had gone up, but that none had returned.

"Narjkhyaw!" said Sasruquo. "It is your privilege to ascend first."

"No, you go up!" replied Narjkhyaw.

"First," countered Sasruquo, "you are older. Second, you have already performed more heroic deeds than I, so you should be first to go up." He stood firm.

Narjkhyaw, without saying another word, gave a lash to his horse and galloped up the rock. The stones hurled off by his horse's hooves were like hail raining down from the sky. He managed to ascend halfway up but then fell and hurtled downward headfirst.

"Ah, poor soul!" thought Sasruquo. "He'll be smashed to pieces."

Narjkhyaw landed, however, without a scratch, cracked his whip once more, and begin to gallop up the rock. His poor horse made its hooves dig into the rock. It forced its teeth to bite into the rock. But it could not climb higher than halfway, and again horse and rider fell. Yet a third time Narj-khyaw tried to ascend, and a third time he and his horse fell. Poor Narj-khyaw. The rock was too much for him.

"No good! You see that I could not reach the top, Sasruquo. That maiden is not destined for me. So be it! You and she have become each other's fate. I could achieve nothing at all!" said Narjkhyaw.

Sasruquo folded both flaps of his cherkesska and tucked them between his thighs and his saddle. Then he crossed the ends of his head cloth over one another and wrapped them around his back. With a cry, he spurred his horse, Bzow, up the rock. With sparks shooting from the rock face, poor Bzow scampered up the rock like a squirrel. At some points he dug in his hooves. At others he gripped it with his teeth. No one knows how many times he slipped or fell, but finally Sasruquo managed to reach the summit.

There he found himself in a beautiful meadow, quite flat, adorned with every type of flower that exists on the face of this earth. But there, scattered among the blossoms, were the bones of the dead. Sasruquo was tired. He dismounted, hobbled his horse, and sat down. A cool breeze began to waft over him. As he sat there resting, gazing about him, an old man appeared next to him. Sasruquo had not seen him approach, nor had he seen from whence he had come.

"You, man! Nart Sasruquo!" said the old man. "I know why you have come. Have no fear! You and the sister of the gods of the hunt are destined to become each other's fate. Do you see the bones scattered about? These are the bones of the dead, which we have tossed away. They are the bones of suitors who have sought her but could not win her. If you do as I say, it is impossible for her not to become your destiny."

The old man sat down and began to talk with Sasruquo. "The brothers of the maiden whom you seek are wicked men. Day and night they stand behind her and guard their sister. Several powerful men have already come here, but no one can have her by force. If she has no desire for a man, he can do nothing. If, God willing, she were to desire a man, then his path would be clear.

"Listen to me well, for I too, alas, have known sorrow because of her! In the world above there is the sky. Down below there is the earth. Apart from one son, I have no one. He too came to woo her, and today he sits beside her. He surmounted that rock face, vanquished her brothers, but made no impression on her heart. 'Until I see the man who wins your heart, the one with whom you will depart, I will not leave your side': that was the vow he made to her. Lo, it has been fifteen years since that time and my son still sits beside her.

"Now pay heed to me, and I'll tell you one by one the things you must do. When you leave me, you will not encounter anything difficult. The gates will be open wide, and her brothers will be in their rooms. My son will be the only one sitting on the balcony of the castle. He will be playing a harp and will not speak with you. Whenever he plays the harp, she sleeps sweetly. All the better for you! Go straight to her room. When you open her door and enter, you will notice first how her hair, so long and plaited, lies all about beside her. Say not a word but go forward and touch your little finger to her tresses.

"'Hey, may my sins fall upon your head!' she will say, awaking. 'I saw in a dream the man who will win my heart. How could you awaken me before I had seen my fill of him?' When she says this, then you will know what to say. Remember, she is yours! She will leave with you, as leave you must, and her brothers will follow you at a distance. They are no cause for fear. But my son will be a reason for worry. He rides a horse that is like yours. Once he sets out after you, he will catch up to you. What I ask of you is this: When he catches up to you, please do not shoot him! Shoot his horse instead! Kill it, and then you will have nothing else to fear. Then go home with your wife!"

Sasruquo thanked the old man and quickly mounted. When he reached the gate, he saw that it was indeed open, and he rode quickly inside. There was not a soul in the yard. He dismounted and tethered his horse. He scaled the wall of the castle and climbed onto a balcony. There sat a young man, the son of the old man, playing a harp. He was strumming a pick across its strings and singing a song. The melody would stir anger at one moment and sadness the next.

> She grows not old; she grows not young.
> Ahahayra, misery![3]
> Who is the man come to her in a dream?
> Ahahayra, misery!
> Who has her heart and soul?
> Ahahayra, misery!
> When will that one cross my path?
> Ahahayra, misery!
> When will we fight man to man?
> Ahahayra, misery!
> When will our swords glint and clash?
> Ahahayra, misery!
> She grows not old; she grows not young.
> Ahahayra, misery!
> Another year passes and still I wait.
> Ahahayra, misery!

Sasruquo stood still and listened to this lament. His heart did not like what he heard, but he held his tongue and went to the maiden's room. When he opened her door, the light she gave off shone on him like the sun and the moon. She was deeply asleep. At first Sasruquo was taken aback. Whatever else he might have thought, he did not think that she was quite so beautiful as they had said. With a changed heart he approached her and with his little finger touched the maiden's hair.

"Hey, may the devil take you, son of the old man! I was just now seeing in my dream Nart Sasruquo. How could you awaken me before I had seen my fill of him?" cried the maiden as she sat up with a start.

"If you can recognize in reality what you saw in your dream, well here I stand. I, Nart Sasruquo! I stand before you," said her suitor.

"I am yours if you can take me away. But, alas, the old man's son is not likely to let me go with you," said the sister of the Ayirgs.

"Don't you worry about that!"

"Even if we get past him, my brothers will not let us go a single step."

"Well, this would befit them."

"Then go below and mount your horse. Take up position at the bottom of the palace, and you will see what I shall do!" she said.

Sasruquo went forth and took his horse. As he passed, the old man's son sat and sang on his harp as he had before. This is what he sang.

> Who climbed the rock on a horse's legs?
> Ahahayra, misery!
> Who could not wake her from her sleep?
> Ahahayra, misery!
> Who did not think to say "Good day"?
> Ahahayra, misery!
> Who came and went all in vain?
> Ahahayra, misery!
> Who gave one more to the skulls piled here?
> Ahahayra, misery!

These words struck Sasruquo's heart like an arrow, but he passed by and said not a word to the harp player and climbed down the castle wall. There he mounted Bzow and rode to the far side of the yard. He gave a mighty cry that shot over the castle like a bullet and set everything ringing. Then the maiden flung open her window and jumped out, falling down from the castle's seven floors. Sasruquo sped toward her and grabbed her just before she was to hit the ground. Holding her across his horse's neck, he sped out of the yard with her.

At that moment the old man's son let out a piercing cry. "He has taken her, the dog! He has taken her! Where are you?"[4]

Immediately two youths appeared, one mounted on a golden horse, the other on a black one. Both set off after Sasruquo as fast as they could ride.

As Sasruquo and his bride rode out of the yard, she said to him, "Don't go back the way you came!"

"Why? Am I a thief? I came openly, I shall leave openly. If I don't follow my old track, can it be that there is only one other that I must take in this world?" asked Sasruquo.

Bzow galloped over the ground like the wind, crossing the wide meadow that lay before the castle. The two youths were hot on Sasruquo's track, with first one then the other in the lead. Yet, however fast Bzow galloped, Sasruquo could not reach the edge of the meadow. He would peer ahead, and to him it would appear that the meadow was not wide, that the edge was near, and yet it would not draw nearer. Instead it seemed that he crossed over the same spot again and again. He was amazed and knew not what to do. Should he stop and take his bearings? But who would give him a chance? The two youths were drawing nearer, their swords unsheathed. There was no place to halt. He goaded his horse onward and continued as fast as he could go.

Then, lo, the horses that were on his track began to tire and falter. Then in another moment one dropped down in a heap and the other fell on top of him! The son of the old man saw all this from his seat on the balcony. When he saw that the two youths could not catch Sasruquo, he jumped down to the courtyard, mounted his own horse, and rode out of the gates in a blur.

Sasruquo looked back and saw that the son of the old man was in pursuit. He saw too, without a doubt, that the horse on which the youth rode was one of the Nart breeds, much like his own. Sasruquo did not like this at all.

"Bzow! Keep it up!" he said with such a voice that it rolled across the meadow and thundered back. At that, when he heard the echo, Sasruquo realized that he had been riding in circles around the meadow.

"This isn't simple. It is not what it seems. It must mean something," thought Sasruquo. But he rode on as before because he had no place to halt and reconnoiter. The youth was in hot pursuit.

Bzow, who had traversed so much ground, who had raced so long, began to grow weary. The horse on which the son of the old man was seated was fresh. It began to close the gap between them. It was then that Sasruquo recalled the old man's words. He turned about and shot at his enemy's horse. The arrow sailed through the air and hit the other horse in a mortal spot. The horse reared up, turned about twice, and fell down, dead.

"Now, if you set off on your return route, you will have no shame. If you do not, then you will go no farther here," said the maiden draped across his horse. When she saw that the old man's son could do no more and that Sasruquo had spared him, her heart grew tender toward Sasruquo. "My dream was no ordinary one," thought the sister of the hunting gods.

Sasruquo found his old track and set off on it. Soon he came to the rock he had ascended. With the maiden held tightly across the horse's neck, he descended without mishap.

At the bottom stood Sasruquo's friend, Narjkhyaw. He rejoiced when he saw Sasruquo returning gloriously, safe and with a wife. Narjkhyaw spun around on the spot, and when they reached him, he helped them dismount and rest. Then they all set off together along the road by which the two men had come.

When they reached the spot where the two men had first met, Sasruquo began to speak and said, "Narjkhyaw, I am the one, it is true, who in your stead fetched the maiden, but you are the elder. You are the one who first scaled the rock. You see what she is like. In my opinion, I think she is fitting for you. Take her as your wife!"

But was this the sort of maiden that could be gotten rid of in such a fashion? One look at her was worth a life. What other balm was there for the fevered mind?

"No! Would that she had been my destiny!" said Narjkhyaw. "Then I would have won her just as you did. There are many rocks far worse than the one I have scaled on my horse, but I could not scale that one. She and you were destined for each other. You are suited to each other. You won her. How could I take from you the woman who is part of your destiny? And in any case, this is not something for any man to do."

Only his conscience and a sense of shame made him speak so. Otherwise, was she really the sort of woman one could turn away?

"If that is how you feel, then fine! Come home with us, then!" said Sasruquo. With his wife held across the horse's neck and his friend by his side, Sasruquo set off for home.

Soon word spread among the folk that Sasruquo was returning home with a bride. All who knew him, all for whom he had done a kind deed, came forward to meet him with joy. With all their hearts and souls they congratulated him and his new bride. All about, the Nart horsemen heard word of this and mounted their horses. They rode out to greet them, and, bustling about, they surrounded the pair and entered the village of the Narts with the two at their center.

When a man had first come to them bringing word of Sasruquo and his bride, his brothers had gathered together and discussed what they should do.

Some said, "What? Are we to give that bastard a wedding feast?" and determined not to organize one, but others were of kinder heart, and in the end all agreed to hold a feast. No one doubted that they had at hand what they needed for a great feast. At once they set themselves to it and readied a great feast. Their kin and friends were all invited. They joyfully prepared all for their youngest brother and his wife.

For seven days and seven nights there were feasting and drinking, singing and dancing. As for Narjkhyaw, he sat at the middle of the table, and all showed him respect.

During the feast the beautiful Gunda caught his eye as she was serving his table. Narjkhyaw remained seated. He did not know what to do. Words failed him, because suddenly he had fallen in love. Later the daughter of the Ayirgs bore Sasruquo a fine son.[5]

From Inal-Ipa et al. 1962, saga 31, pp. 267–77. For a translation and discussion of this and a similar saga, see Dumézil 1978, 147–58.

⊙ This tale is reminiscent of saga 2. This tale also seems to have descended from the account of the Indo-European Divine Twins who rescue the shining Dawn (Ward 1970; Puhvel 1987, 228–29). Her mountain palace, however, is purely Caucasian.

The heroine in this saga parallels Adif (saga 27) and Qaydukh (saga 62) in her luminous assistance to the returning hunters (see also sagas 79 and 80). Note too the radiance of the heroine Gunda in saga 84. Kevin Tuite (personal communication) suggests that the name Ayirg is derived from **(a-)giorgi'*, "Saint George," with "the [South] Caucasian sense of the divine patron of men [who] exploit outside spaces for the benefit of the community." In Abkhaz this figure has become pluralized. Their daughter would thus fit into a broad Caucasian tradition of a radiant female deity (perhaps named Dali) who guards the wild beasts, who is sometimes theriomorphic (often appearing as a deer), and who usually has an uneasy, sometimes hostile, relationship with hunters.

[1] The title of this saga has the Abkhaz / r-tə-pḥá / 'their-dear(?)+daughter', whereas in the body of the saga she is clearly the sister of the Ayirgs, / ayrgʸ-(r)ʕa /, the gods of the hunt.

[2] See sagas 83 and 84 for variants of the tale of the beautiful Gunda, here replaced with the otherwise nameless daughter of the Ayirgs.

[3] The Abkhaz for *misery* is / gʷə- šʸa+ӡa / 'heart-blood+water', literally, "heart's blood."

[4] There is confusion here in the original text. The harpist says that "They have taken her, the dogs!"

[5] The ending is murky. The beautiful Gunda makes an appearance as a maiden waiting on wedding guests. Narjkhyaw is smitten with a love for her that will unfold tragically in saga 84.

While Sasruquo was away engaged in war, his wife did not allow his house to fall into ruin. She carried on and endured.

Her husband was engaged in warfare for sixty years, but she did not lose her love of life. No one ever heard her complain about her toil or loneliness. As for herself, she continued to radiate warmth like the sun and light like the moon. With the passing of time she grew neither older nor younger.

When the war was over, Sasruquo returned home safe and whole. Easy at heart, he returned to living out his days at home. After some time had passed, Sasruquo acquired a son. The babe grew up. Eventually he reached the age when he was quick of foot. If you startled him, you had no chance of catching him. At about that time he went out with his father and accidentally died at his father's hands. Sasruquo remained alone, unable to kill himself. As for the child's mother, she was at the point of following her babe to the grave, but what could she have done? The living cannot kill themselves for the dead. That is the way of the world. She survived too and eventually her spirit returned to her.

Then another fair while went by. Once more Sasruquo acquired a son. "Alas, what has befallen me has happened, but it seems now that my seed will not altogether disappear from the earth," he said, and he rejoiced in the birth of this son as he had never rejoiced before.

The child grew up and reached the age when he could mount and dismount a horse all by himself. One day, as the child was playing quietly outside in the yard, a great white-throated bear suddenly appeared, snatched the child, and took off with him. When his cry was heard, Sasruquo rushed outside and saw what had happened. Right there he dropped on one knee and aimed an arrow at the bear. The arrow flew. The bear dropped the child, who then rolled on the ground.

Sasruquo and his wife rushed to the child, who lay outstretched on the ground. When they reached him, they discovered that the arrow had hit the soft spot of his temple and that their son was already dead.

What were they to do? By heaven, with their own hands they had torn out their own hearts and were left alone in the world! They moaned and they grieved, but they could not bring themselves to commit suicide. Otherwise, their grief knew no bounds. But what is there that time cannot devour? With the passing of time, their sadness waned, and with yet more time they began to forget their grief.

One day, as he was sitting at home, a group of horsemen rode into Sasruquo's courtyard and as a group dismounted before him.

"Welcome!" he said in Abkhaz, greeting his guests, leading them into his house, and offering them seats. "Well then, from where have such well-equipped folk such as yourselves come to visit me?" he asked his guests.

"We are travelers. On our journey we came to your village. We thought, 'Let's go to Sasruquo's. He has performed so many deeds. Perhaps he can tell us a tale or two.' And then too we knew of your having fallen upon evil days, and we thought that we might lighten your heart, cheer you up a bit. So here we are!" they replied.

"If that is how it is, then you have done me a good turn, my guests," said Sasruquo, who then arose and hurried off to set in motion the makings of hospitality. He had some rams slain and set some youths to skinning them and to putting the meat into pots. The pots were then hung over the fire. The meat was hanging and cooking, and Sasruquo had set off for the yard to check the guests' horses. Just then a huge eagle swept down from the sky and seized him. With a great flapping it lifted him up and flew away with him into the sky. No one had seen it come. No one saw it go.

The eagle flew into the remote heavens, bearing Sasruquo in its talons. They passed over dark woods and gleaming expanses of water. Then, in the course of their flight, they came to a vast sea. No one knows how long they flew over it, but finally the eagle set Sasruquo down on the balcony of an Abkhaz-style house, which arose from the sea. The waves broke against the edge of the house. Sasruquo could not see anything on which the house rested.

A woman was sitting on the balcony, sewing, and when she saw that Sasruquo had appeared there, she stood up with a start and came over to greet him. She welcomed him in Abkhaz, embraced him as though he were her brother, and treated him with the utmost hospitality, as though she would have given her life for her guest. Then she led him inside and sat him down. She spun swiftly about and in the flash of an eye had prepared a meal for him.

Sasruquo sat there gazing all around, unable to make a suitable response. From where he sat he could see a child sitting inside, playing. But what a paltry thing is the word *child!* Anyone who saw him would say, "I need not eat or drink. I need only behold him. His eyes sparkle like an eagle's. His skin is as soft and white as milk."

The hostess prepared her guest's meal. She bade him to wash. Then she led him in and sat him down at the head of the table. Sasruquo began to eat. He noticed that as soon as he had entered the child had begun to stare at him, not taking his little eyes off him. He drew near him at one end of the table and continued to stare at him.

"Ye gods, what is it about me that has so caught this child's attention?" Sasruquo wondered. In order to befriend the child, Sasruquo sliced off a piece of the beef on his plate, stuck it on the end of his white-handled sword, and coaxed the child to him, saying, "Come on over here, then, little fellow!"

But as the child came to get the meat, he tripped and fell on the tip of the sword. He died right then and there.

The hostess cried out, "Woe, how could you devour your own flesh yourself?"

"Alas, woe is me! What has happened to me?" said Sasruquo. In despair he went out again on the balcony, not knowing what to do. Before he could take his own life, the huge eagle swept down again, seized him, and flew off with him, climbing high into the heavens.

They traveled thus, with the eagle gleaming in its flight, until it took him back to his yard and set him down precisely where it had snatched him before. He entered the house and saw that his guests were sitting and talking among themselves, seemingly unaware that he had been snatched away and returned. The table had been prepared. The meat was brought out as he watched and they began to eat.

"What is it, my man? What did you stumble on when you went out just now?" his wife asked. "I see that your brows are knitted together in worry."

"What could have happened to me? Nothing!" he replied.

But his wife did not believe him. "You must tell me at once what happened to you!"

Did Sasruquo not know his wife's character? He saw at once that it would be impossible for him to refuse her, and so he replied, "Something did befall me, but give me time, until we finish eating."

He sat down with his guests, ate and drank with them, joked with them, and laughed with them as they wished. Sasruquo sat among them like someone to whom nothing had happened.

When the guests had finished, his wife said to him, "Now you must tell us what befell you."

Sasruquo began to tell them the tale, how the eagle had carried him off from the yard when he had gone out to see the horses, how it flew with him and set him down on the balcony of an Abkhazian house in the midst of the sea, how a woman met him there, how she prepared a meal for him, how he was eating, how, to his dismay, a child fell on his sword and perished, how when this happened he was at a loss as to what to do and went back out on the balcony, how the eagle came again, seized him, and flew back with him.

When Sasruquo had finished his story, his wife let out a shrill scream.

"Calamity! Calamity! How could you bring about the loss of your own seed by your own hands? You have suffered a fate even worse than those that have befallen you before. That was your own son that you killed with your own sword," she wailed, and she decided to kill herself, to blot out her own soul.

The guests were sitting in discomfort, but what could they do? When her spirit revived a bit, they asked her, "How could this be?"

"As you have already heard, whatever offspring I have borne has died at my husband's hands. When this last child was about to be born, I kept this from him. Nor did I tell him where I had taken the babe. When he was born I set off and gave him to the goddess who rules the sea to rear him for me. She reared him and guarded him. Alas, in just one more year I would have brought him back here. The goddess of the sea was my own mother's foster mother. Poor soul! She reared for us the last hope that our lineage would not vanish, and now you see the result!" said the sister of the hunting gods as she rent her cheeks.

The guests thought that what had transpired was a tragic miracle, but they had no power to undo it. What was done was done.

Thus it was. Sasruquo had no one left. While he lived, he lived, poor wretch. And when he exchanged this world for another, no one deemed Sasruquo to be among the dead for the simple reason that

> When a horse dies, its paddock remains.
> When a man dies, his name lives on.

From Inal-Ipa et al. 1962, saga 36, pp. 301–7.

◐ This tale perhaps makes the association between Indo-European Dawn, here in her Caucasian form of a gleaming mountain maiden, and the sea by means of a foster mother, the goddess of the sea.

The slaughter of one's own children parallels that of the Ancient Greek god Cronus, who devoured his offspring as they were born so that they would not overthrow him. This is an echo of an ancient Middle Eastern mythic theme of dynastic struggle among generations of gods (Puhvel 1987, 24–29).

Kevin Tuite has pointed out (personal communication) the themes of a radiant wife in the goddess of wild beasts, perhaps named Dali (see the remarks at the end of the preceding saga), and of a wild animal snatching a child, which occurs among the South Caucasian Svan.

SAGA 80 ‿ *The Light-Giving Little Finger*

Sasruquo was forever wandering.[1] He would travel, circling the world and hunting. He would often set off in search of glory. With drawn swords, with the clash of steel on steel, he and his enemies were always striking at each other's sides. They would always set to with much bloodletting. In this way, when Sasruquo found himself in the midst of trouble, his wife would come to his aid. What she would do is as follows.

When he was tired and exhausted, unable to do any more, Sasruquo would return home. When the night was as dark as pitch and filled with fog, his wife would hold her little finger out the window of her room. The light from her finger would shine out in the gloom of night like a ray from the sun, and it would cast a bright light on Sasruquo. From that point until he entered his yard, his path would be illuminated. When he entered his yard, his wife would quietly withdraw her finger. Then Sasruquo, whole and unharmed, would come into the house and say, "Good evening!" Sasruquo was aware of his wife's help in this way, but he did not deem it worthy of praise.

So one day the Narts held a great gathering. In addition to the Narts, there were representatives from other peoples, and altogether there was a great throng. At this meeting, as they were discussing a matter, Sasruquo and his brothers began to argue over something that had been said.

"What's all this, you! You wouldn't be able to speak to me so haughtily if you recalled all the good deeds I have done for you!" said Sasruquo in anger.

"What's this way of talking you have? Never mind your good deeds to us. Sure, you're a really strong man! Maybe that's because the sister of Ayirg became your wife. Maybe she takes your hand like a child's and leads you up and down so that you can speak insolently to the truly great Narts," said the Narts.

And it was just such a commotion that Nart Gutsayk[2] had been waiting for.

"O you great Narts!" said he, raising his voice so that all the people heard him. "Today is Friday. What I say is true. The horse on which I sit is a charger. A man boasts about his father's hoe. Sasruquo boasts about his wife's little finger. Perhaps, for that reason, you, his brothers, should pity him."

Laughter erupted. They burst themselves laughing. They were so merry that some fell on the floor with laughter while others did cartwheels.

What could he have done, Sasruquo? With his head hung low, he left the Nart gathering and quietly went home. He could still hear their laughter even when he was very far away. When he reached home, his wife immediately saw that he was troubled.

"What is it that you have on your mind?" she said as she embraced her husband.

"My head aches. That's all," and he said nothing more to her.

So, when three months had passed, Sasruquo once again prepared to set off in search of fame. Just as he was about to leave, he said to his wife, "Come here, please!" She went over to him and he sat her down. Then he spoke thus to her. "The light that you cast with your little finger has already aided me many times, but henceforth you must never tell anyone of this help that you give me."

"Ah, you poor fool! Clearly your nasty brothers have been taunting you with having no spirit that is not dependent on your wife," she said and grew very angry.

"One way or another, however it may come to pass, this talk must stop from this day forth," he replied.

"Why do you refuse my slight assistance? From me, who is wholeheartedly for you! Is it simply because they said something to you that you hated? Let it go! Nothing good will come of it. The shining of this little finger of mine is miraculous. If I stop its shining, then in a short while I too will perish," said his wife.

"I'm off now. The giants have scattered my herd of horses and taken them across the Kuban. I must catch up with them and take my herd back home. The giants are not likely to take to this sweetly. There will be battle and much blood. It will be impossible for the giants and me to meet without much gore and blood, as you know. But no matter what trouble I run into, even if right here at the threshold they seize me and tear me limb from limb, don't you interfere with your help. If you do, I'll kill you and then kill myself. Know this!" he said, and then drawing himself up he swore a mighty oath.

What should she have done? The sister of the hunting gods began to cry. She was in pain. To her it was as if her husband were setting off to seek death and oblivion, not fame. But her tears were in vain. Sasruquo had already made up his mind and put an end to the matter. Then Sasruquo set off along his path.

The giants had crossed the Kuban and entered the Abaza Plain, driving the horses before them. When they looked behind them[3], they saw that someone was coming, someone about the size and shape of a raven. Did they really not know that it was Sasruquo? In the twinkling of an eye they readied themselves and set to fighting with Sasruquo.

No one knows how long they fought, but it was not simply a skirmish. The giants fired swarms of arrows at Sasruquo, but he was able to return their fire in kind. In the end Sasruquo defeated all the giants. There was not one left to tell of their deaths. He took charge of his horses again, turned the herd about, and set off for home.

By the time he approached the stone bridge that crossed the Kuban, the heart of night had been split. It was midnight. "Night," you say! What kind of rotten night was this? When this took place it was spring. The rain poured down constantly, and clouds of thick mist had begun to form. If someone had held a branding iron before your eyes, you would not be able to see it.

Meanwhile Sasruquo's wife was at home. Her brows were knitted together in worry as she scanned her husband's route, wondering what news she would hear. Wherever Sasruquo had gone, from wherever he was returning, whenever he reached the stone bridge, she would poke her little finger out her window, and its light would at once shine on her husband and his path. Then joyfully he would cross the bridge and come to her. Now she recalled Sasruquo's oath. But she couldn't find the patience, the strength to subdue her worry. Then she thought, "Perhaps he is already at the bridge, already across," and so she stuck her little finger out the window.

In fact, at that moment Sasruquo was drawing near the bridge, driving his herd before him. As he stopped at the foot of the bridge, his herd took fright in the darkness and began to shy away from the bridge. So he let out a shriek like an Abkhaz stallion and set to running among the horses, but not one would set foot on the bridge, not even by chance. Then when there was nothing else left to do, he set about catching the horses one by one and putting halters on them. Then, after tying them one to another, he set foot on the bridge, leading his horses. As he reached the middle of the span, with his nervous horses prancing behind him, his wife stuck her little finger out. When her bright light shone on the horses, they panicked and bolted over the side into the water, taking Sasruquo, who was tangled up in the halters, with them.

The Kuban was in its spring flood stage and was flowing in torrents. Sasruquo and his horses fell right in the midst of the foaming waters. His wife saw what misfortune had befallen him.

"Woe! Wretched me! How did this lapse befall me?" she said and let out three heartrending screams. Then in a flash she ran out to where the disaster had struck. Soon she was atop a boulder at the foot of the bridge. There she allowed her little finger to protrude from her sleeve and lit up the Kuban. She saw nothing of Sasruquo, only two horses.

"Oh, are you anywhere about?" she called and the echo sounded, "Are you anywhere about?" Her voice resounded through the night, hither and thither, losing itself among the boulders, bouncing off them. She looked but could see no sign of him. He had sunk beneath the deep water.

"How can I see you? Because of me you have perished!" and again she let out three heartrending screams. In despair she threw herself from the top of the boulder into the foaming waters. Where she fell there protruded a huge rock, and when she hit this she split it in two. Covered in its dust, she plunged headlong into the waters.

Thus did the Ayirg's only sister, a woman without parallel on earth, perish at this spot. She sacrificed herself for her husband, Nart Sasruquo. But meanwhile, nothing had happened to Sasruquo. He had eluded death.

From Inal-Ipa et al. 1962, saga 39, pp. 317–23.

๑ This saga is a variant of the Circassian tale of Adif (saga 27) and the Abaza one of Qaydukh (saga 62). With its somewhat contrived death of the shining woman, it is an inversion of the usual Caucasian account [KT]. The shining woman, termed Dæl in Svan and Dela 'god' in Chechen, is a goddess of wild animals encountered on summits. She takes up with hunters, who in the end fall to their deaths in mountain ravines. By contrast, in this account and the preceding one, she is only the sister of the hunting gods. Although her husband survives, she herself jumps to her death into the river, splitting a large craggy rock, in memory of the original hunter's drop into the mountain's hidden depths. See the remarks at the end of saga 78.

[1] The first paragraph of this saga reads:

> Sasruquo's wife used to give birth to children as precious as gold, but it was impossible for each and every one of them not to die at the hand of their father, Sasruquo.

So by his hand perished the three youths who were born to his wife. Why should a man like Sasruquo have come by such a fate as this?

Unfortunately, this theme is not taken up again (see saga 79), but rather the saga recounts the tale of the illuminatrix and her ungrateful husband (see the Circassian saga 27).

² Compare this name /gʷətsákʲʲa/ (for /gʷəcákʲʲa/) with perhaps /a-gʷɔ́ckʲʲa-ra/ 'the-frankness', and Abaza /gʷɔ́ckʲa/ 'frank, blunt'.

³ These details place Sasruquo's abode in the steppes north of the Kuban and far from present day Abkhazia.

SAGA 81 ✑ *How Sasruquo Tamed the Wild Stallion*

After Bzow died, Sasruquo would not sit astride any other horse out of respect for his dead steed. Go or come where he might, he traveled on foot.

In those times the only breed of horse that knew what it meant to be ridden was the Nart breed. Other types of horses did not know what it meant to be mounted by a rider. Also, apart from the Narts, other peoples did not know how to ride horses.

One day Sasruquo heard that the Narts were holding an assembly beyond a great river. He felt bitter about it, saying, "What are these folks up to that they didn't invite me?" He made up his mind not to go at all, but later, with his heart unable to stand it, he changed his mind and set off for the gathering.

He traveled until he came to the bank of the river, where he halted. The water rolled along in a furious torrent, churning this way and that. He tried to cross at various spots, here and there, but could not find a ford. As he gazed over the waters, he noticed below him a wild horse grazing. He went up to it and begged it, if possible, to take him across the river, but the horse did not understand a single word. The Nart horses understood speech. The wild one did not. That was Sasruquo's error. In frustration, he grabbed the horse and caught hold of it. For a bit, he thrust into its mouth some twine made of mulberry bark and with all his force mounted it. Right there it entered the water with Sasruquo on its back. This was just what Sasruquo had wanted.

He made the horse advance until it reached the middle of the river, and then he turned it to face the flow of the flood. The horse thrashed against the torrent, raising waves that crashed, one against the other. Soon the horse grew tired and halted. That horse, which before had been so noisy and wild, a real destroyer of the world, began to go quietly along in whichever direction Sasruquo pulled with the reins of bark twine. Then Sasruquo pointed the horse's head toward the far bank, urged it along, and in this way crossed the river. Thus he finally reached the assembly.

At this gathering there were people other than Narts. The Narts felt shame before the others because Sasruquo had ridden up to the assembly on a wild horse.

"What are you doing, you? If you said that you would ride a horse again, don't you think that we would have found you a fine gelding?" Nart Siyt said.

From where he was sitting Nart Gutsakya said, "Leave off, lads! Leave him alone! Now is the moment when he has gotten just what he deserves."

Sasruquo said not one word.

The other people, however, looked on Sasruquo's arrival in a wholly other light. They had never thought that it was possible to break a wild horse, nor that a person could ever sit on one. They approached Sasruquo and asked him what he had done to tame the wild horse.

Sasruquo explained to them how he had done it. These folk rejoiced greatly and showed him their gratitude.

From that day onward all peoples began to tame wild horses and to ride them.

From Inal-Ipa et al. 1962, saga 38, pp. 314–16.

✑ This tale offers a unique insight into what must have been an early trick for taming a horse.

SAGA 82 ✑ *How the Narts Cultivated Fruit*

What the Narts lacked was of little consequence, save for their lack of fruit, for they possessed nothing in the way of fruit cultivation. This was greatly distressing to them. The only ones at that time who had fruit were the giants, but can you imagine them giving anything to humanity? Therefore, the Narts lacked fruit. The Narts, with their large households, wanted to have every type of fruit. Therefore they resolved, even if half of them should die, that they would attempt to find every variety of fruit and to bring it back for planting in profusion so that everyone could eat his or her fill.

Since the giants and the Narts were enemies, the Narts had to do battle for the fruits and wrest them from the giants. The Narts knew this full well, but they were not the sort to be deterred from a goal once they had set upon it. So they launched a war on the giants for the fruits of the earth. The first year they were unable to win the fruits. Again in the second year they failed. And yet once more in the third they failed. They were unable to carry the fruit trees away with them.

As a rule the Narts would not take Tsfitsf[1] with them to battle. In the fourth year, however, as they were about to set off to do battle with the giants, Tsfitsf pestered them to take him along, but they refused, saying, "We cannot leave our mother alone with no one here at home. You stay with her!" Make what you want of this excuse; they simply wanted to defeat the giants themselves and win all the glory.

"Fine," said Tsfitsf, "but when are you returning?"

"If we are still in one piece, we will return in three months' time," they replied, but as fate would have it, when three months had elapsed, the Narts did not return. So, as the fourth month opened, Tsfitsf prepared himself for battle. He donned his armor, mounted his steed, and set off in search of his brothers. Tsfitsf met them as they were traveling along the road home. They had achieved nothing.

"What's the matter? What has befallen you?" Tsfitsf asked.

"We were unable to fulfill our goal. We achieved nothing," they replied.

"Come on, now, lads! Have no fear, Nart warriors!" said Tsfitsf to his brothers. "You must turn back this instant!" And so saying, he shamed them into turning around, and, riding at their head, he led them back to battle. The Narts, in shame, followed behind.

The land where the giants lived was encircled by a massive stone wall. When they arrived, there stood before them a great iron gate, the only opening into the land. Tsfitsf gathered his brothers around him and spoke to them thus: "Set Sasruquo before this gate. An evil wind will arise. Thunder and lightning such as no one has ever seen before will come. But no matter what happens, you are not to lose heart! When the great tempest strikes, the gate will open. When it opens, with no weapons other than your swords, you must fall upon the giants!" Saying this, he was gone in a flash.

No sooner had he vanished than an evil wind arose. Thunder and lightning began to strike all around so that the whole earth shuddered. Then before long, the iron gate swung open and there stood Tsfitsf in the opening, sword at the ready!

"Forward, Nart heroes!" he cried, and with sword held aloft he led them into that land, with Sasruquo second, and the other Narts behind.

The giants did not know what had befallen them. Rushing to and fro, they fell into confusion. Before word of what had happened had reached them all, the swords of the Narts had done their work. The heads of giants rained down, one upon another, squashing those underneath. Those few giants who remained saw that they could do nothing to resist the onslaught of the Narts and so surrendered as prisoners.

In the land of the giants richly laden orchards stretched as far as the eye could see. All types of fruit were there. As for the fruit hanging from the tress, why, the smell alone would have satisfied your stomach! They shone where they hung and melted in your mouth! Wherever you gazed, your eye saw fruit hanging from bent branches of apple, pear, and peach trees. As for the vines, there seemed to be an infinity of them.

The Narts rested and then took one specimen of each type of tree. With a huge number of trees they set off for home. Back home they planted all the trees that they had brought. All proceeded peacefully in these efforts until it came to the planting of the vine. Then, for reasons no one knows, they began to quarrel over where it should go. Their tempers flared and they grew angry with one another. Then Tsfitsf pronounced a curse over the vine: "Whoever drinks wine in excess, like a man who does not fit into his own skin, may he know wrath like that of Sasruquo! But whoever drinks wine in moderation, like one happy with his lot, may he know joy like that of Tsfitsf!"

This is why drink has the power to create anger.

The fruits brought back by the Narts are those now found in Abkhazia: the apple, the pear, the grape, the peach, the fig, the cherry—you complete the list! Before this, Abkhazia knew no fruit. Tsfitsf performed a wonderful deed!

From Inal-Ipa et al. 1962, saga 27, pp. 236–40.

๑ Kevin Tuite (personal communication) notes that the fruit-hoarding giants are contrasted to the cereal-cultivating Narts through a sort of preternatural abundance. The stone wall surrounding their land might be directly associated with the megalithic circles found in the highlands of Abkhazia, called the /(a-)c'ang°ára/, and with the mythological aborigines of Abkhazia, the /(á-)c'an/ ["(the-) Atsan," perhaps linked to /(á-)c'an/ 'down; underneath'], considered to have been either dwarves or giants.

---

[1] "Tsfitsf" is Abkhaz /c°ɘc°/ 'whittler', the form /a-c°ɘc°/ 'shavings, whittlings' used

as a name. He is a mild-mannered counterpart of the frenzied Sasruquo. Like Sasruquo, he is rejected by his brothers and stays by his mother, spending his idle time whittling on firewood by the hearth. He is apparently the Abkhazian original, with Sasruquo being imported from the North.

However formidable it may appear, the name is easy to pronounce if one simply says *tsits* while making an *f* throughout.

SAGA 83 ◌ Khozhorpas

The beautiful Gunda, whom they called Lady Hero, had made a vow that she would marry no man save he who could seize her and throw her to the ground in wrestling.

From where the sun rises to where the sun sets, the finest youths sought betrothal to the beautiful Gunda. To all who sought her hand she explained her vow. An army of youths was constantly beseeching her to be theirs. As soon as she told them her vow, they would wrestle with her, grappling for an opening, but it was not easy to find a man who could defeat Gunda. She would shame those whom she hurled to defeat. Either she would cut off their ears and stick them atop the fence posts that ran around the great yard of the Narts or she would brand them with a hot iron and then let them go.

Gunda had already thus shamed ninety-nine youths when word reached her of a mighty man named Khozhorpas. He had set out from the west to seek her hand.

When he came before her, she said: "I wish that you would withdraw. I fear that you will prove incapable of overcoming my vow. If you look at the Narts' fence, you will see what the results have been for those who have tried before you." Gunda then explained to him her vow and swore that she would not forgo it for him.

"However that may be, I too am a man of this world. I have heard about you and have come from a distant land. I am not about to return without my strength having been tested against a woman. You will see if I can win your friendship. Come, let us wrestle!" He hunkered down to begin to grapple with her.

"If you are determined to try, then so be it! But you must know this:

when I have hurled you down in defeat, do not think that I won't put my mark on you. Don't you see, impaled on these stakes, the ears of those youths whom I have already defeated?" And saying this she again showed him the ninety-nine stakes on which were impaled the ninety-nine pairs of ears.

But Khozhorpas, too, it seemed, was a wonder. Paying no heed to these tangible signs of the misery of his predecessors, he strode up before her and stood there. Then suddenly the two rushed together and began grappling with one another, each seeking an opening. They wrestled a good while until each had worked up a sweat in the other's grip. Those trees on which they exhaled bent over and stayed bent. They laid bare the whole huge field. The earth shook. The sun stood still and watched them.

At that time Lady Satanay, the mother of Gunda, had no peace either. She was pacing up and down, eating at her heart.

At last, mustering all his strength, Khozhorpas started to swing Gunda up into the air. He lifted her up, and twisting, twisting, he carried her into the center of the great yard. Then, having spun her about his head, he slammed her flat on the earth, that valiant woman who, during her whole life, had never before been shown the earth by anyone.

News soon spread far and wide that Khozhorpas had triumphed. A great festival was held among the Narts. "Well, despite what we may have said in the past, we have now gained a brother-in-law to win the friendship of our sister," they said.

Lady Satanay too rejoiced. "My daughter has finally gained a husband," she said and treated Gunda's defeat as a cause of great joy. She had fattened a bull for the day when her daughter would acquire a husband, and now she led it out, cast it down, and slew it. She then organized the wedding.

Having won as his wife the beautiful Gunda, the only sister of the great Narts, Khozhorpas was delighted. After the wedding festival, he turned about and with his new bride set off for home.

From Inal-Ipa et al. 1962, saga 26, pp. 233–35.

◌ Only in the Abkhaz corpus is Gunda said to be one of the Narts (see also saga 85). In the Ubykh saga 89, Satanaya mourns her youngest son, Yarichkhaw, because he has died seeking the hand of Gunda.

In Abkhazia and up to the river Kuban stood many castles of the Narts. Of that multitude two have survived to this day for humankind to marvel at.

One of the Narts' great white castles stands at a spot called Akalamkhishra, the "White-Headed Reed-Bed." They say that inside that castle stands a golden table, and on that table rests a golden dish. It was the sort of table that if you left something on it and then went out, when you returned the object would have disappeared. At the back of this castle is a door on which is written: "Here is where goodness is, but it is not possible to enter here."

The other great castle of the Narts is in Abkhazia, in the village of Tquarchel.[1] It stands on a high hill called Narjkhyaw, and the castle takes its name from this hill. So does a famous hero of those times.

Narjkhyaw was a shepherd. He was raised in the forest. They used to say that he had never seen a house with a door. He was a fearsome man and unlike the Narts.

Narjkhyaw had his abode in Tquarchel, in the castle with the same name. He had a stone wall encircling it. If you go there, you can still see it today. Even now the chimneys and fireplaces of the castle stand. Whenever he bounded off of Castle Narjkhyaw, he would land on the peak Ayserra. Whenever he bounded off of Ayserra, he would bound onto the peak Kun's Yard. And whenever he bounded off of there, he would bound onto yet another mountain. This was the manner of his traveling, be he on horse or be he on foot.

Narjkhyaw did not keep his wife in Castle Narjkhyaw. She dwelled in Castle Ghartskiyket. Narjkhyaw spent a good deal of time going to and from her castle, but for most of the time it was Castle Narjkhyaw where he had his abode. Narjkhyaw and his wife had a chain running to and fro between them with which they used to communicate whenever they wanted to eat. So, if they wanted to eat, they would shake it, and then they would come together to share a meal.

So it was, until one time Narjkhyaw's wife ate without shaking the chain. Narjkhyaw was hungry. He wanted to eat. He waited and waited, but his wife did not shake the chain. After a while he realized that his wife must have had her meal without shaking the chain to invite him. Narj-khyaw grew very angry that his wife had broken the understanding that they had. He stood atop the hill, lifted a huge stone (it was no ordinary stone), and hurled it with all his might so that it would crash down on the castle standing in Ghartskiyket and kill his wife. But what happened was for the best. The stone did not touch the castle but fell by its side. That stone, even today, in truth, lies on the hill Ghartskiyket and is called the Stone of Kwajar.

When that stone landed, it shook the earth. Narjkhyaw's wife ran out and saw the stone. She realized at once that Narjkhyaw had thrown it in anger. What was she to do? With some retainers she went on foot to Narj-khyaw's, hair unkempt and barefoot, to beg for his forgiveness.

Narjkhyaw had acted in anger and now regretted what he had done. When he saw his wife coming to accept blame, he did not let that blame stick to her but instead forgave her. They say that when women bare their feet and undo their hair in times of mourning, this derives from Narj-khyaw's wife, and that prior to her women did not know this practice.

So time passed, until one day Narjkhyaw's wife died. After some time he conceived a desire to marry again, but finding a woman suitable for him was no easy task. Narjkhyaw went to his mother and asked her, "Mother, I seek a wife. Whom should I marry?"

"There is a woman who befits you, though I don't know whether you will win her," replied his mother.

"Who is this woman I might not be able to win? Where is she?" he asked.

"A white crystal tower that reaches to the sky stands within the iron wall of the one hundred Nart brothers. No bird enters this wall. There they have set their only sister, Gunda the Beautiful, but they will give her to no ordinary mortal. You may think that you are a powerful man, but you have never visited the Narts and had a good look at them, for then you would have seen the true measure of your manliness. Today they are holding a festival. The one who will carry off their sister from this gathering is a man's man, a real hero."

Narjkhyaw said no more to his mother. Had he not already seen Gunda the Beautiful? Were the tender feelings of his heart not directed toward her? He took out his father's prancing steed from its stable and mounted it. He shouted to the horse and leaped over the house. He shouted at it again and leaped back.

"Mother! I must see the manliness of this people into whose walls, by your words, no one can enter and whose sister no ordinary mortal can win," he cried. He set his spurs to the horse and rushed out of the yard like a bullet in the direction of the Narts.

Thus it was that just as Gunda the Beautiful was betrothed to Khozhorpes of the West, and as the wedding was to be held soon, Narjkhyaw of the East set off to win her.

As Narjkhyaw was traveling, he came upon three brothers who had fallen to blows among themselves over some quarrel.

"What are you fighting about?" Narjkhyaw asked them.

"Can't you see the reason for our dispute? We have our father's inheritance—a sword, a whip, and an old shepherd's cloak made of felt. We cannot agree on how to share it, so we have come to blows," they replied.

"Pray, bring hither the objects of your dispute. I shall divide them among you," he said. He took the objects and smashed and tore every one, then threw the pieces on the ground before them.

"Do you agree with this?" he said.

"We agree," they replied when they saw what he had done, and he remounted and continued on his way.

As Narjkhyaw continued resolutely, he came upon a pair of men who had stuck each other into the ground up to their knees as they wrestled.

"What are you arguing about, wretches?" he said, and he rode between them, separated them, and then continued on his way. But after he had ridden only a little way, he looked back and saw that they were still fighting and had stuck each other into the ground, this time up to their waists. He turned back and rode between them again, and this time he said, "If you won't stop it, then this is what you deserve." He caught hold of each by the scruff of the neck, yanked him out of the ground, and threw each in opposite directions toward his home. Then, after uttering a threat, he continued on his way.

As Narjkhyaw went farther, he came upon yet two more men who were fighting, this time over a chain.

"What is it that you are arguing over?" Narjkhyaw asked them.

"We are arguing over a chain that our father left us," they replied.

"What do you mean? Is this not shameful? The chain belongs to the eldest," he said. Then he separated them and set off once more on his way. But as with the others, he had not ridden far when he looked back and saw that these two also were fighting again, pulling the chain this way and that. Narjkhyaw dismounted, ran over to them, separated them, and snatched the chain from them. Then he snapped it in two and gave half to each one. They then grew calm and he set off on his way once more.[2]

That day the Nart brothers were gathered in the yard of their home. They were amusing themselves with a game—jumping and throwing a ball. They never gave thought to the idea that someone could beat them. Only Nart Sasruquo was absent. He was off on a hunt.

Lady Satanay gazed out and saw a horseman racing toward them like a bullet. But the word *horseman* can hardly describe what she saw!

"Narts, my sons!" the lady called. "You have never known shame. Now, finish your game of ball. We have a guest."

The Narts, who had been playing ball since morning, were all worked up and excited. "If a guest comes, we'll see him later," they replied and paid no attention to what she had said.

Even Gunda the Beautiful had had a premonition since morning that on this day a fearsome fellow would come among the Narts. She stood up and called to them, "Hey there, my great brothers! My upper lip senses something bad. Bolt fast the gates! Today a foul man is determined to come among you. If he comes, you and he will derive no good from each other."

"Ha! Fancy that! Who would challenge us?" replied the Narts. But they knew that their sister had the power of prophecy, and so they did not need her to repeat her warning. The Narts set to and bolted fast the great iron gate that stood in the middle of their castle's wall, a wall over which not even a bird could fly. The gate was suspended before the door of their house so that no man could gain entry. In this way they heeded her words and then returned to their game.

So they played on until afternoon, when they cocked their ears and could hear a horrible noise coming from a great distance in the East. Then suddenly a great cloud descended on them, and they grew dazed and collapsed, one upon another. Then a foul wind blew up and struck them, blowing half of them against their own wall. This was the breath from the horse of the man destined to come among them. As they gazed about, they suddenly caught sight of a horseman whose every line and movement showed steely will.

As he approached, he left sharp tracks along the whole length of the trail. As he drew near the gate, he spread thunder and lightning.[3] Some of the Narts went to the gate with the intention of keeping him out. Together they stood with their shoulders against the gate. But the red-faced giant,[4] who had appeared as quickly as lightning, paid no heed to anything at all. He rode onward without pause and struck the gate with his horse in full gallop, unable to rein it in, that horse whose head was in the air.[5] The gate shattered and fell inward. Three Nart brothers crawled out from underneath its ruin, but three remained pinned under it.

Narjkhyaw had come. When she learned who it was, Gunda the Beautiful hid herself. Narjkhyaw brought his fierce steed to a halt as best he could and dismounted.

"Good day, there, great Narts!" the guest said, raising his voice, but he received no answer of "Welcome! Greetings!"

"Greet me well or greet me badly, I have come," said Narjkhyaw.[6]

When the guest dismounted, a few of the Narts felt ashamed and went to take his horse away for him. They led it to the house and tied its harness to the iron tethering post, which was fixed firmly in the ground. The other Narts, though, continued to play ball as before.

As soon as they had tethered the horse, it began to gnaw with relish at the crude iron where it had been tied. The tethering pole could not support the weight of the harness and began slowly to sink into the ground. After a while, when it did not see its master, Narjkhyaw's steed began to neigh, and paw the ground. Then it reared its head, and the tethering pole, which by now had sunk deep into the ground, was yanked out as though nothing held it and was flung far away. Upset and with its head high in the air, the horse burst into the vast yard of the Narts.

"Hey! Good day!" Narjkhyaw called to them, but again the Narts acted as though they had not heard him and gave no reply.

"Great Narts!" shouted Lady Satanay once more. "Leave off playing ball. A guest is among us. To judge by his and his horse's adornment, he is a powerful man. Let there be no cause for surprise here today!"

But the Narts again paid no heed to what their mother had said. They chased after the ball, which had rolled to the bottom of the yard, tackling each other along the way.

Narjkhyaw went up into the guest room by himself and sat down. Several Narts came out one by one, and then two by two, and sat down beside him.

"Narts, I come to seek your sister's hand. Where is Gunda the Beautiful?" Narjkhyaw asked.

"Gunda is here," they replied.

"If she is here, I wish to see her. Pray, summon her hither," he said.

So they brought her. When Gunda the Beautiful entered, she was crying and her eyes were streaming with tears.

"What is the matter? Why are you crying, beautiful Gunda?" asked Narjkhyaw.

"Why should I not cry?" replied Gunda the Beautiful. "My three brothers were left beneath the gate when you entered. We cannot lift it off them, and so they are dying. They had such fine reputations, and now you have ruined these."

"Phew! I hadn't realized that," replied Narjkhyaw. "Don't worry about it!" And he went, kicked the ruins of the gate off them, and released them. The Narts who had been trapped beneath it helped each other to their feet, dazed and bruised.

When Narjkhyaw returned from the gate, those whom he had released came with him. Because they had seen what sort of man he was, they began to flatter him.

Then Gunda the Beautiful brought the iron bench on which the hundred Narts used to sit and bade Narjkhyaw to sit on it. When Narjkhyaw flopped down on it, the four legs of the bench cut into the ground and slowly sank farther and farther with a creak, up to the spot where Narjkhyaw was sitting. Narjkhyaw did not like this and rose. Gunda the Beautiful not only could not lift the bench but could not even budge it from the earth. Two Narts came over, but they too, try as they might, could not free the bench. Finally, Narjkhyaw placed his little finger along the side of the bench and pressed it upward. With utter ease he lifted the bench out of the ground. The Narts were ashamed.

"Sit down! Why are you standing up?" said Gunda the Beautiful quickly to hide the embarrassment.

"If I sit here again, I'll have to raise the bench up a second time," said Narjkhyaw. He took out his shepherd's felt cloak, stood his fur hat on it, and sat down that way.

The hosts then saw what a wonder they had as a guest. Whether they wanted to or not, they had to tend to him. They took from Narjkhyaw his iron bow and arrows and his armor. The Narts helped each other to carry them to the central iron pillar that held up the house. There they hung them where they hung their own weapons and armor. But as soon as Narjkhyaw's weapons and armor were hung from the pillar, it began to sink into the ground. It could not withstand the weight and began to creak and groan. The Narts took down Narjkhyaw's things and laid them on the ground.

Then Narjkhyaw arose, plunged his stick into the ground with a thud, and hung his weapons and armor right there.

When they saw him do this, the spirits of the Narts sank. "A miracle has apparently brought him among us. If it occurs to him, he could kill us too as though we were one person, don't you see?" they said among themselves. They feared him and decided to find some way to kill him. They talked among themselves and decided to try poison. So, in a twinkling, one Nart went to the mountains while another went to the seashore. The first returned with a red mountain snake, the second with a red seashore snake. Then they pounded the snakes' venom, blood, and flesh and boiled them into a broth. Then they secretly added this broth to the wine.

That night they all sat down to feast. They presented their guest with the best portions of meat. Then they placed before him a cup and a reed bowl full of wine, the wine that had been poisoned. They all sat beside him and urged him to drink, but Narjkhyaw grew suspicious.

"Hey, you wretches! They say that an elder is next to God. First take this wine and offer it to your father," said Narjkhyaw, sensing what was in their hearts.

In shame they took the mug and placed it before their blind father. With a loud slurp he tasted it, and when he had swallowed a mouthful, the old man stiffened and fell backward. As best they could, they quietly lifted him, carried him out, and buried his corpse. Then they returned with the cup and set it before Narjkhyaw again.

"Narts, where is your mother? I don't see Lady Satanay. From this moment I consider her my mother too. This cup is mine, but I cannot take hold of it before her. I want her to hold it to her lips first," said Narjkhyaw.

"Hold on to it there! Our mother has gone out," said the Narts.

"If that is so, Siyt, after your mother you come next in seniority in this house," he said and offered the drink to the Narts' eldest brother.

At first Siyt politely declined, but Narjkhyaw persisted. If Siyt did not drink when a guest had offered him his portion, then it would be a great shame. So, finally he took it, raised it up, and drank from it. For a while Siyt withstood the poison, but then he arose, left the hall, and collapsed just outside.

After this, Narjkhyaw raised the cup and drank, using his mustache as a strainer. He lifted both the cup and the bowl to his lips and drained them dry without leaving a drop, having filtered through his steel mustache and teeth the pure wine so that it would not bother him. Then he picked the snake bones out of his mustache and tossed them into the reed bowl with a rattle. All this meant nothing to him, and so his stomach gave off not even a grumble.

When Narjkhyaw had caught sight of Gunda the Beautiful, shimmering, his heart was enraptured by her.

"I must marry her, Lady Mother," he said, speaking first with the mother of the Narts, Lady Satanay. Then he turned to her children and spoke thus, "You are the one hundred Nart brothers, people who are capable of much. I am a single man, but I consider myself a real man. As I said to you earlier, I have conceived a desire to become related to you. Your sister, Gunda, pleased me. I want her as my wife. Give her to me! I shall marry her."

And the Narts rose and said to him, "You are a fine man. We won't withhold our sister from you. We would give her to you happily, but how? She is betrothed to Khozhorpes. If he hears of this, both you and we will have a bad future."

"If she is betrothed to Khozhorpes, I am in no hurry. If it pleases you, inform him. If he comes, we will see each other, for both he and I are men," announced Narjkhyaw.

"He lives far away. He is a traveling man and has gone off to a lofty mountain to hunt," said the Narts.

"So then fetch your sister and give her to me!" ordered Narjkhyaw in anger. He waited a moment, but when he saw that no one was moving, he grew even angrier. "I have fallen upon a pack of beggars!" he blurted out and jumped up. "If you see your brother-in-law, put him on my track. If he catches up with me, we'll talk!"

He quickly went to the golden crystal tower in which Gunda lived, smashed his way in, and seized her. He held her under his free arm and mounted his horse. Before her brothers realized what was happening, he had draped her over the horse's neck, shot across the yard, and with ease leaped over the iron fence. He landed in the meadow outside and rode off. So he set off with bright Gunda, her brothers looking on, and disappeared with her. Wherever he went, thunder and lightning followed, and his horse's tracks cut deeply into the trail.

The Narts had thought all along that the guest would not dare anything against them, and so they were taken aback when they realized what had happened. They donned their armor, mounted their horses, and set off on the trail of the one who had taken their sister. They followed him for three days and nights, but to no avail. They could not overtake him.

Now, Nart Sasruquo had not been at home during all of this. When he received word of what had happened, he shot home like a gust of wind and asked his mother for permission to follow them. When she gave him her leave, he mounted his steed and set off after Narjkhyaw. Sasruquo caught up with the Narts and overtook them. He set off on the trail of

Narjkhyaw, who by now had been riding for nine days and nights, but he too could not overtake him.

As for Khozhorpes, he knew nothing of what had happened. There was no way to get word to him, though the Narts tried all they could.

First, they made up their minds to try a crier. The younger brother of Nart Khmish, Nart Misa, had a ferocious voice. He took up position on a high hill, turned toward the mountains in the West and called to Khozhorpes, "Hey, wretch, wretch, wretch! Khozhorpes! Now is the moment when valor is needed. Gunda the Beautiful, betrothed to be your wife, has been stolen by Narjkhyaw, who has run off with her. If you are seated, arise! If you have arisen, then make haste! Wretch, wretch!"

Second, they dispatched a runner to search for wherever the Narts' brother-in-law might be and to say to him, "A wondrous fellow unexpectedly came among us. Like a shot he closed in on the gate of our iron wall. On horseback he reduced our iron gate to rubble. The pillar where one hundred men used to hang their armor could not support his armor. The bench on which one hundred men used to sit was driven into the earth when he alone sat on it. Then he said he wanted our sister and struck a pose, puffing himself up. Gunda the Beautiful, your betrothed, was snatched away by Narjkhyaw in such a fashion that we could not use our strength. If you are asleep, awake! If you are awake, make haste! We could do nothing against him. You must hasten as fast as you can."

If it had not been for Gunda the Beautiful herself, neither the voice of the crier nor the words of the runner would have reached Khozhorpes. When she realized how things were unfolding, she cried out herself twice, with all her might, in a shrill voice, and Khozhorpes heard her voice clearly from where he was far away.

Narjkhyaw continued as he had before. His horse raced over the ground like a hound, leaving behind it furrows in the earth, a clear trail.

As soon as Khozhorpes heard the shrill cry of Gunda the Beautiful, he readied himself and climbed on his steed, which was swifter than the wind. Moving swiftly, he set out on Narjkhyaw's trail. He sped along, and finally, with a crack of his whip, he overtook his foe just as the latter was about to reach the summit of Chamhara, at the spot known as Apshera, where seven roads meet.[7]

When Narjkhyaw looked back, he saw that Khozhorpes had already closed in on him so closely that he could recognize him with his own eyes.

Khozhorpes called, "Hey! So you'll slay me and be on your way again.

But don't think that I'll let you go free so easily. Unless you are carrying off the lady just to wear her headdress, you will halt, like a true man."

"Hey, just you come on like that! Here I am," replied Narjkhyaw. "You are the tracker. Shoot!" He continued as fast as he could, just as before.

They were within shouting distance of each other, but there was still some way between them. Khozhorpes came on relentlessly, folding the vast field beneath him, with nothing holding him back. Just as they rode into Svan Field,[8] just as he was gaining on the pair, something shone on him like the dawn. This was shining Gunda, still held across the neck of Narjkhyaw's horse. They reached a spot where the two foes could see each other clearly. Khozhorpes reined in his horse and raised his voice, "Who are you to slay me and then go on your way?"

"Hey, hey, Khozhorpes! Here I am! Come forward!" yelled Narjkhyaw.

"Let her go if you will! Don't force us to kill one another," replied Khozhorpes.

"No, battle is our only escape here," countered Narjkhyaw.

The foes met. Standing face to face, they challenged each other. In those days the weapons were catapults, double-edged spears, and bows and arrows. Both men decided on ferocious battle right in the middle of Svan Field, first with bow and arrows.

"You are the pursuer. Yours is the first shot. Shoot!" cried Narjkhyaw.

For a goodly while they shot at each other, their blood boiling. With the little finger of his right hand Narjkhyaw deflected the arrows flying toward him, piling them in a rhododendron bush[9] that was by his side. Khozhorpes caught the arrows aimed at him in midflight and stopped them.

Khozhorpes' soul was seated in the center of his right foot. If an arrow were to penetrate it, his soul would be released. Narjkhyaw kept aiming at his foe's right foot, but he could not strike it. As they continued the battle, their arrows became used up.

"I'll go and make some more arrows and return with them for both of us," said Narjkhyaw, but Khozhorpes refused.

"You have a woman with you. I'll make the arrows and bring them for us," Khozhorpes said, and he went, made more arrows, and returned with them. He unfurled his shepherd's cloak and dropped them on it. The two men then sat beside each other as they apportioned them out. Then they returned to their places on the field and resumed fighting.

Once more their supply of arrows was exhausted.

"This time I'll go, make arrows for us, and bring them back," said Narjkhyaw. He went off, made some arrows, and brought them back. He too unfurled his cloak, and they sat beside one another as they apportioned the arrows between themselves. Once more they took up positions and began to fight.

Narjkhyaw became heated and his shooting grew stronger. Taking careful aim, he loosened an arrow. It flew forward and split Khozhorpes' head in two.

Holding his head together, Khozhorpes shouted to his foe, "If you are a man, Narjkhyaw, let us hold a truce for a while! Wait for me! My head is hit. I'll go to Aynar the smith and come back with my head hammered back together again."

"Go! Don't rush! I'll wait for you here. I too have suffered a wound on my thigh. Before you return, I'll put it right," said Narjkhyaw.

Khozhorpes set off for the smithy, holding his split head together firmly with both hands. When he arrived, he put his head down before Aynar the smith and said, "You must quickly hammer it together for me. Narjkhyaw and I are doing battle on Svan Field. He is waiting for me."

Aynar the smith began his work and hammered Khozhorpes' head together for him. Where he hammered, he fitted a patch of brass, drove in a nail, and fastened it. He molded an iron brace around it and made it fast. Hammering away, he fitted bolts in place and made them tight, not allowing his split head to come apart.

Khozhorpes returned with his reconstructed head. Without delay, both resumed their places and their battle.

Khozhorpes shot an arrow and wounded Narjkhyaw's left hand, rendering it useless. The second arrow that he had sent right after the first, however, was caught by Narjkhyaw in his right hand and crumpled to bits, which he sprinkled over the ground. Narjkhyaw had also shot off an arrow, and this one flew forth and shattered Khozhorpes' knee.

"Ah, wretch!" said Khozhorpes. "Again, let us have a truce! Wait while I go to Aynar the smith and return with my shattered knee rejoined!"

Narjkhyaw granted him the truce. Khozhorpes went once more to Aynar the smith, had his knee mended, and returned once again to do battle. They resumed their fight. When it was clear that they would get nowhere with arrows, they turned to their double-edged spears.

Khozhorpes let fly a spear. "Where did it go?" he cried.

"Don't you see where it has gone? It has hit my leg and put my thigh out of joint," replied Narjkhyaw.

"The next shot is yours. Throw your spear!" cried Khozhorpes.

Narjkhyaw's spear caught Khozhorpes in the head and broke it.

"Where has it gone?" asked Narjkhyaw.

"Don't you see where it has gone? The head and intellect are what makes a man. Again my head is shattered. If possible, wait for me once more! I'll go mend my head and come back," said Khozhorpes.

"Fine! I'll wait for you," replied Narjkhyaw.

Khozhorpes went once more to Aynar the smith and returned with his head patched up. It was his turn to shoot, and as soon as he reached the field, he let fly another spear.

"Where has it gone?" asked Khozhorpes.

"I didn't see it over here," said Narjkhyaw. Then Narjkhyaw let fly a spear. It struck the patch in Khozhorpes' head and sheared it off.

"Where has it gone?"

"It struck the patch on my head and sheared it off," replied Khozhorpes.

"Then do you want anything more?" asked Narjkhyaw.

"Give me time just once more," pleaded Khozhorpes.

"Fine! I'll give you time," answered Narjkhyaw.

When Khozhorpes could no longer help himself, Narjkhyaw picked up Gunda the Beautiful once more, chose a road, and set off. His strength was almost gone, but before too long he reached a huge mountain. He came to the foot of the pass Humwa, where seven roads meet, but he was unable to go farther. He gripped his wounded leg. He managed to get as far as White Reeds and froze there, unable to move.

The mother of the Narts, Lady Satanay, was a woman whose words found fulfillment. She arose and uttered a curse, "Narjkhyaw, you who gave no happiness to my daughter, you who caused Khozhorpes' shrill cry to ascend to the heavens! With nothing holding you from above, with nothing supporting you from below, turn into a sight miraculous to behold! Both you and your horse and my daughter, Gunda the Beautiful, turn into a gentle whetstone, just as you are holding her at this moment, beneath your arm! Turn to stone! Crystallize! Until Judgment Day may you stand so in midair with nothing able to shift you! Once each year may you awaken! With horsemen traversing you above and travelers passing beneath your horse's stomach, may you sink slowly to the ground! When your horse's stomach touches the ground, may the millennium start that very day!

"May Gunda the Beautiful take the name Nantpara Hill! As long as beauty exists in the world, as long as our earth possesses sweetness, may her name not pass from memory! Honey surpasses all other food and drink. May all bees have her as their guardian! May their guardian deity have the name Anana Gunda![10]

"Khozhorpes, you, my child, may you grow in the guise of a rhododendron by every stream! May you stand there for the people, with your most beautiful blooms. Every spring, with its perfume in the air, may the rhododendron remain to bring joy to people!

"May happiness constantly attend the abodes made of plaited rhododendron twigs, and may they last long! May the rhododendron bear your name in nature's order. May it stand and fill the world, never losing its leaves, neither in winter nor in summer! Once a year let the people celebrate the festival of the rhododendron in your name!"

They say that Lady Satanay's words came true.

Nart Sasruquo and his horse, flying over the ground in their pursuit, continued as before. Lo! Lo! They were on the point of catching up, but even so, poor Sasruquo failed to reach the man who had snatched his sister away while their souls were still in them. When he drew near them, he looked up at Narjkhyaw, and without uttering a word and while still moving straight toward him, he unsheathed his keen sword and struck out. But when the blade struck that which was newly made into stone, the steel gave off sparks that lit up Sasruquo's face. He saw what had happened. He stopped and sat there, astride his horse, his head held low in dejection.

All had undergone the fate ordained for them by Lady Satanay. Gunda the Beautiful had turned to stone, all cold. She became the bees' guardian deity, known as Anana Gunda. She remained on Nantpara Hill as a wondrous token.

Khozhorpes became part of nature and the Festival of the Rhododendron took its name from him.

Narjkhyaw, with Gunda held under his arm, and his horse were turned to stone, and they are suspended in midair at the place where seven roads meet, turned to stone with a smooth covering of moss. That monument will not descend to the ground until Judgment Day, they say. But they also say that there is not long left before it descends to the ground, that already a traveler on foot cannot pass beneath it without crawling.

From Inal-Ipa et al. 1962, saga 41, pp. 331–50.

⌀ This saga is a darker version of the winning of the maiden (see also sagas 78 and 83). It is also an example of the sort of myth that typically refers to certain locales that are notable and endeavors to provide a folk history or explanation for these. Gunda's radiance recalls that of a number of heroines: Adif in saga 27, Qaydukh in saga 62, the daughter of the Ayirgs (plural) in saga 78, and Sasruquo's wife in 79, who is said to be the sister of the Ayirg (singular) in saga 80 [KT].

[1] Tquarchel is a small city in the mountains of southern Abkhazia. It is primarily a mining center and underwent a long siege by Georgian troops during the Georgian-Abkhazian War of 1992–93. The name might be derived from the verb "to take as a prisoner of war," shared between the two otherwise unrelated languages (Abkhazian / a-t'q'°a-rá /, Georgian / t'q've /), and may hark back to a time when captives were used to work the mines.

[2] A chain seems an odd item to fight over. Perhaps this is the chain of the hearth, from which kettles were hung. In Ossetian tradition, this chain is the abode of the god Safa, the god of the hearth.

[3] This suggests that Narjkhjaw was originally a storm god, who has been displaced by Sasruquo.

[4] The red face mentioned here is unique among the Nart corpora and suggests old links with such figures as Rudra of the Rig-Veda and the "fiery face" of the Baltic god of thunder and lightning, in Lithuanian Pérkūnas (Puhvel 1987, 224).

[5] This celestial horse head is seen in Abaza in the horse of Totrash (saga 60) and in Circassian (saga 23). In Ubykh (saga 86) it is the head of the approaching Bardanuquo (paired with Ubykh Tutaresh [Totrash]), which reaches into the sky.

[6] In saga 85 this is said by Sasruquo. This and the following saga use a wind to portend the approach of the mighty horseman.

[7] *Apshera* is / a-pšʸa-rá / 'to bless, sanctify'; perhaps it is repeated in the name of the Apsheron Peninsula, which juts out into the Caspian Sea in northern Azerbaijan. This peninsula forms the southeastern end of the Caucasian mountain chain.

[8] The Svans are a people distantly related to the Georgians, who live in the high mountain valleys of northwestern Georgia, southeastern Abkhazia, and southern Kabardino-Balkaria.

[9] Khozhorpes is called the rhododendron boy (see the comments at the end of saga 89).

[10] *Ananda Gunda* means "Grandmother Gunda."

SAGA 85 ◌ *An Account of the Narts*

Among the Narts were seven brothers. Their sister was named Gunda. The youngest brother was named Khmish. Although he sought the sister of Yarchkhyaw, Lord of the Atsan,[1] he, alas, would not give her to him. Sasruquo knew of this, but he did not meddle in their affairs.

Once Khmish and Yarchkhyaw set off together on a hunt. They spotted some deer clinging to a craggy slope. Yarchkhyaw shot at them and killed one. Khmish took offense and spoke to Yarchkhyaw thus: "You know how we Narts regard ourselves, that before us no one does anything. Why did you kill it before me?"

"I did not know that. I had not realized that you were nearby. But come here! I offer the companion's share to you," he said.

"Hey! Should I take against my will the bit of companion's share of that which you killed? Are you forcing me to do what no Nart has done?" he said.

"Ha! You wicked Narts are a lazy, low-down race! Once again, whom do you not hold in contempt?"

When Yarchkhyaw said this, Khmish drew up to him in a flash and said, "I shall show you if we are lazy!" and he grabbed a fetlock of the deer in a tight grip, impetuously flayed the carcass up to the head, and stuck the hindquarters on the point of his pike. Then he set off to return.

Later, when he entered the compound, Sasruquo, who was sitting atop the balcony, looked and saw him.

"Hey, you luckless one! Surely you did not kill this. If you had killed it, would you not have brought the head and neck? Why don't you know that we do not settle for bringing the companion's share? You have brought disgrace!" he said.

"I did not kill this. The one who killed it is Yarchkhyaw. When I said to him, 'Why did you kill this before me?' right off he did not say good words to me, but instead he said to me thus: 'Why is it that I should give my sister to the lazy, low-down Narts?'" Khmish said.

Would Sasruquo stand about on hearing this? He climbed into the saddle of his fiery steed and set off. Did Yarchkhyaw not know what Sasruquo was like? Could he not have known that he would not forgive him for what he had said to Khmish? He said to his sister, "You should be ready."

The breath shooting from the top of Sasruquo's steed began to blow like the wind into his yard. Could he not have known why Sasruquo was coming? He opened the gate and stood waiting for him. Sasruquo entered the yard.

"*Wah!* I look upon you with favor!" said Yarchkhyaw.

"Whether you regard me with favor or you do not regard me with much, I have come!" he said, and he rode his steed straight up to the palace.

"Where would you seat me, luckless Yarchkhyaw?"

"I defer to your valor. If you wish, I can seat you here or in the shade."

They brought a bench, but as he sat down it could not support him. They brought another one, but that one could not support him either. A third was brought, but how could that one hold him?

"Release my horse and tether it to the hitching post," he said.

Yarchkhyaw drew up to it, seized the bridle, and pulled, but how could he make the horse obey? "Well!" said Sasruquo, and then he jumped back on his steed in one smooth, powerful bound, as though he himself were a racehorse.

"What did you say to Khmish?" asked Sasruquo.

"What did I say? We were together, hunting. I did not see him, and inadvertently I killed a deer. When he said 'Why did you kill it?' I said, 'I had not realized that you were nearby.' Thus, from its fetlock to its head the dog flayed it and took half."

"Then what did you say?"

"I blurted out, 'The Narts are a lazy, low-down bunch,' but I did not mean much by the phrase. It escaped me."

"Cross over to here!" said Sasruquo, and he took Yarchkhyaw prisoner. What person could possibly talk back to him, Sasruquo?

Setting his sights on Yarchkhyaw's sister, he said, "Come here!" Swiftly seating her on his horse, he carried her off.

Sasruquo behaved in this way.

Told in 1928 by Bartsets Shulayman, fifty-two years old, of Barmesh to A. N. Genko and published in Bgazhba (1964), 379–80.

◌ This saga is an inversion of the preceding account about Narjkhyaw (a variant of this name). Charachidzé (1968, p. 166) has noted that Abkhazian myths are often inverses of those found elsewhere in the Caucasus [KT]. Instead of seeking the beautiful but betrothed Gunda, Yarchkhyaw must give up his own sister. Instead of being a savage and mighty warrior, he is the presumptuous and arrogant lord of a race of water sprites. Khmish, who in the Circassian tradition is depicted as an elder, the father of Pataraz, here is the youngest of Gunda's seven brothers. Instead of taking a water sprite, Lady Isp, as a wife against the wishes of the Narts while on a hunting trip with the little people, he is humiliated while hunting and has his wife brought to him by Sasruquo, who is intrusive in this myth, as a form of vengeance. The account may be old, since Sasruquo can be seen as being in the process of coming to dominate this account, as he has so much else in the Abkhaz and Abaza traditions. After all, Sasruquo is always set apart from the other Narts, whereas here he is associated with the seven brothers and may even be one of them. Whether this myth precedes the usual accounts of Yarchkhyaw / Narjkhyaw in the Nart sagas is open to question. This myth is crucial to an understanding of the origins of Khmish and Pataraz, and its use of Yarchkhyaw / Narjkhyaw may be old, but it does not bear directly on the latter's efforts to win Gunda. This inversion of Khmish and Lady Isp may be a reflection of an older account more in line with the usual portrayal. In this protomyth, Khmish may have taken Lady Isp against the wishes of both the Narts and the Atsan because he had been bettered in the hunt by the prince of the little people.

[1] These are little people (se my comments at the end of saga 82).

THE UBYKH NART CORPUS

Analyzed and Re-translated by
John Colarusso
from the Ubykh

Earlier Translations into French by
George Dumézil and
Hans Vogt

Long ago, in the land of the Adyghey, there was among the Narts a certain Satanaya. This young woman had a tower house[1] from which, if she peered out, she could see wherever she wanted. Nearby flowed a river. Satanaya also had three servant girls. Going down to the edge of the river, they would wash their clothing. From time to time Satanaya, going down to the edge of the river, would sit on some large rocks at the water's edge, right where they did their washing. If it happened to be a warm day, she would say "there is no one here," and she would undress herself and slip into the water.

In this way, a certain cowherd of the Narts, by the name of Sosna, would often spy on Satanaya from afar, from the other side of the river. One day Satanaya had again gone down to the riverbank, undressed herself, and entered the water, whereupon Sosna, keeping himself hidden, drew near to where Satanaya was in the water, naked. She had gone into the water naked, unaware of what he was about to do. Then suddenly Sosna seized Satanaya and took her virginity, there in the water. Then he swam back to the far shore, making a furious splashing.

Satanaya was very depressed by what had befallen her. Not knowing what to do, she swam ashore, and deep in thought she walked back to her house. For several days she brooded and said to herself, "What has befallen me has never befallen anyone else before. What will I do with myself?" After a while she could no longer bear it and said, "I shall tell this secret of mine to Tlepsh." And she sent her servant girls to call him.

Tlepsh was a master of whatever he did. He was constantly working at his forge. When Tlepsh came he asked her, "What do you wish, Satanaya?"

"Alas, Tlepsh, what has befallen me has not happened to anyone else. I cannot tell anyone my secret except you. It is like this. One day I was bathing myself and had entered the water. Sosna came, seized me while I was naked, and did to me what he should not have done. I thought, 'Except for you, Tlepsh, there is no one who can find a remedy for my plight. Except for you, there is no one who will keep my secret hidden.' I have confidence in you and so I have called for you. Except for God, there is no one who knows of this matter."

Tlepsh said, "That is no problem. I shall find a remedy for you. Simply wear a large shirt so that those who see you will not know when your belly becomes large. After nine months I shall return." Then he went back to his forge.

When two months of her term remained, he went down to the water's edge without anyone seeing him. He cut through one of the rocks on which she had been sitting and hollowed out of it just enough space to hold an infant. Then he placed the top back on it so that the two halves fitted smoothly. Then, for the benefit of the Narts, he said, "O Narts! A rock by the water's edge on which Satanaya used to sit is trembling, and a voice is coming from inside it." When they gathered to look, he made as though a voice were coming from inside it.

The Narts were amazed and said, "How can this be?"

When nine months had passed, Satanaya began to have labor pains. At this time Tlepsh returned to her and said, "O Satanaya! When you give birth to the infant, go to the river. I have cut through one of the nearby rocks on which you used to sit and have hollowed it out just enough for an infant to fit inside. Lift off the top of the rock and set inside this infant to whom you will soon give birth. Then put the top of the rock back on. At that point I shall arrive. You then go back to your house and rest."

Several days later Satanaya gave birth to a baby boy. Without anyone seeing her, she brought him to the rock about which Tlepsh had told her and placed him inside it. Then she replaced its top.

That evening Tlepsh arrived. He shouted and said, "Ah! Look over there! There is a voice coming from inside that rock." The Narts soon gathered together. Tlepsh went up to the rock, and hitting it with his hammer, he removed the top part of the rock. When the people looked inside the rock they saw a new infant sitting inside it. Fire had descended on him and he was aflame.[2] With his iron tongs Tlepsh grasped the infant by his two thighs and dunked him in and out of the passing water three times. The fire that had descended on him was quenched. Then he set the infant down on the bank and called to Satanaya, "O Satanaya! An infant has come out of this rock. If you take and rear him, he will become a son to you."

Satanaya drew near and Tlepsh handed the infant to her. The Narts standing there were greatly amazed. Tlepsh said, "I shall name him Soseruquo," and so they all called him Soseruquo.[3] With the infant in her arms, Satanaya returned home and the Narts dispersed.

Satanaya reared Soseruquo. He reached the age of twelve or thirteen, and one day he asked his mother, "O Mother, these so-called Narts, these big people, will I become big like them?"

She said to him, "O my son, although you will not become big like them, all of them will fear you and you will kill them."

Eventually Soseruquo grew up and reached the age of twenty. Mounting his horse, he would ride through the regions of his domain and appropriate land. The Narts began to fear him because he would always strike and slay those who had entered the land he had staked out as his own. Despite their hostility, Satanaya loved one of the Narts, a certain very heroic Nart by the name of Bardanuquo. She hoped to marry him. So she made three servant girls keep a watch for him, by day and by night, to see if he should happen to pass by or enter that domain.

One day one of the servant girls ran in and said, "Someone is coming hither. His head is in the sky and smoke rises behind him. Fire comes out of his mouth."

"What are you saying?" Satanaya replied. "Tell me the truth!"

Thereupon the servant girl said, "A certain horseman is coming hither. His bearing is as straight as a knitting needle. The hooves of his horse scattered the earth and raised the dust behind him. His mustache glitters like gold."

Satanaya grew joyful and said, "No! If that is so, then he is Bardanuquo. It must be he for whom I have waited all these days." At once she summoned the man who was her cowherd and said, "Now go before this horseman who is riding hither and invite him here."

The cowherd went before that horseman, showed him due respect, and said, "Welcome! You are invited to come to us."

"Wherever that is, I do not want to go there. But if you know where I might find a hero, tell me!"

When the cowherd replied "That, I do not know," the rider struck him twice with his riding crop and set off again on his way. The cowherd ran as fast as he could to Satanaya and told her what had happened.

"Alas, go again before him," she said, "and I shall come along as well. Say, 'Come to us! Satanaya prays very much and wants to see you. She says, "I would be happy if he were to come and eat one mouthful,"' tell him."

When she had finished, the cowherd set off again before the horseman, and Satanaya followed close behind. "O our guest, please come to us! Satanaya has killed a lamb. She said, 'He will taste its soup' and waits for you. She sent me here again."

Thereupon the horseman said, "I do not want woman's small talk. If there is any hero about, tell me!" and he set off on his way again.

Just as he was leaving, Satanaya arrived and called out to him, "Alas! Bardanuquo! If you are a true hero, then look behind you just once!" As Bardanuquo turned about to look, Satanaya took off her clothes and showed herself to him naked.

When Bardanuquo beheld her thus naked, he said, "*Pfu!* It would be better than this if you were dead!" He then turned his horse about and set off again on his way.

Satanaya had done what she did because she wanted Bardanuquo very much. She returned home dejected and with a broken heart. Soseruquo was lying asleep in the house. In sorrow Satanaya went to him and kicked him with her foot. "You lie here sleeping and do not know who enters your domain! You don't even know who leaves it!"

When she said this, Soseruquo replied, "O Mother, what has happened? Was that horseman who passed by Bardanuquo? Would he not listen to what you said? If he would not come here for your sake, then I will go to him and bring him back for you. If he will not come back willingly for me, then I will bring his head back." He arose, mounted his horse, and set off after Bardanuquo.

After a long, hard ride he drew up behind him and said, "May you find good roads, Bardanuquo! Where are you going? Where are you riding from?"

Bardanuquo replied, "If there is a heroic man in this country, I want to meet him. I am seeking such a one."

Soseruquo replied, "If that is the case, then there is no problem. Let us ride together to the Narts and ask them."

So, riding together they came to the Narts. When the Narts saw them approaching, they grew frightened. Soseruquo went among the Narts and said to them secretly, "This man will kill each and every one of you. If you listen to what I say, you will escape from him."

The Narts replied, "Very well!"

Whereupon Soseruquo said, "If you all agree, then kill a sheep and prepare it for us to eat. When you sit down at the table, fill the hollow wine cup and give it to Bardanuquo. He will drink that all at one time, without taking it from his mouth.[4] As he is drinking that, I shall take a firebrand from the fire and burn his face."

The Narts replied, "Very well!" and they did as Soseruquo had suggested. They made ready the table and sat down side by side. While they were eating, they had the large wooden wine cup brought in and gave it to Bardanuquo. As Bardanuquo took the cup with both hands and began to drink, Soseruquo jumped up, snatched a brand from the fire, and held it to Bardanuquo's face. Even as his face was being burned, Bardanuquo drank the wine, not taking it away from his mouth until he had finished it. When Soseruquo saw this, he let the firebrand drop to the floor and dashed out of the house, setting off again on the road. Even though Bardanuquo was furious, he was ashamed to follow in pursuit because the other was so small. "May God do evil unto your mother!" he called after Soseruquo. He finished eating, then slowly mounted his horse and set off again on his way.

Having ridden only a little way, Soseruquo changed his appearance and came before Bardanuquo once again.[6] Soseruquo asked him, "Where are you going, Bardanuquo? What happened to your face?"

Bardanuquo replied, "I was sitting among the Narts and an evil baby burned my face. I don't know whether he was a man or a devil, but I was ashamed to go after him."

Soseruquo, deceiving him, then said, "May God do evil unto that one's mother! What happened was nothing. Turn around and together we will ride back to the Narts. Otherwise they will say of you, 'He was afraid and ran away.'" He persuaded him to turn about, and together they rode back to the Narts.

Again, just as before, the Narts made ready the table. Just like the first time, Soseruquo explained to the Narts, "If you do not kill him today, you will not escape from him again. Now in order to kill him attach two swords firmly in this doorway, and once again give the wine cup to him. Again, as he is drinking this, I will burn his face all over with a firebrand. This time he will become angry and set off after me. I shall run and dash underneath the swords. But when he comes he will be in a rage and will not see them. As he passes through, they will strike him in the chest and cut him through the midsection. Then you will survive."

Again the Narts did as he said, and together with Soseruquo and Bardanuquo they all sat down at the table. They ate awhile, and then they brought in the great wine cup and gave it to Bardanuquo. Taking it with both hands, he began to drink. As he was drinking, Soseruquo drew out a firebrand that was fully aflame and thrust it into Bardanuquo's face. However much it burned him, Bardanuquo endured it and did nothing until he had finished the wine. When he had drained the cup, he took it from his mouth and said, "May a dog shit in your mother's mouth!" and full of fury he went after Soseruquo. Soseruquo ran outside through the door, bounding beneath the swords, but in his fury Bardanuquo did not notice them. He thought to himself, "I shall bound out through the door and seize Soseruquo," but when he hit the door the swords cut him in two through his midsection. His upper portion toppled to the ground outside, and his legs remained in the house. In an instant Soseruquo turned about, cut off Bardanuquo's head, then mounted his horse and returned to his mother.

"O Mother!" he cried. "Although I was not able to bring Bardanuquo himself, I did bring you his head!" and he let it drop to the floor before his mother.

When Satanaya saw this, she was grief stricken and grew angry with her son. "Would that the milk I gave you from my breasts had been a poison to you! Why did you do this?"

Soseruquo replied, "What should I have done? He would not come back at my request. I said, 'I shall show him to you,' so I have brought you back his head."

His mother then said, "O my son, the time of your death has arrived. You will not live much longer. There is one whom they call Tutaresh who is Bardanuquo's brother. Wherever you may flee, he will find you."

Several days passed and Soseruquo was in the courtyard when a strange bird flew up and alighted on a post. "This bird is very beautiful," he said to himself. "I shall try to catch it," and so he began to creep up on it.

While he was doing this, his mother looked out and saw him. "O my son, do not touch it! That is not a bird but a demon that they call Zhembik,[7] the daughter-in-law of the Narts." Upon hearing this, Soseruquo grew frightened and spent his time in worry.

One day, as he was at one of the boundaries of his domain, he saw a horseman coming toward him in the distance. When he saw him he became frightened. He turned about and set off for home. As he was riding back, he saw a beautiful bird sitting in the road. "This bird is even more beautiful than the one the other day. I shall catch this one and bring it back for my mother." Saying this, he caught the bird and placed it in the space between his coat and his chest. He teased the bird and said, "Don't tell anyone that I killed Bardanuquo." When he returned home he said, "O Mother, I have brought a bird for you that is prettier than the one the other day."

She asked him, "All right then, where is it?"

When Soseruquo reached into his coat, however, he could not find the bird. "Alas!" he said. "It is no longer here, Mother!"

Then his mother said to him, "As I have told you, that is not a bird. It is a demon. Now the time of your death has drawn near."

Thus, one day soon after, as Soseruquo was again seated on his horse and at the limits to which his land reached, he saw a horseman approaching him from afar. He said to himself, "I have seen this horseman once before. Whatever he would do, let him do it! I shall rush upon him!" and so he gave his battle cry and rode forth.

He rushed on the other rider and rammed the breast of his horse into the other's, and yet he merely bounced off the oncoming rider and spun around twice, having no effect. Soseruquo now looked at him more closely and saw that he was asleep in the saddle! When Soseruquo saw this he became terrified, turned, and rode back. At the sound of his hooves the rider awoke and angrily rubbed his eyes. With his eyes he followed Soseruquo as he rode off into the distance. Then he set off after him, and no matter how hard Soseruquo rode, the other gained on him until he came up behind him and seized him. As the other drew out his sword to slay him, Soseruquo said, "O my enemy, please do not kill me today! Please grant me a reprieve until the Narts' day,[8] when we shall meet on Mount Haram and do battle!"

The other said, "If that is what you wish, then very well!" and he released him.

Soseruquo, whose skin had become the color of a corpse's, returned home. When his mother saw how he was, she asked him, "What has happened, my son?"

"Alas, Mother!" he replied. "Today I encountered a horseman and attacked him. He neither heard my cry nor felt the impact of my charge but sat on his horse asleep. I saw how he was and had turned to come back when he awoke, rubbed his eyes, and, not letting me get away, caught up to me and seized me. As he was about to kill me, I extracted from him a reprieve until the Narts' day." And then he asked his mother, "What day is the Narts' day?"

She said, "O, my son, the one whom you encountered is Tutaresh, Bardanuquo's brother. Even though you will not escape from him again, I shall once more tell you something that might enable you to deal with him. But if you cannot handle him, then you surely will not escape from him a second time. The Narts' day is Thursday. Today is Wednesday."[9]

Soseruquo then said, "If that is so, then our day is tomorrow, don't you say? It is indeed very near! All right then, if it must be that we do battle tomorrow, tell me what I ought to do, Mother!"

"O, my son," she replied, "tomorrow, as early as possible, hang handbells all over your horse, mount it, and climb to the summit of Mount Haram. Tutaresh will then come there. While he is ascending and is still below you, give a cry from above and, striking your horse, rush down on him. Tutaresh's horse will panic from the sound of the bells. He will try to make his horse stop and will try to rein it in. The horse will collapse under him, and it is then, if you can, that you must do something. If you fail then, you will not have another chance."

Soseruquo did as his mother said, and very early the next morning he ascended Mount Haram. A little later Tutaresh came and started to climb the mountain. Tutaresh had not yet reached the top when Soseruquo cried, "I am coming! Hold yourself well!" He struck his horse, and a great clangor rolled down the hillside from the handbells. Then, as he rushed down on Tutaresh, the other's horse panicked and tried to bolt. Tutaresh grew furious at his horse and pulled mightily on its reins, trying to make it turn about, but he pulled so hard that he broke its neck and both fell down together.

When Soseruquo saw Tutaresh lying on the ground, he rode down on him to strike him, but from where he lay on the ground Tutaresh struck at Soseruquo and cut off his two legs at the thighs. Soseruquo screamed in pain but then said, "This does not count. If you are a hero, then we will fight with the discus."

"Very well!" replied Tutaresh, whereupon he struck at Soseruquo with his discus. Soseruquo struck the discus with his head and deflected it.

Then Soseruquo said, "Now I shall send it back, and you must deflect it with your head!" and he hurled it at Tutaresh.

When Tutaresh tried to deflect the discus with his head as Soseruquo had done, the discus cleaved his head into two parts and he fell over dead.

Some nearby Narts had seen what they did and how they fought. They greatly feared both Tutaresh and Soseruquo. Soseruquo had killed many Narts, and for that reason they were all his enemies. They had seen from afar what had happened to the two and so approached the hill. They found Soseruquo still clinging to life, his legs severed. They seized him and dropped him into a deep cavern at the base of Mount Haram. Then they placed stones over the cavern's entrance. Soseruquo screamed loudly and long, and his voice could be heard issuing from that cavern for years. After a while his screaming finally died down inside the cavern.[10]

This is how it happened: the manner of Soseruquo's birth, the way of his heroic deeds, and finally the manner of his death.

From Dumézil, 1960c, "Récits oubykh, IV," "Sawsereqwa," a Kabardian tale in Ubykh, pp. 432–48, teller Tevfik Esenç.

⊘ Not only is this saga an account of Soseruquo's birth and life, but it also serves as a cautionary tale: the scorning of the love-struck woman by the overly brutal hero (see also Abaza saga 64, where Soseruquo passes up a lovely maiden and so meets his doom). Bardanuquo, as with his Circassian counterpart, Shebatinuquo (see sagas 11 and 12 in the Circassian section), confuses brutality with valor. The Ubykh form of the name points to an original * / bartinuquo /. This is an enlarged version of the encounter between Sawseruquo and Totaresh (saga 24), Totrash / Sotrash (saga 60), bringing in Bardanuquo as a brother to the latter. Tutaresh's glittering mustache is reminiscent of the golden jaws of the hero Indra, of the Rig-Veda of Ancient India (see saga 24, note 20). The encounter between Sosruquo and the sleeping Tutaresh is closely parallel to that between the two Russian heroes Ilya Muromets and Svyatiogor, who is riding along asleep on his horse (Bailey and Ivanova 1998, 16–17).

In a variant of this story (Dumézil [1931], story 12, pp. 167–70, and revised in 1959a, pp. 64–65; Hadaghatl'a [1969], 2:146–47), Soseruquo has an amicable rivalry with a giant named Sofu, characterized as having manly power, Ubykh / tə́t-x̌°a / 'man-power'. His name is derived from the Circassian / śaawa-x̌°ə(-ž̌') / 'page.boy-white(-color)', and this figure relates to such white-colored forms as the Germanic Wodan and Hindu Shiva. They habitually wrestle, trying to tear each other's clothes off, perhaps as a form of humiliation, but matters turn deadly when Sofu drives Soseruquo seven spans into the ground with a blow from the back or spine of his one-sided sword and then tries to behead him. Soseruquo seeks and is granted a reprieve, saying that it is their day to talk, not to ruin their friendship (!) (note the odd sharing behavior of the two enemies in Abkhaz saga 84), and that they should meet again on Haram Hill, Ubykh / haram /. Upon his return to his mother, he refuses to tell her what happened, though she sees that something is wrong, since he is covered in dust. Instead, his horse tells all: "This night feed me well with sweetened and salted feed. Please, on my tail attach handbells. Tomorrow I shall bring back for you the head of our enemy. I shall return your son's honor." The tale unfolds as this one does: Soseruquo arrives early and casts a fog atop the mountain. Sofu's horse is injured by its rider when it tries to flee the sound of Soseruquo's bells, having its neck broken in Dumézil's versions, and having its lips an jaws torn in that of Hadaghatl'a. Sofu is cut down, despite his pleas for a reprieve, while struggling to raise his injured mount. Sofu's horse is enlisted to return to Satanaya, called "the little woman," bearing Sofu's headless body, and it uses its hoof to implicate Soseruquo, who bears Sofu's head.

---

[1] This tower house is a "raised house" (/ za-c°əya-q'áśa-q'a / 'one-house-raise-past') and suggests the tower houses once commonly found in the Caucasian highlands.

^{2} This miraculous state suggests that the infant owes some of his parentage not merely to Sawsna and Satanaya but also to Tlepsh's divine and fiery intervention. Like Tlepsh's metalwork, the infant is afire and must be quenched and tempered. The Ubykh locution (/á-mӡˀa ø-fá-tˀ°ə-gˀə ø-lá-tˀ°-q'a / 'is the-fire it-down-fall-and it-there-be-past') means that the fire has descended into the infant from the heavens, much like a thunderbolt.

^{3} *Soseruquo* may originally have meant "son of Sosna" (see the end comment in saga 60). Ubykh preserves a "long" pronunciation of this name, with four syllables, / sǫwsərəqˀ°a / [sosərǔquo].

^{4} The cup is supposed to be passed around, but Soseruquo is counting on Bardanuquo's arrogance and expects him to hog the cup.

^{5} See saga 84 n. 4. This is literally a "fiery face," like that of the Baltic god of thunder and lightning, in Lithuanian Perkúnas (Puhvel 1987, 224).

^{6} Soseruquo is a trickster figure with shape-changing powers.

^{7} The demon bird (see Vogt 1963, 236), Ubykh / ӡəmbəkˀ-γ°ənd°ə́ / 'Zhembik-bird', adds a touch of supernatural foreboding, which, while rare in the Circassian and Ubykh Nart sagas, is common in those of the Abkhaz and Abazas.

^{8} "Narts' day" (/ nart-n-a γa-mˣˀa / 'Nart-obl-pl their-day') is an obscure reference to some sort of holiday, perhaps originally reserved for battle, since in Iranian it would have meant "heroes' day."

^{9} The Northwest Caucasian people have a seven-day week, and Saturday is the original Sabbath. The Abkhaz and Abaza days show an old root for *day* / -ša / (now / mša /, built on the same root, or / čnə / 'day') and the remains of an original system of counting, much as in Russian, where Tuesday, Wednesday, Thursday, and Friday are clearly derived from "second," "third," "fourth," and "fifth," respectively.

	West Circassian	Kabardian	Ubykh	Abaza	Abkhaz (Bzyb)
Monday	bλəpˋa	bλəśḥa	wətˀ°afą́q'a	šˀaxˢa	aśˀ°axˢə́
Tuesday	γ°əbӡˢ	γ°əbž	átˋq'ˀ°amˣ°a	ʕˀaša	ayˀˀáša
Wednesday	baraskaźəy	baraźəy	bráskˢa	xaša	áxaša
Thursday	mafakˋ°	maˣˀakˀ°	wətˀ°ákˋ°ačˢa	pšˢaša	apšˢaša
Friday	baraskašˣˀ°a	maraym	áśˢˣa	xˀ°aša	axˀ°aša
Saturday	šambatˋ	śabat	śabá	sabša	asábša
Sunday	tḥaawəmaafa	tḥamaaˣa	məˣˀ°áməˣ	mčaša	amčə́śša

Tuesday was clearly the second day in Ubykh, Abaza, and Abkhaz, and Abaza and Abkhaz show that Wednesday, Thursday, and Friday were third, fourth, and fifth. Ubykh retains this sense only for Friday. West Circassian has 'seven-nose', or "tip of the seven," for Monday, and Kabardian has 'seven-head', both indicating the start of the week. Thursday is "middle day," with the forms pointing to an original * / maaˣˀ°a-kˀ°ə / 'day-middle, core'. In Ubykh / wətˀ°á / may have originally meant "week" (now / məˣˀá-a-γa / 'day-conn-locus'), so that Monday is / wətˀ°a-fá-a-q'a / 'week-sever-conn-cut' (compare / -fá-q'-/ - 'sever-cut', "to strike" but also "to set a day for something"), and Thursday / wətˀ°á-k'°ač'a / is 'week-tail', "the trailing part of the week." Both Circassian and Ubykh suggest an original system wherein Thursday, perhaps also originally the fourth day, also denoted the halfway point of the week.

Abkhaz also shows a name for Thursday, / mš-pq'a /, which means "day-cut," with "cut" here referring to sacrifices of animals (Akaba 1984, 73) [KT], hence the cognate verb in Ubykh with its added sense of "to set a day for something" (namely, a sacrifice).

[10] Here the saga ties into an old topography myth accounting for the roar of an underground river at the base of a mountain.

SAGA 87 ☙ *Another Birth of Soseruquo*

Others say that long ago in Circassia, in the land of the Adyghey, there was a clan, the Nart tribe. The Narts had a cowherd. He grazed his cows on a mountainside.

There was also a maiden from among the Narts called Satanaya. A river flowed past the base of the mountain on which the Nart herdsman stood. The maiden would go to that river to wash her clothes.

One time, from where he stood, the herdsman saw something wrapped in a rag floating down the river. He called to Satanaya and said, "O Satanaya, the river is bringing something! You should pull it out of the water."

When Satanaya scanned the water's edge, she saw a small sack wrapped in a rag by the riverbank. She pulled it out. The maiden knew what was inside. As quickly as possible she stuck it underneath where the double fold is, under her belly's navel.[1] When nine months had passed, a soul entered into it and it became a baby boy.

The child possessed both beauty and goodness. He grew up and was called Soseruquo. They said that he grew to be a very manly hero among the Narts, but he made many enemies and they pursued him by day and night. His enemies had killed his grandfather.[2]

One day his enemies caught up with him, and they fought with the discus, the "returning wheel." He was grievously wounded. Some of his friends found him and carried him back to his house. They went to find someone to care for and bandage his wound. They asked him whom they might seek and he said, "You all go ask my mother. She will know best."

They went and told her everything, and she said, "Make brine and pour it into a tub. Then set him down in the brine."

"That is impossible!" they replied. "It will harm him."

"What do you take me for? Do as I said!" she commanded, and so they did just as she had said and set him in a tub of brine.

As the brine began to sting, he started to sing a song:

> Two friends love one another.
> In the morning the rose sweetens your heart.
> The warm rain makes the meadows fertile.
> If the yeast is good, it will give the beer strength.
> If the wife is good, she has no price.
> What can a noble virgin sew?
> What harm is there if the shoe is narrow?
> He who does the deed does not bear the praise.
> What harm is there if the pigs do not grind what they eat?
> What is goat hair good for?
> In addition, would you count the wheat?[3]

When several days had passed and he had emerged from the brine, he sent his mother, Satanaya, back to her house. He set her down in a carriage in which he had placed rings of thorns on the four walls.[4] When the carriage bounced along, the thorns kept sticking into her skin. So in this fashion she returned to her own house.

An Ubykh rendering of an Abadzakh West Circassian tale, from Dumézil 1931, story 5, pp. 136–41, teller Hikmet bey of Kirk Pinar after Chichit Ömer of Yanik.

⊘ This saga is an odd variant of the usual conception of Sawseruquo / Sosruquo. The odd reprisal of the thorn-lined carriage may have some link to the use of the root / k°ə / 'cart' to refer to maidens in saga 12 (Circassian) and saga 89 (Ubykh).

[1] This is a euphemism for female genitalia. Satanaya is making herself pregnant with this water-born wayward "seed."

[2] This scrap of pedigree merely serves to reinforce the euphemistic nature of Satanaya's pregnancy.

[3] This song is a list of what seems to be Ubykh adages, some of which remain unclear. The first line may suggest that homosexuality, otherwise scorned throughout the Caucasus, is in some sense natural. This might be in accord with Soseruquo's own marginal status. The fourth relates to the belief that a beer's intoxicating power arises directly from its yeast or grain source. The fifth affirms that a good wife is priceless, literally without bride-price. The sixth hints that a highborn bride will not be adept at household skills. The eighth claims that credit for a good deed is rarely assigned to the one deserving it, a bleak view of

human affairs frequently assumed in warrior cultures. The ninth reflects older pagan values by questioning the Muslim interdiction against eating pork, the flesh of a ruminant that does not chew its cud. The tenth suggests that some things are utterly useless, and the eleventh suggests that some efforts are futile.

[4] Dumézil (1943, 98 n) remarks that the Circassians view these as being wild rose thorns (Satanaya's iconic flower), placed in two circles inside the carriage, one high and one low. Even though she has cured Soseruquo, he takes revenge on her for her callous disregard of his suffering. One might note that both Satanaya and the Ancient Greek Aphrodite share parallels not only as fertility figures who mate with a shepherd but, as this saga shows, as figures who know how to treat combat wounds.

SAGA 88 ⟋ *The Death of Soseruquo*

In the time of the Narts there was a man of short stature whom they called Soseruquo. This man was very clever, and when he wished, he could strike fear into the Narts by changing his form. As he wished, he could change himself into a wild animal, a shoe lying in the road, or a sack, and when in distress he could conjure up a fog[1] and then strike the Narts and kill them. Because he was hidden in the fog, the Narts could not see him and were unable to strike back and kill him.

The venerable Saquuna,[2] mother of the Narts, was very wise. One day the Narts said to her, "If we do not kill Soseruquo, he will not allow us to live. Tell us how we may destroy him. If we succeed in killing him, then we will be free and will survive."

Their mother said to them, "If it is so that you have not been able to kill him, then fetch the iron discus, stand on the hill above his house, and call to Soseruquo. As he comes out of the house, yell to him and say, 'We will throw the iron discus. If you are a hero, then use your fist to hit it and send it back up!' and then let loose the discus."

As their mother had said, the Narts went to the top of the hill and threw the iron discus down on Soseruquo, but he simply hit it with his fist and sent it hurtling back toward them.

The Narts went to their mother again. "He threw back the iron discus. What should we do?"

Their mother said, "If that is so, then call again to Soseruquo and say,

'Once more we will let loose the iron discus. Once again, if you are a hero, hit it with your elbow and send it back!'"

Doing just as their mother had said, the Narts let fly the iron discus, but Soseruquo hit it with his elbow and sent it hurtling back at them.

The Narts went to their mother one last time and said to her, "Alas! We cannot destroy him. Whatever we commanded, he did. If we do not kill him, we will no longer be able to live."

Their mother said to them, "If it is indeed true that you will no longer be able to survive, then I must tell you that there are no bones in Soseruquo's thighs. The flesh there will not be able to withstand the iron discus. It will cut off his thighs and he will die. Then you will be saved."

The Narts said to Soseruquo, "Strike it with your thighs and send the discus back up!" Then they let fly the discus. Soseruquo tried to stop it with his thighs, but it cut through them.

When that happened, Soseruquo cried out and said, "Those wild beasts who dwell in the mountain forests and would eat meat, now let them come hither and eat meat!"

First came the wolf. To eat of Soseruquo's flesh, however, was more than the wolf could bring himself to do. He did not eat it but rather gathered it together. As the wolf was about to withdraw, Soseruquo said to him, "Wherever you go, may your heart be like my heart! May they see you as they see me, and may those who see you fear you! When you turn back to go, may your heart grow as brave as a dog's heart!" The wolf then turned back into the forest.

After him came the hare. He too could not eat of Soseruquo's flesh and also gathered it back together. Full of compassion for Soseruquo, the hare stopped and stood by him. Then Soseruquo said, "As I fooled the people whom I encountered and escaped from them, may you become such so as to escape the clutches of those who pursue you!" Thereupon the hare returned to the forest.

All the wild animals of the forest came, one after another. Not one among them ate of his flesh. All took pity on him and withdrew from him. At the very end came the vulture. He took hold of Soseruquo's thighs and began to eat away at the meat.

Then Soseruquo grew furious and cursed the vulture. "When you are about to lay eggs, may you lay them in the remote reaches of the mountain forests, where no man can go. May you lay your eggs through your mouth! May Almighty God ensure that when it is time for your eggs to begin hatching, your little ones hatch while your breast is still on top of them! When hatched, may each of your little ones stab at your two eyes and eat them!"

The vulture flew into the sky. This then was the manner of Soseruquo's death.

From Dumézil 1957, 1–4, teller, Hüseyin Çavuş.

     ◐ This is an animal fable, much like saga 3 (Circassian). See also saga 64.

[1] Conjuring up a fog must be a vestigial power of the storm god; perhaps it refers to a cloud from which lightning bolts would issue. This is a good example of an odd, almost nonsensical detail that must reflect an ancient and coherent complex of imagery.

[2] *Saquuna* is the native Northwest Caucasian form of *Satanaya*, / śa-q°ə-na /, Circassian / śa-q°ə-na / both 'hundred-son-mother', "mother of (a) hundred son(s)."

Saga 89 ◐ *Yarichkhaw*

Long ago, in the time of the Narts, there was a noble lady of the Narts called Satanaya. Her husband had gone off to battle and had been killed. He left behind a small child named Yarichkhaw. Satanaya nourished that child and reared him by herself.

When he was twenty years old and quite robust, he was walking along a road and saw sitting there two small children playing with one another. He went up to them and knocked their heads together. The children became angry. "You may know how to knock our heads together, but you don't even know how to use the weapons your father left behind for you. Your mother has them and is hiding them," the small ones said to him. "You do not even know how to use those things that were left behind by your father! Those which your mother keeps hidden from you!"

Yarichkhaw rushed back home and said to his mother, "What are those things that were left by my father and that you are hiding from me? Why won't you give them to me?"

His mother replied, "Alas, my son! You are still small and would not be able to wield them."

When he continued to pester her, she said, "If that is the way you are going to be, then follow me!" She went into the horse stable and dug in the ground. She showed him the horse she had hidden from him by burying it underground. Then she also gave him the sword and lance that his father had left behind.

Yarichkhaw led the horse out and draped a saddle over it. Then he took his weapons, mounted the horse, and rode out into the steppe. Seven times he rode up into the sky and back down again. The horse bucked and kicked, but it could not throw Yarichkhaw off. Then he returned to his house and said, "Mother! Is there any man in this land more heroic than I am?"

His mother said, "Alas, my son, there are the seven Nart brothers.[1] They could drown you in their spit or smother you with their breath!"

Then the youth replied, "Oh, God! If I don't go near them, it won't happen, will it? So I shall go to them straightaway!" As he said that, he mounted his horse and rode off to encounter the seven Nart brothers.

He entered the domain of the seven Nart brothers, which was seven days' ride from his home. From afar they saw him. "Some horseman is approaching very rapidly!" they said.

Soon one of their servants said, "A horseman approaches!" Then they said, "Oh, God, he has arrived!" He entered their courtyard, and the seven brothers came out to welcome him. He dismounted and thrust his lance into the ground.

"Welcome!" they said. "We shall take the lance out of the ground." Then the seven brothers pulled on it, but try as they might they could not pull it out.

"May he who called you heroes hold a handful of your shit!" sneered Yarichkhaw, and then he pulled the lance out of the ground and entered their house.

They offered him a chair. "Please have a seat," they said, but when he sat down the chair broke and sank into the earth to a depth of seven spans. When they saw this, they offered him a place on the floor and he sat. Their sister emerged. She was called Gundba the Beautiful. She was unique. Up and down, whatever was to be done, she did for him. The brothers said to themselves, "Oh, God! Here is a man who has come to devour us. We will not escape from him."

When evening came they asked him, "Our guest, what will you eat? What will you drink?"

"As my meal after the journey, a cow that has been barren for seven years; this will be my portion along with my bread. Seven cauldrons full to the brim will be my portion of porridge. The cow's skin filled with millet beer will be my drink," he said.

"That is no problem!" they replied and they sent for what he had asked. First they found the barren cow, killed it, and roasted it. Then they made the porridge and beer. When they brought them in and set them before him, he began to eat. Fifteen days he sat there. Bite after bite he ate the meat, and then he started on the porridge. When all was gone, he washed it down with the beer.

"Oh, God, we will never be able to escape from this man!" they thought. Then while sitting with him, they said, "O our guest, we would like to eat with you the meat of a game animal. Tomorrow we shall leave you and go to hunt some big game."

"Fine!" he replied. "I shall await your return here."

So the next morning the brothers set off for the hunt and traveled up into the mountain forests and meadows. Having gone some distance, they encountered a wild boar. They struck at it and wounded it. The boar turned on them and chased them into the top of a knotted tree. Whenever they tried to come down, the boar would rush at them. They were stranded, unable to return, and they remained in the tree.

A day passed and they had not returned. Yarichkhaw asked himself, "Has something happened to them?" and so he set off to track them. After a while he heard a voice.

"Alas, do not draw nearer!" it said. "There is a wild boar beneath us and it will devour you!"

"Where is it?" he called, and then he saw the boar milling around beneath the knotted tree. He unsheathed his sword and approached it. When it rushed at him, he smote it and cut its head off.

"You can come down now," he called to them. "May he who called you heroes hold a handful of your shit!" Then he helped them down. Together they returned to their house, carrying the boar on their backs.

Yarichkhaw rested for several days and then said, "Well, now I shall return home."

"O our guest," they said to him, "if it is so that you must leave, then what thing would you like as a parting gift? What object? What food?"

"I don't want just anything, neither gifts nor provisions," he replied. "I want your sister, Gundba the Beautiful. If you will give me your sister in marriage, then I shall return with her as my bride."

"Alas! We would gladly give her to you, but we have already taken bride money for her," they replied. "We have already betrothed her to one called Quazherpish. Today Quazherpish will come for her with his bridal party, and he will not allow us to survive if we gave her to you instead."

"I shall deal with him myself then," he said to them.

Since they feared him, they led their sister out to him and set her on the horse behind him. Then they took a sheepskin cloak, a *burka,* and placed it over them so that she was hidden. Then Yarichkhaw set off on the road.

While returning home, he came upon Quazherpish traveling along the road with his wedding party. Yarichkhaw asked him, "Where are you bound?"

"I go to wed Gundba the Beautiful, the sister of the seven Nart brothers," he replied. "She has been betrothed to me, and I shall bring her back as my bride."

Yarichkhaw said, "If you saw her ring, would you recognize it?"

"Oh, God, I would recognize it even if I saw it from a distance of seven days' journey."

When Quazherpish said this, Yarichkhaw drew Gundba's arm out through the opening in the cloak from beneath his cloak and showed Quazherpish the ring on her hand.

"Having killed me in this way, where will you go to escape my vengeance?" cried Quazherpish. "Where will you go to escape my vengeance?"

"If you seek revenge," replied Yarichkhaw, "then as the eldest the right of the first blow belongs to you!"

Then Quazherpish shot an arrow and slashed Yarichkhaw's thigh and foot. When Yarichkhaw unleashed his arrow, he wounded half of Quazherpish's head. In this fashion they fought for seven years. His mother, Satanaya, would say as each year passed, "O God, turn them to stone where they stand!" Thus she prayed, and the two turned to stone where they stood at the end of the seventh year.

Yarichkhaw remained seated on his horse with Gundba the Beautiful behind him and an infant in her arms. Quazherpish became a great open cavern that loomed over them.

They say when the day comes that Yarichkhaw on his horse sinks completely underneath the ground, the end of humankind will be at hand. My grandfather recounted to me the following: "We passed underneath the Yarichkhaw formation. Twenty years later we chanced to pass by it again. It had subsided into the earth to the point where we were unable to pass underneath it again."

After they died, Yarichkhaw's mother herself, Satanaya, composed a song in grief and pity for her son.

You remained as the last of the Nart race.
I made you grow big by always caressing you.

My unique son, my Yarichkhaw.
Poor Satanay ahaha, no! no! Sarasana Satanay, ahahaha.

Seated upon your horse I made you go out.
I hung down from you your sword and your lance.
Because of Gundba the Beautiful you became a corpse.
Poor Satanay ahaha, no! no! Sarasana Satanay, ahahaha.

I hung down from you your sword and your lance.
You remained the last of the Nart race.
My unique son, my Yarichkhaw.
Poor Satanay ahaha, no! no! Sarasana Satanay, ahahaha.

Her unique son was killed.
She tore again and again her hair.
She beat again and again on her two thighs.
Poor Satanay ahaha, no! no! Sarasana Satanay, ahahaha.

From Dumézil, 1955, tale 6, pp. 34–39; 1960b, p. 74; and Vogt 1963, "Les Nartes," story 10, pp. 58–63, teller Tevfik Esenç.

◐ More elaborate versions of this tale, with its closing doomsday theme, are found in the Abkhaz sagas of Khozhorpas and Narjkhyaw, sagas 83 and 84.

Yarichkhaw (Narjkhyaw) is a defective doublet of Sawseruquo, chiefly lacking his trickster nature and having more of a savage one [KT].

The Ubykh names look particularly old, / yárəč̣ˀχ̣aw/ and /q°ążarpə́š/, /q°azarpə́šˀ/, but their etymologies remain unclear. The latter is supposed to refer to the rhododendron. Dumézil (1960b, 75 n) traces the Ubykh / yarəč̣ˀχ̣aw/ back to the Abkhaz variant / yarč̣ˀχ̣aw/, itself supposedly from Ossetian / aræxʒaw/ ← ? / aræx-ʒaw(ma)/ 'many-things' (Abaev 1996, 59, 389–90), and / q°ążarpəš/ (ignoring the other form from Vogt) back to Ossetian / xožirpəs/ 'rhododendron boy', but the latter has no etymology within Ossetian, 'rhododendron boy' being literally in Ossetian / fugæ-læppu/ (Iron dialect) or / fugæ-biccəw/ (Digoron dialect). Given the Abkhazian variant / narǯˀχ̣ˀáw/, the Ossetian does not look like the source for the first name. This name cannot be separated from its Circassian forms, / yarəš̌ˀˀáq°a(-χ̣áaf)/, / yaš̌ˀˀarə́q°a/, and / yarəš̌ˀˀq̇ˀáw-χ̣áaf/ (/χ̣aafa/ 'brave'), with perhaps the truncated form / ʔahrə́š̌ˀˀ/ (see saga 34 n. 7).

The Abkhaz form of the second, / x°až̌°árpəs/, does resemble the Ossetian, but the Abaza / q̄°əž̌°ə arpəs / seems to point to an original initial stop and a compound name (see saga 47, n. 1). From this and the complex Ubykh form, the source looks as though it may have been more like */qoži arpəś/ or */qoži orpəś/, perhaps Iranian in origin but not Ossetian.

Gundba the Beautiful, /g°ə́nd°ə a-nə́x̣°a/, however, is clearly linked to the Circassian /ak°áanda/, both pointing to an original */(a-)k°ənda/, linked to the root /k°ə/ 'cart'; see the Circassian saga 12.

[1] Both Dumézil (1955, 1960b) and Vogt (1963) refer to these brothers as Yarichkhaw's maternal uncles, which would make Gundba the Beautiful his aunt.

SAGA 90 ∽ Three Brothers, Their Sister, and a Nart

In olden times there were three brothers who had a unique sister. They nourished this sister of theirs with the marrow of roe deer. They called her the exquisite maiden. The Narts heard of this girl, and a certain Nart came and abducted this unique maiden.

The three brothers and their mother were left behind. They pondered their plight, not knowing what to do, until the eldest brother put on his armor and set off to find his sister. He roamed about until he finally saw her inside the house of a Nart.

His sister's heart broke when she saw him. "Why did you come? Even if I had died, why should you get yourself killed?"

"My heart could not bear it," he replied. "It does not matter to me if I die." After he said this, they sat talking together for a while, whereupon a monkey boy[1] came in. Because of the hospitality that had to be shown to a guest, it said "Welcome!" and then went out again.

Not much time passed when the Nart himself entered. "Welcome!" he said and seized the brother's hand in such a grip that it was crushed to powder. The brother fell over dead. Now only two brothers and the mother remained.

A year passed and the middle brother's heart was sorely grieved. As his eldest brother had done, he put on his armor and set off to find his brother and sister. After traveling for a long time, he saw his sister in a Nart's house, just as his brother had done.

His sister said, "Why did you come? The Nart killed our eldest brother. Why did you come?"

"What should I have done?" he replied. "I shall meet my death where my brother met his."

Again the monkey boy entered and said "Welcome!" and then went back out. Soon after, the Nart came and said "Welcome!" Then he seized the brother's hand, and, just as with the first, he crushed it into powder and the second brother fell down dead. Their sister sat brooding and weeping day and night.

One day the youngest brother said to his mother, "I have gotten very dirty. Set some hot water to boil for me. I shall wash myself."

His mother boiled the water and then said, "If you want to wash yourself, then wash yourself!"

"Please hand the water to me!" he replied. As his mother extended her hand, he grabbed it and thrust it into the boiling water.

"Why are you scalding my hand?" she cried.

"Show me right now my father's armor and weapons, his horse, and whatever else he left behind for me!" he demanded.

"Don't scald my hand! I shall show you all straightaway!" she cried, and he released her hand from the water.

His mother opened a door leading underground and showed him his father's legacy: his armor, weapons, and horse. He donned the armor, strapped on the weapons, mounted the horse, and set off.

He traveled far, as had his brothers, until he rode into the courtyard of the Nart.

Crying bitterly, his sister ran out to meet him. "Why did you come? Will you make these Narts kill every last one of us?" she said, weeping. Then she remembered the dictates of hospitality and said to her brother, "Come in!"

After she had spoken, he said to her, "Please do not grieve so over these things. Tell me, what is there that is so heavy that this Nart will not be able to lift?"

She showed him a huge chunk of iron lying in the courtyard and next to it the trunk of a giant tree that the Narts had brought in. Then her brother seized the chunk of iron with one hand and flung it far away. Then with two hands he seized the tree trunk and threw it across the yard.

When she saw this she said, "God has looked upon us again! You will be able to do something."

Then he gathered all the wood he could find lying about the courtyard and filled up the fire trench[2] inside the house. He kindled it and made a huge fire. He took some iron spits that were in the house and set them in the fire so that their points were heated.

When they had begun to glow red, the monkey boy came and said "Welcome!" As the monkey boy turned around to leave, the youngest brother seized him and flung him through the middle of the window. He landed with such force outside that he died. He was lying on the ground when the Nart returned. He looked at the monkey boy and saw that he was dead. Then he entered the house and said "Welcome!" He took the brother's hand, but this time he seized a mighty hand, not like the ones before. They began to grapple with one another, and holding on to one another, they tumbled outside.

In the time of the Narts, when people wrestled, they would drive one another into the ground like posts. The Nart lifted the maiden's brother and brought him down against the earth in order to drive him into the ground, but he was unable to drive him into it.

Then the maiden's brother lifted the Nart, and when he slammed him down, he drove him into the ground to his knees. He pulled him out and lifted him again, and again he slammed him down, this time driving him into the ground to his belly, up to his belt. Once again he pulled him out and lifted him, and again he slammed him into the ground, this time to his neck. Then the brother took off his own belt and bound the Nart's two hands with it. He went into the house and seized the red-hot spits. Then he brought them out and thrust them into the Nart's eyes, his nostrils, and his mouth, and so burned him. In this fashion he killed the Nart.

Afterward, he set his sister on the horse and loaded her baggage on it. Then he returned home. When they drew nigh their mother, he set his sister back down. They rejoiced in one another and sang a lament.

This tale was told by Kemal Effendi of Kirk Pinar as recorded in Dumézil (1931), story 2, pp. 115–23, and then reworked in his 1959 Études oubykhs, *52–54, according to Tevfik Esenç.*

🖎 The lament in this saga has not survived. The tale shows strong parallels with the preceding one of Yarichkhaw, particularly the theme of the young hero tormenting his mother in order to obtain his father's legacy. In the abduction of the maiden, it shows strong parallels with the Circassian tale of the Life-Giving Princess (Circassian saga 3).

Most striking, however, is its resolution of the odd but typically ambiguous moral stance toward the Narts into one of outright enmity. Dumézil interpreted this in the following way: "This is the only tale which gives the accurate image of an Ubykh Nart, who is not a hero in the Circassian or Ossetian manner, but is more like the primitive and barbarous giants of the type of the *devs* or 'yeniž' [= Ubykh

/ yanɜ́ż / '(cyclopean) giant']" (1931, p. 123). Dumézil may well have been correct in seeing an ancient retention of Northwest Caucasian enmity toward the Iranian archetypal hero embodied in the Nart. Certainly the villainous aspect of the Narts that runs through so much of the tradition, the odd enmity between so many of the heroes and the rest of the Narts, may reflect ancient ethnic animosities.

Given the envy that sets the rank and file against the hero, however, as, for example, in the Rig-Veda between Indra and his Maruts, or in Greek between Achilles and the rest of the Achaeans, or even in Germanic between Sigurd and his in-laws (Magnusson and Morris 1980, 112–16), such a grim moral perspective on the Narts may be abetted by separate and ancient roots within Indo-Iranian lore itself. The manner of wrestling has parallels in Central Asian lore, particularly that of the Hungarians, and seems to be of much later origin.

[1] The original tale has / za-mamun-nayš°-g°ara / 'a-monkey-boy-certain', which Tevfik Esenç (Dumézil 1959a, 53 n. 4) considered strange and replaced with / za-mamuna-š°-g°ara / 'a-monkey-small-certain'. This may originally have represented a juvenile wild man, in light of the account of a wild man (Colarusso 1980) given in the following saga.

[2] The Ubykh has / məʒˠá-x̌°a-gˠəʒa / 'fire-long-big', where / -x̌°a- / is used only with "fire" and / lák'°əma / "ear" (as with a donkey). It may be cognate with proto-Circassian */ zaʁ°a / 'straight, even' (Kuipers 1975, 62, §88). This suggests a fire trench of the sort attested in *Beowulf* and used by the pagan Germanic peoples. This makes sense in that the Ubykh actually reads that "he filled the inside of the house" with wood but then sat in it awaiting the Nart. The fire trench has clearly been forgotten, but the notion of filling a large portion of the house to make a fire has not.

SAGA 91 ෨ *The Adventure of Marchan Shaghy*

Long ago there was a hunter called Marchan Shaghy.[1] He killed a buck when he was in the mountain forests.[2] Evening having fallen, he spent the night on the mountain. He lit a fire and was roasting the inner organs[3] when he heard a voice. He climbed into a nearby tree and hid himself, taking with him the innards he had been roasting. He draped his cloak over another old tree.

A wild man, covered all over with hair, approached. The wild man looked around. He mistook the tree on which the cloak was draped for a man and threw himself on it.[4] The hero, seeing this from where he was sitting in the tree, primed his pistol and shot at the wild man. The wild man caught fire and went off, running into the woods.

After this, Marchan Shaghy returned to his fire, roasted the organs, and ate them. He said to himself, "In the morning I shall find this creature whom I have wounded, wherever he may have gone to."

At dawn he set off after him. He traveled far and wide and came upon a beautiful small plain. When he looked all around, he heard a voice saying, "What did you come here to do?"

When he looked all around again, he saw a giant who had been tied down. The bound giant called to him, "Come here! Bring me a digging stick[5] made from the plant that blooms first but brings forth fruit last."

Marchan Shaghy went and brought back with him other sorts of digging sticks for the giant.

"These won't do," the giant said.

Then he set out again and began to cut off part of a dogwood. Another voice said, "You must not cut this off!" He looked all around but could not see who had said this. He returned to the giant and said, "I did not find it."

"If you found it and did not bring it back to me, then may God turn you to stone right where you stand!" roared the giant. "How are things in this land?" the giant went on. "Do the sheep bring forth lambs? Do the honeybees multiply this year?"

Marchan Shaghy replied, "They are reproducing, but it will be neither much nor little. Why do you ask?"[6]

"If I had gotten hold of the digging stick, I would have dug up my sword," the giant replied. "Then it would have been possible for me to do that which I promised."

Marchan Shaghy knew that if the giant found his sword, it would mean the country's destruction. The giant was not free.

If he had gotten back his sword, he would have done whatever he wanted, and when that happened it would be the end of the world and the final doom of humankind.

From Dumézil 1955, tale 5, pp. 30–33, revised in 1960b, p. 74, tale 5, teller Tevfik Esenç from Haji Osman köy, Turkey.

👁 This tale is called "Un Prométhé oubykh," and it does recall variants of the giant atop the mountain, such as Circassian sagas 34–37. It is coupled, however, with an odd account of an encounter with a wild man of the Caucasus. For an account of such lore in the Caucasus, see Colarusso (1980). Generally such lore is nonmythical, the creature being known only to huntsmen, who consider it rare and dangerous.

[1] Ubykh / marčą́n šá(a)γə /. The Marshans, with 'sh' instead of 'ch', are the Abkhazian royal family.

[2] He is said to be on a / ɬaχá / 'montane forest' (Vogt 1963, 144), as opposed to a mountain pasture / səpqʸə́ /, which, when suffixed with / gʸəȝa / 'big', can also mean simply a "large (bare) mountain" (as opposed to / x̄ə-š°á / 'grazing-place', 'pasture' from / -x̄- / 'to graze').

[3] The organs are in Ubykh / c°a-gʸə-c°°ạba / 'skin-heart-liver', considered a delicacy (compare West Circassian / g°ə?aś°°ə?a /, a rhyming compound derived from */ g°ə-ś°°ə?a / 'heart-liver'). Georgian shows / gul-γviȝli / 'heart-liver', and the related Svan shows / q'wiža-i-gwi /, 'liver-and-heart', both with the sense of the "tastiest portion of meat" [KT]. These suggest, at the least, very old borrowings between Northwest Caucasian and South Caucasian, and they may even be ancient cognates between two language families that otherwise have diverged widely.

[4] Perhaps the wild man (/ ɬaχa-tə́t / 'montane.forest-man') mistakes the cloak for another of his kind, since it is a / č°ʸ́k'°a /, the shaggy and wide cloak made of sheep's wool, often called a *burka*.

[5] The term / γ̧ą́nca / now means "fishhook." Originally it must have been a curved digging tool. The (West) Circassian cognate / ḥaánc'a / means "wooden spade" (Kuipers 1975, 80, §113).

[6] The bound giant is an antifertility figure, a personification of nature's destructive forces. The hero appears to mollify him by his noncommittal answer to the question about the world's abundance.

SAGA 92 ◑ A Marvelous Sword

One of the Khanuquo[1] princes said, "I shall go where no man has been able to go before," and for three or four years he prepared for a great journey. Then he traveled on his horse, passing back and forth over countrysides and seas until finally he spotted an island in the sea. "I shall go to this island, where no one has set foot before," he said. So he cut across the water, came ashore, and climbed the island's summit.

He dismounted and began to look around. While exploring, he came upon a sword. He said to himself, "No man has been able to come here as

I have done. How then did it get here? If in fact no one has been here before, then this sword must be truly special!"

He prayed long and hard. Then he arose and carried the sword with him back to his home.

When he brought it back, the Khanuquos placed it inside a coffer. Once each year they would open it and gaze on the sword. It would let them know if there was going to be a war. The Khanuquos preserved that sword until the destruction of Circassia.[2]

From Dumézil 1931, story 16, pp. 175–77, revised in 1959a, story 16, p. 67. The teller was Ilyas bey of Yanik, Turkey, rendering a tale by Chichit Ömer.

This saga is an interesting addition to the beliefs that seem to have constituted the ancient Iranian cult of the sword (Littleton and Malcor 1994). It seems to have persisted in the Northwest Caucasus down to 1864, the year in which czarist forces defeated and then expelled most of the Circassians, Abazas, and Abkhaz and all of the Ubykhs.

[1] This name is derived from *khan* and must represent an old ruling family that may have traced its origins back to the Mongol Empire.

[2] The Ubykhs consider themselves / á-dəĝa / 'the-people', or Circassian, an interesting instance of ethnic unity crossing over a substantial language barrier. Similarly, the Svans consider themselves Georgians despite profound differences between their language and that of their remote kinsfolk to the south [KT].

BIBLIOGRAPHY ∽

ABBREVIATIONS USED IN THE TEXTS

GENEG   Hadaghatl'a Asker (/ḥadaɣaλ'a askar/) (in Russian, A. M.
Gadagatl'). 1967. *Geroičeskij épos Narty i ego genezis.* Krasnodar
knizhnoe izdatel'stvo, USSR.

Hadaghatl'a (year), vol. (number), saga (number)
Hadaghatl'a Asker (/ḥadaɣaλ'a askar/). 1968–71. *Nartxer*
(/nahrt-ha-r/) [The NARTS] (in various Circassian languages and
dialects). Vols. 1–7. Miyeqwap'e [Maikop], USSR: Adyghejskogo
Nauchno-Issledovatel'skij Institut.

M-S   Meremkulov, Vladimir, and Shota Salakaja. 1975. *Narter'a, Narty*
(/nart-rʕa/. Karachai-Cherkessia: Karachaevo-Cherkesskij
Nauchno-Issledovatel'skij Institut.

Abaev, V. I. 1990a. "O sobstvennyx imenax nartskogo éposa." In *Izbrannye trudy,*
by Gusalov, 243–60.

———. 1990b. "Nartovskij épos osetin." In *Izbrannye trudy,* by Gusalov, 142–242.

———. 1996. *Istoriko-étimologicheskij slovar' osetinskogo jazyka.* Vols. 1–6. 1958,
1973, 1979, and 1989. Reprint, Moscow: VIKOM Publishers.

Akaba, Lili Kh. 1984. *Istoricheskie korni arxaicheskix ritualov abxazov.* Sukhumi,
USSR: Alashara.

Aliev, A. E. 1994. *Nartla / Narty, Malkar-Karachaj Nart épos* (in Karachay-Malkar and
Russian). Moscow.

Allen, W. Sidney. 1965. "An Abaza Text." *Bedi kartlisa, revue de kartvélologie* 19–20:
159–72.

Arans, Olga R., and Christine R. Shea. 1994. "The Fall of Elpenor: Homeric Kirké
and the Folklore of the Caucasus." *Journal of Indo-European Studies* 22:
371–98.

Ardzinba, V. G. 1985. "Nartskij s'uzhet o rozhdenii geroya iz kamenija." In *Drevn-
jaja Anatolija,* edited by B. B. Piotrovskij, V. V. Ivanov, and V. G. Ardzinba, 128–
68. Moscow: Nauka.

———. 1988. "K istorii kul'ta zheleza i kuznechnogo remesla (pochitanie kuznicy
u abxazov)." In *Drevnij Vostok, étnokul'turnye svjazi,* edited by G. M. Bongard-
Levin and V. G. Ardzinba, 263–306. Moscow: Nauka.

Ascherson, Neal. 1995. *Black Sea*. New York: Hill and Wang.

Bachrach, Bernard S. 1973. *A History of the Alans in the West*. Minneapolis: University of Minnesota Press.

Baddeley, John F. 1969. *The Russian Conquest of the Caucasus*. 1908. Reprint, New York: Russell & Russell.

Bagov, P. M., ed. 1999. Adəĝɛzɛ psaλaλɛ / *Slovar' kabardino-cherkesskogo jazyka*. Moscow: Diroga.

Bailey, Harold Walter, Sir. 1959. "Iranian *Arya*- and *Daha*-." *Philological Society Transactions*: 71–115.

———. 1980. "Ossetic (Narta)." In *Traditions of Heroic and Epic Poetry*, edited by A. T. Hatto. Vol. 1, *The Traditions*. London: Modern Humanities Research Association.

Bailey, James, and Tatyana Ivanova. 1998. *An Anthology of Russian Folk Epics*. Armonk, N.Y.: M. E. Sharpe.

Benveniste, Emile. 1959. *Etudes sur la langue ossete*. Paris: Klincksieck.

———. 1973. *Indo-European Language and Society*. Translated by Elizabeth Palmer and edited by Jean Lallot. Coral Gables, Fl.: University of Miami Press.

Benveniste, Emile, and Louis Renou. 1934. *Vrta et Vrθragna, Etude de mythologie indo-iranienne*. Paris: Imprimerie Nationale.

Bergé, Adolf Petrovich, ed. 1866. *Sagen und Lieder des Tscherkessenvolks (von Shora Bekmursin Nogma)*. Leipzig: O.Wigand.

Berzeg, Sefer E. 1998. *Soçi'nin sürgündeki sahipleri Çerkes-Vubihlar*. Ankara: Kafkasya.

Bgazhba, Khukhut S. 1964. *Bzybskij dialekt abxazskogo jazyka*. Tbilisi: Publisher of the Georgian Academy of Sciences of the USSR.

Bielmeier, Roland. 1977. *Historische Untersuchung zum Erb- und Lehnwortschatzanteil im ossetischen Grundwortschatz*. Frankfurt am Main: Peter Lang.

Bjazyrty, Alyksandr. 1993. *Narty Tayræg'ty Istori* (in Ossetian, Nart narrative history). Dzæwdzhyx'æw (Vladikavkaz), North Ossetia-Alania, Russia: Ir Publishers.

Blanch, Lesley. 1960. *The Sabres of Paradise*. New York: Carroll and Graf Publishers.

Bremmer, Jan. 1976. "Avunculate and Fosterage." *Journal of Indo-European Studies* 4:65–78.

Brooks, Willis. 1995. "Russia's Conquest and Pacification of the Caucasus: Relocation Becomes a Pogrom in the Post-Crimean War Period." *Nationalities Papers* 23:675–86.

———. 1996. "The Politics of the Conquest of the Caucasus, 1855–1864." *Nationalities Papers* 24:649–60.

Buck, Carl Darling. 1933. *Comparative Grammar of Greek and Latin*. Chicago: University of Chicago Press.

Burkert, Walter. 1985. *Greek Religion*. Cambridge, Mass.: Harvard University Press.

Bzhedukh Hisa (/bźadəɣ° ʕəysa/). 1980. "Nart Tutaryšre šyntypšymre Jatxyd"

(/nahrtˤ tˤəwtˤahrəšˤʸra šˤʸəntˤəpšʸra yahtˤ̊əd/) (in Bzhedukh West Circassian, The tale of Nart Tutarish and the Prince of Shinte). *The Circassian Star* (New York) 3, no. 5:32–33.

Charachidzé, Georges. 1968. *Le système religieux de la géorgie paienne: Analyse structurale d'une civilization.* Paris: François Maspero.

———. 1986. *Promethé en la Caucase: Essai de mythologie contrastive.* Paris: Flammarion.

Chirikba, Viacheslav A. 1991. "On the Etymology of the Ethnonym /ápˢwa/ 'Abkhaz.'" *The Annual of the Society for the Study of Caucasia* 3:13–18. Columbus, Ohio: Slavica Publishers.

Colarusso, John. 1980. "A Wild Man of the Caucasus." In *Manlike Monsters on Trial, Early Records and Modern Evidence,* edited by M. Halpin and M. M. Ames, 255–64. Vancouver: University of British Columbia Press.

———. 1984a. "Epic, Nart: North Caucasian." In *The Modern Encyclopedia of Russian and Soviet Literature,* edited by H. Weber, 7:1–14. Gulf Breeze, Fl.: Academic International Press. Also in electronic form in *The Grolier™ Multimedia Encyclopedia.* 1995. Version 7.0.2.

———. 1984b. "Parallels between the Circassian Nart Sagas, the *Rg Veda,* and Germanic Mythology." In *South Asian Horizons.* Vol. 1, *Culture and Philosophy,* edited by V. Setty Pendakur, 1–28. Ottawa: Carleton University, Canadian Asian Studies Association.

———. 1988. "The Narts" and "The Blossom of Lady Satanaya (Hatiquoya West Circassian)" (a Nart saga). *Newsletter* (Kavkaz Cultural Center of California) 2, no. 6:6, 9.

———. 1989a. "The Woman of the Myths: The Satanaya Cycle." In *The Annual of the Society for the Study of Caucasia,* edited by Howard I. Aronson, 2:3–11.

———. 1989b. "Myths from the Forest of Circassia." *The World & I* (December): 644–51.

———. 1989c. "Prometheus among the Circassians." *The World & I* (March): 644–51.

———. 1991. "Circassian Repatriation." *The World & I* (November): 656–69.

———. 1992a. *A Grammar of the Kabardian Language.* Calgary, Alberta: University of Calgary Press.

———. 1992b. "How Many Consonants Does Ubykh Have?" In *Caucasian Perspectives,* edited by B. George Hewitt, 145–56. Munich: Lincom Europa.

———. 1994a. "Circassians." In *Encyclopedia of World Cultures,* by Friedrich and Diamond, 85–91.

———. 1994b. "Nahrt λəx̌ºəźər-λ'əbλan" (The Nart hero as knight). In *Nart éposymra,* by Gadagatl', 64–67.

———. 1994c. Foreword to *From Scythia to Camelot,* by C. Scott Littleton and Linda Malcor. New York: Garland Publishing.

————. 1994d. "Proto-Northwest Caucasian, or How to Crack a Very Hard Nut." *The Journal of Indo-European Studies* 22:1–35.

————. 1995. "Abkhazia." In *Central Asian Survey,* edited by B. George Hewitt and John Wright, 75–96. London: Hurst.

————. 1997a. "Circassians." In *Encyclopedia of American Immigrant Cultures,* edited by David Levinson. New York: Macmillan.

————. 1997b. "Phyletic Links between Proto-Indo-European and Proto-Northwest Caucasian." *The Journal of Indo-European Studies* 25:119–51.

————. 1998. "Dumézil and the Details: An Analysis of the Comparative Technique in Linguistics and Mythology." *Cosmos* 14:103–17.

Dalgat, U. B. 1972. *Geroicheskij épos Chechentsev i Ingushej.* Moscow: Nauka.

Davidson, H. R. Ellis. 1964. *Gods and Myths of Northern Europe.* New York: Penguin Books.

Davis-Kimball, Jeannine. 1997. "Sauro-Sarmatian Nomadic Women: New Gender Identities." *The Journal of Indo-European Studies* 25:327–43.

Delaney, Frank. 1994. *Legends of the Celts.* London: Harper Collins Publishers.

Dillmann, François-Xavier. 1979. "Georges Dumézil et la religion germanique: L'interprétation du dieu Odhinn." In *Georges Dumézil à la découverte des Indo-Européens,* edited by Jean-Claude Riviere, 157–86. Paris: Copernic.

Dirr, Adolf. 1920. *Kaukasischen Märchen.* Jena: E. Diederichs. English translation by Lucy Menzies. 1925. *Caucasian Folktales.* London and Toronto: J. M. Dent & Sons.

Dumézil, Georges. 1929. "Le dit de la princesse Satanik." *Revue d'études armeniennes* 9:41–53.

————. 1930. *Légendes sur les Nartes.* Paris: Institut d'Etudes Slaves.

————. 1931. *La langue des Oubykhs.* Paris: Champion.

————. 1934. *Ouranós-Váruna: Etude de mythologie comparée indo-européenne.* Paris: G. P. Maisonneuve.

————. 1941. "Le nom des Arya." *Revue de l'histoire des religions* 124:36–59.

————. 1943. "Légendes sur les Nartes: Nouveaux documents relatifs au héros Sozryko." *Revue de l'histoire des religions* 125:97–128.

————. 1948. *Loki.* Paris: G. P. Maisonneuve.

————. 1952. *Scythes et Ossetes.* Paris: Payot.

————. 1955. "Récits oubykhs [I]." *Journal asiatique* 243:30–33, tale 5.

————. 1956. "Noms mythiques indo-iraniens dans le folklore des Osses." *Journal asiatique* 244:349–67.

————. 1957. *Contes et légendes des Oubykhs.* Vol. 60. Paris: Travaux et Mémoires de l'Institut d'Ethnologie.

————. 1958a. "L'epopée Narte." *La Table Ronde* 132:42–55.

————. 1958b. "Arí, Aryamán: A propos de Paul Thieme 'arí, Fremder' (*Zeitschrift der Deutschen Morgenland Gesellschafts* 117:96–104." *Journal asiatique* 246:67–84.

————. 1959a. *Etudes oubykhs.* Paris: G. P. Maisonneuve.

———. 1959b. "A arí, Aryamán (*Journal Asiatique* 246:67–84)." *Journal asiatique* 247:171–73.

———. 1960a. "Les trois 'trésors des ancêtres' dans l'épopée Narte." *Revue de l'histoire des religions* 157:141–54.

———. 1960b. *Documents anatoliens sur les langues et les traditions du Caucase.* Vol. 1. Paris: G. P. Maisonneuve.

———. 1960c. "Récits oubykh 4." *Journal asiatique* 248:431–62.

———. 1965. *Le livre des héros: Légendes ossètes sur les Nartes.* Paris: Gallimard.

———. 1968. *Mythe et épopée I: L'idéologie des trois functions dans les épopées des peuples indo-européens.* Paris: Gallimard.

———. 1970a. *The Destiny of the Warrior.* Translated by Alf Hiltebeitel. Chicago: University of Chicago Press.

———. 1970b. *From Myth to Fiction, the Saga of Hadingus.* Translated by Derek Coltman. Chicago: University of Chicago Press.

———. 1971a. *Mythe et épopée II: Types épiques indo-européens: Un héros, un sorcier, un roi.* Paris: Gallimard.

———. 1971b. *The Destiny of a King.* Translated by Alf Hiltebeitel. Chicago: University of Chicago Press.

———. 1973a. *Mythe et épopée III: Histoires romaines.* Paris: Gallimard.

———. 1973b. *Gods of the Ancient Northmen.* Edited by Einar Haugen. Berkeley, Calif.: University of California Press.

———. 1978. *Romans de Scythie et d'alentour.* Paris: Payot.

———. 1986. *The Plight of a Sorcerer.* Edited by Jaan Puhvel and David Weeks. Berkeley, Calif.: University of California Press.

Dzidziguri, Shota. 1971. *Gruzinskie varianty Nartskogo éposa.* Tbilisi: Merani.

Friedrich, Paul. 1978. *The Meanings of Aphrodite.* Chicago: University of Chicago Press.

Friedrich, Paul, and Norma Diamond, eds. 1994. *Encyclopedia of World Cultures.* Vol. 6, *Russia and Eurasia/China.* Boston: G. K. Hall.

Fritz, Sonja Gippert. 1994. "Ossetes." In *Encyclopedia of World Cultures,* by Friedrich and Diamond, 297–302.

Gadagatl' [Hadaghatl'a], Asker M., ed. 1994. *Nart éposymra Kavkaz bzesh'enyg'emra* [Nart aposəmre kavkaz bześ'enəɣemre]/Nartskij épos i Kavkazskoe jazykoznanie (The Nart epic and Caucasology). Societas Caucasologica Europæa, Sixth Colloquium, 23–25 June 1992, Maikop. Maikop, Republic of Adygheya, Russian Federation: Adygheya Publishers.

Gammer, Moshe. 1994. *Muslim Resistance to the Tsar.* London: Frank Cass.

Geldner, Karl Friedrich. 1951. *Der Rig-Veda.* 3 vols. Cambridge, Mass.: Harvard University Press.

Gerstein, Mary R. 1974. "Germanic *Warg:* The Outlaw as Werewolf." In *Myth in Indo-European Antiquity,* by Larson, Littleton, and Puhvel, 131–56.

Gonda, Jan. 1960. *Die Religionen Indiens, 1: Veda und älterer Hinduismus*. Stuttgart: Kohlhammer.

Grassmann, Hermann. 1964. *Wörterbuch zum Rig-Veda*. 1872. Reprint, Wiesbaden: Harrassowitz.

Graves, Robert. 1955. *The Greek Myths*. New York: Penguin Books.

Grigolia, Alexander. 1939. "Custom and Justice in the Caucasus: The Georgian Highlanders." Ph.D. diss., University of Pennsylvania, Philadelphia.

Grimal, Pierre. 1990. *A Concise Dictionary of Classical Mythology*. Edited by Stephen Kershaw from the translation by A. R. Maxwell-Hyslop. London: Basil Blackwell.

Gryaznov, Mikhail P. 1969. *The Ancient Civilization of Southern Siberia*. Translated by James Hogarth. New York: Cowles Book Co.

Gusalov, Vitaly M., ed. 1990. *Izbrannye trudy*. Vladikavkaz, North Ossetia, Russia: Ir Publishers.

Güterbock, Hans G. 1961. "Hittite Mythology." In *Mythologies of the Ancient World*, edited by Samuel Noah Kramer, 139–75. Garden City, N.Y.: Doubleday.

Hadaghatl'a Asker (/ḥadaɣaλ'a askar/) (in Russian, A. M. Gadagatl'). 1967. *Geroičeskij épos Narty i ego genezis*. Krasnodar, USSR.

———. 1968–71. *Nartxer* (/nahrt-ha-r/) (The Narts) (in various Circassian languages and dialects). Vols. 1–7. Maikop, USSR.

Hat'ana A. A., and K'erashya Z. I. 1960. *Adyghabzem yzexef gush'y'al'* (Adyghey language self-contained dictionary). In Russian *Tolkovyj slovar' adygejskogo jazyka*. Maikop, USSR: Adyghey Book Publishers.

Held, Warren H., Jr., William R. Schmalstieg, and Janet E. Gertz. 1987. *Beginning Hittite*. Columbus, Ohio: Slavica Publishers.

Henze, Paul B. 1992. "Circassian Resistance to Russia." In *The North Caucasus Barrier*, edited by Marie Bennigsen Broxup, 62–111. London: Hurst.

Hewitt, B. George. 1998. *The Abkhazians: A Handbook*. New York: St. Martin's Press.

Hewitt, B. George, and Elisa Watson. 1994. "Abkhazians." In *Encyclopedia of World Cultures*, by Friedrich and Diamond, 5–10.

Holthausen, Ferdinand. 1948. *Wörterbuch des Altwestnordischen*. Göttingen: Vandenhoeck & Ruprecht.

Inal-Ipa Sh. D. (/ynal y-pa š. d./) et al. 1962. *Nart Sasryqwej pšyn' wa žwi zažw'wyk jara jašcwej* (/nart sasrəq'°əy pš'ənʕ°aź°əy zaź°ʕ°ek' yara yaš'čay/) (The Nart Sasruquo and his ninety-nine brothers). Various Abkhazian dialects. Aqua (/aq'°a/) [Sukhum], USSR: Alashara Publishers.

———. 1988. *Prikljuchenija Narta Sasrykvy i ego devjanosta-devjati brat'ev*. Sukhumi, USSR: Alashara Publishers.

Iskander, Fazil. 1983. *Sandro of Chegem*. Translated by Susan Brownsberger. New York: Random House, Vintage Books, an Ardis Book.

Khamytsaeva, T. A., and A. Kh. Bjazyrov. 1990. *Nartæ/Narty*. 2 vols. Ossetian and Russian. Moscow: Glavnaja Redaktsija Vostochnoj Literatury.

————. 1991. *Narty, kommentarij.* Vol. 3. Moscow: Glavnaja Redaktsija Vostochnoj Literatury.

Khodorkovsky, Michael, and John Stewart. 1994. "Don Cossacks." In *Encyclopedia of World Cultures*, by Friedrich and Diamond, 103–7.

Knipe, David M. 1967. "The Heoric Theft: Myths from Rgveda 4 and the Ancient Near East." *History of Religions* 6:328–360.

Knobloch, Johann. 1991. *Homerische Helden und christliche Heilige in der kaukasischen Nartenepik.* Heidelberg: Carl Winter Universitätsverlag.

Kuipers, Aert H. 1960. *Phoneme and Morpheme in Kabardian.* The Hague: Mouton.

————. 1975. *A Dictionary of Proto-Circassian Roots.* Lisse, Holland: Peter de Ridder Press.

Lak'oba, Stanislav. 1998. "History: Eighteenth Century–1917." In *The Abkhazians*, by Hewitt, 67–88.

Lang, David M. 1954. "Caucasian Saga." *Asiatic Review* 50, no. 182:149–52.

Laroche, E. 1960. "Hittite *arawa-'libre.'*" *Latomus: Revue d'études latines, Collection Latomus.* Vol. 45, *Hommages à Georges Dumézil.* Brussels.

Larson, Gerald James, C. Scott Littleton, and Jaan Puhvel, eds. 1974. *Myth in Indo-European Antiquity.* Berkeley, Calif.: University of California Press.

Lincoln, Bruce. 1981. *Priests, Warriors, and Cattle.* Berkeley, Calif.: University of California Press.

Littleton, C. Scott. 1966. *The New Comparative Mythology: An Anthropological Assessment of the Theories of Georges Dumézil.* Berkeley, Calif.: University of California Press.

————. 1982. "From Swords in the Earth to Sword in the Stone." In "Homage to Georges Dumézil," edited by Edgar C. Polomé. *Journal of Indo-European Studies*, monograph 3, pp. 56–67.

Littleton, C. Scott, and Linda Malcor. 1994. *From Scythia to Camelot.* New York: Garland.

Littleton, C. Scott, and Ann C. Thomas. 1978. "The Sarmatian Connection: New Light on the Origin of the Arthurian and Holy Grail Legends." *Journal of American Folklore* 91:513–27.

Lockwood, W. B. 1972. *A Panorama of Indo-European Languages.* London: Hutchinson University Library.

Lotz, John et al. 1956. *The Caucasus.* Human Relations Area File, no. 35, Columbia, vol. 1. New York: Columbia University, Language and Communication Research Center.

Luzbetak, Louis J. 1951. *Marriage and the Family in Caucasia.* Vienna, Austria: St. Gabriel's Mission Press.

Lyons, Marvin. 1977. *Russia in Original Photographs, 1860–1920.* London: Routledge & Kegan Paul.

Magnusson, Eiríkr, and William Morris. 1980. *The Story of the Volsungs and Niblung.* Facsimile of 1870 edition. Totowa, N.J.: George Prior Pubs.

May, Robert, trans., Tamir Salbiev, Ossetian ed., John Colarusso, English ed. 2002. *The Ossetian Nart Sagas*. Caucasian Series. Madison, Wisc: Turko-Tatar Press.

Meremkulov, Vladimir, and Shota Salakaja. 1975. *Narter'a, Narty* (/nart-rĩa/). Karachai-Cherkessia: Karachaevo-Cherkesskij Nauchno-Issledovatel'skij Institut.

Miller, Vsevolod Fedorovich. 1972. *Osetinsko-russko-nemtskij slovar'*. 3 vols. The Hague: Mouton. 1927. Reprint, Leningrad: USSR Academy of Sciences.

Myzhaev, Mikhail I. (1994) "Predstavlenija o mire v adygskom geroicheskie épose 'Nartxer.'" In *Nart éposymra*, by Gadagatl', 57–63.

Nachq'yebia-Ipa, S. M. 1988. *Apsua bezhshwa aomografkwa rzhwar* (/apwa bəzš°a aomografk°a rž°ar/) (Dictionary of homographs in the Abkhaz language). Aqua [Sukhumi], Georgia: Alashara.

Namitok, Aytek. 1939. *Origines des Circassiens*. Paris: P. Geuthner.

Nat'ho, Kadir I. 1969. *Old and New Tales of the Caucasus*. New York: Private printing.

Nickel, Helmut. 1975a. "Wer waren König Artur's Ritter? Über die geschichtliche Grundlage der Arturssagen." *Zeitschrift der historischen Waffen- und Kostümkunde* 1:1–18.

———. 1975b. "The Dawn of Chivalry." *The Metropolitan Museum of Art Bulletin* 35:150–52.

O'Brien, Steven. 1982. "Dioscuric Elements in Celtic and Germanic Mythology." *Journal of Indo-European Studies* 10:117–36.

Odell, Kathleen. 1977. *Mission to Circassia*. London: Heinemann.

O'Flaherty, Wendy Doniger, ed. and trans. 1981. *The Rig Veda: An Anthology*. New York: Penguin.

Olrick, Axel. 1922. *Ragnarök: Die Sagen vom Weltuntergang*. Translated by Wilhelm Ranisch. Berlin and Leipzig: Walter de Gruyter.

Özbay, Yismeyl Özdemir. 1990. *Mitoloji ve Nartlar* (Mythology and the Narts). Ankara: Kafdagi Yayinlari 1.

Özbek, Batiray. 1982. *Die tscherkessischen Nartensagen*. Heidelberg.

Paris, Catherine. 1974. *La princesse Kahraman*. Langues et civilisations à tradition orale 8. Paris: Société d'études linguistiques et anthropologiques de France.

———, ed. 1992. *Caucasologie et mythologie comparé*. Special no. 23 of Société d'études linguistiques et anthropologiques de France. Paris: Peeters.

Pedersen, Holger. 1931. *The Discovery of Language*. Bloomington, Ind.: University of Indiana Press.

Perry, John R. 1986. "Blackmailing Amazons and Dutch Pigs: A Considertation of Epic and Folktale Motifs in Persian Historiography." *Iranian Studies* 19:155–65.

Pisani, Vittore. 1947. *Crestomazia indeuropea*. Turin: Rosenberg & Sellier.

Polomé, Edgar. 1953. "L'étymologie du terme germanique *ansuz* 'god, sovereign.'" *Etudes germaniques* 8:36–44.

———. 1974. "Approaches to Germanic Mythology." In *Myth in Indo-European Antiquity*, by Larson, Littleton and Puhvel, 51–65.

———. 1982. "Indo-European Culture, with Special Attention to Religion." In *The Indo-Europeans in the Fourth and Third Millennia*, edited by Edgar C. Polomé, 156–72. Ann Arbor, Mich.: Karoma Publishers.

Propp, Vladimir. 1968. *Morphology of the Russian Folktale*. Translated by Lawrence Scott. Austin, Texas: University of Texas Press.

Puhvel, Jaan. 1987. *Comparative Mythology*. Baltimore, Md.: Johns Hopkins University Press.

Raevskij, D. S. 1985. *Model' mira skifskoj kul'tury*. Moscow: Nauka.

Renou, Louis. 1957. *Vedic India*. Translated by Philip Spratt. Calcutta: Susil Gupta.

Rice, Tamara Talbot. 1957. *The Scythians*. London: Thames and Hudson; New York: Praeger.

———. 1965. *Ancient Arts of Central Asia*. London: Thames and Hudson; New York: Praeger.

Ridley, Richard R. 1976. "Wolf and Werewolf in Baltic and Slavic Tradition." *Journal of Indo-European Studies* 4:321–32.

Rolle, Renate. 1980. *Die Welt der Skythen*. Frankfurt: Luzern. English translation by F. G. Walls. 1980. *The World of the Scythians*. Berkeley, Calif.: University of California Press.

Rosenkranz, Bernhard. 1978. *Vergleichende Untersuchungen der altanatolischen Sprachen*. The Hague: Mouton.

Salakaja, Shota Kh. 1976. *Abkhazskij Nartskij épos*. Tbilisi: Metsniereba.

Sanazaro, Jacobo. 1506. *La vita: [A] sito de Zichi chiamati Ciarcassi: Historia notabile*. Rome: Aldus Manutius.

Shaban, Kube. 1959. *Adegha Folklore*. Paris: Private printing.

———. 1981a. "X"ymyš'yquo Peterez" (/ xəməšˤʾəqˤa patˤaraz/). Ms., 6 pp.

———. 1981b. "ʡˤaꭗˤ ꭗˤˤəblɛwəɮˤ'" (in Bzhedukh West Circassian). Ms., 2 pp.

Shamanov, Ibragim Magomedovich. 1994. "Balkars." Translated by Paul Friedrich. In Friedrich and Diamond, 51–54.

Shapiro, Michael. 1982. "Neglected Evidence of Dioscurism (Divine Twinning) in the Old Slavic Pantheon." *Journal of Indo-European Studies* 10:137–66.

Sturluson, Snorri. 1971. *The Prose Edda: Tales from Norse Mythology*. Edited and translated by Jean I. Young. Berkeley, Calif.: University of California Press.

Toporov, V. N. 1968. "Parallels to Ancient Indo-Iranian Social and Mythological Concepts." In *Pratidānam*, edited by J. C. Heesterman, G. H. Schokker, and V. I. Subramoniam, 108–20. The Hague: Mouton.

Tripp, Edward. 1970. *The Meridian Handbook of Classical Mythology*. New York: Meridian.

Tsutsiev, Artur, and Lev Dzugaev. 1997. *Severnyj Kavkaz, 1780–1995, istorija i granicy*. Vladikavkaz: Proekt-Press.

Tuite, Kevin. 1996. "Further Thoughts on Dal, Thetis, and Their Semi-Divine Offspring." Paper delivered at the Black Sea Conference, McGill University, 25 January 1996.

————. 1998. "Achilles and the Caucasus." *Journal of Indo-European Studies* 26:289–343.

Vernadsky, George. 1943. *A History of Russia.* Vol. 1, *Ancient Russia.* New Haven: Yale University Press.

Vogt, Hans. 1963. *Dictionnaire de la langue oubykh.* Oslo: Universitetsforlaget.

Volkova, Natalia G. 1994. "Karachays." Translated by Paul Friedrich and Jane Omrod. In *Encyclopedia of World Cultures,* by Friedrich and Diamond, 158–62.

Ward, Donald J. 1970. "An Indo-European Mythological Theme in Germanic Tradition." In *Indo-European and Indo-Europeans,* edited by George Cardona, Henry M. Hoenigswald, and Alfred Senn, 405–20. Philadelphia, Penn.: University of Pennsylvania Press.

Wasson, R. Gordon. N.d. *Soma: Divine Mushroom of Immortality.* New York: Harcourt, Brace, Jovanovich.

Watkins, Calvert. 1972. "*dieu-* 'god.'" *Indo-European Studies: Special Report to the National Science Foundation,* 4–30. Cambridge, Mass.: Department of Linguistics, Harvard University.

Weekley, Ernest. 1967. *An Etymological Dictionary of Modern English.* New York: Dover. Reprint of the 1921 John Murray edition, enlarged with a biographical note by Montague Weekley.

Wikander, Stig. 1938. *Der arische Männerbund.* Lund: Ohlsson.

9 780691 169149